AFTERWARD
Murder of a Soldier

Terri Schlack

Black Rose Writing | Texas

©2024 by Terri Schlack
All rights reserved. No part of this book may be reproduced, stored in a retrieval system or transmitted in any form or by any means without the prior written permission of the publishers, except by a reviewer who may quote brief passages in a review to be printed in a newspaper, magazine or journal.

The author grants the final approval for this literary material.

First printing

Some names and identifying details may have been changed to protect the privacy of individuals

ISBN: 978-1-68513-485-3
PUBLISHED BY BLACK ROSE WRITING
www.blackrosewriting.com

Printed in the United States of America
Suggested Retail Price (SRP) $28.95

Afterward is printed in Minion Pro

*As a planet-friendly publisher, Black Rose Writing does its best to eliminate unnecessary waste to reduce paper usage and energy costs, while never compromising the reading experience. As a result, the final word count vs. page count may not meet common expectations.

ACKNOWLEDGMENTS

It is beyond words to explain how we got through the years after Ryan's death. I heavily leaned on my husband Rich Schlack and our son Adam. They kept me from going to a darker side.

Sometimes a person finds strength from something that is written. I am grateful to these writers for their work that sometimes comforted me, gave solace or stated an insight that touched me. Thank you to Paul E. Babb, Robert Blecker, Ellen Brenneman, Harlan Coben, CPT Simeon Ecuyer, Gwen Flowers, Edgar A. Guest, and William Landay. A note of thanks also goes to the "Heroes" Season 1, Episode 2 (a quote from Mohinder Suresh) writer(s).

Meghan Tokash was the prosecutor in Ryan's murder case. She was there for us before, during and even long after the trial. Her suggestions for the book were much appreciated. She was part of a commission which resulted in President Biden signing of the Sexual Harassment/Assault Response and Prevention program. It is a step in changing the old military judicial system. I am honored to know this woman.

AFTERWARD
Murder of a Soldier

FOREWORD

What is justice? This is an age-old, vexing question—one of great debates among jurists, the criminally accused, those victimized by crime, and the public. Justice varies like raindrops or wheat grains. It is vexing. As humans, we try our best to create systems of punishment to mete out justice appropriately after findings of guilt, and often our best efforts fail.

It was early July 2009 when I drove from Fort Lee, Virginia, to Fort Hood, Texas—excited to begin my new job as Senior Trial Counsel for III Corps. According to the Army's public facing website with information for newcomers to the post, Fort Hood is nicknamed the Great Place "because of the quality of life the post and area offer Soldiers and their Families."

As a fledgling trial counsel, only a week after my arrival, I had my first homicide case. The news was profound: a young service member's life cut short. For what? By whom? Tenacity soon overtook my initial sadness as I grabbed my "Manual for Courts-Martial" and drove off to the Fort Hood Criminal Investigation Command (CID) Office.

As assistant prosecutor to the 1st Cavalry Brigade Trial Counsel, I was tasked with preparing the sentencing case for the court-martial. This meant learning everything possible about Ryan and his family so that if convicted, a panel (military jury) could sentence his killer appropriately. Once Ryan's killer was convicted, the military judge instructed the panel members—as all military judges do—that they could sentence the accused to no punishment all the way up to the jurisdictional limits of the court-martial, in this case, life without possibility of parole. The sentence was a shock to the Schlack family which was only exacerbated by news of subsequent trials with similar facts but widely disparate sentences. Was Ryan's life less valuable than the victims in those cases? What could be done?

In 1984, Congress created an independent U.S. Sentencing Commission to reduce sentencing disparities and promote transparency and proportionality in sentencing in Article III United States district courts. But for the United States Armed Forces—governed by Article I—any scrutiny of military sentencing came nearly three decades later. Established by the Department of Defense General Counsel, the Military Justice Review Group (MJRG) conducted a comparative review of military justice principles and procedure with those used in United States district courts. In its 2015 report, the MJRG advocated to amend Article 56 of the Uniform Code of Military Justice to include sentencing parameters and sentencing criteria similar to state and federal civilian courts.

Last year, I had the honor of serving on the Secretary of Defense's Independent Review Commission (IRC) on Sexual Assault in the Military. Published on July 2, 2021, among its 82 recommendations, the IRC advocated for judge-alone sentencing in all noncapital general and special courts martial and the establishment of sentencing parameters. My colleagues and I agreed with the MJRG. We concluded, "It is clear that the current discretionary practice of sentencing accused anywhere between no punishment and the jurisdictional maximum of the court is absurd." Though the IRC's tasking was confined to a review of sexual assault in the military, the recommendation—supporting the MJRG's own recommendation—will impact the entire military justice system.

The advent of sentencing parameters is a watershed moment in military justice. Parameters will provide court members with an actual confinement range setting an upper confinement limit and a lower confinement limit. Determining the value of a case is no longer a blind stab for court-martial panel members. Going forward, trained military judges will levy sentences according to delineated parameters—akin to guidelines used by federal district court judges nationwide. That it took the military such a long time to reform is little consolation to the Schlack family and victims situated in similar past military cases.

In the days after Ryan's death, following his murder, Wisconsin News Station NBC26 posed the question: Can justice truly be served in this case? A vexing question to be sure—one which no answer will ever satisfy. But sentencing parameters are a beginning. A beginning that I am certain the Schlack family would champion.

Meghan Tokash
Attorney, New York

BEFOREHAND

In November 2008, Ryan wrote the following on OkCupid.com, an on-line dating service:
The Skinny
User: funnytallguy4u
Ethnicity: White
Height: 6'8"
Looking for short-term dating, long-distance pen pals
Don't smoke
Rarely drinks
No drugs
Age: 29
Sex: Male
Preference: Straight
Current Residence: Oshkosh, Wisconsin
I am tall, funny and smart.
Sign: Cancer (but it doesn't matter)
Education: High School Graduate
Job: Military
Income: $20,000 - $30,000
Kids: Doesn't want children
Language: English

My Self-Summary
I'm a shy gamer guy. I'm not the type to spend my life in Mom's basement, though. I'm in the Army, and I work out almost every day. I have a good sense of humor.

What I'm doing with my life:
Right now, I am in the Army, serving in Iraq. As soon as I get out, I'm going back to school and see how things go from there.

I'm great at:
Reading people, games, listening, soldiering (sexy, eh) being funny

The initial impressions of me:
My stunning profile picture. I'm in Iraq and it's hard to look like the Fun-Spontaneous-Guy-Everyone-Wants-to-be-Around here. I'll fix it soon.

My favorite books, movies, music, and food:
Music: I like everything from Abba to Metallica to Mozart to ZZ Top. Pretty much everything but rap and country.
Movies: I liked Howard the Duck. If you find a movie I haven't watched, you'd be 3 steps from the Holy Grail.

Six things I can't live without:
My bike, music, games, car and my mind (some would argue this point)

I spend a lot of time thinking about:
Things I'd rather be doing

The most private thing I'm willing to admit here:
Anything you are brave enough to ask. I am very open.

You can message me if:
You can wait to see me 'cause I'm not going anywhere soon.

CHAPTER 1

2009

It is a Thursday in mid-July, which usually means another hot and humid day in Wisconsin. Ryan packs his belongings for the trip back to Fort Hood, Texas. Some things he left at home while on his second tour to Iraq included CDs, DVDs, and gaming books. He missed these types of things while in Iraq, so is eager to have it all with him again.

His father Rich and I notice that Ryan doesn't seem to be in a hurry for the 1200-mile trip ahead of him. Rich is a little worried that he is missing daylight. As Ryan is coming down the stairs, Rich meets him at the bottom of the stairs. "You are kind of poking around here instead of getting a good start for your trip," Rich comments with worry in his voice.

Ryan ponders a moment as he keeps walking through the kitchen, then says, "I think, Dad, I will visit Chuck Reynor after he gets off work. I'll likely hit the road later in the afternoon and drive until I think I need to pull off the road."

"You always were a night owl," I quip, grinning at him as I am cleaning the kitchen.

After loading the boxes and duffle bag in his car, Ryan goes upstairs one more time and comes down with a full laundry bag. Meanwhile, his dad is in the living room playing Solitaire on his iPad while I am in the kitchen emptying the dishwasher.

"Gee, I guess I could've done laundry," he says to me as he pauses in the kitchen.

"Why didn't you do it here?" Rich calls out. "You could have done it in the comfort of your own home instead of a big, noisy, old laundry room fighting for the machines."

Ryan mutters and shrugs, saying, "I can do it when I get back to Hood. I have enough clean clothes to last me."

I chuckle then respond to Rich, "It will give him something to do once he's back. What else would there be to do?" Ryan smiles, and I wonder what he is thinking.

"That about does it," Ryan says. "Everything fits in the car."

Rich and I give Ryan hugs and kisses. Trying to hug our tall son is a bit of a stretch for me, so standing on my toes, I give him a motherly hug and a kiss. Rich gives him a hug and pats on the back.

Rich and Ryan go out the door. As I walk behind them, I stop and stand on the step leading into the garage, noting how similarly Rich and Ryan are built. Rich is several inches shorter; both are broad shouldered, straight postured and with military haircuts. Rich's red hair has long ago turned white while Ryan's is light brown.

Rich stops midway in the huge garage as Ryan continues to walk to his car to throw the laundry bag in it. Ryan hesitates just a second, then comes back to me and gives me another hug and kiss. A warm feeling comes over me because of the unexpected affection Ryan has just shown. He is usually not one to show endearment. He looks me in the face, sees my tears, and quietly says, "Aw, Mom."

"Drive safe. Before we know it, you'll be home in September," I whisper.

Rich and I watch from the driveway and wave as Ryan drives off. He has already dropped the top on his red Mustang convertible.

Walking back into the house, I say, "I am so glad Ryan had a month home. He spent two weeks with his friends before we got home from Europe. By the way, I wonder what he and his buddies did to celebrate his 30th birthday last week. I'll ask Adam what they did."

"Yeah, it was too bad his leave wasn't after we got back, but I guess that's how it's done now. The entire unit goes on leave," Rich explains.

"Let's review our trip photos and select ones for the album. We have them all printed, right?"

The two of us spend some time to work on our "European Trip: Once in a Lifetime Vacation" photo album. We spent a lot of time carefully planning our European trip. Nothing can go wrong, or can it? A week before we leave, we find out Ryan will be home arriving on the same day we leave. The only thing to do is roll with it. Besides, he'll still be home for almost two weeks more when we get back.

Looking at each photograph, I recall our trip of a lifetime. This adventure started in the middle of June, arriving in Paris, France. We used boats and busses but also did a lot of walking to see everything we could. We spent lots of time at the Eiffel Tower, even taking the typical photo of the bottom of the Tower looking up. I know I'll enlarge it and put it in the perfect place on the wall above the stairwell.

One night we stayed very late to watch the ten-minute flickering of lights on the Eiffel Tower. Most everyone was sitting on the grass waiting for the spectacle. Two police officers walked up to us and started a casual conversation. Rich wondered if there was an ulterior motive.

There was a government building that reminded me of the White House, a stunning glass-topped building. Experiencing the Seine River bridge, Louvre, and Notre Dame was wonderful. We spent a day at Versailles which is beyond amazing. Of course, we went to every museum we could find in Paris.

Oh, the funny stories we will tell of the tiny hotel with the tinier elevator; only one suitcase and I could fit in it. Then there's our discussion the first evening on tipping, which was interrupted by a Parisian sitting at the next table. She assured us tipping five Euro would get us a kiss from the waiter.

Stops at Bayeux and Normandy were definitely on our agenda. Our trip included a stop in Brugge, Belgium, and a boat ride tour there.

Then it was on to visiting cousins in The Netherlands and taking us to a windmill factory, a castle, and a community with four windmills showing the different purposes. Rich and I took the car to Amsterdam to roam the Van Gogh Museum and the Royal Palace. Oh, did I mention the Red Light district? A person can't visit The Netherlands without riding down the canals.

We left my cousins and drove to Bastogne, Belgium, passing a WWII German Cemetery. It puzzled me why this was unexpected. After all, the Germans needed a place to bury their dead.

After dropping off the rental car in Paris, we flew into Munich, Germany, rented another car, and headed for Garmisch-Partenkirchen staying at an American Armed Forces Resort. Enjoying the smell of our hot cups of coffee, we would sit on the deck every morning looking at the Bavarian Alps. What a very surreal experience. Because we live on the flat eastern side of Wisconsin, these mountains were breathtaking.

We toured through the Bavarian Alps, the state of Tirol, Austria, Switzerland, and Liechtenstein. We never tire of a couple of our favorite places we've visited while living in Germany, such as Neuschwanstein Castle and Eagle's Nest. Then there was Vipiteno, Italy, walking to take in a different culture and architecture.

The trip was very memorable, but in the end, we couldn't wait to get home. On the flight back, we talked about things to do with Ryan while he's home. The thought of Ryan's return in a few months is overwhelmingly joyful.

CHAPTER 2

Waking up quite early on Friday, I think about what needs doing. I should work on housecleaning, laundry and getting the motorcycles ready because on Sunday we leave on a 700-mile trip to Branson, Missouri. We'll rendezvous with friends and have a couple of enjoyable days.

The phone unexpectantly rings, and it's Ryan. "Hi, Mom, can you guess where I am?" he says in a giddy voice.

I reply, "Gee, I don't know what time you left, so I'd guess Missouri."

"Nope," he laughs. "I am 40 miles from the Texas border and decided to pull over."

"Wow, you really flew, didn't you? Are you tired?" I ask.

"Yeah, I am," he replies.

"It's a good thing you pulled over. Take a little nap because you have plenty of time to get back to the post. And, for crying out loud, get out of that Mustang and walk around to stretch. Your tall self must be feeling so cramped up in that convertible. I still don't know how you can steer it with your knees knocking on the steering column!" We both laugh. I chuckle when I think about how he has the driver's seat pushed back as far as it goes. His friends refer to it as a three-seater convertible since there is no seating space behind the driver.

"It's not too hot yet, so I'm stopping to take a nap and stretch a bit."

We say our goodbyes. A thought that I didn't say 'I love you' jumps into my head. However, we'll stay connected through the phone until he returns home in two months.

I also hear from our second son Adam. "Mom, I'm calling to let you know I am heading to Wisconsin Rapids today," he says as he is chewing on something. "I have my stuff packed and will be back on Sunday. It should take me a couple of hours."

"That sounds like a great idea. Are you going by yourself?" I ask.

"Yeah. I don't know how much room my friends have at their house for guests," Adam responds.

"Say hello to them for me, okay? Drive safe! Love you," I reply.

"Love ya, Mom."

Adam is nearly as tall as Ryan. He would have beautiful soft brown curls if he'd grown out his hair, but he prefers it quite short. Living away from home resulted in poor eating habits, making him a heavyset guy with an unkempt look. His calm demeanor, his warm personality and his humor make him very likeable.

We have made the decision to clean the house today. This afternoon, we will wash our 1994 Honda Gold Wing touring bikes, get the air checked in the tires, and go to a gas station to fill the tanks. I reminisce at times about bike trips when I work on my bike.

Rich has had motorcycles on and off since he was 15. He began with a Rex 100, and by the time we met, he had a 450 Honda. In fact, when we moved to Texas, he was the one to suggest I get a motorcycle. No objections from me; it seemed exciting.

I do not fit the movie image of a female motorcycle rider but can handle the 850 pounds of bike quite well because of my height and long legs. I began my first adventures in 1976 on a 250 Kawasaki. By 1994, I graduated to my Gold Wing, and that's when we did serious riding. My proudest moments are riding the SaddleSore (1000 miles in 24 hours) and the BunBurner (1500 miles in 36 hours) with friends. These bike marathons test your stamina, and I love a good challenge. The two of us managed to tour almost all the lower 48 states. Our two sons no longer find it cool to ride on the back of our bikes with us. What I do know is riding with a group is my favorite way to travel and being last in line is my favorite spot.

Saturday, we are being lazy. I only need to do the laundry and pack clothes for the trip. We decide what we want to take along and set those aside to stuff into soft luggage bags that fit into the motorcycles' side saddles.

With the last load of laundry finished, I fold clothes on the table. The thought pops in my head that I rarely fold clothes on the dining room table. Usually, I plop the basket on the carpet and fold the clothes while watching the news channel. I bring up the last clothes, add the missing items to the piles, and put away the rest.

Around 2:00PM, I decide to relax for a while in the living room. Rich is watching some arbitrary show on television. I know sitting and driving the motorcycle tomorrow means no wiggling around, so I stretch out and push back my Lazy Boy.

Suddenly, a car races past the house and from my angle, I can't be sure it pulls into our short driveway. The street we live on is a block and a half long, so people take note when a car is moving too fast.

"Rich, do you see someone pull into the driveway? They were flying but then seemed to brake fast, and I think they are in our driveway," I state.

As I am saying this, he's getting out of his Lazy Boy, saunters across the living room to the front window and observes what is going on outside. He suddenly freezes for a slight moment, then slowly takes a step back. There is a strange expression on his face.

"Do you see someone? Do you know who it is?" I ask curiously.

"I don't know," Rich replies quietly. His tone is a concern to me.

Leaving the recliner, I walk through the dining room and enter the foyer to look out the front window. In an instant, I glimpse a sergeant's rank on a jacket sleeve. I wonder if one of Ryan's friends might stop by to introduce themselves or check if Ryan is still around.

Rich opens the inner wooden door. His posture slumps and his face turns pale. I can't understand why Rich is acting so strangely. The master sergeant opens the outer glass door and asks if we are the parents of Ryan Schlack.

Rich takes a step back allowing a chaplain, a master sergeant, and an army specialist to enter the house. I hear Rich say, "Oh, God!" while stumbling backward into the living room. Two soldiers rush in and grab for Rich as he's about to fall. It then registers in my brain that there are three soldiers at my door. I just stare and try to look to Rich for reasons these soldiers are here; yet I have an awful, awful feeling. I know what three uniformed soldiers coming to visit means, and I don't want to believe it.

"Is Adam here?" the master sergeant calmly asks.

Rich replies, "Adam is out of town."

We gesture to the soldiers to come in and all of us walk through the foyer toward the dining room. The master sergeant continues, "Can you tell us where Adam is?"

Rich answers, "Adam is visiting a friend in Wisconsin Rapids. What is this all about?"

The chaplain now speaks. "Let's sit down. Can you call Adam to tell him to come home? How long will it take him to come back?"

Heading to the kitchen wall phone, I whimper hoarsely, "I'll call Adam. "

As Rich comes into the dining area, he states, "It's a two-hour drive." He looks distraught but is rallying to take control.

Adam answers his phone after what feels like forever. "Adam, you have to come home," I say as composed as I can manage. The army specialist walks toward me and watches me as I grab the kitchen counter.

"Mom," Adam quietly asks, "what's wrong?"

I can barely hold it together when I answer, "I think I know, but I can't say it out loud. I just can't. If I say it out loud, I'm afraid it will be true." I could not hold it in any longer.

Adam softly responds, "Mom, is Dad there? Let me talk to Dad." I hold the phone out to Rich, and he takes it from me.

"Adam, something has happened to Ryan. Come home and we'll talk then," Rich places the phone back on the receiver.

The chaplain suggests, "We'll wait for Adam and then give you the details."

Rich turns to the chaplain and, in a firm voice says, "We need to know now."

"I think it would be better if we wait in case someone might have questions that we might be able to answer," the master sergeant replies. Rich and I sink into the kitchen chairs, folding our hands on the table.

"We aren't going to wait. Adam is a couple of hours away. You will not leave us hanging," Rich demanded. "You need to tell us now."

CHAPTER 3

So, it begins. The words. "We regret to inform you that Ryan was fatally wounded last night around midnight. He was taken to the hospital and died there," MSG Fredrick Davis explains. Rich and I both put our heads down on our arms and sob. The master sergeant might have said more, but I didn't hear it. I think about when Ryan left for Texas just two days ago. That's when I had last seen him alive.

Rich is thinking they don't have, they can't have, the right person. They are making a huge mistake. This isn't happening to us.

Once we compose ourselves a bit, the master sergeant relays what he knows. "It seems Ryan was doing laundry at the barracks when he got a phone call inviting him to a party at a friend's house. He told the first caller that he didn't think he'll come. Following a few additional phone calls, he eventually made it to the party. He died shortly after midnight on July 18 at Darnell Army Hospital at Fort Hood, TX."

MSG Davis pauses a moment to let us absorb this information. Then he continues, "A casualty officer will assist your family in any way you'll need help. You should do nothing until the officer calls you tomorrow."

Meanwhile, Adam is doing his best to drive home. It seems like the road becomes longer. Thoughts run through his mind, and he rationalizes that worst-case scenario is Ryan has hurt himself in a car accident. Adam knew Ryan is not a skillful driver, so the accident was severe and has permanently incapacitated Ryan. He thinks about different ways he can help his parents. Should he move back home? He refused to think of Ryan as no longer living.

I didn't pay attention to how long the soldiers stayed. Rich and I remain seated in the chairs trying to make sense of what we heard. Time passes. We wonder out loud what we should do.

Since we were told to do nothing until we hear from the Casualty Assistance Officer, we decide we should at least contact our siblings. There are four brothers and one sister in my life. We keep in touch with each other and tend to follow the adage, "No news is good news."

Starting with the oldest, I call Jerry who is 14 years older than me and lives in Texas. Jerry knew Ryan better than any other family member. Whenever Ryan was stationed at Fort Hood, Jerry and Rita would invite Ryan to their home for the weekend or holidays occasionally.

Jerry answers his phone and does the usual initial greeting. When I hear his voice, I start shedding tears and try very hard to be clear because this is the most difficult thing I have had to explain. He listens as I tell him what I know. After I finish, a lengthy silence follows.

"This is so difficult to believe," he slowly begins. "You say Ryan was on the base when it happened? Do you know if the shooter is caught? How can this be? I am so, so sorry to hear this, Terri. I can't imagine what you are going through."

"There are many questions we have, as well," I murmur. "I'll let you know more when we find out so, we will talk again, Jerry. Goodbye."

Gib lives about 25 miles south of us. He is seven years older than me, and we seemed to get along the best while growing up. In hindsight, I kind of missed him when he left home to enlist in the Air Force.

After telling what I know, he asks, "Do you want Mary and I to come over?"

"I, … We…, I don't know. My mind is not working, and I don't know what I want. Maybe we're not ready for that. I don't know."

Gib firmly says, "Yes, we are coming over. We'll be there in half an hour." At this point, I am in no shape to object or have a thought about them coming.

When I call Vince, no one answers. A minute later, Vince calls me back with a chuckle in his voice saying he wasn't fast enough to pick up his cell. I tell him about Ryan. He offers condolences but doesn't know what else to say. Even with Vince being four years older, we had nothing in common until we could hang out together and hit the beer joints.

The youngest, Glenn, is five years younger than me. I always think of Glenn as being the quiet one; not that words come easily when given such news. He tells me to keep him posted.

Shirley breaks down which makes me cry, too. Being 11 years older than me, we found it impossible during our younger years to find common ground except for sharing a bedroom. Now, it is our children that is the common link. I can't answer her questions. I knew her feelings of the loss of her son would come flooding back. This news cannot be softened. Another similarity we have is her son's unfortunate demise to melanoma at 30 years old. Ryan had just turned 30.

Rich holds off calling his sister because she is out of town today. He says he'll try tomorrow. That's when he will call his brother in California, too.

Gib and Mary arrive and, of course, hug one another tightly, which feels like a bit of the weight is now shared. We all sit in the living room. Our conversation is raising questions to which we have few answers.

Later that afternoon, Adam pulls up in the driveway and sees a car he doesn't recognize. Adam walks in from our garage. Right before he opens the door, he works to make himself emotionally strong for his parents. Taking a deep breath, Adam enters the house. He looks terribly worn when he walks in, and his face shows he knows something is very bad. I hear him say softly, "Hello, Mom and Dad."

Rich and I go to him. I take Adam's arm and lead him to sit on a dining room chair. Adam's worst fears came true. Ryan has died. Caressing his face, I try to compose myself so I could be clear.

"Adam, this afternoon there were three soldiers who came to our door. After asking them in, Dad and I were told that Ryan was at a party. There was a commotion or argument or something, I'm not sure, but somehow Ryan got shot. He died at the hospital. We don't know any more right now. We hope to find out more details tomorrow."

Wanting to be close to him, I put my forehead on his. I wish I could take away the pain he is feeling. It is obvious Adam is holding back his emotions, trying to be strong. I pause a moment to give him time to process what I said.

Walking back into the living room, I sit down in the green Queen Anne's chair, but Adam stays seated a few seconds longer. He is thinking as bad as he feels, it is harder on his parents. Then he rises and shuffles into the living room as Mary walks toward him and hugs him tight. Hearing him sob, I so want to be there for him, to hold him like Mary is doing.

Rich tells Adam that we are to do nothing until contacted. Gib and Mary depart, leaving the three of us in solemn togetherness.

I realize I must reach out to the friends waiting for us tomorrow. It's a good time for me to call since they're probably done biking today. I sob as I wait for Mark to pick up his mobile phone.

"Mark, this is Terri," I say stifling my crying.

Mark chuckled, "What's going on? Terri, what's so funny?"

I say, "We won't be coming to Branson, Mark."

"Why?" he says, a bit more calmly as he realizes I am not laughing.

"We heard today that Ryan got shot and died," I answer, weeping and trying to get my breath.

"Oh, geez, Terri. I am so sorry. I can't believe it. What happened?"

"We got little in detail. Hope to hear more in the next coming days. I just thought I would call so you won't be looking for us," I whimper. "We'll let you know more when we know. I gotta go, Mark. Please, tell the others."

In the evening, I send email to several close motorcycle friends because I wanted them to hear it from Rich and me, not some newscast that gets it all wrong.

> 7/18/2009 6:44PM
> To: GWRRA Friends
> From: Rich & Terri
> Subject: From the Schlacks
> Mark, please forward to whomever I missed.
>
> In May, our oldest son, Ryan, returned from his second tour in Iraq and was recently home on leave. He left last Thursday back to Ft. Hood, TX, where he would remain until he got out in September. This afternoon, we were told that Ryan was at a party at a friend's house last night. For some unknown reason, someone brought a gun to the party, and whether it was used in anger or by accident, someone fatally wounded Ryan. He died at the hospital.
>
> This is all we know at this time. I will let you know about the funeral arrangements.
>
> Terri and Rich

After Adam calls his friends in Wisconsin Rapids to tell them what happened, he leaves to go to his apartment. He lives on the second floor of a house owned by Chuck who was a good friend of Ryan's. Adam walks into Chuck's first-floor apartment and has a brief conversation, then Adam goes upstairs. He is thinking he should call ABC Wholesale, his place of work. He gets the voicemail.

"Hi, this is Adam Schlack," he begins, but then blubbers. "My brother was killed last night." He doesn't remember what else he says to his boss.

His boss calls a bit later, asking, "How long do you want off?"

Adam replies, "A week, I think."

"You got it," the boss says. And that was it.

Adam doesn't want to be alone, so went back downstairs to Chuck's place. A nephew of Chuck's dropped in so Adam invited him upstairs to play video games awhile. Meanwhile, they could hear people gathering in Chuck's apartment to celebrate a friend coming to town. Eventually, they go downstairs to the party.

Kerry, Chuck's girlfriend, was coming out of the first-floor apartment. She sees Adam and says, "Oh, hello, Adam. I'm just running to do some shopping."

"I'll walk you out to the car," Adam sighs.

"How are you doing?" she asks because she thinks he is not himself. She gets into her car.

Adam's eyes get misty, then murmurs, "Ryan was murdered last night." Kerry is so stunned it prompts Adam to ask her, "Are you okay to drive?" A few words of condolences are said, and Kerry drives off.

Walking back into Chuck's apartment, Adam joins the crowd where there is laughing and talking. Cal Jones and his girlfriend arrive shortly afterward, and everyone is greeting them. Cal sees Adam and laughs. "Dang, I am sorry I missed Ryan. I heard he left on Thursday."

Adam's only response was a simple, "Yes, you did." Now he ponders how to tell Ryan's fate to the group of friends.

After a moment, Adam calls out, "Hey, everyone, can I have your attention?" It took a moment for the whole group to settle down and look at Adam. Adam solemnly says, "Ryan was murdered last night." A long silence ensued. Chuck's five-year-old son walks up to Adam and tips his head straight back to look Adam in the face. He asks, "Did you like him?"

Adam smiles a little and quietly responds, "Nobody could push my buttons like my brother. Yeah, I liked him."

One good friend of Ryan's wasn't there, so Adam calls Grant and asks him to come over using the ruse of the party. At first, Grant didn't feel like it, but Adam can be persuasive. Grant pulled into the driveway where Adam met him. Exiting the car, he says, "For cryin' out loud, Adam, what is so important that I had to be here? You can't have fun at a party without me? Is the refrigerator empty of beer so I have to make a beer run?"

"Grant, Ryan was murdered last night," Adam calmly informs. Grant is a big guy, so when he starts swaying, Adam thinks he may need to catch Grant from falling.

"Did they catch the killer?" Grant questions.

Adam replies, "They know who it was."

Right at that time, Adam's fiancée Ann pulls up and shouts, "Hey, Adam, you're home! I thought you were coming home tomorrow." Grant walks into the house while Adam takes Ann by the hand and walks up to their apartment. After closing the apartment door, Adam hugs Ann fiercely and says, "I love you, Ann."

Ann looks confused until Adam says the words, "Ryan was murdered last night."

She responded to Adam's hugs with hugs of her own.

In our living room, Rich and I sit, recalling what was said, questioning each other with unanswerable inquiries, and finding solace in silence.

We go to bed, but neither of us sleeps. We are in such turmoil; a feeling of loss and a dizzying number of questions. At one point, there is a waterfall of tears running down my face. Holding hands, we try to give each other the strength it will take to face another day. It is the longest night I have ever endured.

CHAPTER 4

The sun is now rising and finds Rich and I getting up and making some coffee. Questions and more questions fill our heads. How did someone manage to bring a gun onto the base? Or was the gun at the house? What caliber gun could it have been? No one else was shot, were they? What housing area was this in? How far away was the hospital? What was the response time of the military police and ambulance? Has the shooter not been caught yet? The guys at the party should know who it is. Whom should we contact for information and updates? Is the casualty officer responsible for keeping us informed?

Starting with funeral homes seems like a good idea. "I think we should look in the phone book to find the first two funeral homes nearest our house," I suggest.

Rich responds, "I would feel more comfortable if we drive past the funeral places to see where they are and what they look like to help make our decision. So, Terri, yeah, find out addresses for the two closest funeral homes."

"Let's wait to go look at funeral places after this sergeant meets with us," I say. "I should call Adam to ask him to come over, too."

To pass the time, I browse the computer and find Channel 10, a Texas station (KWTX), with a post online.

One Fort Hood Soldier Killed in Shooting On Post

"(July 18, 2009)–Fort Hood officials are investigating the shooting death of a soldier on post overnight Friday. A Deputy Public Affairs Officer for Fort Hood told News 10 a soldier fired shots into a crowd gathered at a home in McNair Village at Fort Hood sometime after midnight, Friday. Officials aren't identifying the soldier yet, but someone shot him in the hip. They took him to Darnell Army Medical Center, where he later died from his wounds. The public affairs officer says the suspect, a soldier, fled the scene but was apprehended by Fort Hood Police at 10:15 am Saturday morning at Fort Hood's main gate. The authorities have not disclosed a motive for that shooting."

"Wait a minute. McNair? That is not far from the hospital! How come it took so damn long to get to him!" Rich says angrily. I know enough to leave him alone when he is fuming until he calms down. That question should be directed to the arriving sergeant.

SGT Keith Wills calls and says he is to be our casualty assistance officer. He lives in Green Bay, Wisconsin, which is about an hour away. He asks if he can come and have us sign some papers. Rich tells him, yes, we will be here.

I call Adam to find out how he is doing. Then say, "A casualty assistance officer is coming named SGT Wills. Dad and I think you should be here, too."

"Okay. Can Ann come?" he asks.

"Yes, sure, if she isn't working or if she can get off work. You two are engaged, and she should be involved, I guess." It turns out Ann didn't want to come. I fleetingly wonder if it is because she is not comfortable with us. Adam and Ann never come over to visit us or to do something together, so we feel like we don't know her very well.

SGT Wills arrives and we all sit at the table. He reminds us what his job is and proceeds to lay out some forms. There is the "Authorization for Disclosure of Information–Members of Congress" and the "Authorization for Disclosure of Information–Third Parties", to name two. Immediately, I spot incorrect information such as our last name was spelled "Schleck" and Richard's middle initial has an "E". We reluctantly sign them. Wills said he'd get that straightened out and return tomorrow with a corrected copy. I am wondering why we are signing erred information, but I go along with it. What do I know?

Wills briefly discusses benefits, obtaining Ryan's belongings, and issuing a death certificate. I write down a list of items he says we need to gather to take care of all the upcoming paperwork. The funeral home has to be one that would take Ryan's body. Will informs us Ryan's body is now in San Antonio having an autopsy done. He mentions if we want him to go to the funeral home with us, that would be fine. The meeting with the sergeant lasts for an hour.

After SGT Wills leaves, Rich feels he should tell his sister Ellen today. She is five years older, and the two are close because of their childhood. But it was Ellen's husband Jim who answers the phone. Rich is reluctant to tell him, but Rich's voice is a giveaway when telling bad news. Jim prodded it out of him. Later, Ellen called, and they talked awhile.

Overhearing the two talk about their older brother Jack, I realize Rich has had more than his share of family deaths. Rich was five when their mother died. His Dad was still in the army and couldn't care for the kids. So, Ellen and Rich got shuffled around until an aunt and uncle gave them a home, although a tumultuous one. A car accident killed his brother Jack when Rich was fourteen. When we were dating, his father, long retired from the army, died in an apartment fire. Now, his oldest son is murdered.

Rich then has to call his older brother as awkward as it might be.

"Hi, Tom," my husband says as Tom answers the phone.

"Oh, hi," Tom responds.

"I am calling to tell you that my oldest son Ryan had been shot and died at Fort Hood."

"Sorry to hear that," Tom says.

Rich continues, "We don't know details, but will let you know when we find out."

"Yeah, you do that," Tom answers.

"Well, I gotta go. There are so many things to do. You take care. Bye now," Rich ends the conversation. Tom replies with a "Bye."

After Rich's phone calls, the three of us drive to the two funeral homes to look at the physical building. Fiss and Bills-Poklasny Funeral Homes meets our needs because it was closer, and we liked its appearance. Upon arriving home, I call the funeral home and am directed to Ben Jackson. We arrange to meet tomorrow morning at 11:00AM, after Will's meeting with us.

The afternoon crawls along. Donna Vosters calls me. She is an educator who teaches fourth grade. Her classroom is across the hall from mine. "Terri, this is Donna. Is everything all right?"

"Why, Donna, why are you asking?" I quip harshly.

"Is Ryan alright?" she asks. "Barb asked Gordon about something she heard. Gordon called me."

"How would Barb know?" I ask. "Who told her?" It dawns on me I am taking things out on Donna. I try to calm down and share what we know.

To this day, I cannot understand why I feel I put up a wall between us. I intended to tell her in my own way and time. She's a good friend and we're a great teaching team. Donna doesn't deserve to be treated like this. It continues to bother me throughout the day.

It is a good time to do something productive, so we shop for suits for Rich and Adam. JC Penny might have something for Rich. Surprisingly, the store has suits to fit Adam, too. The clerk patiently waits as they search for something they like. Rich ends up with a teal-colored shirt which blends well with the pinstripes on a charcoal black suit. The tie he finds adds to it. Adam's suit is black. He decides Ann and he will go shopping for shoes, a shirt, and a tie another time.

Later in the evening, I find Donna sent an email. She explains my sister-in-law called a teacher we used to work with, and that teacher called Gordon, my principal.

Often, Rich and I sit in silence, not knowing what to do or say. I regret the conversation with Donna and must take action. An email sounds like a good idea.

7/19/2009 10:57PM
To: Donna
From: Terri
Subject: I'm so sorry

I must apologize. Rich said I sounded angry or upset with you and you didn't deserve that. I thought there might have been something found online, and how would Barb know and ten other thoughts popped into my head. It irritated me that I didn't have that control. I'd rather wanted to call you myself.

The thought never occurred to me about my sister-in-law Mary alerting people in Fond du Lac. I thought about you and planned to tell you myself instead of you hearing it from someone else. Can you please pass it on to Gordon, Zoey, and any other school folks? Everyone at work should know.

Please accept my apologies. I'm hoping to have information about the funeral tomorrow. If you don't hear from me on Monday, it means we couldn't get a date pinned down because of moving Ryan's body. I know you are here for me.

Thanks, Donna. I'm sorry I came across so harshly. Thank you for emailing me. Thank you for your thoughts.

Love, Terri

I know we are in for a busy day tomorrow. Even knowing that, we go to bed but don't sleep. Rich gets up later to watch some television downstairs and a half hour later I follow. Occasionally, one of us returns to bed, but sleep eludes us.

CHAPTER 5

Oh, my word! What a way to start a Monday! A centipede is walking right across my kitchen floor. Where did that despicable thing come from? Where there is one, there are more! I've never had those creepy things in my house before. Mortified is not a strong enough word I would feel if people came to the house. How dare these creepy bugs show themselves! I am an excellent housekeeper! After I step on the one, I call the Orkin Company to set up an appointment. I am overjoyed they can come tomorrow.

It's important to gather the necessary paperwork Wills mentioned. After finding some items at home, we go to the bank. The safe deposit box has everybody's birth certificate, our marriage license, and the rest of what we thought fit the description on the list.

Adam and Ann arrive a short time before SGT Wills, the casualty officer. Wills gets down to business and lays out the corrected forms to sign and a huge binder on the table. It is called "The Days Ahead: Essential Papers for Families of Fallen Service Members". The sergeant identifies helpful binder sections for organization and checking. Wills states he needs the funeral home to sign forms for receiving Ryan when the casket arrives by plane. We are running late for the funeral home appointment, so I call to tell Mr. Jackson we'll be a half hour late.

Ben Jackson greets us at the funeral home door at around 11:30AM. He shows us to an office and asks us to sit down.

"First," Ben begins, "let's choose the Outer Burial Container. There's not much of a choice, so selection is easy."

Wills clears his throat and says, "You will not be financially responsible for the care of the embalming and the preparation of Ryan. He will be in his uniform. This 'Disposition of Remains Statement–DA Form 7302' needs to be filled in. It gives you options what you would like the government to assist with."

We choose Option 1, which involves preparing, dressing, casketing, and transporting the remains to the funeral home for subsequent interment in a civilian cemetery. Mr. Jackson clarifies what the funeral home is responsible for.

"I'll give you this Register Book for guests to sign in. Now for the 'Thank You' cards," Ben continues. "Here is what we offer. You'll see about ten different styles, so look them over." The card the four of us decide on has hues of purple flowers and the card itself is light lavender. Inside it says: "During a time like this; We realize how much our friends mean to us... Your expression of sympathy will always be remembered."

Next, Rich, Adam and I talk about the service. People are aware that Ryan attended a couple of churches, but he has never explicitly claimed membership in any one church. Our decision is to have a religious representative to conduct the service. Ben suggests Pastor Cane, a retired pastor, who charges $100.

With Ben's assistance, a newspaper notification is written. Ben suggests getting a picture of Ryan for the newspaper.

SPC Ryan Richard Schlack

"SPC Ryan Richard Schlack, age 30 of Oshkosh, passed away on Saturday, July 18, 2009, in Ft. Hood, Texas. On July 12, 1979, he was born in Nuremberg, Germany, the son of Richard and Terri (Huber) Schlack. He was a 1998 graduate of Oshkosh West High School. Ryan was in the US Army having served five and a half years. His hobbies included bicycling, playing video games, and watching movies. His memory will be cherished by his parents: Richard and Terri Schlack and one brother: Adam (fiancée: Ann Baker) Schlack all of Oshkosh.

Funeral services will be at 11 a.m. Friday, July 24, 2009, in the Fiss & Bills-Poklasny Funeral Home, 865 S. Westhaven Drive, with Rev. Christopher Cane officiating. Burial will follow with full military honors at Riverside Cemetery. Friends may greet the family from 9 to 11 a.m. in the funeral home."

SGT Wills leans over to Mr. Jackson and in a low voice says, "You will have to make arrangements to pick up Ryan at the airport. At last check, Ryan will arrive on Wednesday."

"What day would you like the funeral?" Ben says turning to us.

"How will Friday work out?" Rich asks.

Adam interjects, "Wouldn't it make more sense to have it on a Saturday when more people would come?"

I give him a stern look. "This isn't about everyone else's schedule," I say. As Adam looked at my expression, he knew there will be no further discussion. Seeing his face, I think I am a bit rough on him.

"That will be fine. Friday, July 24th. I will call the cemetery officials and work with them to get a plot in the veteran's area of Riverside Cemetery," confirms Ben. "Let me get you some easels with stands to display pictures or whatever you feel is appropriate."

Meanwhile, Wills is making phone calls to arrange an honor guard.

As we are walking out of the funeral home, Adam leans over to me and says Ann and he are going home. We both hug Ann and Adam and tell them we will see them later.

Rich and I decide a luncheon should be served after the services, so we head to a place that serves superb meals called Kings Banquet Hall. The menu we choose is a Hot Sandwich Buffet with roast beef in gravy, ham, mashed potatoes, tropical fruit fluff salad and marble sheet cake for $9.75 per person. When questioned, we estimated around 100 attendees.

It surprises me that the funeral home did not offer what I call prayer cards. It's a card with a religious picture on one side and a brief biography and a picture of the deceased on the other. Long ago, it was standard to have this available for the visitors. Although I didn't want a prayer card per se, I want to offer a memento for those who came and to put in the "Thank You" cards. It is a tradition I have experienced with other funerals.

Rich and I go to Kinko's to see if they could help. A poem I brought along seems perfect.

HIS JOURNEY'S JUST BEGUN
By Ellen Brenneman

Don't think of him as gone away –
His journey's just begun,
life holds so many facets –
this earth is only one...

Just think of him as resting from
the sorrows and the tears
In a place of warmth and comfort
where there are no days and years.

Think how he must be wishing that
we could know today
How nothing but our sadness can
really pass away.

And think of him as living in the
hearts of those he touched...
for nothing loved is ever lost and
he was loved so much.

The next task is finding a suitable photo for the newspaper. Of the few photos we have of Ryan as an adult, we find a picture of Ryan leaning against a building on the Central Texas College/Tarleton Campus located near Killeen, Texas. It is a favorite of mine. Ryan has on a black baseball cap and a gray t-shirt. He has such a beautiful smile on his face, which is special because it was tough to get him to show that smile.

The clerk and I talk about the rectangular traditional card shape and the color card stock it should go on. She offers to try a couple colors. She also tells us to return in a couple of hours to see which one we like best. Right before we leave, a thought occurs to me. I turn to the clerk and ask if the card can be bookmark-shaped cards; long and rectangular.

She smiles and says, "Sure. He liked to read I take it." I nod to her and smile.

As we head home, we talk about what else we can do today. I remember we need to contact the McClone Insurance Group about canceling Ryan's auto insurance. At home, I call them and are told that we cannot cancel over the phone. Later, I am checking on emails and find one from the agency.

7/20/2009 1:28PM
To: Mr. and Mrs. Schlack
From: McClone Agency
Subject: Ryan's Auto Policy
Mr. and Mrs. Schlack:
I spoke with the Progressive Insurance Company. The company has changed the name on the policy to Estate of R. Schlack. They would like a copy of your Power of Attorney that he would have given you. The policy will stay in force as long as you need it. The car is covered port to port. Also, just recently, Ryan added collision to the policy. There is a premium currently due because of that endorsement in the amount of $418. You can pay that at our office, and I can upload that payment to Progressive.

Progressive and the McClone Agency extend our deepest sympathy for your loss.

CHAPTER 6

Today, I should also shop for something to wear for the funeral, so later in the day I call my friend and neighbor Joyce to see if she'll go with me. We leave about 4:30PM to the Appleton Mall. Since it's a Monday, the mall shouldn't be busy.

"I want to thank you for the meats, bread and cheese you dropped off. It was very thoughtful," I say as I get into Joyce's car.

"That's okay, Terri. It's the least I can do," she smiles a little. We talk about nothing important as we drive the half hour to the mall.

As we arrive, Joyce asks, "So, what are you thinking you would like? Are you thinking of a dark color? A dress?"

"My ideal outfit would be a black or dark suit with a skirt, I think," I answer.

But that seemed to be a huge quest because we were not having much luck. We walk into the third store this evening. As I try on things, Joyce continues to look for more outfits, and I find nothing fits right or it doesn't look good on me. At this point, I am ready to give up and conclude I'll have to find something in my closet. Just then, Joyce walks into the dressing room carrying a black pants with a jacket having white lapels lay over the slightly larger black lapels.

"Oh, Joyce, I think you found it! I really like this. Oh, geez, I hope it will fit me," I said and can't contain myself. I quickly put it on and step out of the dressing room.

"You look great in black. I like it on you, but I don't like how the pants fit. They are too baggy. Let me see if I can find a smaller pair,"

Joyce said smiling. But, alas, there were no smaller sized pants in the store.

"Gee, this would have been perfect. Maybe we can find pants in another store," she adds.

"I think I have the answer. Let me call my sister to see if she can help me. She has been sewing for years, so I don't think this would be too difficult," I explain as I buy the outfit.

I phone Shirley and ask what she is doing this evening. After explaining the problem, Shirley tells me to bring it over and let her look at it. It is 7:30PM by the time we get to Shirley's. After a bit of small talk, we get down to the reason we are there.

"Terri, try the outfit on and let's see what I can do," Shirley says. Slipping into the bathroom, I come out to model my purchase.

As she is examining the pants, Shirley comments, "I think I can take it in. The side zipper will be tricky. I'll get my pins. The jacket looks fine."

While Shirley is pinning the pants, Joyce says, "When was the last time you ate something? Let's grab something to eat. I bet you haven't eaten much."

I hem and haw, then Shirley says, "Yes, go. You can take the pants off now. The adjustment will take some time. Cinders Restaurant is close by."

Off to Cinders we go to get something to eat. Joyce orders a burger and fries with a drink while I order just fries. I eat a few. I am just not hungry. Our conversation focused on family or neighborhood news and anything else except what is currently happening.

We get back from eating and Shirley has me try on the pants. We all agree although I have no buttocks, the pants seem to fit better. I suddenly feel very worn out. It is 9:30PM, and all I want to do is to go home. I express how tired and worn out I feel, so I hug my sister and thank her for the help on the pants.

An hour later I am home and, although I feel exhausted, still have the urge to e-mail friends and family about the funeral date and time.

Replying to McClone's at 11:30PM, my email states Ryan did not give us Power of Attorney, and we are hoping the Army will help us with this. My husband and I will come to pay the bill at some point.

The television and newspaper reports come in from Texas and Wisconsin. Most have similar information like the one from WBAY Channel 2 Green Bay (10:30PM):

"Someone shot and killed an Oshkosh soldier at Fort Hood. We are told from the family it happened at a party on the US military base. According to the military, Specialist Ryan Richard Schlack was killed during a weekend party at Fort Hood, Texas, on Saturday.

The Oshkosh native received an assignment to the 1st Cavalry Division. His family says he entered the military in 2004 as a computer technician and served several tours in Iraq. His father tells Action 2 News Ryan had just returned to Texas to serve his final two months after being on leave in Oshkosh. According to Ryan's dad, Ryan was asked to attend a house party over the weekend.

Several people got into an argument and that's when a person involved got a gun, a battalion commander at Fort Hood tells Ryan's dad. Questions still remain, even among Ryan's family, about what happened next.

The Associated Press reported that the gunman fired into the crowd, while Ryan's battalion commander informed the family that Ryan got shot when he attempted to intervene between the two fighting individuals. Either way, it appears he was not the target.

The ABC affiliate in Waco, TX, reported Monday night that the suspect, Barto Abadia, turned himself in Saturday morning after the shooting.

Ryan's family tells us he was supposed to leave the military last May but was called to serve another tour in Iraq.

The funeral for Specialist Schlack will take place this Friday in Oshkosh. Visitation is from 9 to 11 a.m. at Fiss & Bills-Poklasny Funeral Home on Westhaven Drive, after which Schlack will be buried with military honors."

CHAPTER 7

I doze in the Lazy Boy with the television set on all night. Rich goes to bed to try to sleep but gets up often and sits in the living room. Around 9:00AM, as I'm about to doze off, the phone rings. Rich turns the television to mute and answers it, then turns on the speakerphone.

I overhear CPT Stone introducing himself as Ryan's company commander.

"I want to extend my deepest condolences to you and your family. I can't imagine the shock of hearing about such a tragedy. If there is any way I can help from here at Fort Hood, please call me," CPT Stone begins.

"Thank you, sir. We appreciate you calling and for your offer," Rich says. "Yes, we have a concern about Ryan's car. Where is it parked now? What do we do about it?"

Stone answers, "I can tell you it is still parked at the home where the incident took place because no one can find the keys. I assume the car will be sent separately."

"I'm almost sure we have a set of keys here. Let me find a way to get them to you, sir," Rich volunteers.

"Oh, one more thing," the captain softens a bit. "I am pleased to inform you Ryan will be given a promotion posthumously to sergeant. I feel it is appropriate."

Rich ends the conversation with, "That is great. Thank you, sir, and thank you for your call. Goodbye."

"Did I hear that right? Ryan is getting a promotion?" I ask excitedly to Rich.

"Yeah, and it's a good thing, but it is typically done," Rich tells me matter-of-factly.

Now that I am more awake, I send an e-mail to MaryAnne and Connie about how much I appreciated Connie's advice in an email she sent a few years ago.

> 7/21/2009 9:49:26 AM
> To: MaryAnne
> From: Terri
> Subject: Just sharing
> To MaryAnne,
> I know you know what happened and I am sure Connie knows, too. I want her to know she's on my mind every day, along with the situation with her son. Too many people I know have buried their children. My friend in Indiana with her daughter shot accidentally, my sister with her son dying of melanoma, and Connie with her son's suicide. I took Connie's advice she gave me some time ago. She said to hug your boys every time I could and tell them more often than usual that you love them. Connie has no idea what a comfort it is to know I was more open to my sons about my feelings for them. As a result, they seemed to open up a bit.
> Right before Ryan left, we kissed and hugged and he went to his car, threw luggage in it, and walked right back to me and gave me another kiss and hug. He had never done that before. I will treasure that moment forever. Please thank Connie for me. It was the best advice I have ever received.
> Terri

Right after the phone call, Rich gets ready for the day. He takes the Mustang keys to the Ford dealership and requests a copy. They tell him they can't do it. We decide to mail the keys, insure it, and register it to the company commander.

Adam had told us that his friend's girlfriend has an aunt who has a flower shop in Appleton. Rich and I hadn't talked about any particular flower shop, so we told Adam that we would take the offer. We would meet him there in the afternoon.

When we arrived at the store, we didn't expect a little group to meet us there. The group composed of Adam, Ann, Chuck, and the couple who arranged this. The owner closes her store, so we have privacy, which I think is very thoughtful.

We all sit in a circle in the middle of the floral shop as the proprietor asks questions and jots notes. I now notice the smell of the room full of flowers. It's a relaxing, tranquil sort of odor.

"All I am thinking is I want a big red, white and blue floral arrangement," I begin.

Ann jumps in with, "The rest of us have been talking about this, and we want an arrangement that looks like a 1980s Nintendo console done with carnations. Ryan was into gaming."

The friend chimes in, "We also want a wreath on an easel with the flowers being all the friends' favorite colors including Ryan's, which is forest green."

Adam says, "I think I would like an easel arrangement using red, white and blue flowers with 'BROTHER' in gold script."

The owner asks us to look around to see if anything catches our eye. She has a nice array of arrangements spread around the store, but most are small compared to what I would like. By this time, I also feel pressure, distraught, antsy. I can't seem to focus. The kids are talking and probably making other suggestions than the Nintendo controller. Suggestions include a Ford Mustang symbol or a game-related image they would all enjoy.

Occasionally, the owner would come up to me, sigh and put my hands in hers. She would have a sad, consoling expression on her face. The first time she does this, I am thinking how sweet; that she is trying to calm me because I must look overwhelmed. But then it happens so often I feel irritated and think she is faking it all. Am I such a cynic?

Out of nowhere, I no longer wish to stay. I don't want to do this. I want to leave, oh Lord, do I want to leave, but I haven't picked out any flowers. Looking frantically around, a photo on a computer screen catches my attention. It has a pretty basket arrangement of red, white and blue flowers.

"I like that arrangement," I tell the shop owner as I point to it.

She gives me a funny look and says, "That one?" like she didn't believe me.

"Yes, that one. It's very pretty with the red, white and blue floral arrangement," I reply. "I would like 'SON' on a fat ribbon, too." The pressure of feeling trapped is now so strong. Nonetheless, I must complete this. Everyone ordered and walks to the exit door, so I hurry. I desperately want to go with them. Quickly finalizing the purchases, I never once look at the final invoice.

We get home and Rich finds a pan of caramel bars tucked in the door from friends Leanne and Ken. I smile and thank her in my heart for this most welcome gift on an awful day. I jot a thank you email off to Leanne and Ken. There are some comfort foods that work.

When the Orkin representative comes, I meet her at the door and tell her immediately that we are dealing with a funeral. I didn't want this to be a surprise to her and hoped she isn't put off. I know she feels awkward, and I give her credit for being very gracious about it. The Orkin rep is knowledgeable and goes right to work. She finishes quicker than I imagine.

As my husband and I settle in for the evening, a man phones us, saying, "Is this Mr. and Mrs. Schlack? Ryan's mom and dad?" I cautiously reply that it is.

"My name is Ethan Jaks. My home is where it happened. The commanders told us not to contact you and to leave you alone, and anyone who did would get in trouble. I decided to take a chance. I figured you'd want to know."

"Ethan, we are so very grateful that you contacted us because not knowing is tearing us up. We do not think we are being given the full information," I anxiously say. I whisper to Rich to pick up the other landline.

"We were having a party at my house because the next day we were going back to work after our tour in Iraq. I called Ryan to tell him about the get-together. He said he might come. Somebody called him again about 10:00PM, but Ryan said he was in the middle of doing his laundry.

"Later that evening, the party was in full swing. Everybody was drinking. In the house, Barto Abadia and Greg Owens got into an argument. Two of us tried to calm both guys down. Greg got so angry, he punched a hole in the wall. Ryan arrived around 11:00. Greg and Barto start yelling again at each other, so finally a couple of us separated them. Spence and I took Barto out the back door, and Ryan and another guy took Greg out the front door.

"I try to talk to Abadia and tell him to calm down. Finally, Abadia said he was going to leave, so he walks down the driveway and across the road where he had parked his car. I went back into the house to order pizza online. Abadia came back up the sidewalk. I heard something going on so got to the front door and heard a gun lock and load. I didn't see the gun, but saw a flash. I was thinking it was a 9 mm or a 45 cal. At the same time, Ryan pushed Greg over real hard. They both fell over. Ryan said he was hit and started hollering. Some guys went to go get towels, and I went into the house to find my phone to call the ambulance. I couldn't find it, so went running next door to ask them to call 911. They already had called. Ryan was still conscious and talking. We didn't see much blood, so thought the bleeding had stopped. Ryan was still talking as he went into the ambulance. We thought he'd be okay. The next morning, we found out he didn't make it.

"I'm so sorry. I figured you'd want to know what happened."

Rich and I thank him many times for telling us. Jaks gives us his phone number and said his mother would be coming this weekend to spend time with him. He seems pretty shaken up.

Rich says he thinks he'll get some sleep tonight, so goes to bed after the 10:00PM news. Whether he sleeps, I am not sure because he is up an hour later, and we talk more about what Jaks told us.

CHAPTER 8

It is after midnight when we head upstairs to bed. My mind is filled with thoughts on what to do and how to proceed. Thoughts constantly swirl in my mind. At some point, I can't stand it, so I get up.

Very early on Wednesday morning before the sun is thinking about coming up, I am at the computer composing an email to co-worker Donna, Principal Gordon Rogers, and the school secretary Zoey. Surely, others are wondering, and I don't want people getting wrong facts. The email keeps me busy until Rich gets up.

7/22/2009 3:37AM
To: Donna, Gordon and Zoey
From: Terri
Subject: From Terri
Please pass this on to anyone who'd care to know.

Days seem lengthy, but time surprises me when I check. Time isn't important. It's funny how the clock doesn't rule when I eat or sleep. I realize half the day is gone before I think I should eat. I think I eat a lot, but when I look at my plate, I have more of a sandwich or tons of fries left over.

Neighbors and friends bring food which saves me from going grocery shopping. I don't want to be around people right now. You have no idea how thankful I am for that simple gesture.

My eyes are sore, and I know I should sleep, but closing them doesn't make it happen. More thoughts in my head, more questions, more memories swirl.

The media talks about Ryan - every morning phone calls from the TV stations. Rich and I talked about what to do about the media. Facts should be out there. Rich felt it was important, so we deal with it. We'd answer questions, we decided, but no interviews. We can't bring ourselves to do that.

One time, I didn't know that one channel recorded us as we were speaking to them. Rich said later he was suspicious. I was so angry. And, of course, during airing it on TV, the particular station cut off my thoughts in mid-sentence, so what I said didn't make sense. Idiots! But now I am more attentive. At least I hope I am. I pass on some of the tasks to the company commander at Ft. Hood so give the media his number.

I know the dreaded day is coming. We're told Ryan's body will arrive here on Thursday, too close to the funeral day. Haven't been told if it will be Milwaukee's or Green Bay's airport. Appleton's airport, which is a half hour down the road, does not handle coffins. The funeral home wants him here on Wednesday. An autopsy was done at Lackland Air Force Base in San Antonio, not Fort Hood. I don't know why. An FYI, there will be a soldier to escort Ryan at all times, 24/7 until he is turned over to the funeral home. A funeral detail is being sent from Missouri for Friday. They will assist with the military honors.

Sergeant Wills visits us daily, providing paperwork and informing us of events and expectations. Supposedly, everything goes through this guy. Wills says even the army commanding officers are to get this guy's permission to call us. Any questions? Yep, it's his job to get the answers. It takes the pressure off us.

Rich checks on the computer a lot for information. Talking to the party host has given us a clear picture of the new information we were seeking. The soldier said if his commander found out about him calling us, he'd get in trouble, whatever that means. He felt compelled to call because Ryan was such a great friend to him, helping him "through his divorce and other things going on in his life." We are so very proud to be parents of such a fine son. The soldier also said some were talking of coming up on their next long weekend to meet us. Does he know how far Wisconsin is from Texas?

The soldier was beyond shocked when he was told Ryan had died. He said when the ambulance picked Ryan up, Ryan was still talking and conscious. The wound wasn't bleeding profusely. The soldiers at the house thought they had it stopped pretty much. What happened? The hospital is less than a mile. I don't know why I am suspicious something went wrong. We won't get the police report for a while yet.

I think about my sister whose son died of skin cancer, my close college friend whose daughter was shot, and Connie whose son committed suicide. As everyone says - no parent should have to bury their child. I watch parents have a tender moment with their little ones and hope they cherish that moment. Simple moments in times past with my son are oh, so powerful now.

Love,
Terri

About 5:00AM Donna sends email letting me know people are thinking of us and they are asking what they can do. She has no answer but asks them not to call us, to respect our privacy. She says she is there for me, which there is no doubt.

I respond by telling her I just feel helpless and don't know what anyone can do except when the school year begins. I know I'll need a little TLC.

A meaningful email from Connie pops up on the computer.

7/22/2009
To: Terri
From: Connie
Subject: To You
Dear Terri,
Words cannot express how deeply saddened I am by your loss. I am so glad you got to experience the closeness of the hugs and kisses that

mean so much to a mother. To this day I tell Stephen and my daughter-in-law those hugs are the "bestest" feeling in the whole world.

I remember at the end of the school year, MaryAnne subbed in your classroom so you could spend time with Ryan when he came back from his first tour in Iraq. How wonderful for you! It seems so senseless for him to have served two tours in a war-torn country and then come home safely and be killed in such a senseless way trying to make peace.

As a mother, you will always have the memories of him to help you through the days, months, and years ahead. Nothing but time will ease the pain and hurt you are going through right now. Each day you will think of him and the wonderful man he became. But if you believe in a greater power, no matter how unbelievable this nightmare seems, know that it is part of a greater plan and someday we will know why. I've always thought you were a very strong person and your strength will help you through this as well.

I am keeping you in my thoughts and prayers, as are many people. As a mother who has lost a son, though I know the circumstances were different, I think I know a little how you feel. If you ever want to talk, know that my door is always open to you, at any time, day or night.

Take care and God be with you,
Connie

CHAPTER 9

What a busy morning we are having with emails and phone calls. CPT Grady Stone calls and apologizes about his not being able to attend the funeral because of the start of the pretrial hearing also called an Article 39. He will, instead, send representatives from the company.

Shortly after that, my cousin from The Netherlands calls.

"Hello," I say as I answer the phone.

"Terri? Oh, Terri, this is Nel. Your brother Vince called us to tell us of the awful news. I am so very sorry for you. My heart breaks for you."

"Hello, Nel. It's upsetting and hard to handle. It doesn't seem to be real," I respond.

Nel continues, "I hope the person who did this is caught and punished severely."

I reply, "The people at the party already know, so it's just a matter of time."

"Terri, we are heartbroken and will hope this will be handled. We love you and think of you often. We so enjoyed your visit earlier this summer. Take care, sweet Terri. Keep us informed, okay?"

"Thank you so very much for calling. It was so sweet of you to do so. Goodbye and say hello to Wim."

"Take care of each other, Terri. Goodbye," Nel says.

Shortly afterward, the Reverend Christopher Cane calls wanting to talk about Ryan, but I get the feeling over the phone that he is half-interested, so I didn't share too much. Instead, I refer him to Ryan's friends to get other viewpoints.

I find out later that Reverend Cane contacted a couple of Ryan's friends and talked for an hour at a restaurant about Ryan. The guys felt like they gave the Reverend some "good stuff". Adam was also contacted, and he talked about Ryan's personality, spending time together especially as kids, the similar interests such as gaming and movies and more.

Jodi had called and asked if I would like her and her mom to put a display on the bulletin boards. It's not a priority, but sure, I'm grateful. Ellen and her daughter Jodi say they will come in the late morning. Prior to their arrival, I get the family photo albums then spend time looking for pictures of Ryan.

Jodi and Ellen arrive before I know it and get to work selecting pictures from the pile I hand them, then put together two bulletin displays. One board is of Ryan growing up and the other is military or recent pictures. Jodi cut out letters and placed them on each board. People who will come to the funeral probably know Ryan at different stages of his life and will get to see him in his youth and as a young man. The women finish up, and I think it is a lovely display depicting our son.

"Let's go to lunch," Rich says. "There's a nice restaurant right down the street."

Rich and I take the two to Mr. Cinder's, a favorite place of ours. Four of us chatting about nothing important when the thought strikes me.

"We will be offering lunch at King's Banquet Hall, but I want to be sure to order enough food," I begin.

"Well," Ellen replies, "Jodi does just that as part of her job at the church."

"Yes, I do," Jodi smiles. "Let's figure it out." She digs out a pen and uses a napkin as a writing pad, then starts by asking about my family and relatives. Then she lists relatives on the Schlack side. Next, a list of friends and neighbors as Rich and I name people in the categories. Jodi estimates roughly 100 for the lunch. It was reassuring to have someone verify the guess we already told the banquet hall.

Ellen and Jodi leave shortly after, so Rich starts looking for news articles about Ryan. The news made it into the "Army Times", the "Chicago Tribune" and publications in towns close by. The "Oshkosh Northwestern" carried the obituaries.

In a phone interview today with the "Appleton Post-Crescent," Rich shared some things such as, "He knew all these people at the party. Everyone had served in Iraq with him. It wasn't like they were strangers.

"My son considered going back for a third tour, but instead would return to Fox Valley Tech to finish an electronics degree. He had hoped to move on to the University of Wisconsin- Oshkosh, to pursue an electrical engineering degree. I want people to know he was a good guy.

"...I think he wanted to get back with his close friends around here...

"The hardest thing for the family to deal with is the senseless way my son died. When they told me he had been shot, I thought they had the wrong person.

"The military had changed my son over his five years of service. I now saw him as more outgoing and friendlier. He'd been gone for the past five and a half years and became quite an interesting fella."

Shirley calls to ask if Dick and she can come over. About an hour later, I open the door and as my sister and husband walk in, I fall into her arms, asking, "How did you do it? How could you bear it?"

As I shed tears, she comforts me with, "You put your faith in the Lord. It is in His hands." I finally get calm and invite them in. Dick brings in frozen pizzas with him and puts them in the freezer. We talk about what we know so far about how Ryan died. We also share what is going on in our families.

Shirley and Dick are here when we get a call verifying details of the event; on how Ryan pushed Greg out of the way and took the bullet. Rich thinks we have two separate sources giving us a clear understanding of what occurred. We talk a little more about what we are just told.

Shirley and Dick decide to leave. Rich and I need to do something, anything that gets us out of the house. Rich suggested going to Kinko's and pick up Ryan's memorial bookmark cards. We asked for 125, but the clerk makes a lot more. She says they aren't cut all neatly, so gives those to us, as well. I'm pleased with the result.

As is my habit, I check emails and see Wills forwarded an email regarding Ryan's Flight Itinerary.

7/22/2009 15:13
To: SGTWILLS@conus.army.com
From: usarmy@conus.army.com
Subject: Flight Itinerary for SGT Schlack, Ryan R. (Unclassified)
Depart: 23-Jul-2009 11:55
Delta Airlines Flt #1572
San Antonio, TX
Arrive: 23-Jul-2009 15:20
Atlanta, GA
Depart: 23-Jul-2009 19:18
Delta Airlines Flt 1274
Atlanta, GA
Arrive: 23-Jul-2009. 20:25
Milwaukee, WI

It will be about 8 or 9 PM by the time Ryan's flight arrives in Milwaukee. It's close because it's Thursday night and the funeral is on Friday. Oh, geez, Thursday is tomorrow already! There is nothing to be done about that now.

Later, I read an email from my niece which perks me up a bit. Michelle sends copies of her e-mails when she "conversed" with Ryan while he was in Iraq. She is right in thinking I would like to read it. It gives me more insight into Ryan as a young man. It is also just a year ago when this exchange occurs.

Thurs 7/16/08
Dear Michelle, Thanks for the card. This was my first time getting cards this way, and yours was by far the best. I had a great day and I hope you do, too. Ryan

Wed 7/16/08
Dear Ryan, I'm so glad you've received the eCard. And even more glad you had a great birthday. So how hot is it there? Michelle

Thurs 7/17/08
Michelle, it gets about 120–130 degrees but I work in AC so I don't mind so much. With the arrival of my PS3, I now live in relative luxury. I'm taking lots of pictures and I'm sure my parents will show everyone what it's like here when they get 'em. Now that I have internet in my room, just email me with any questions.

Sun 7/20/08
Ryan, that's fantastic that you have AC. What a relief. I'm glad to hear you've got it "somewhat easy" compared to others. I know being far from home is never all that easy. How long is your stint there? Michelle

Tues 7/22/08
Michelle, I'm gonna be here either for a year or 15 months. They haven't told us, but we're guessing a year. Looks like my pictures never made it home. I'll have to be more careful with them. How's life treating you back home? Ryan

Michelle writes on Thursday, the 24th, about her successful life, her husband's MBA graduation, and her two children. She then goes into detail about how she met her husband Lee and made suggestions for how Ryan can meet girls.

Fri 7/25/08
I can't send the pix via Internet because there may be a security issue. It's probably why my first set didn't go through. I carry them with me, and they will arrive with me.
I didn't know you had kids! My best friend has a three-year-old and Adam's girlfriend has a five-year-old, so I get second-hand experience with kids. When I'm home, that is.
My available technologies are pretty good. I have an in-room Internet line good enough to download videos, make phone calls, and I have a

webcam, but I don't know how to use it. My room came with AC and for $90 I found a mini-frig and a decent size TV. The parents sent over my PS3, so I have video games and HD movies. I'm working on getting my War Hammer game over here, too. I turn in the laundry, and it takes only one day to get done. (Last time it took 4 days.). Movies reach bootleg stores within a week or two of their release. The picture is usually fuzzy, but that's what you get for two bucks. I even had my bike brought over so I can ride around when I want (but it's difficult with a weapon strapped to my back.)

My average day is pretty boring. I get up between 6 and 7, have breakfast and go to work, where I sit in a tower until evening (can't say when I start or stop). Then I come back and either get on the computer or play video games until about 2:00 am (yes, I only sleep about 4 hours). If you want to get into a chatroom, I should be available noon to 3 (your time). I hope that gives you a better idea of what it's like here and I look forward to your messages. Ryan

The next day, Michelle describes Lee physically and says Ryan met him at his grandma's funeral. She asks if Adam is serious about the girlfriend and is impressed with Ryan's tech skills. Michelle proposes noon as a suitable time for their talks. Picturing him on a bike with a weapon is hilarious, she thought. She asks about the tower job, talks about marrying into a family, and is surprised he manages on about four hours of sleep.

Mon 7/28/08
I've got a Skype account, and today would have been good, but I don't have your number. I'll save my questions, so we'll have something to talk about when I call. See you then. Ryan

Mon 7/28/08
Tomorrow (Tuesday) won't work for us. My name is "Shelly" on Skype. Do you go by Ryan.Schlack on Skype? Michelle

Tues. 7/29/08

Yes, Ryan.Schlack. I guessed yours, but my search didn't find you and said it was for business. Where do I look? Ryan

Tues 7/29/08

I added you as a contact on my Skype account. Let me know if it lets you know I did that.

Tues 8/12/08

I found you and added you as a contact, but every time I call, I get a machine. When's a good time to call? Also, in about 2 weeks I should get my own Internet cable so I should be online more. (I got to share this one with my roommate).

Tues. 8/12/08

We typically have the computer off and when I am on the computer, I don't always have Skype running. So, it is best to schedule a phone call. I tried leaving you a voice mail. Let me know if you get it. The best time for me to talk is between 9 -10 pm CST, however I realize that may not work for you. I thought you said something about being available around noon CST. We could do that here. We are available.... Michelle

I make it a point to contact Michelle. "Michelle, thank you so much for the copies of your conversations with Ryan. I am surprised you still had them. What is a bigger surprise is all the stuff he told you and never mentioned to us."

"Oh, Aunt Terri, I am glad you got to read them. His living in such a different world is so interesting to me. By the way, have you ever read Ryan's MySpace.com? It's another on-line dating site."

"Michelle, wait," I say as I get up from the chair and walk to the desktop computer. "You know how technologically challenged I am, so do you have time to walk me through it, please?" I get a step-by-step direction and it is as she described.

"The date on this is July 2009. Does that mean he did this in the same month as when, as when…" I couldn't go on.

Michelle finishes my sentence, "Yes, the same month of his passing." I am trying to keep calm. I thank Michelle for helping me with this and we say our goodbyes.

Ryan on MySpace.com:

Hello, my name is Ryan, and I am 29 years old. I am in the Army and I'm deployed right now in Iraq. I'm smart, funny, and many other descriptions I could tell you. Yes, it's a cop-out answer, but I wouldn't be here if I didn't wanna meet you.

Interests:

General: I like music, driving, games, road trips, biking and sleeping

Music: Anything. I mean it. Anything from Abba to Mozart to Metallica to ZZ Top

Movies: EVERYTHING. I think I've seen three movies I didn't like.

Television: I haven't had a TV for years.

Books: I read lots. Terry Goodkind, Dan Abnett, Stephen King

Details:

Here for: dating, serious relationships, friendship

Hometown: Everywhere

Body Type: 6'8", average

Religion: Christian

Children: Someday

Education: Some college

Occupation: Soldiering

Income: $30,000 - $45,000

I knew most of it, but his response to having kids was unexpected. I recall the one I read some time ago saying he didn't want children.

Into the night Rich and I talk about all what occurred today, sometimes in the bedroom and other times sitting in the living room. Two more days before the funeral. Can we do this?

CHAPTER 10

Thursday morning, Rich checks the mail and more sympathy cards arrive. Also in the mail, we get condolences from different army personnel and political people. We read them then put them into a bag with a US Flag flying across the front and backside of it. I save them to get addresses later for the sending of thank you cards.

Rich suggests we display Ryan's promotion letter and the condolences from government officials. We get out gold wrapping paper to cover the last bulletin board.

Another piece of mail didn't surprise me and yet I can't say I expected communication. Not so soon, anyway. It is a card and note from Greg Owens's sister:

Dear Ryan Schlack family,
I didn't know Ryan or his family. My name is Marcy and my brother Greg Owens was with Ryan the night his life was tragically taken. We are so aware of the fact that it could have been any of those boys taken that night–including my brother. But unfortunately, it was your Ryan–and for that, our family is so heartbroken for your family. There has not been one second since that night you guys aren't in our hearts and prayers. My brother truly cared for Ryan and considers him a loyal friend. He's deeply confused and anguished about God's motives. We have no answer for why it was only Ryan, no one else.

So, I just wanted to let you know though we may never meet, your family will always be in our hearts, not just now during this trying time, but for always.

Please take this as a memorial for Ryan from our family.

A check is included with the note. I don't have any information on how to contact them, except through the address on the envelope. Rich says to wait until after the funeral and see if we can get a phone number or something.

As I walk into the living room, I can't believe what I see. How did I miss that? Rich hears my raised voice. "My carpet has a big stain in the middle of the floor! What is it? How did it get there? I'm calling a carpet steam cleaners."

Why is waiting for someone to arrive feels like eternity and puts your nerves on end to where you can't stand it yet you must? Finally, two men come to my door in the afternoon and I show them to the living room. Upon inspecting the stain, a man explains that water caused the wood under the carpet to turn brown. He asks me when the carpet was cleaned last.

"Yes, another pair of guys from your company steam cleaned the living room and stairs. I don't recall when it was done. Just clean it," I respond, frustrated.

"Ma'am, there is nothing we can do."

"Okay, then I guess that's it then," I answer in a resigned manner.

After the cleaners leave, I tell Rich what they told me. "Guess all we can do is get a new carpet," Rich mutters.

"What else can go wrong?" I cry. Rich takes me in his arms and holds me.

It is one day before the funeral. Rich, Adam, and I go to see the gravesite because Mr. Jackson tells us it is prepared. We want to know the location of the site before the funeral. It is found along one of the roads in the cemetery near a tree.

At 5:30PM Rich, Adam, Ann, and I meet Mr. Jackson and the Honor Guards at the funeral home to prepare to go to the General

Mitchell International Airport in Milwaukee, Wisconsin. Three vehicles are ready to travel–the hearse, a van with the eight Honor Guard soldiers, and our car. It is a quiet, somber two-hour ride except for the radio playing old music from the 70s and 80s. My thoughts are drifting, and I suspect so is everyone else's.

The first thing we are directed to do is to go to a particular cargo area. Mr. Jackson says he knows where to go. We make stops at a couple of loading docks. It takes three tries, then finally get headed in the right direction.

As we drive along a narrow road toward the offices for cargo business, we are greeted by about 30 Patriot Guard members lined up on either side of the drive, each standing with a 3' X 5' flag. It is a humbling, honorable, awesome sight. A feeling washes over me of patriotism and love for country.

The Patriot Guard is a network of men and women who simply honor soldiers who have died by standing along the drive with large US flags. They also ride motorcycles, but I'm not sure if that's a requirement.

Ben Jackson leaves us to talk to someone, then comes back. "The flight is late by about half an hour," Ben informs us. It seems a very, very long half-hour.

I quietly say to Adam, "I am concerned about the Patriot Guard standing there for so long. Why not go to the Guard and inform them that they don't have to stand there because the plane will be late and it's dark? I feel it isn't safe to ride a motorcycle at night."

So, Adam jogs off in the direction of the Patriot Guard. He was thinking how impressive this is so he takes a picture. Some even shake his hand. Adam shouts, "Thank you" to the Guard members.

While he is gone, the vehicles get ready to drive onto the tarmac. Ann has the sense to call Adam on her cell, and Adam barely makes it back in time.

He quickly comes to me and whispers, "They said they didn't mind. They will stay as long as necessary. They are very insistent."

Security inspects each vehicle with mirrors and a dog. Ben finds out how close we can get to the plane and how they go about delivering Ryan to Ben's waiting hearse. The four of us are told to ride in the van with the Honor Guard and leave our car where it is.

The Honor Guard is already sitting in the back. Rich takes the front seat next to the sergeant. Ann and Adam sit in the second-row bench seat. I am the last in line boarding the van.

"Do you want to sit here, too?" Adam asks as he looks at me.

"I could sit on your lap," I quip. I hear a bit of laughter from the back rows and think I break the tension. Was this appropriate? Tension burdens us all. Humor offers relief.

There is little talk in the van. Rich asks the young Honor Guard men where everyone is from. These young men, possibly privates or specialists, were in the army for a short time, except for the sergeant in charge. The sergeant had slashes on his sleeve which indicated he'd been around for quite a few years, most likely being a career soldier.

Through a checkpoint and gate, the hearse and the van pull through. It's likely a quarter mile long ride. We get out of the van and onto the tarmac to stand and wait until everything is prepared. There are even a couple security people with us. I have forgotten the routine when deplaning with a coffin on board, so I think that we are waiting for the passengers to deplane.

Suddenly, I hear the Honor Guard being instructed to walk to the baggage belt on the plane. The four of us stand there looking a little lost. Finally, a security guard tells us to go ahead toward the plane. As we walk, there are faces of people looking out the plane windows. Why aren't they off the plane yet? Oh, yes, it is customary to hold up the passengers until the deceased is off the plane. Only the soldier accompanying Ryan's casket is allowed off.

When we get closer, Ryan's casket is sitting at the end of the baggage belt and the Honor Guard arranges themselves to move the casket from the moving belt to the hearse. It is surreal seeing a casket knowing your son is in it. I try not to cry, but some tears escape.

Adam now realizes this is real. Ryan's gone and he won't hang out with him anymore. He understands that he was only listening to words, but that didn't make it true. But now, it is different, and he sheds tears.

A man in a Delta uniform walks up to us, hands Rich a medal and says, "We present you with this medal from Delta Airlines. It is to honor Ryan's service to his country."

Another worker comes up behind him. "All the airline people who handled the casket signed this sympathy card." He hands me the card. How very remarkable. How very kind.

With impressive precision, the Honor Guard lifts the casket gently and walks to the open back door of the hearse. Walking nearby is an officer who I assume accompanied Ryan's casket from San Antonio. He is of medium height, physically fit and dressed in his uniform. Later we find out he is Warrant Officer (WO2) Gerald Williams. He is also the officer in charge of Ryan's shop. WO2 Williams gets in the hearse and rides with Ben. We all get back into the van which takes us to our car.

The three vehicles along with security, police cars and SUVs drive past the Patriot Guard at the entrance. It is so unbelievable to think that these strangers came to stand. I feel honored, appreciative, and have a great deal of respect for what they do.

At the end of the line of Patriot Guards, a woman is taking pictures. We learned from the Patriot Guard that she was on the same flight. She learned at the end of the flight that a soldier was on board, being carried to his final resting place.

There are four vehicles in the lead of our convoy. The on-ramps are blocked, and the escorts lead until we get to Hwy 41. Motorcycles are in front of the escorts when we first leave the airport. Of course, they are the Patriot Guard escorting us. The drive back to Oshkosh is somber.

Around 11:30PM, we pull onto the street the funeral home is on. Already we can see flags line the driveway and part of the parking lot with more Patriot Guard standing along the sidewalk to the door. Fourteen Patriot Guard members hold flags outside. It is an awesome sight.

Again, the Honor Guard carries Ryan into the funeral parlor. The four of us wait in the sitting room until Ben signals us to follow him. While walking towards the room, he turns and warns us that Ryan looks pale without make-up.

It is truly shocking to see your son like that. He is already in his uniform in a very nice casket. What a helpless, deep-down-in-the-heart sadness I feel. It is unimaginable, this weight. The finality of it; that feeling will be with me for a long time, no doubt.

Holding Ann's hand, Adam is bracing himself for what is coming and squeezes her hand more tightly. Like his parents, he can't help but cry. He realizes Ryan isn't wearing glasses. Why not? He tries not to let this bother him. Shouldn't he look like he's sleeping even without all the incident details? Adam murmurs, "I am so very proud of him."

For no reason, all the things I wish I had said the last time I saw Ryan floods my thoughts. Did he know I love him? Did he know I worried so very much about him, and it is only out of love and the strongest hope that he will have a good life? And now, it is ended. How can I deal with this? I remember thinking of the last few months and how he seemed happier and surer of himself. I had such hopes he'd reach whatever goals he set for himself. But now, it is gone. No chance. I wonder what would have been. That is taken from him. How unfair.

We leave the funeral home about 1:00AM. We should sleep, but it wasn't meant to happen.

CHAPTER 11

I set my alarm for 6:30AM, but we are both awake long before then. Rich and I drift around getting prepared for the day.

The phone rings. "Mom, it's Adam," he begins.

"Adam, you are supposed to be here in a few minutes, at 8 o'clock. What's going on?" I comment while glancing at the clock.

Adam sighs and explains, "Mom, my car won't start. I can't figure out why. We'll take Ann's car, but we are going to be a little late, okay?"

While waiting for Adam and Ann to arrive, I put tissue, hand sanitizer, lens cleaner and spray into my new pink Amsterdam day bag. I don't know why I put a small purse in the day bag.

I call Joyce. "Joyce, I haven't eaten, so am assuming my breath is raunchy. I brushed my teeth. Anyway, I don't have breath mints. Do you have something?" I am more panicked than I need to be probably because I feel like I'll forget something.

"Yes, Terri. I will be right over," she replies and runs through our backyard with breath mints. She comes in the house, hands the breath mints to me then hugs me. I hoarsely say "thank you" and she is out the door.

Finally, Adam arrives and rushes to get dressed.

"Very fine, Adam. That periwinkle shirt with the black suit. It looks great on you," I say. "Did you get a tie?"

"No, Mom, I didn't. I am hoping Dad has one I can borrow," Adam answers.

"Yeah," Rich slowly says, "I think I might have something."

I turn to Ann. "Ann, did you get your hair cut and styled? It looks very attractive on you."

She's wearing a navy-blue dress with a short jacket. A simple necklace and earrings are her only jewelry.

It is getting late, but we make it to the funeral home a little after 8:30AM. People are there already. Thirty-one Patriot Guards are standing with flags to the entrance. A row of small flags lining the driveway can't help but catch your eye.

When we all walk into the funeral home, it seems everything is starting at once with not a minute to take a breath. 1LT Chloe Meyers, the second in command of Ryan's unit, approaches me. "Hello, Mrs. Schlack. I am First Lieutenant Chloe Meyers and Ryan was in my unit. I want to present you with this gift from the shop." She hands me a stuffed brown bear dressed in an army Class-A uniform. Rich and I thank her.

Next, the Patriot Guard Senior Ride Captain Wayne Midlands introduces a few Gold Star Moms. These are mothers whose children died in the Gulf Wars. They present me with gifts such as a Gold Star Flag and a Gold Star pin for each family member, which is unexpected. Next is the mother of Rachel Bosveld, the first Wisconsin female and the fifth Wisconsinite who was killed in Iraq. I take a step to hug her as we are being introduced. Thinking of what these mothers are dealing with overwhelms me. These mothers are younger than me, giving me hugs and introducing themselves. One thought that slowly creeps into my brain is–but Ryan didn't die over there. A fellow soldier shot him. He was shot on US soil. I cannot be in the same league as these mothers.

Adam and Ann gaze at the room, admiring the flowers. They find Ryan's photos on a board and Adam has an idea. Putting it into motion may be tricky.

Mr. Jackson takes the stuffed teddy bear from me and walks over to place it above Ryan's head inside the casket lid. It is an unexpected, sweet gift.

Seeing the room filled with plants and flowers of all kinds and colors is absolutely breathtaking. We walk around, looking over the array of plants and flowers, and then spend a few minutes at the coffin. The sweet flower smells were so comforting in the large room. It is then that I see the floral arrangement I had ordered. I absolutely hate the arrangement. It turns out to be a little basket with a small arrangement of red, white, and dull blue flowers and it dwarfs compared to the surrounding flora. The red, white, and blue flowers were not as large or attention-grabbing as I imagined. So now questions are in my head. Why wasn't I aware of the size of the arrangement I selected? Wouldn't the florist have known I wanted a gigantic bouquet? Why didn't she show me her best first? What was I thinking? I'm frustrated, but what can be done now?

Shirley's family sent a dish garden that was eye-catching and was placed at the head of the coffin. Adam's "Brother" arrangement was so perfect. The Nintendo controller didn't turn out all that well. It turns out only a handful of us know what it should resemble. There had to be 30 arrangements of greenery and flowers. A garden surrounds us, framing the room.

Adam planned to stand by the photo boards and tell stories but was wondering to himself if that is appropriate.

It is getting to be 9:00AM, so I get the tissues and water bottle from my day bag and put them behind me. Rich, Adam, and I arrange ourselves by the casket as friends and relatives form a line.

We stand for two hours, talking and accepting condolences and expressing heartbreak. My brothers and sister with some of their adult children are here. They traveled from states far and wide. It is a comfort somehow, even though we live in different states. Ryan's and Adam's friends including Ryan's drama class schoolmates, a few parents of Ryan's friends, many of my co-workers, a couple from school management, a couple guys from Rich's work even though he had retired, neighbors, friends from Gold Wing Road Riders Association and others. The funeral home had to set out more chairs as the room became standing room only.

Ben Jackson finally comes to us and says, "It's 11:00. We need to start."

By this time, I have to go to the bathroom, so promptly take care of that. I am so hoping I wouldn't embarrass myself coming back into the room while everyone is already settled.

While in the bathroom, a female Patriot Guard comes in. She doesn't speak to me, but they have protocol to follow. I quietly comment, "My husband and I are interested in participating in the organization. It is wonderful what you all do."

She hesitates, then replies, "I'll tell Wayne and he'll get information to you. I'm not supposed to talk to anyone."

Sure enough, as I walk into the viewing room, everyone is seated and waiting. Ben rushes to me and escorts me to a seat. The Reverend Christopher Cane begins. None of what I told him is in his sermon or prayers. None of what the friends or Adam told him is in his sermon. What a disappointment. Adam considered speaking about Ryan, but thought it would cause a scene. It is a very general one-size-fits-all sermon, but at this point, what can we do? What would one expect of a retired pastor who didn't know Ryan? The prayers and a presentation take about twenty minutes.

An announcement from Ben is made to the friends and family that a lunch will be served at King's Banquet Hall. Slowly, people walk past the casket one more time. Rich, Adam and I follow at the very end. We pause a moment at the casket.

Standing there, thoughts run through my head like I'm conversing with him. "Ryan, God, I hope you know we love you. You and I had our disagreements in the past but hoped before you left for Ft. Hood, you can agree we worked things out. During your teen years, I knew you were angry with me a lot, but I did what I thought was best. When you were to come home in September, I hoped we could form a better bond than in the past. You sure are a different young man than when you went into the army. I so wanted to get to know you. You seemed to have a direction and confidence I had not seen before. There were a few letters from friends of yours that told me a different side I never knew. People were impressed with your writing ability in high school, your humor that made people forget their problems, and over and over about what a good friend you were."

Bending over, I kissed Ryan on the forehead. After Rich and Adam spent time with Ryan, we then walk outside. Rich and I are standing near the front of the hearse. I don't know what I am thinking. Why aren't we heading to the cars for the cemetery? Don't we get into our cars and wait for the hearse to move?

I lean over to Rich and whisper, "What is going on? Did we forget to do something?"

He whispers back, "The casket isn't out yet."

I feel embarrassed that I didn't realize we are supposed to wait for the casket to go into the hearse. Rich must think I lost it. Of course, I have not seen the pallbearers yet. Soon after, Adam, Chuck, Paul, Grant, John, and Michelle, aided by Greg because Michelle was very pregnant, carries the casket to the hearse. Chuck, Paul and Grant are Ryan's Wisconsin friends, while John, Greg, and Michelle are Ryan's cousins.

Beforehand, the funeral director states to the pallbearers that the casket would be very heavy which may cause concern. The pallbearers are told to wheel the casket to the hearse then lift it into the vehicle. Adam was thinking as he lifted the casket that it was not nearly as heavy as they were led to believe.

The procession out of the funeral parking lot begins with the Patriot Guard on their motorcycles. Next is Dave, a friend and a police sergeant, with his squad car. Following is the hearse, then the family and then the others who came to the service. All the intersections to the cemetery are blocked. I don't know if that is typical, but it is so considerate. As the hearse passes the traffic controllers, many salute. It makes me feel so proud yet it's so surreal. Apparently, cars are still coming from the funeral home as we get out of our car at Riverside Cemetery which is a five-and-a-half-mile drive.

I see the canopy near the burial site. It is drizzling, so I grab three umbrellas from the car. The four of us sit on covered chairs under the canopy. Since we don't need them, I hand the umbrellas to persons behind me and offer the umbrellas to anyone who needs one. There is a kind of lost feeling that overcomes me and an urge that I want my family members nearby. A glance over my shoulder tells me they are here.

When everyone assembles, the Honor Guard takes Ryan's casket out of the hearse. It is quite an experience to see the care, professionalism, respect, and precision of the mannerism in doing this task.

Reverend Cane begins his presentation of which I am half-listening. My ears perk up when he says, "We want to say, 'Thank you, Brian'" and the crowd collectively inhaled sharply due to the Reverend's error; A signal that means "Hey, you made a mistake."

Adam was shocked and thought he didn't hear correctly. Afterward, Adam tells me he thought the preacher did not take his job seriously, that he could not remember Ryan's name. After all, Adam says, "It would be the last time Ryan and I would be above ground together. This was a serious moment for me."

I firmly speak up to the reverend, "It is 'Ryan' if you please". Adam was so glad that I corrected the paster.

Soon after, Rich's sister Ellen leans over to me and whispers, "Terri, look behind us. They are doing the lone soldier."

I am puzzled by this since I never heard of soldiers doing any "lone soldier" for army funerals. Try as I might to ignore her comment, my curiosity gets the best of me and I stand up, turn around, and only see one soldier standing too far away to be part of any ceremony. There are seven Honor Guard soldiers marching up the road toward us. Adam, Ann and Rich stand now, too. I am feeling angry at myself as we sit down because I still can't figure out what Ellen is talking about.

It gets silent, and I know the 21-gun salute is about to occur. Gun salutes at veterans' funerals always struck me as excessively loud. Why inflict that on the grieving? But this time, it is somehow different. Yes, I am startled at first, but I handle it well. Taps follow.

After the folding of the Flag taken from the casket, the process of presenting to the sergeant and then to 1LT Meyers is precise and deliberate. I realize the lieutenant is walking toward me. Feelings I can't describe envelope me and that surreal feeling is back. She is squatting in front of me, placing the flag on my lap slowly, deliberately saying, "This flag is presented on behalf of a grateful nation and the United States Army as a token of appreciation for your loved one's honorable and faithful service."

As I listen to the words, I am leaning forward and rest my head on her shoulder. I think afterward I should have sat up straight and sucked it in like in the movies. But then, I can't believe every mother or wife reacts like you see in the movies.

Later, I recall what the lieutenant recited. Did she say, "On behalf of the President of the United States, the United States Army and a grateful nation, please accept this flag as a symbol of our appreciation for your loved one's honorable and faithful service." I silently cuss the president who changed that speech.

Adam's hand is now resting on the flag. Rich's hand follows. The ceremony ends.

The four of us get up and walk toward the encasement. I put a hand on it and pause to whisper, "I love you and will miss you so very much."

Then I am hearing Ellen asking me if I see Ryan's name on the encasement. I didn't want to talk. I just want to get in the car.

She is talking again. I get irritated, so I sharply say, "Yes, Ellen, I see." I still feel a bit upset about the "lone soldier" thing. The sergeant appears and offers his arm, then walks me to the car. I am so grateful for a moment of solitude.

The sergeant gives Rich an encasement for the coffin's flag that was draped over it. It is a beautiful and well-crafted wooden case with Ryan's name and rank of "Sergeant" on it. I am handed the shell casings from the 21-gun salute.

Many family and friends gather at King's Hall next to the Hawthorne Inn. The inviting smell of the tasty meats and fresh-baked buns waft around us. Rich, Adam, Ann, and I go from table to table to visit briefly, tell what we know and answer questions. I sit and eat a bit, probably more than I ate in the last 48 hours. Rich, Adam, and Ann chose to swing by the buffet once in a while to grab a finger food.

After the guests leave, Rich, Gib, Mary, Shirley, Dick, and I regroup then go to the funeral home to handle the flowers and plants.

"Rich, can you please take pictures of all the plants and flowers so I can write a thank-you card later?" I ask. At the gravesite I recall there is a yellow arrangement, the Nintendo mockup, Adam's basket, the friends' arrangement, and our basket.

I feel overwhelmed and say, "There are just so many plants and flowers! If I take them all, my house will look like a flower shop. Besides, there's no room to put all these plants and flowers."

Ben suggests, "There is a nun's retirement home next door. I know people have sent flowers over there. What do you think? It won't be any bother for us to do that for you."

What a great idea! I cannot see myself just tossing them. Decisions must be made. It is strange that I want all those green plants, but I do. I feel at the moment I can part with the flowers because I do not have a green thumb. I don't worry so much about the green plants.

Loading up Gib's truck, Shirley's car, and our vehicle, we make quite a procession. Following Gib, I smile at all the leaves blowing around in the back of the truck as we pass them. The plants all arrive safely. We bring most into the kitchen and place the large ones around the house. Already planning ahead, I will bring a few large ones to school in the fall where I can appreciate them. Rich is overwhelmed by the plants and relieved when I tell him some will go to school with me. I will hold off telling him they will come back home when school is out in June.

After the plants are put throughout the house, my brother, sister, and their spouses leave soon after. Rich and I settle in with Adam and Ann. After a while, Adam gets a call from Lewis Zane, a high school friend of Ryan's, who wants to come over. He would like us to see home videos he taped while Adam and Ryan made a mini-play. I see the fun Adam and Lewis are having watching and commenting as the video plays. It is good for Adam to "step away" for a short time.

After we say our goodbyes to Lewis, Adam says, "Mom and Dad, I guess Ann and I are leaving, too. Or do you want us to hang around?"

"No, you can go home. We'll talk in the morning," Rich replies.

It is just as well because I feel exhausted. While the videos played, Rich nodded off a little. We doze in our Lazy Boys for a short while then watch the news channels. As usual, we sleep for an hour or two. Then discuss it all once more at night.

CHAPTER 12

The day after the funeral is yet another long, unbearable day. Rich and I sit in our Lazy Boys for long periods of time not saying a word. Thoughts of Ryan, the account of what happened, the funeral, our unanswered questions are on our minds. We share deep thoughts and frustrations, overwhelmed by emotions when a loved one passes. Rich and I both sometimes fall asleep, which is probably good. There are no phone calls in which to respond. No one visits. What is there to say? The endless tears will not bring him back; will not solve anything.

Checking emails, we see Wayne Midlands from the Patriot Guard send the Patriot Guard website for us to peruse. It lists the dates and times of the mission and from all over the country, condolences and kind words from Patriot Guard members are posted. There were about ten pages of thoughtful comments. The end contains a description of the local groups' contributions to Ryan's funeral.

The newspapers interviewed family and friends and wrote very nice articles about what happened to Ryan. There must have been only one photographer since all the newspaper photos of the funeral were similar.

Adam spent most of the day with his friends. In the evening, the group goes out and finds the last bar Ryan went to before he left home. It is a complete dump in Adam's estimation.

Rich goes to bed, but I stay up because my mind will not stop replaying some things, be it what occurred today or what has to be done.

I crawl into bed about 6:00AM on Sunday.

Rich rolls over and is asking, "Are you just coming to bed now?"

I whisper, "Yes. I just couldn't sleep. Let me sleep, okay?"

"Sure," he says, "but I think I'll get up."

Phone calls and more phone calls. I can't stay in bed due to the phone ringing. It's about 10:00AM.

"Shirley called a few minutes ago," Rich says as he sees me trudge to the coffeepot. "Your family would like to gather before everyone goes home. Glenn set up a place and got a semi-private room. I think we should go. We don't have to eat."

"I don't know," was my reply. "I am not quite ready to go out in public. I guess, though, I would like to thank everyone for coming to the funeral. Everyone is probably getting ready to go home tomorrow. We should say our goodbyes. Sure, let's go."

There were 16 of us at a long table. Everyone was pleased with what they ordered. The conversation slowly gets lively by the time coffee is served after dinner. There are a few laughs when the topic becomes "when I was a kid". We can always count on some funny stories from Jerry. This prompts others to tell about silly incidences.

It is time to say our goodbyes and wish everyone safe trips home as we head out of the restaurant. Rich and I both agree it was a good decision.

For the next couple of days, I go through the sympathy cards. I discover some people put in beautiful poems of loss. One poem is from Edgar A. Guest entitled "Plain People" which has God explaining to you that He will "lend you for a little while a child of Mine". It gives a different perspective to those who lose a child.

Rich suggests I write to the company commander in hopes it will arrive in time for the memorial for Ryan. Rich didn't know if it had occurred already or not, but to mail it anyway.

Dear Captain,

The Schlack Family would like to express our gratitude for your support during this time of grief. It's comforting to have a reliable contact for questions and updates. We appreciate the presence of company representatives and those who knew and worked with our son through 1LT Meyers and WO2 Williams.

We would like to have you share the following with the men and women of the Rough Riders:

"Hammer the Americans hard enough and you forge the best weapon in the world." (Captain Simeon Ecuyer...in a letter written to Colonel Bouquet during the siege of Fort Pitt, 1783.)

It takes a special courage to volunteer to do the unique job you have chosen. Each one of you needs to know how grateful this country is for this selfless act. Countless people stand in awe of what you do for your country. Those of us back home should never take you for granted. Know that in our own ways, we show our support and teach the next generation the importance of what you do.

"For all his bluster, it is the sad providence of man that he cannot choose his triumph. He can only choose how he will stand when the call of destiny comes, hoping that he'll have the courage to answer." (Mohinder Suresh, a fictional character in Heroes, Season 1 Episode 2; a favorite show of Ryan's).

Ryan was with friends and fellow soldiers. We are confident in the actions taken during Ryan's injury. A cruel twist of fate happened in an instant, which no one could have predicted. We want you to know that you are not blamed for the end result. All the "If I had done this..." or "I wish I'd done that..." won't change anything, so we ask that you do not dwell on "ifs". Take comfort in knowing you did your best.

Know that you will always be in our thoughts and held in high regard. We know Ryan valued your friendships above all. May God bless and keep you all safe.

Sincerely,
1SG and Mrs. Richard Schlack (Ret.)

Final Inspection
By Paul E. Babb, Sr.

The soldier stood and faced God,
Which must always come to pass.
He hoped his shoes were shining.
Just as brightly as his brass.
"Step forward now, soldier.
How shall I deal with you?
Have you always turned the other cheek?
To My Church have you been true?"
The soldier squared his shoulders and said,
"No, Lord, I guess I ain't.
Because those of us who carry guns,
Can't always be a saint.
I've had to work most Sundays,
And at times my talk was tough.
And sometimes I've been violent,
Because the world is awfully rough.
But, I never took a penny,
That wasn't mine to keep...
Though I worked a lot of overtime.
When the bills just got too steep.
And I never passed a cry for help,
Though at times I shook with fear.
And sometimes, God, forgive me,
I've wept unmanly tears.
I know I don't deserve a place,
Among the people here.
They never wanted me around,
Except to calm their fears.
If you've a place for me here, Lord.
It needn't be so grand.
I never expected or had too much,

But if you don't, I'll understand."
There was a silence all around the throne,
Where the saints had often trod.
As the soldier waited quietly,
For the judgment of his God.
"Step forward now, soldier you've borne your burdens well.
Walk peacefully on Heaven's streets; you've done your time in Hell."

I also send a short email to my brothers and sister thanking them for Sunday night and to Glenn for arranging this. It allowed us to step into another facet of our lives which enabled us to take a deep breath to forge ahead another day. The fact that we are not a close-knit family does not negate the fact we know we love each other. My email sign off is, "By the way, many people are in awe of our family–I mean, it was noteworthy, and they couldn't believe how many tall people there were in one place. We sure can WOW a crowd, can't we?"

On Monday, Adam went back to work driving his straight truck. Ryan lingers heavily in his thoughts day after day. Songs on the radio would bring thoughts of the things they did together. He tries to act as normal as he can when he's at work. He isn't sure he's pulling it off.

CHAPTER 13

It has been six days since the funeral when I ask, "Rich, how are you sleeping?"

He replies, "I don't sleep the whole night. Sometimes I turn on the bedroom television for a while. I notice you aren't in bed until early in the morning."

"Yes, I have tried going to bed earlier, but don't sleep. I force myself at 4:00 in the morning to head upstairs. But I do try hard to get up about 9 or 10 o'clock. I appreciate you not disturbing me. Due to my brain jumping between thoughts, I don't anticipate developing a healthy sleeping habit for a while. I can't stop it."

A college friend sends an email today. Some years ago, Cyndy's daughter shot herself fatally, or so the witnesses said.

> 7/30/2009
> To: Rich & Terri
> From: Cyndy
> Subject: Checking In
> Good Morning my Dearest Friends,
> I just traded in my cell phone because it was acting up. I didn't expect the new one to go out quite so quickly. Sorry.
> I will try to call you in a couple of days, and I want to spend a few days with you very soon. Right now, things are hectic for you. I am glad that you have friends and family in the area. You mentioned how good it was to talk and hear from some of Ryan's friends. Those connections

are precious. I have contact with some of Catherine's friends and it is like some kind of live link to her. That may sound strange to you.

Our hearts go out to your family. Please call me anytime you need to talk.

I will try to share whatever advice I can. Of course, you can tell me to be quiet, too! I sing out of tune, so my advice or thoughts may be out of tune also! Mike talked at first, then, was done talking. I couldn't stop talking. We reacted differently. It's hard to be supportive when you're in so much pain. I know I am selfish and wasn't strong for Mike. I knew it and still couldn't change it. I pray that the two of you will be good to and for each other.

Our thoughts and prayers are with you, know that.

I will be in touch.

Cyndy

My cousin Nel, from The Netherlands, sends an email. I am so very fond of Wim and Nel. She apologizes for her English because she feels she cannot find the words, but she does a great job. Nel comments about what a sad thing to happen after our traveling in Europe. Both send much love.

Michelle, my niece, sent us something that she found on Facebook. A news article of sorts under "Fallen Heroes". It is dated a few days ago.

Saturday, July 25, 2009
Army SGT Ryan R Schlack

"US Army SGT Ryan R. Schlack is remembered as a good soldier who did his work and got the job done.

The 30-year-old Oshkosh man was laid to rest in a funeral service Friday about a week after he was shot and killed by a fellow soldier during an altercation at an on-base party in Fort Hood, Texas.

An estimated 150 people, including family, friends and military personnel attend a funeral for Schlack at Fiss & Bills-Poklasny Funeral Home in Oshkosh. Schlack was later buried with full military honors at Riverside Cemetery.

'Ryan did his part. He always did what he was supposed to do. It's a big loss and we will definitely miss him,' said US Army Chief Warrant Officer 2 Gerald Williams, who attended the funeral and had served with Schlack in the 27th Brigade Support Battalion, 1st Cavalry Division.

Officials from the US Army said Schlack, who served 5 ½ years in the Army, was posthumously promoted to the rank of sergeant.

The Reverend Christopher Cane, who officiated at the funeral and burial, had words of comfort to those who knew Schlack. "As we go through all of this together, putting to rest our friend who served our country, we want to say, 'Thank you, Ryan,' for what you did," he said.

Oshkosh resident and GWRRA member, who said she knows Schlack's parents well, said Friday was a tough day to get through. 'Nobody should have to bury a child.'

Two dozen members of the Patriot Guard Riders stood watch holding American flags outside of the funeral home prior to the service. They also drove their motorcycles in the funeral procession to Riverside Cemetery.

'We come with utmost respect and compassion,' said Kaukauna resident Wayne Midlands, a veteran of the Vietnam War and a member of the Patriot Guard Riders. 'We feel it is our duty and obligation to pay respects to the veterans and also the families and to be here in time of need.'

SGT Barto Abadia is charged with murder in the death of Schlack, who is a 1998 graduate of Oshkosh West High School. Schlack and Abadia were members of the 1st Cavalry Division and had recently returned from tours in Iraq.

Schlack's father, Richard Schlack, said his son's commanding officer told him Schlack had been at a party last Saturday less than an hour when an argument broke out. Abadia is accused of leaving the party and coming back with a gun. When Schlack stepped in to calm things down, Abadia shot him in the hip. He died July 18 at a Texas hospital.

Schlack entered the military in 2004 as a computer detection systems repairer and arrived at Fort Hood in 2005. He served two tours in Iraq where he was assigned to the 27th Brigade Support Battalion, 4th Brigade Combat Team, 1st Cavalry Division."

I read the article over again to be sure I read how Ryan got shot according to them. Yes, the writer of this article got it wrong. How do I get the story right?

CHAPTER 14

I take time today to respond to Greg Owens's sister's letter:

August 2, 2009
Dear Family of Greg Owens,
Thank you for your condolences, your memorial gift, and your letter. It means a great deal to us that we have a way to communicate with you and your son/brother Greg. The soldiers were told they would get in trouble if anyone contacted us personally.
My family wants so much for Greg to know our hearts go out to him. We, too, think of him and the others so very often. We hold hope that time will alleviate the confusion and anguish that torments Greg. There should be no feelings of guilt because he or the other men, for that matter, survived this tragedy, this incomprehensible tragedy that is so difficult to understand. There never may be any answers to the many "Why" questions. From what we can surmise, during the attempt to diffuse the situation, Greg was talking rationally with Ryan and was not the antagonist. We firmly believe everything that could have been done to prevent the argument and then, to help Ryan, was done. We put the blame squarely on Barto Abadia. He had the gun. He made the choice to retrieve it from his car. Whether the gun fired accidentally or on purpose, the fact of the matter is Abadia wanted it to become part of the issue. Who could have predicted what would happen next?
Our hope is that Greg becomes the best person he can be; to make a difference and to make something of his life. He should hold dear the

memories he has of Ryan and know that Ryan held his friendship in high regard.

"Blessed are the peacekeepers; for they shall be called children of God." Matthew 5:9

Sincerely, Rich and Terri Schlack

Now is the time to email my long-time pen pal in Washington State. I should get a written note to her right away.

8/3/2009 8:37PM
To: Susan
From: Terri
Subject: Guess what
I received your card today. Thank you.

As I said, I was in a panic and must have deleted my emails explaining what happened, so I didn't have a record of who I sent it to.

We are still working on getting Ryan's things home and canceling phones, the Internet, car insurance and whatever else we find he had payments on, if any. I decided to go to a math workshop next week because I am needing to push myself back to work. I don't feel excited or anxious or anything about the coming year. But I know I need to do this. On the other hand, Rich seeks house projects. He's been on unemployment since March and actively searching for a job. We are realistic no one will hire someone his age. Adam doesn't say much. He has Ann to talk to, so I think he's confiding in her. That is the news from here.

Hope your school year goes well.
Love,
Terri

We are glad to get a call from CPT Stone. "Have you heard anything about Ryan's shipment?"

"No, we haven't and are wondering about it," Rich informs him.

"I'm calling the trucking company. I'll get back to you," the captain says exasperated, then hangs up.

Within fifteen minutes, Stone calls us back. "I found out Ryan's belongings left on July 30, Thursday, and the car left on Saturday, August 1. It should take 5-10 days. Along with Ryan's possessions here at Ft. Hood, there should be a videotape of the memorial service held at Hood which is packed along with the commanders' challenge coins. The unit's belongings from Iraq are not here. It comes back on a ship, so that will take longer."

"Thanks so much, CPT Stone," Rich sighs.

I write a letter to Nel and Wim. Her adult children speak and read English very well, so I know she will ask one of them to read it to them both. I mention the news article I included in the letter about the funeral, addressing the inaccuracies in the incident description. I confess at times, I think Ryan is at Fort Hood yet. We know we must get back to living because Adam needs us, too. School starts for me, and I am not excited to begin as other years. I thank her again for the call and email and that I feel the hugs across the ocean.

8/3/2009 10:42PM
To: Terri
From: Shirley
Subject: hi

I won't ask how you are doing 'cause I know the answer to that. I am thinking that you are probably close to the day of reckoning. By that I mean that later all the hoopla is over, reality sets in that Ryan is not coming home again. You may find yourself angry–and maybe even angry at Ryan. I recall talking to Dan a lot–sometimes in anger and frustration. And maybe you will not feel any of those things. Like you said, it comes in waves.

Just wanted you to know you're constantly in my thoughts. And we are continuing to pray that God helps you both through this.

I would like to go out for lunch sometime soon, just the two of us. I know that you are kept busy with your motorcycle club and such. But let me know if this is something you would like to do. If not, that is okay.

Thinking of you–Blessings, Shirley

Also, a curious letter arrived today from a name I don't recognize. As I put it on the table to read tomorrow, I read the first line. I know I wouldn't sleep unless I read the rest.

July 30, 2009

Dear Mr. and Mrs. Schlack,

My name is Will Hendrickson, and I was a classmate and graduate with your son Ryan at Oshkosh West High School. I wanted to write to you in regard to the sincere sorrow that I feel about your son's passing. Regretfully, I would rather have said some of the things that I am about to write to you personally face to face because I feel it would have been more appropriate in my opinion, but I was in Arkansas for job training the days of the wake and funeral. I really did not know your son that well, however I knew him by face, and I had him in a couple of classes. Even though I did not know Ryan all that well, I knew that he was probably a pretty good guy for more than a couple of reasons. For example, in one of the classes that I had him in during high school, he really came out of his shell and opened my eyes as to who he was. The class was a speech class and over the course of the spring 2004 semester, each student in the class had to give three speeches. What was really neat about the class was that it forced people to open up and show themselves. Up to this point in school, Ryan said very little, so when he went up in front of the class to give his first speech, I was pretty curious as to who he was and what his speech would be. After Ryan gave his first speech, I really appreciated hearing him speak. Some of the things that I could not get over were how brilliant and interesting he was as well as how good natured and caring. After Ryan's first initial speech, I kept asking, "Where in the world has this kid been?" and "Why in the heck didn't he speak more? On that day, he gained my utmost respect. He was brilliant, interesting, and a good-natured person.

Another reason that I know that your son was all the things listed above and probably more, is how he accepted and dealt with things. To make a long story short, I cannot tell you how angry it makes me in regard to the circumstances in which he died, but just like in the class I had with your son, in the end he really proved how big of a person he really was. I wish more people would have noticed his good qualities. Again, I am sincerely sorry for your loss. If there is anything that you need, please let me know. I would be honored to help you. May the road rise up to meet you. May the wind be always at your back. May the sunshine warm upon your face.

Sincerely, Will Hendrickson

In my heart, I thank this Will Hendrickson for his letter. It helped to give insight to my son and his high school life. I wept and wept after reading it.

CHAPTER 15

It seems no matter what, I cannot sleep. Rich can go to bed and may get up once for television but goes back to bed. It is a week and a half since the funeral and the news frenzy, the sympathy cards and self-imposed sheltering are over. I'll consider my options.

8/5/2009 7:57PM
To: Shirley
From: Terri
Subject: Re: hi
Hello Shirley,
Thank you for the offer of a lunch, but no thank you. We are keeping our camping reservation for Thursday through Sunday near Ft. McCoy before the "school stress" starts. However, we are also expecting some of Ryan's things to show up soon. So, we are playing it by ear. Ryan's commanding officer also said the memorial for Ryan was standing room only in the chapel. They even videotaped it and will send a copy. I thought that was very thoughtful.

On Monday through Thursday (Aug. 10–13) I am attending a math workshop to learn more about how to teach math the way the district is encouraging all of us to do. I have some knowledge about it and began exploring concepts last year, but the district is eager to move forward quickly.

The week after, I hope to get into school to start arranging things. I manage 4th grade math supplies and aim to improve organization by using labeled boxes for easy access. Becca and Donna will help when they can, but Donna's got her own room to set up.

As you can see, I am immersing myself in school. This is what I do. I must admit I cannot feel the same about starting this year as other years. I'm pushing myself to start and hoping to regain excitement. I don't know; I just don't know.

We received sympathy cards from a group called "Soldiers Angels". Strangers who lost a child in Iraq or Afghanistan are members. Every day I shed tears for them, as well.

Well, that is it on this end.

Terri and Rich

Shirley thanks me for the update and is glad to hear I keep busy. She asks that one day she could see the video of the memorial service.

Today is the day we arranged long ago, another lifetime ago, to go camping at Fort McCoy. What gets us up is an early morning call from SGT Wills calling to let us know Ryan's things will be delivered today. The truck is crossing into Minnesota.

Rich in turn, asks, "SGT Wills, can you tell us anything about the life insurance money and the death certificate?"

"Yup, yup, right on that," Wills mumbles. "Well, that's what I have for today. Goodbye."

More time is spent writing thank you cards and inserting the bookmark remembrance card of Ryan. The American Flag gift bag overflows with funeral cards and mailed condolences.

With the upcoming math in-service, there's something on my mind I need to convey to Donna.

8/6/2009 10:04AM
To: Donna
From: Terri
Subject: Just a note
I went to school and met up with Zoey. I picked up the books I ordered in June that relate to this class.

Ryan's things and the car are being dropped off sometime this afternoon. I don't have that on my mind anymore. Then we leave for the weekend.

I started this sentence five times and can't think of how to say it. I know you only want the best for me. I know you are a protector and your need to do so has been evident in the past. But now it's time to let people act, say, or do whatever, so they feel comfortable around me. I think if the people who haven't seen me yet can't express how they feel, then there will be this uptight, stagnant block when I'm around and that would be worse because I know I would be the cause of the uncomfortable feeling.

I may very well tear up, or maybe not. Whatever happens will happen. Sometimes something I see triggers it or a thought triggers it. If it happens next week during class, I will leave the room, but don't follow me as is your instinct. I can compose myself better when by myself. I think the others will accept this because by now I am sure 90% of them know. The others will soon learn. As I said, I know you are looking out for me, but I'm ready to let the process take its course.

See you in class.
Terri

I already went food shopping for camping, so the food bags are ready. All I need to do is fill the cooler prior to leaving. I water all the plants, toss out the two dead plants, email people and clean the bathroom. We eat lunch somewhere in all that and try to stay busy.

By 1:30PM I take a nap. Rich decides to call the truck driver at 2:30PM. He gets an answering machine. About ten minutes later, I feel I must try. Just as I pick up the phone, the truck driver calls for directions because he is now in Oshkosh. In less than fifteen minutes he is parked in front of our house. The tight packing in the semi-tractor trailer made unloading the car challenging, but the skilled driver managed it smoothly.

The sight of the car sends chills down my spine. Neither of us says anything as the driver parks it. Rich gets in and parks the Mustang on the far side of the driveway. What boxes are Ryan's are put in our garage.

Rich comments, "Gee, I thought there would be more boxes than this."

"Rich, remember that some of Ryan's belongings are from storage in Texas and some are his items from Iraq. I am guessing this is from Texas because of the car and bikes arriving," I respond. "I agree that there should be more, especially his WarHammer or Dungeons and Dragons tiny models he's always painting. Some boxes might contain them, and we'll investigate upon our return."

Once Rich and I secure Ryan's things, we pack up the camper and take off for the two-hour trip to the Pinewoods Campgrounds near Fort McCoy.

While heading to the campgrounds, Rich raises a point. "We need to make a decision about Ryan's car."

"I know I don't want it sold to someone in Oshkosh. I couldn't bear to see it driving by," I reply firmly. I recall Rich's ability to point out the motorcycle he sold to an Oshkosh resident. "As it is, if I see any red Mustang, I have a meltdown."

"Okay, I can see that. I'll see if I can talk to someone who knows interested buyers."

The weather isn't ideal for camping due to occasional rain. The sun peaks out on occasion, and we sit under the tall shady trees. Camping consists of using the outside grill for brats, hamburgers, and hot dogs. We go to Wal-Mart or a hardware store and, in the evening, watch a video.

The GWRRA motorcycle group put together a game this year called, "Where Are We Now?" Participants are given coordinates to different places in Wisconsin and once there, you must find the answer to a question. A person can't find answers on the internet because the questions are so well done. So, we will try to look for a few spots using our truck. The coordinates take us to Black Earth, Blue Mound and Cassville, Wisconsin.

After this adventure, we have a spaghetti dinner. Rich insists on my spaghetti one time while camping. I just shake my head. Tonight "Wild Hogs" is our entertainment, a movie we enjoy tremendously. Once in bed, naturally, I can't sleep. Since we are near a military base, "Taps" plays, and I cry.

Saturday is a hot one. Rich and I plan a trip to Warren and Neilsville to work on the "Where Am I Now?" game. Mark and a couple of others come to visit. They were on their motorcycles and found themselves in the area. At least that is their story. The topics of conversation are an array of motorcycle bikes and parts, places people plan to go with motorcycles this summer or next year and gossip.

Later that evening, Rich and I pack up to get ready for the trip home. Our movie selection is "In Regard To…" with Jennifer Aniston.

CHAPTER 16

Rich brings in the mail that was sent while we were gone. "Terri, look at this once. Do we know anyone by that name? Open it and maybe it will tell us more."

In the envelope is a sympathy card and it is signed by who I assume is the Class Reunion Rep because she signs it with her name and the "Class of 1998".

After reading the card, I share, "Oh, Rich, it is from a representative of Ryan's high school graduating class. She is extending sympathies on behalf of the class, and she continues to tell us when the news was out, there were emails circulating and stories of how each knew Ryan. She says Ryan will be remembered as a unique, funny, smart and an all-around nice guy. Furthermore, she revealed that countless people wished they had made the effort to know him better. They are proud to have had a hero in their class and send their wishes for peace and comfort to our family."

Rich comments, "I am sure Ryan was shy in school and kept to himself. It is very considerate, though, of the class rep to send us a card acknowledging him."

It is the second week of August. I usually head to school to clean and reorganize, envisioning the room's decoration and leaving personal belongings.

In my school mailbox, I find a handwritten letter.

Dear Mrs. Schlack,

I am very sad about the loss of Ryan. When my mom got your email, I started to cry.

I know you were very proud of Ryan and all that he has done. I remember in 4th grade you talked about how proud you were of Ryan.

I am sorry about the loss.

Best of wishes,

Samantha, One of your former students

Rich and I most always go everywhere together. We have turned into a homebound couple lately and rarely went places. The day comes, as I knew it would, that I have to go out in public by myself. It is because of a 4-day district in-service I am interested in and signed up for last spring. As I am driving to Fond du Lac, I begin to have second thoughts, but convince myself I can do this. Donna and maybe other teachers from Roberts School will be there, so I won't feel alone or uncomfortable.

As I walk closer to the meeting room, I can't believe how jittery I am. Stepping into a line for signing in, I am uncontrollably shaking so much that I can't hold the pen, much less write my name. A teacher sitting next to the sign-in pad is looking sorrowfully at me. She is reaching for my hand, but I quickly scribble the best I can and walk away. Scanning the tables, I see Donna and Tim and a chair between them, instantly knowing they were saving it for me. I feel such a sense of relief. I say a quiet little thank you and feel I can manage this.

The instructor begins. I am not really listening because I am catching up on news with Donna and Tim, but suddenly something catches my ear. No, I didn't hear that. My God, no. Oh, Jesus, she asks that we go around the room telling the group something about our summer. I sit trying to form a plan. What do I do? What do I do? I don't want to be rude.

I beg my partners, "Donna and Tim, after Donna tells her story, just skip me and you talk, Tim, ok?"

But as my turn is surely coming, panic sets in big time. Trying to be quiet and not be noticed, it is all loud to me. I slide back my chair and say, "I can't do this," hoping I wasn't speaking too loudly.

Walking out of the meeting room, I barely make it through the door when the tears start to flow as I walk down the hall. Perhaps ten minutes later, I'm composed and can go back to the room, hoping the summer stories have ended.

I am embarrassed, but I can live with that. I think if people didn't know what is going on with me, they will soon find out. As I walk to my seat, I get a few touches on the sleeve from teachers I pass. Stopping to talk is not an option. People are tiptoeing around me, and I realize it is awkward for them.

The in-service gradually becomes a comfortable atmosphere. By the end, we all converse easily across tables and during breaks.

Online, I come upon the August 6 Fort Hood Sentinel article about the memorial they had for Ryan.

Long Knives Remember Fallen Soldier

"Soldiers from the 4th Brigade Combat Team, 1st Cavalry 'Long Knives' attended SGT Ryan Richard Schlack's memorial ceremony on July 29, at the Fort Hood Red Team Chapel.

Schlack, who was assigned to the 27th Brigade Support Battalion, 4th Brigade Combat Team, 1st Cav Div., died July 17 from a gunshot wound.

'Weeks after his return from Iraq, he laid down his life so that his fellow soldier might live,' said Lieutenant Colonel, commander of the 27th BSB. 'Schlack died because of a split-second decision. He died because he chose to step in and protect his fellow soldier and literally take a bullet for his friend.'

The 30-year-old computer detection systems repairer from Oshkosh, WI, recently returned from completing his second tour in Iraq with his battalion. During his five years of service, Schlack was awarded the Army Accommodation Medal, two Army Achievement Medals; two Army Good Conduct Medals, the National Defense Service Medal, the Iraqi Campaign Medal, with Arrowhead Devices, and two Overseas Service Ribbons.

'His positive attitude and outlook on life was second to none,' said SPC Ethan Jaks, one of Schlack's closest friends assigned to the 27th BSB. 'No matter the time and place, you could count on him to brighten your day.'

Schlack had planned to return to Wisconsin after completing his enlistment to pursue a degree in engineering."

Before things get too hectic at school, we start opening Ryan's boxes. Among Ryan's belongings that were delivered on August 5 are two bikes which Ryan bought while in the army. One is a "Giant" and the other a "Trek". We want to have them checked over, so we take Ryan's bikes into a bike shop. When we pick them up, we ask each other what we should do with them. The bottom line is that Rich nor I could sell them or give them away. The decision is made to keep them for our personal use.

For the first couple of weeks, Rich and I drive to the gravesite every day. With going back to work the last week in August and still working on Ryan's business, it is becoming overwhelming. It may seem like we are bad parents, but it is so damned difficult to deal with your son buried in the ground, six feet under, thinking about his body decaying as time goes by. I still can't sleep, and the pressure is unreal.

A couple of days after our unloading Ryan's boxes, Wills phones us. I immediately put him on speaker phone so Rich can hear. "Mrs. Schlack, I have something for you, and I can deliver it today if you both will be home. I need to review everything with you to ensure everything is in order."

"Yes, SGT Wills, we will be home all day," I reply.

After hanging up, I ask Rich, "What does Wills mean by 'go through it with us to see everything is in place'? He never told me what it was."

Rich just shrugs and says, "I have no idea, but I guess we'll find out when he comes."

"The way Wills was talking," I continue, "it seems extremely important for him to come all the way from Green Bay today and deliver it."

Sergeant Wills arrives later in the day. He struggles to carry a large box into our house. The container is three feet long, eighteen inches wide and fifteen inches tall. We have him put it in the living room. With great ceremony, Wills gets out a pad and pen like he's going to list or check off items.

Wills stands over Rich as he kneels down and begins to open it. "I am responsible for making sure you get everything." He went on and on about this.

Inside is a beautiful maple colored wood footlocker with the Army emblem on its center which I am sure is compliments of the US Army. The interior of the footlocker is all felt-lined with a shelf resting on the top. I briefly wonder why Wills wouldn't know what it is since he is the guy who helps families during a veteran's death. Maybe this isn't from the army.

"Ok, then, everything looks good," Wills says. That is a strange thing to say, since nothing is really in it. What is he checking the footlocker for?

Rich stands up, faces Wills and says, "By the way, how are the death certificate copies coming? Also, the Casualty Report and the life insurance? We would like to finish up our end of the paperwork. We can't finish until we get those things."

"Oh, don't you worry about that," Wills blusters as he walks toward the front door. "I'm working on it." With a wave of his hand, he heads out the door.

Other tasks require attention. Rich is on the phone almost daily trying to cancel Ryan's cell phone, Internet and find out outstanding bills from any companies.

Carrying out an idea, Rich has set up a meeting with the JAG office at Ft. McCoy for Monday the 17th. We have quite a few questions about Ryan's money, insurance for the car, what taxes we need to pay and court proceedings. We want to know if we must go to probate for getting Ryan's money out of the bank.

CHAPTER 17

Wills calls on Friday. "I have all what you asked for and will mail it today. I'm calling so that you are aware it's on its way."

Rich breathes a sigh of relief. "Okay, that sounds good. We do need to take care of Ryan's business."

Rich now is gathering Ryan's things that he will put into the wooden footlocker. Things such as Ryan's uniform, his medals, a booklet with pictures of the funeral procession someone sent us, the binder from the Army "The Days Ahead: Essential Papers for Families of Fallen Service Members" and the Memorial service video held for Ryan at Fort Hood. The footlocker will then be placed at the foot of the bed in what was Ryan's bedroom.

On Friday, Donna texts me. It says, "I have a meeting on the day we were going to meet at school and work in our rooms. Would you want to change to Thursday the 20th?" Then a separate text obviously written shortly after the question says, "You know, Terri, there are things that you will have to do and things you can let go of. One of those things is the Open House. You should think about having a specialist cover that evening."

I had read her text later in the day, then replied.

Date: August 14, 2009
To: Donna
From: Terri
Plans change. Rich got an appointment with the JAG lawyer at Ft. McCoy on Monday the 17th. We need to be there at 2:00 and it's a two-hour drive. I also will be looking to get my hair cut this week. If I get away

early enough, I may go in for a bit on Monday morning. I'll not know until I wake up. On Tuesday is my lunch with neighbors and/or the haircut. Don't think I'll make it on Tuesday because maybe we can take care of some stuff as a result of Monday's meeting. So, I plan to go Wednesday–Friday because I think my vine idea (get it, fine idea?) will take a while to put up. Becca knows about my plans. So, donuts on Thursday?

Re: Open House. Here's the thing. I want to "break the ice" as soon as possible. I dread it, but I think I shouldn't back out because the first day of school may be tougher if I do. That's my take on it. It could be the kids roaming the school on Open House won't say a thing because they've forgotten. And if they do or say something, I need to deal with it.

See you on Thursday, I guess. Terri

The Judge Advocate General (JAG) representative tells us we need to fill out an affidavit since the total value of Ryan's property was less than $50,000. We need it notarized and that should take care of getting Ryan's car under our name so we can sell it and getting the two bank accounts closed. That form seems to be the one to solve issues like that. Another thing is to send along copies of the death certificate and the Casualty Report. That should do it. It is a very informative meeting and I feel confident proceeding.

The first thing Rich does when we get home is to contact Ryan's banks. All South is very accommodating, but Pentagon Federal says they have to wait 90 days before releasing funds. We talk about what deductions he might have and are told the Master Pay Account would tell us.

It is time for me to focus on school. There is still the sleep I can't seem to get, and I worry that I will have no energy for school. My mind fills with things that need to be done before the kids come. Rich lets me sleep in, but I pull myself out of bed by noon. That means I have had maybe six hours of sleep, but it's something. There needs to be a way to go to bed at a normal time and get up at the 5:30AM alarm for school.

I know going to work is what I need to do. It is so hard to sit home because all I do is think about Ryan and think about how Rich and Adam are doing, and it worries me. I don't know how to help them.

There is no way to relieve the pain. Working will keep me sane, although will I be effective?

I go to school on Wednesday, the week before school officially starts. I stop in the office to greet the staff that's there. Zoey the secretary and Principal Rogers call me into his office.

"How is everything going?" Gordon Rogers asks.

"It's going as well as can be expected with a few glitches," I reply.

"Do you feel you need some time off? We will get a substitute to begin the year for you," he says with concern.

"No, I need to be working, so my whole day is not consumed with worry and sadness. Besides, you know the first days are very important to establish routine," I say.

"So, if someone asks you how you are doing, what do you say?"

I think for a moment and answer, "I will say 'I am fine' but I would be lying. I can tell you that. People hesitate to pressure someone in distress. No, that's not quite accurate. To bring up something painful."

As I exit the office, Tim comes in with his young sons in tow. The oldest one waves at me, and I ask how his summer was.

He said, "Fine, how was yours?" just as normal as can be. I think he forgot unless Tim never said anything.

I pause because I didn't anticipate him saying that, then say, "I've had my ups and downs."

He says quietly, "Oh, yeah." Hanging his head, I know he feels embarrassed, poor thing.

Tim jumps in with, "I'll bet that European trip was a blast." So, we talk a few minutes about that as I'm walking out the door.

"Rich, shouldn't we have gotten Wills's package of papers by now?" I ponder aloud as I sit in our living room trying to relax.

"Yep. I'm calling him." Rich picks up the phone and dials.

Wills says adamantly, "I did mail it on that Friday, the day I told you I would. Might I suggest you give it a day or two yet? If you don't get it, then call me."

The next day I go to school to decorate the classroom. I borrow a fairly good-sized monkey that I hang in the upper corner of the room and then make vines extending from the monkey. What are vines without leaves? I didn't know what I have in mind but couldn't stop making leaves and vines.

8/21/2009 4:44PM
To: Terri & Rich
From: Michelle
Subject: hey, hey
Hey Rich and Terri,

I have to apologize for not writing sooner. We have been thinking so much about you and we continue to pray for you. But I needed to write to you for some time to ask how you are holding up.

I was totally blown away by the incredible funeral Ryan had. It was pretty overwhelming for so many reasons. Mostly just the honor and tribute that the military bestowed on him was incredible. But also, the realization that he died so senselessly at such a young age. And I must admit that attending his funeral made me think of my own brother. It's so hard to grasp.

When I spoke to Ryan at Grandma's funeral, I was so impressed with how much confidence he exuded. He had changed so much from when I had last spoke to him. Quite a guy.

We continue to keep you in our prayers. How are you doing? I'm guessing school starts soon, if not already. Will you be starting the school year on time? A friend of ours who recently lost her young husband had said that going back to teaching after the summer break is helping her get back into a routine... perhaps get her mind off the situation a bit. I'm sure you can drive yourself crazy thinking about it. So many thoughts and emotions swimming round and round.

We love you guys, Michelle

Happily, Rich finds a buyer for the car who lives a couple of hours away in Milwaukee. My stomach is twisting in knots as I watch the car being driven away. I feel I betrayed Ryan somehow because that car was his pride and joy.

We get something from Wills, but the insurance information is not among the papers. I'm beginning not to trust Wills. I get a hunch and look at the envelope's postmark date. It was mailed on Thursday, the 20th, yesterday.

CHAPTER 18

It is August 24, the first day of school for teachers. I get about five hours of sleep but there is so much to do at school, I won't have time to think how tired I am. Things kick off with a district staff gathering at the high school auditorium where the superintendent gives a pep talk and recognizes those who have taught in the district for 30 years. Usually, a member of the Board of Education welcomes us all and then a guest speaker or entertainment wraps up the meet. We go back to our schools for more meetings.

Teachers can work in the classroom on some days, but there are more meetings and occasional in-services throughout the week. My friend Becca comes to help, and we plaster the walls around the room with vines and leaves. I am obsessed with this.

What I should realize is I am going contradictory to "Room Appearance 101", one of those 5-minute lessons in a teacher's education course. A teacher should never overload the students' senses with too much crowding of a multitude of décor on the room walls. This year I suspect a failing grade in this.

One workday, the reading specialist and the school counselor come into my classroom.

"How are you doing? Are you ready for the kiddos?" the counselor asks.

"Terri, we are concerned and want to know if you feel you can handle it," the reading specialist says in a worried tone. "The first days can be overwhelming."

"Thank you for your concern, but you both know the first days are critical for classroom management," I calmly state. "Routine is very important. Some students struggle with organization when switching classrooms for the first time."

The reading specialist jumps in, "There is a new reading strategy I will be teaching to the primary grades. Would you be interested in me coming to demonstrate? It will take a few weeks."

Since I will be teaching reading to all the three fourth-grade classes, I suggest, "If you would teach this strategy to two classrooms while I watch, I'll teach it to the third class. How's that idea?"

"That will work out great! We'll get together so I can give you the gist of it and find out when your reading classes are," the reading specialist replied.

I am busy. I lay out a guide for daily lesson plans for the first week, dig out books each student will receive, clean out my desk and back room, setup computers and whatever else needs doing. Many tasks must be completed to ensure a smooth-running classroom. Make name tags for each child's desk, assign a number to each student, put books s/he will need on each desk, put the child's assigned number in each textbook, post a class list on the door, and number the hooks in the hall where jackets and backpacks will be kept. Then there is getting with the other fourth-grade teachers to determine recess and find out if that time interferes with another grade, receive the specials' (art, music and PE) schedules, figure which subjects and what time you teach them then make large room posters of the schedules for each day of the week.

There is more figuring of schedules if two or three teachers in the same grade level want to departmentalize. Of course, copies of class lists go to the specialist teachers and to the teacher for the learning disabled, so each can figure when to pull the identified students from class. If it doesn't run together smoothly, the only thing to do is start over.

8/25/2009 8:13PM
To: Michelle & Lee
From: Terri
Subject: Re: hey, hey
Michelle,

Don't apologize for not writing. Things happen. It's good to hear from you whenever you can write. I started working again last week, but I have flexible hours. I knew I had lots to do especially when I get carried away decorating the room. I officially went back on Monday, the 24th. Days of meetings and a workday with this Friday and Monday off. I think Rich is looking at getting out of town. I worry for him, as he has no place besides home for other thoughts. I have work. He doesn't have anyone to talk to here. Work keeps me busy, but thoughts and people who want to talk bring me back. I know. It will take time. I realize this.

Paperwork, waiting for Ryan's belongings from Iraq and more paperwork has become a frustrating waiting game. We cannot put off this part of our responsibilities. The sergeant assigned to us has faded in his commitment–okay, he does have to do his two weeks now for the Reserve. We are supposed to get someone assigned to us from Ft. Hood to let us know about the trial. Haven't heard anything yet except it may start in September.

It's crucial for Adam to begin the search for wedding halls promptly to ensure a nice place for September. Oh, well, so the wedding will be next October? Or in 2011?

Thanks for checking in. Hug your babies for us.
Love, Terri and Rich

Open House at school occurs on the 26th of August, a Wednesday. At the "Meet and Greet," parents and students can see the classroom, meet the teacher, and ask questions. Although rooms and teachers may not be fully ready, the aim is for each teacher to have a presentable room. In my pith hat and jungle jacket, I look pretty good greeting parents and the students.

At the home front, Rich and I decide to follow through on our needs to settle Ryan's business since it is apparent Wills is an idiot. Rich gets in touch with the coroner in Texas. "Hello, my name is Richard Schlack, and I am calling to ask for copies of Ryan Schlack's Death Certificate. Is it possible to mail it to us?"

The coroner replies, "I cannot send it directly to you, no. I have to send it to Wills, and I have done that already. You will have to ask him for it. I'm sorry this hasn't been done."

The next call is to Army Accounting to find out about the life insurance. After some jumping hoops, Accounting told Rich, "You should expect information in the mail. I would think an army representative would take care of this for you." Rich thanks him for the information.

I bought some Melatonin for a sleep aid and tried it last night. I am dragging today.

Ryan's shipment from his apartment, which was in storage while he was in Iraq, arrived last Monday, the 24th. I am gone to work, so Rich starts to separate the items in logical groupings and places them in the basement. Adam will handle the stacked electronic games and systems, as Rich and I are unfamiliar with them. Supposedly, this is the shipment that carries the memorial tapes, but we didn't find it. I have to remember that we haven't gone through everything yet, so I can only hope.

Rich must have been shopping online and browsing nearby a concrete statue shop. He decides to order a bench from a local concrete business. We already know what it will look like. It has the army insignia, stars on the seat with a little phrase, "I am a Soldier". The bench legs have the "Support our Troops" and ribbon design on it. It will be ready in about three weeks. We plan to put it out on the front lawn near the house until the cold weather comes rolling in.

I sometimes feel guilty about the trip coming up, but I have come to the conclusion Rich suggests trips because it is getting away from the house and there are sad feelings hanging in the rooms and just maybe it's his way of coping with Ryan's death. I could be wrong about this because he is a guy who needs things to do. When he is home, he sits in his Lazy Boy a lot during the day. On a trip, he's driving, reading maps, going to places and staying busy.

Green Bay is our destination for the Green Bay Arts. Rich explores photography artists, and I occasionally look for unique lawn ornaments. From Sturgeon Bay, we visit Washington Island for half a day and explore Door County, a favored vacation spot for Milwaukee and Chicago residents.

CHAPTER 19

Here it is. September. The month Ryan would have been coming home to start his future. In those rare moments of free time, my thoughts drift to Ryan and the possibility of having him nearby once more. This will be a long month.

I have not updated my family in a while concerning the latest news, so I send an email out.

9/5/2009. 9:58PM
To: Family
From: Terri & Rich
Subject: I'll bet you're wondering
Just thought you'd like an update. The items Ryan sent back from Iraq have been in Texas for a couple of weeks. Rich called the transportation company, and they were told arrival should be on Sept.11; the date Ryan was getting out of the Army. We really don't understand the wait. We are not authorized to change the shipment date. Frustration.

We were told by the company commander that a video of the memorial the battalion had for Ryan would be in with this shipment. We acquired a list of what was being sent with the second shipment, but the videotapes are not on the list. Frustration.

Yesterday, the sergeant who I believed knew what he was doing brought the paperwork that should have been started early. The more I learn about his responsibilities, the more frustrated I become with him.

September 8-9 is the date set for the grand jury. We are not allowed to go.

We do know the prosecutor's name and number because he has called and Rich talked to him about a week ago. He says this is the only case he is working on, so giving it his full attention. There are some concerns about the drinking at the party and how additional details are coming out of what happened that night. Ryan's actions remain as reported. It is finding out after Ryan was shot that we are finding out more.

The trial will probably be after October according to the prosecutor. I'll let you know. There is something the prosecutor said that is of concern. We would like to attend the trial. We'll go to the courtroom, but we can't assist with Abadia's sentencing if found guilty. At least that is what I understand. The prosecutor asks us to find individuals to speak at the sentencing about Ryan's impact. He will clarify when we are there. Friends at the party can't speak because they are witnesses and will be called to testify. We will ask the prosecutor to see if we can contact any of those guys to see if they can name or find anybody who wasn't at the party that would speak. Rich, Adam, and I will participate if we can, of course. I doubt any of Ryan's friends from Wisconsin can afford to take time to fly down to Texas. I wonder if videotaped speeches would be admissible. I will find out. If we can't go in to see the trial, then we will ask what is going on when the prosecutors come out during breaks.

Rita and Jerry, I am hoping that you two would consider speaking on Ryan's behalf because I know Ryan did visit you and spent Thanksgiving with your family. Maybe you can get input from any member of your family. It's just a thought.

I just don't have the excitement for this school year. If it weren't for a friend or two, I know the classroom would not have been ready enough for the Open House which was on Aug. 26. I have to give myself a firm talking to most mornings even to get up. Neither of us gets a good night's sleep. Someone is always up, it seems. Rich now handles all the running around and phone calls to get things done. Our frustration grows when more paperwork is needed for tasks we believed were already handled, as both he and I are equally meticulous about these matters.

Rich considers going back to school, volunteering or finding a part-time job. He does need something to think about and do. We both feel like Atlas, burdened with the world. People say time heals, but we have to manage it in the now. It's impossible to see light at the tunnel's end.

Thanks for listening.

Terri and Rich

It is 3:30AM, and I am still awake. I was doing fairly well with sleep the last few days. I feel strongly tonight that I should start a journal. I am not really sure why, but maybe it will help. Rich tells me he is thinking of putting together a photo album covering Ryan's military career. That seems like a worthwhile project for him. Maybe it can be used in court.

Nothing seems to be simple. The Pentagon Credit Union has still not sent the balance of Ryan's bank account, even though we did everything they told us to do. Wills was to get the life insurance paperwork started after the funeral. Wills didn't think anything needed to be done, but then he talks about paperwork coming from somewhere. Wills finally brought the papers last week on Thursday for Rich to sign.

Things that are going... not necessarily right, but making progress is the headstone to order. I was able to go with Rich on Friday to the Veteran's Affairs Office.

While discussing it with someone named Judy at the VA's Office, Rich insists, "We can have either granite or marble, right? Veterans' gravestones in the cemetery vary. There's got to be another stone used, not just marble."

Judy replies firmly, "All the headstones in the veteran's area are marble." It is obvious by her tone she will not reconsider.

Rich and I then talk about what will be on the gravestone. We all agree on most ideas such as the name, rank, when he was born, the date he died, and the battle operation he was in.

"There's one more line. Do you have any thoughts?" Judy asks.

"I suppose 'Loving Son & Brother'" Rich suggests. "Terri, what do you think?"

Pausing for a moment, I can't decide if I should say what my idea is. There won't be a do-over. I begin cautiously. "I feel every gravestone has 'Loving' lines. Of course, that person was loved. I want a statement about Ryan. What do you think of 'Blessed Are the Peacemakers'? To me, it tells that Ryan fought in a war for peace and, at the party, his attempt to help quell the arguing between the two guys."

Rich is quiet for a moment thinking this over. "Yes, I think I like that. Let's do it."

Judy says, "Hold on. Let's see if all the information will fit on the stone." She works on her computer a moment and tells us it will fit.

The All-South Credit Union sent the balance after receiving the documents.

In the mail today, I receive a flyer advertising decorative wreaths. One catches my eye called the "American Tribute Wreath". It's 24 inches with red, white and blue flowers on a green background, so I order it. It will go on our front door.

CHAPTER 20

It is mid-September and finally the recorded Memorial Service done for Ryan at Ft. Hood arrives sent by the new company commander. He sends four of them. Rich tries the first one, and it doesn't work, so he takes it to a camera shop, and they can't get it to work.

The second DVD works just fine. Rich viewed it before I get home from work. When I get home, I immediately ask Rich to put the tape in the player. The quality isn't 100% but it is viewable. Many nice things were said about Ryan. It makes me cry. He made impressions on many people; most notable was the constant mention of what a good friend he was and how tall he was. Two friends spoke. One was Ethan Jaks. His home was where the shooting took place. The video wasn't clear on the other soldier's name tag. This soldier also felt Ryan was a good friend who would help you out in any way he could.

On another front, I lose count of how many calls we have made to Wills and to Ft. Hood about the second shipment. Rich begins tracking it down on his own. Finally, he discovers it's no longer in the Texas warehouse, with no further information available. I don't know how Rich did it, but he finds the second shipment stored in a warehouse in Green Bay, about an hour down the road. Something else which Wills was supposed to keep track.

Rich calls the warehouse, and they confirm the shipment has been there awhile so off Rich goes to Green Bay. More clothes and games and small figurines and carrying cases for these figurines are packed in Rich's car. The shipment also includes the commanders' coins from

Ryan's memorial. I breathe a sigh of relief. These coins are only given to soldiers under special circumstances. It has the commander's unit insignia on it. We already planned to get a display case and put the fifteen coins in it.

The prosecutor updates us on the situation. "The grand jury just finished up on Friday. Now, it has to go to the division commander, brigade commander, and the corps commander for their recommendations. That will take 2-3 weeks. It sounds like 'pre-meditation' is not under consideration. This will affect the sentencing, of course."

Rich is certain of an upcoming trial. We wonder when that will be. What else is needed to set the trial date? It seems the days move so slowly.

School has been in session for five weeks. I change the room décor monthly to reflect the holidays. I've done this for so long, I simply put up the decorations. Major holidays have more, while other times have less. This time, I don't feel any excitement about putting up the Halloween decorations. Too many memories with the boys during Halloween.

I recall one year Ryan came up with the funniest costume. Actually, this story comes out every Halloween.

"What will you be doing tonight, Ryan?" I ask him.

"I am putting something together. I am still trying to figure it out," Ryan replies.

"Oh, you plan to go trick-or treating? Seriously?" Rich says, surprised by this.

When it is time to leave to do some trick-or-treating, Ryan comes into the living room and models his costume. All three of us look at him and burst out laughing.

Adam tries to talk while laughing. "What are you? I mean, what do you call this new look?"

Ryan explains in a serious manner, "Well, there is Batman, Superman and Spiderman, so I will be Fanman." Yes, he managed to have a large square fan attached to himself. We laughed about that for a long time and every Halloween after.

In the classroom, the bulletin boards and doors have skeletons, witches, and ghosts. The students do help assemble the giant eight-foot spider web frame and then tie on the spider web. Finally, the huge spiders are placed on the web and place it so it leans on the classroom window.

I'm thinking about throwing away the old decorations by month's end. If I retire, why would I want them? Some are not in great shape anymore. Yep, I am already imagining that Halloween decorations will be trashed.

It is only October, but I feel a decision has to be made about my teaching next year. At least I can make inquiries about retiring. I sent a note to my friend MaryAnne, who is involved with the union and would have knowledge about this.

10/3/2009 11:20AM
To: MaryAnne
From: Terri
Subject: a question
Hey There Girlfriend,
I have been giving this some serious thought, weighing the pros and cons. Considering recent events in my life, I am seriously contemplating retirement this year. I need to find out about health care insurance. To whom do I speak to regarding payment, duration, health information for decision-making? Should I go to the Instructional Service Center or directly to the Wisconsin Education Association Insurance?

The email continues with telling MaryAnne that the fact Abadia was drunk is in his favor, believe it or not. Wasn't coherent or something. I don't know. I can't imagine the trial will start real soon either. I end by thanking her for the homemade tomato soup she brought to school. Absolutely delicious!

MaryAnne sends an email back relaying her experience when she retired and advice about whom to see.

In mid-October, Adam and Ann go to a wedding event. The groom is a friend of both Ryan and Adam. Actually, Ryan was supposed to be a groomsman for the wedding.

Adam calls us the day after the wedding. "Awe, Mom, they did something so neat!" Adam begins. "Sitting on a stand in the church entryway, was a large poster with three photos of Ryan and the words 'In Loving Memory SGT Ryan Schlack 7/12/79-7/18/09'. Not only that, on the back of the wedding agenda handed out, they have a picture of Ryan smiling in his uniform with 'In Memory of SGT Ryan Schlack - Forever in our hearts'. I brought home an agenda so you can see it. Oh, by the way, I wore Ryan's army boots to the wedding. It seemed an appropriate tribute that wouldn't take the shine off their wedding day. Don't worry, I wore a nice shirt and pants."

"Yes, I would like to see the agenda," I answer. "Did you have a good time at the wedding?" Adam begins to share with us what the wedding day was like. I've never heard of this type of tribute done at a wedding before, but I think it is incredibly sweet and thoughtful.

A few days after that, I went to the basement to get more tissue paper. Halfway down the steps, I holler, "Rich, we have a problem! I think the sump pump gave out."

"Oh, great," my husband grumbles as he comes down the stairs behind me. Over half the basement was covered with about 1/4 inch of water in places; just enough to create a mess.

"It looks like the large area rug is ruined and the small carpet pieces," I comment. "Can you help me pick up all the stuff on the wet parts of the floor? Let's put them in the garage for now."

Rich gets brooms and large rags and we proceed to clean up the floor. We did as much as we could that night. Thank goodness we had Ryan's things up on tables or shelving. The few boxes on the floor absorbed some water which may have saved the items inside.

Despite getting the sump pump working again, Rich chooses to buy a new one. Now there are fans drying the floor. After two days of the fans blowing, we are pleased everything looks good.

I feel I should write the Owens Family to keep them posted, so I send a handwritten letter.

October 24, 2009
Dear Owens Family,

I debated for a long time if I should write again. My husband and I often wonder how your son/brother is doing. Hopefully, time is taking care of the long process of healing.

You may be aware that Article 32 has concluded, and a trial will follow. The prosecutor tells us it is common for the defense to try to push the court date later in hopes of those involved not remembering the facts as easily. The first date was Oct. 28. The prosecutor thought December or January.

My husband and I plan to attend. We are hoping our son and fiancée can also attend. Our hope is to meet Greg and others who attended that night. I don't know if Greg would feel comfortable, but I thought we'd at least offer our email and phone number. I wrote it at the end of this letter. Since you are our only line of communication at this point, please pass this on to him and we'll leave it to him to communicate with us.

We also want to bring any of Ryan's things that the guys might appreciate as a memory. If there is a video game, movie, picture, or something they may know of, we'd happily bring it with us if we can.

Just in case Greg doesn't know, when the man who shot Ryan is found guilty and the sentencing begins, we need to find friends of Ryan's who are not participating in the trial to speak about Ryan to the panel. We are asked to find friends who can talk about how Ryan's death affected him/her; to make Ryan a real person, a valuable human being. If I understand the prosecutor right, if I want to speak about Ryan, I cannot sit in the courtroom. I don't understand the reasoning behind this, but my husband also understands it is this way. If this is true, I am very upset I can't be in the courtroom. I also feel helpless since I don't know who

Ryan hung around with. I desperately need people to talk about Ryan and update me on court proceedings.

But, again, we'll leave it to your son/brother if he wants to get in touch with us.

I can't express how we felt receiving your first letter. We were so grateful to be able to relay to your son/brother that we do not blame anyone there but Abadia.

Thank you for any help in sending this information on to Greg. Hopefully, Greg feels comfortable passing this on to Ethan Jaks and the others. I don't know names.

You are all in our thoughts.
Rich and Terri Schlack

Greg's sister sends an email and expresses her feelings. She also called Greg to let him know what we need. She tells me Greg wrote a letter to us some time ago but hung onto it until he was ready to send it. He'll now send it.

CHAPTER 21

The news media is going crazy today, November 5. All that's talked about is of an unbelievable incident involving a soldier on a killing spree. Nidal Hassan, a US army major and psychologist fatally shoots thirteen people on Fort Hood making it the worst mass shooting on an American military base. There were over 30 people injured. Thank goodness he was stopped by SGT Mark Todd shooting Hassan. Hassan did not die but was paralyzed. The question has to be asked. Did Hassan get a gun on base the same way Abadia did?

I call Adam. "Did you hear what happened today, Adam?" I ask.

"Yes, I am hearing all about it. I am as outraged as anybody else. I thought, how did this happen again? It is a birthday I'll not forget easily," Adam comments.

Judy from the VA Office calls and says, "Ryan's headstone was placed last week sometime. I don't know if you were told or not." Rich thanks her for contacting us.

Rich went to the cemetery and put a flag with a stand next to the headstone. He calls me at work to let me know. I go after work to see it. The marble gravestone is very nice looking. It is a long while before I can stop the waterworks to drive home.

What a surprise we receive in the mail. When I come home from work, Rich greets me with, "It was not expected, but we received $1200 from Ryan's Montgomery Bill money in the mail."

"Oh, you're right. I thought they just keep it," I say. Money is deducted from a soldier's pay for a few years and then given to veterans for education or training. Since he never used it and he has died, the Bill refunds what was paid in.

"And one more surprise," Rich goes on. "It's exactly 90 days after his death and we receive Ryan's money from the Pentagon Federal's account."

"Will wonders never cease?" I say in awe.

Adam calls and we talk a bit. Then he says, "I don't know if I told you, but the day after my birthday, my boss at the warehouse said the news made mention of Ryan and how he was killed.

Observing Veterans Day in November is the first time I tear up in front of my fourth-grade students. Over the speaker, the principal, Mr. Rogers, asks for a moment of silence for the veterans. Following the pledge, I go out into the hall to regain composure but fall short. I am an emotional person and I need to learn to quash the tears coming to the surface. The next instance I think, good luck with that.

It is rough when Mondays come around. I clearly hate Mondays. I don't want to get up in the morning, don't want to work, don't want to be there. Yet, I need to be sure I am functional. On Mondays, I linger just a moment in the office and tell the secretary how I hate today before heading to my room. I don't understand why I do this. What am I expecting her to do?

A few days before Thanksgiving break, a group of teachers are sitting in the teachers' lounge eating lunch. Zoey asks, "Terri, why don't you just retire at the end of the semester? Don't wait until the end of the school year."

"I have to admit the thought crossed my mind, Zoey," I begin, "but I am incredibly torn because it was drilled into me from my first job on that you don't quit. I am in the middle of a contract, and I shouldn't just quit. I have no idea why that was important to me except that I was raised that way."

"There are always exceptions, Terri," Zoey softens her voice.

"Zoey, it would mean I will sit home every day moping around, worrying about Rich and Adam, and maybe sink into a depression I may not get out of. Besides, I will have 20 years here in Fond du Lac at the end of the year. I need this work partly for my own sanity. I know I hate Mondays, but it usually gets a bit better as the week goes on."

As I walk into the house, Rich hands me a letter from SPC Greg Owens. "Do you think it is the letter Greg had written but didn't send?" I ask Rich.

Dear Mr. and Mrs. Schlack,

Without faith anything is impossible and with faith everything is possible. In that I strongly use my faith in God to make it possible to say goodbye to Ryan; without faith I would be lost in this time of tragedy. Ryan was a friend in which I met three years ago upon my arrival at Fort Hood. It didn't take long for me to become friends with Ryan. I soon learned he was from Wisconsin, which is right by my home state of Minnesota. I could tell he shared the same small-town upbringing that I was brought up with. About two months after I arrived at the Unit, SPC Ethan Jaks joined the 704th Support Battalion. Like myself, Jaks became friends with Ryan quite quickly. They both worked in the C and E Sections, while I was the 92 Yankee which was working in Supply. The C and E section was responsible for repairing technical gear or breaking them so they cannot be used for anything. A good example of this gear is night-vision goggles. After working within the Unit, the group of friends grew, and I could tell Ryan felt like he finally had a group of friends who praised his uniqueness instead of looking down upon it. Ryan was truly one of a kind, probably the most kind-hearted, non-self-centered person I ever met. He was always helping me and others. I remember last year before we deployed, we had a Company Ball in which the soldiers had to wear our Class A uniforms. I could never and still to this day tie a tie. Well, Ryan tied my tie for me. I know it seems like a small thing, but it saved me from looking unprofessional in my uniform, so it really meant a lot to me. After that, he gave several of us soldiers a ride to the Ball in his Mustang. He really enjoyed that car.

Ryan worked at the Entry Control Point (ECP) while stationed in Iraq. He was a guard at a gate and worked grueling long hours in the hot Middle Eastern sun. I saw less of Ryan towards the beginning of the deployment which was a bummer. You see, Ryan and I shared the love of Sci-Fi, Horror, and Comedy movies (I still have the Jim Carey movie he lent me right before block leave in my dresser's bottom drawer. I don't have the heart to get rid of it.) We both enjoyed such bands as Foo Fighters, Nickelback, and The Offspring. I remember Ryan would always sing out loud to his favorite bands while driving. I told him never to quit the Army and try to become a professional singer! Towards the end of the deployment, Ryan and Jaks came off ECP and were put back to work in the C and E section of the motor pool where I was working. I saw them every day now, and it seemed like the group was back. I remember every night a group of us would sit on our steps and talk for hours about how great it was going to be once we made it back to the United States.

During our last month of being deployed, Ryan became my running partner. We would run four miles a night. He would always say that he needed to lose some weight because he gained weight during leave in March. It was funny because he had such long legs where two of my steps equaled one of his. Ryan, Jax and I got into the routine of going to midnight chow at the dining facilities (DFAC). I always marveled at his incredible capacity for Coke consumption. He would drink about five cans in one meal! I really miss him a lot.

It saddens me greatly that I'll never get the chance to thank him personally for saving my life. I was so excited when I found out he was back from block leave and was coming over to Jak's. He showed up and was glad to be back with his friends. I wish Barto Abadia was never there that night. He simply had too much liquor in his system and was becoming more and more rude and violent to us. I remember SPC Spencer Vans and I told him to stop drinking and go to bed. Sadly,

Abadia didn't want to hear that and became violent toward me and the other guests. He pushed me and stormed out the back and said he was going to drive home, so Ryan, Vans, and I exited through the front door to make sure he didn't drive while intoxicated. Ryan, Vans, and I were on the front lawn talking about a game called "War Hammer" that Ryan was going to teach me to play, when suddenly Abadia appeared and fired a shot at the same time Ryan pushed me out of the way. It happened so fast that my reaction was to grab the gun from Abadia and give the weapon to Jaks and told him to call 911. That moment was the most numb and scary situation in my life. The gun sounded like a cap gun we all played with as children. I held Ryan like an infant while he laid there dying. We were waiting for the ambulance. I didn't let go of Ryan until he was loaded into the ambulance.

How is it that Ryan could survive two tours overseas yet fall victim to a fellow friend and soldier, Barto Abadia? That is the tragic and most frequent question I ask myself. It's so wrong and unfair. Ryan gave his life to save his friends. He cared for the well-being of others and put his life on the line for me. I feel so guilty wishing the bullet would have struck me instead of Ryan. Today's date is November 10th, and I am still just as sad and guilty as the night he was shot.

In my mind, Ryan is still on extended leave and he will be returning any day now. I wish that were true. I know deep down that Ryan is gone and will never return, and that's what hurts me the most. I will be walking down the street or at work and all of a sudden, I will relive that night in my mind, and it makes me break down. They say a man isn't supposed to cry. To me that is not true. Losing a close friend will do that to anyone. Ryan, Jaks, and I were supposed to take a trip to New Orleans this upcoming Thanksgiving weekend. I can't go without Ryan. It was his plan and idea to go.

Ryan's memorial was a very sad event for me, but I know that we all cared for Ryan and God has plans for your son. I miss his sense of humor and friendship so much. I always considered him a gentle giant. He *towered over me. I am about 5 feet 10 inches and 135 pounds. He had a great love for life and for those around him. It's with great sadness and a heavy heart that I say goodbye to Ryan and only wished that one day I could be as kind and helpful to others as Ryan was. I feel deeply for his family and could only offer you the comfort that God has plans for us all and that Ryan is in a better place away from all the hate and violence. One day when I feel comfortable, I wish to visit Ryan's gravesite and honor my fallen friend.*

Greg Owens

What a beautiful letter. It makes me ache for him for all he is going through.

CHAPTER 22

It is already December. Falling snow melts by day's end. I come home from work and Rich informs me the prosecutor called.

"Okay, what did he say?" I ask.

"Remember when we got the impression we may not be able to sit in the courtroom during the court proceedings? The prosecutor mentioned a possibility of us being able to sit in, with the defense's consent. Terri, without military secrets, why can't we sit in? Now, it is up to the defense."

A few days later, Rich phoned a coroner at the San Antonio Army facility where the autopsy was done. "I am sorry to tell you that I sent it to SGT Wills within weeks of the incident. Wills should have sent it to you long ago. I will try to track the autopsy paperwork down and give you a call back." Rich thanked the coroner.

Unfortunately, we are not home, so this doctor leaves a message on the answering machine. "Wills is out of town on emergency leave and will be back on Friday. I will fax the autopsy to Wills who should then get it to you by Monday or Tuesday. Officially, you probably know I cannot send it directly to you. I'm sorry this is taking so long."

Days later, I send an email to Greg telling him we received his letter. The email continued with the fact we are looking forward to meeting him if he is okay with that, and that we may not be able to sit in on the proceedings but hope I'm wrong. My email went on to say the shooting on Nov. 5 was heartbreaking, and I hoped Jaks and he weren't anywhere near the area. I'm writing to make sure the guys are okay.

Finally, I shared with him what was written on Ryan's gravestone:

> Ryan R. Schlack
> SGT US Army
> Jul 12, 1979–Jul 18, 2009
> Operation Iraqi Freedom
> "Blessed are the Peacemakers"

I admit to Greg that the last line has a double meaning for us.

Rich gets busy and writes another letter to the National Personnel Records Center to try to verify and receive Ryan's medals. The last letter from the NPRC says they did not receive some form. We filled out what we were told to fill out and mailed it some time ago. Rich cites the Request Number and the person who signed the previous letter. Well, now they will check on it.

I managed a late-day appointment to visit my physician assistant. While there, I begin to tell her about Ryan. "I feel so depressed all the time. It is such a horrid feeling. I am tired of feeling this way," I finally say.

She advises, "I am going to put you on an anti-depressant called Alprazolam."

"I'm not sure about that. My husband and my friend both were on anti-depressants and describe the weird feeling they got from it. My husband stopped taking them. I am worried that during the trial I won't be on top of what's going on. I need a clear head."

"We have time to adjust the dosage as needed," she explains. "Don't worry. You can't go on like this, that's for sure."

Could these pills also help with sleep deprivation?

We haven't placed anything at Ryan's gravesite for Christmas yet. We have no idea what to put there. Driving around the cemetery to see what's done, I tell Rich, "It seems holiday flowers such as poinsettias, lilies, and roses are the typical thing to do. Let's go to Stein's to see what they have."

I find a nice-looking arrangement of a few red and a few white poinsettias with some greenery in a large gold-colored plastic vase with a long pick on the bottom so it could be pushed into the ground. I saw that at the cemetery, so I assumed the groundskeeper would find it acceptable. Rich and I can put it at Ryan's gravesite on Saturday.

Christmas Eve Day at the doctor's office, I talk about the upcoming trial. She has a health concern.

"Terri, my thought is this hysterectomy will alleviate your current problems. How do you feel about having it done based on what you know about when the trial will be held?" she proposes.

"I don't want to be in a situation that would prevent me from attending that trial. What if a complication occurs? The trial keeps getting pushed into the next month. There isn't a lot of time given between the day we are told and the beginning date of the trial. Will I be well enough to fly out there and sit if the court date is close to recovery time?" I respond in frustration.

"This is not a real emergency. How about surgery after the trial?" the doctor suggests.

I didn't care about that idea, but it makes the most sense. All this postponing causes me stress. Initially set for September, the trial was rescheduled to October, then January, and finally February. I hope I can hold out that long.

Rich, Adam, and I talk about going to visit Ryan's gravesite on Christmas Day. I feel devastated he won't be here to share Christmas. There are so many things I think about such as what his future would have been like. What decisions would he have made about his life? One person Ryan kept in touch with was a cousin, and she thinks he would have gone to tech school for computer repair. According to her, Ryan was going to tell her something that would surprise her when he got home.

Adam came over to continue to help check Ryan's game systems by playing the games. He came upon a game called "BioShock". Shortly before Ryan went back to Fort Hood, he had been showing Adam how to play it. Adam found a few other things he would like. One item is a

DVD called "Yes, Man" and the other a cartoon show named "Avatar". Since Adam is now an adult, he didn't find the cartoon interesting at all. Why would a cartoon be so good? Ryan had said his friends and he thought it was so good. Ryan told him he had the whole set, so when he comes back from Hood, they will watch it.

I ask Adam to get on Ryan's Facebook. Some names came up that aren't familiar. Maybe these guys can help with the sentencing portion to testify on Ryan's behalf, so I write the names down. The problem is are they Army friends or hometown friends? I think I know the hometown friends.

It is 11:45PM Christmas Eve, and I can't sleep. I've been trying to stay busy and focus on tasks to avoid becoming too emotional.

The first Christmas without Ryan. He would make it home for Christmas more often than not. Adam arrives with Ann and her five-year-old son. There is the opening of Christmas presents and assembling of toys. Later, Rich and I know where we need to go to make this day complete; to make it about family.

It has snowed a bit enough to cover the ground. A light dusting is on Ryan's gravestone. Mostly, we are huddled around the stone. It still seems wrong somehow that now we are only three. That Ryan is not in Texas or Iraq or some faraway place, but here. After a while, we quietly leave as I brush away the tears. Each of us touches the stone gently as we each say, "I love you."

CHAPTER 23

2010

The new year! It's here, but nobody in this house is even excited about it. We didn't even watch television for the celebrations.

I never realized it, but I tend to wait for Rich to say, "Let's go to the cemetery." My guess is that he just doesn't think to ask. When we do go together, I feel Rich is my support while we are there. He gives me strength. I handle it better when I go with him. It could be though, he wants to go alone. Today, I am having a bad evening and the subject comes up.

"So, I'm kind of wondering, Rich. How often do you go to the cemetery? Just curious," I ask.

Rich thinks a couple seconds and replies, "I go maybe every couple of days to the cemetery."

Wow! Does that make me feel lousy! Why do I not go more often? Yes, I do go on my own, but I have a tough time the following few days. Why did I think he would tell me the days he went? Why wouldn't he ask me to go with him? I ask him every day how his day is going. He never tells me he went to the cemetery. His answer is most always that he did nothing.

Since the funeral, I think about and talk to Ryan in my head most every day. It's my way of communicating, and it helps or maybe comforts me. Standing and staring at a gravestone just leads to feeling rage sometimes at how Ryan died.

Shall I make a resolution for 2010? The next day, I go to the cemetery. All the way there, I sob and as I get closer, it gets worse.

Because of a river of tears, I can't see, so I turn down the wrong cemetery path, which means having to circle around, then park the car near Ryan's site. Good thing I have to stop. Sitting in the car and sobbing uncontrollably for a while, I finally compose myself. I leave the car, standing by his gravesite, talking to Ryan about my daily thoughts and imagining his responses. All the way home, I tell myself I will not depend on Rich. There is no reason to.

Finally, we hear from the US Human Resources Command which explains that they are aware of our request regarding Ryan's medals, but due to the number of requests and the difficulty of some cases, it may take six months before they get to it. They appreciate our patience.

In late January, standing by the grave, Rich says, "It doesn't change anything. It doesn't bring Ryan back, or change the events, or make me feel better or more at peace or anything. It doesn't change anything."

This is one of the fewest times he opens up. There is a great sadness in his eyes. I feel for him because he is right. Thinking of Rich sitting home alone in his Lazy Boy, thinking and thinking and not coming up with the answers to his questions. Should I stay home and be there for Rich? Can I make a difference in my fragile state?

The Nurse Practitioner orders some pills, in her words, "to take the edge off". I take a couple. I wasn't going to, but as I think about the upcoming trial whenever it is, I need to be halfway composed and alert. The antidepressants take a week or two to kick in.

A weird thing happened last night. My cell phone was ringing, but I didn't get to it on time. I did not recognize the number, so I call it back. It rings, then quits, so I look it up on the Internet. It is a number that comes from Ft. Hood, but originally the phone was purchased in Georgia. I knew Ryan met some guys from Georgia at a place he'd been; maybe Ft. Hood. I call it back again and leave a message about me being Ryan's mom and to call me. Nobody ever calls back. So now I am worried I scared the caller off. I need to think in terms of the caller's importance of contacting us again.

Then we get a call from MAJ Frank Michaels, our attorney. He leaves a message on our answering machine. He says he needs addresses and phone numbers of our family. Rich suggests I call him to ask all the questions we have. MAJ Michaels is in his car but did manage to answer a few of our questions.

"I am not sure how this works, but shall I gather photos and/or letters from family and friends to present during the sentencing phase?" I ask.

"By all means, do that," he replies. "Also, you, your husband and your son can write victim impact statements as well. By the way, Abadia's mental evaluation is finished. There are two versions; the short version is what the prosecutor gets, and the long one is given to the defense and judge. The gist of the short version is that Abadia has a mental defect that was exasperated by alcohol which caused him not to appreciate his wrongful doing. We are getting two psychologists to refute that. According to the long form, the trial should be as early as February 16th.

It suddenly slaps me in the face that this is real. It is truly beginning, and I need to be prepared, so we need to get our act together for this. Thoughts are flying through my head. The trial is now possibly in February.

With the mass killing by Major Hassan who killed thirteen people and injured thirty-one people at Ft. Hood last November, I don't know what to expect now. Will Hassan's trial supersede Abadia's?

CHAPTER 24

I send an email to my brother Jerry. The email explains the prosecutor's consideration of the letters from family and friends. I explain I wasn't sure who in his family knew Ryan well enough to write something, but could he forward my request to them? The email continues:

I am writing to ask for help, but if you don't feel comfortable enough about doing this, I understand. I hesitate to write, but then I would regret it if I didn't.

I do know Ryan went to see your daughter Donna and her family, but don't know how often, and I really don't know how well her family got to know him. That is why I would understand if you don't feel comfortable with this. The prosecutor wants you to write about how your life changed now that Ryan is gone. Please also share the admirable qualities you saw in him.

If you should decide to write something, please send it to us by February 1, so we have plenty of time.

If maybe the whole family would want to write something together, you could collaborate it if you are available. In one email I sent you, I informed you that Rich, Adam, and I were not able to be present during the trial to listen to the proceedings. Well, we kept asking the prosecutor about this until finally he told us that it is up to the defense to say yes or no. So far, we don't know the answer to that. Ann, Adam's fiancée, will not be speaking at the sentencing because she feels she did not know Ryan well enough. Therefore, she will sit in the courtroom. I asked if you and

Rita might consider sitting in the courtroom in case we can't. This offer still stands. I will leave it to you.

Terri and Rich

I write to Ryan's aunts and uncles for the same request. Trying to e-mail MAJ Michaels, I couldn't get it to make sense in a concise way, so I end up calling him.

"Yes, MAJ Michaels, this is Terri Schlack. How are you doing?" I begin.

"Hello, Mrs. Schlack, we are doing well and you?" MAJ Michaels responds.

"Well, as well as can be expected, I guess. Say, the reason I am calling is I gave you a few names we came across who seem to have known Ryan, although I don't know them. Please check if any of these men would be willing to speak during the trial's sentencing phase, unless they need to speak during the trial itself."

"Yes, I have the names. I will see what I can do," he says.

Then I get on a roll. "I want to get things right. I know we only have one chance, so I apologize for asking, but I need to know. Regarding the photo album, how will it be presented? Who will see it? Will it be shared with the jury openly or during their private discussions? I am trying to decide upon a small photo book with 4X6 photos or a large album with 8X10 photos, although large photos will catch people's attention and are right in their face. Should photos focus on Ryan's adult life or should there be his life span?"

"Mrs. Schlack, I don't wish to be rude, but just an FYI. In the military, a jury is known as a panel. You couldn't have known, but you will hear that term a lot. As for the photo album, you can set it up any way you wish. It may be easier to carry along if it is in a smaller album, but larger 8X10s get attention like you said," MAJ Michaels replies. "The photos will be at the disposal of the panel and the defense will take a look to see if there are any photos they object to having in the album."

"Okay," I continue. "Then I want you to know I have asked Ryan's buddies here in Wisconsin if they'd care to write something and they said they'd try to get something to me. My brother lives in Texas. Ryan went to visit him and his adult children, but I'm unsure of the frequency. I know Ryan never minded the drive to the houses which are quite some distance from Fort Hood. I contacted them to request their help in this."

"Mrs. Schlack, that sounds great. The purpose is to get the panel to see Ryan as a human with a life to live," MAJ Michaels commented.

"Wisconsin weather in January through March can be miserable with snowstorms and flights possibly cancelled. So, when the person who does the arrangements is setting it up, I hope she is aware that getting us there a day or two early would be better than coming in late, okay, MAJ Michaels?" I say, a bit embarrassed by this request.

"We will work that out when we know the court date is set in stone. Mrs. Hammons is great at her job," MAJ Michaels comments with pride in his voice.

"And finally, Rich was stationed at Ft. Hood for several years in 1975-76 and then again in 1984 until 1990, and we are comfortable with the area. You see, we lived in Copperas Cove. I don't know where you'd arrange for our stay, but a place with a kitchenette would be nice. We are talking about renting a car, too, so don't let distance be a factor."

"Again, no problem, Mrs. Schlack. Mrs. Hammons will set everything up for you, but if you have an issue, please bring it up to her," MAJ Michaels stated.

"Well, MAJ Michaels, this is all I have for now. And thank you for all you are doing. I can't tell you how much we appreciate your efforts in this," I stress to him.

"That's okay, and just ask me anything. I am here to help," he says. "Goodbye, Ma'am."

CHAPTER 25

One day after talking to MAJ Michaels, I call Chuck Raynor and his wife, along with three others of Ryan's Wisconsin friends to see if they might write something that has to do with how their lives have been affected with Ryan gone. They all said they would.

Later that day, Lewis Zane phones and begins, "Hello, Mrs. Schlack. I seem to be struggling with your request. I have a question."

"Sure, Lewis, I will try to answer it," I reply.

"Well, about this victim impact statement I am writing. How much does it influence the penalty, specifically the death penalty?"

"Lewis, from what we've been told, the death penalty is not completely off the table, but is highly improbable due to Abadia's inebriation. You see, being drunk is more likely to affect the sentencing, thus the death penalty will not be considered. I find that maddening, but that is what we have been told."

"So, there are other things that take into consideration when looking at issuing the death penalty, right?" he asks.

"Oh, yes. There are other things we probably won't see, like a doctor's findings from tests or maybe what the investigators discover. The panel has an opportunity to look over a lot of documents to determine what to recommend."

"Okay, thanks, Mrs. Schlack. I'll get at this statement," Lewis comments, and seems to be more relieved.

On the 27th of January, MAJ Michaels calls back and talks to Rich. MAJ Michaels explains, "The Army will fly the family members down to Fort Hood and pay for car rental. The Army will arrange lodging, but you'd have to pay for it but getting military rates. The trial is looking like mid-March."

I can't tell you how disheartening and crushed I am feeling. I just want to hang my hopes and sights on a finish line. March is a lifetime from now.

A decision that can't be put off is to take the anti-depressants, so I began today to take those pills. I don't think they're helping today. I cry driving home from school which happens a couple times a week, tear up talking to one of Ryan's friends about the trial, and it being delayed yet another time.

The family's victim statements about Ryan are coming in. I expect more by February 1st.

From my brother, Jerry:

I am Ryan's uncle on his mother's side, the Huber's side. Our hometown of Little Chute, WI, has big families and pretty much everyone knows everyone. Family ties run deep. I am the oldest of six, and my sister Terri, Ryan's mother, is the fifth, 16 years younger than me. We have about 150 first cousins, and we keep up on the maladies of them and their family. We grew up with few fatalities and no killings. Terri married Rich and he, like all the other in-laws, became a loving part of our family. We all get along together, even from one generation to the next. Even though Rich did twenty-two years in the military, and I became a corporate transfer victim, the Schlacks and my Huber bunch remained a part of this family relationship.

Then, about 5 years ago, Ryan was stationed in Texas at Fort Hood, about 85 miles from our home. So, it was just natural that my wife Rita and I occasionally brought him to our home for R&R - home cooking, a room, big cable HD TV, snacks, refreshments, and a nearby theater. He crashed. He came to our Christmas gathering and played with my grandchildren. Santa brought him gifts. I drove up to Fort Hood to get a box of games he wanted shipped to Iraq on one of his deployments there. He and I exchanged emails. Ryan and I talked about his life and his plans. Later, when he bought a car, he drove down to my daughter's place to hang out with my oldest grandson. They both loved games. It is exactly correct to say Ryan was special to my Huber bunch in Texas, nineteen of us. Three of us went to his huge Wisconsin military funeral. We are close hearty bunches who try to bear up under such a tragedy. Why was Ryan snuffed out while trying to help?

Ryan looked much like me, walked like me, and had a quiet self-confidence, too. We are not fighters. We do not need to be. We can get along with our laid-back demeanor and presence. I never heard Ryan raise his voice. Ryan was quiet and unassuming. I miss him.

From my brother Gib and his wife, Mary:

To Whom It May Concern:

Ryan Schlack, the son of Richard and Terri Schlack, was our nephew. Ryan was a shy, quiet young man, but one who readily spoke about his army career and his hopes for the future.

It has been our privilege to have Ryan in our family. He was a serious youth, more into video games and the like than into intense relationships. But when he came to our home or when we visited him, he was always welcoming with a smile and a hug. He was a listener, a planner. He loved electronics and watching him manipulate his way through games and programs was amazing.

Ryan was so different from our sons, but so similar in many ways. All of our sons are tall and Ryan was the tallest. All of our sons are very handsome as was Ryan. When we saw Ryan the last time, we were reminded of how much he resembled our youngest son. The resemblance was so strong that we had a difficult time looking at Ryan in his casket. Our sons followed their father into the Air Force; Ryan followed his father into the Army. Our sons respected his choice to enlist in the Army and they were proud to say that they were related to him.

Ryan was blossoming into a wonderful young man. His service experiences were helping to round out his personality and give him character and depth. He had recently developed an internet relationship with our niece and was chatting regularly with her about how to meet *girls, what girls liked, and how he might try to develop a relationship. He spoke at family gatherings and in emails about how he was looking forward to finishing his military commitment and going to college.*

There's a point in a boy's life when he chooses to become a man and looks forward to what the future might have to offer. Ryan finally knew what he wanted and was on the cusp of becoming all that he could be. It's really hard to understand how all of his potential could be snuffed out by a senseless, brutal attack of someone he trusted to be his friend.

Without Ryan, our family will never be the same. He will always be missing. He won't be at future family gatherings playing cards or games; he won't be laughing with his cousins or his brother; he won't be there this coming fall when his brother gets married; he won't be there if his brother has a child; he won't be there to help his parents as they get older; he won't ever get married or have children.

We'd like the panel to know that Ryan was well loved by the family and by others who knew him. He was polite, thoughtful, kind, and respectful. He gave his life.

I am so glad that cousins from Texas and Illinois Ryan got to know found it comfortable to participate in writing victim statements.

From Ryan's cousin, Donna (Jerry's and Rita's daughter):
My name is Donna Santos, and I live in a large well-known city in Texas. I am a first cousin to Ryan Schlack. Growing up, I can only say I knew of Ryan rather than knowing Ryan. Distance and age played a big factor in me not knowing Ryan during our childhood.

My memories are limited to the Schlack family taking a vacation to California to visit my family, as well as a few sprinkled summer trips my family made back to Wisconsin to visit relatives. It was not until adulthood and Ryan's move to Ft. Hood that I can say I truly got to know Ryan. He would join my family for holidays as well as come to my house for visits.

It was during this time that my teenage son, Gregory Santos, began developing a true friendship and mentorship with Ryan. My son has always been very inquisitive. Gregory was interested in hearing firsthand Ryan's life's experiences in being in the military and serving our country overseas. They would talk about what war is like and the politics that surround it. Ryan was able to provide a perspective that was unique and new to my son. They spent hours playing the board game "Risk", a game Gregory loved but found very few people that shared this interest.

As a single mom currently raising two teenage girls and a teenage son, I am always looking for people who can positively enrich my kids' lives. Ryan was one of those people. I appreciated him opening up and sharing what can often times be difficult experiences. He was loving, patient and understanding in providing my son with answers to what can seem like endless questioning. My heart grows heavy when I think of how Ryan could have continued to mentor my son and be a positive role model, especially at a time when role models are scarce. He was a wonderful man and my life, as well as my kids' lives, have been enriched by getting to know him. He will greatly be missed.

From Ryan's cousin, Michelle (Dick's and Shirley's daughter):

Watching Ryan transform from a teenager into a man was quite impressive. When Ryan was a boy, I remember seeing him at Christmastime. He was a tall, thin kid that walked hunched over. He made little eye contact with others unless you initiated a conversation with him. When we gathered at Christmas, he was quiet and stuck close to his brother Adam. I knew the two of them were quite close and had quite a strong bond as brothers. He and I would speak here and there, but it was tough to find a common thread since we had a 9-year age gap.

A couple of years passed without seeing Ryan. I had gotten married, moved to St. Louis, and I could not always get back for the annual Christmas celebration with my mother's extended family. I heard Ryan joined the Army. One Christmas when he was home on leave, it was quite noticeable that he had really come of age. From what I had heard, he stood tall. His body had grown from a very thin to a very strong, brawny one. He had confidence, and he wasn't the reserved, timid boy I had remembered. From the stories I had heard from my family, the Army had really developed his confidence.

In July 2006, Ryan's mom, my aunt, had suggested sending birthday cards to Ryan while he was in Iraq. So, I went ahead and mailed him a care package with cookies and some games. I was a bit curious to meet this newly transformed cousin of mine. At my grandmother's funeral in 2007, I was finally able to see Ryan. He stood tall and self-assured. He was a strong, well-built, handsome young man. I approached him and we had a wonderful conversation about how he was doing in the military. I could tell he was happy and enjoying his army life. He told me he was going to be buying a car, and I could tell that this was a huge accomplishment. He looked me in the eye when he spoke, and he was now carrying well-deserved pride in his achievements.

Ryan was then deployed a few months later for his second tour to Iraq. My mom had reminded me again of his birthday, so I had sent him an eCard that he must have gotten a big laugh out of because he emailed me back on July 16, 2008, to tell me that "mine was easily the best." Little did I realize that in just roughly a year he would be gone.

Ryan and I started some email conversations shortly after his 29th birthday. I was asking him about his life in Iraq and about his luck with dating. I had shared with him my story of meeting my husband who is a programmer. My husband Lee is more on the shy side. We had met on the Internet which was a great way for a shy guy to meet girls. I had used that information as an opening to ask Ryan if he was pursuing any dates. I tried to let him know that he was a fine catch, so he really ought to start asking some girls out. After some time, Ryan did finally start to open up with me and share that he had asked a girl out while he was in Iraq. He was also pursuing some Internet dating. Since he had access to the Internet on his base, he was able to do that. I remember specifically one night that Lee and I had sat down and conversed with him over Skype on tips and hints he might want to use when writing his profile for internet dating. Ryan was very open to our suggestions. He even let us look at his profile he had set up online on an Internet dating site.

At Christmastime, Lee and I sent some homemade cookies and some books on dating and girls. A short time later, he was coming home for a week or two and told us he had met a girl online that he was going to meet when he came home for his leave. I waited to hear how it had turned out, but in the typical Ryan style, he kept quiet. I regret that I never did get to ask him how it all went, because it was just a few months later that I got the tragic news of Ryan's death.

It was such strange news to hear because it seemed like Ryan had just come to a place in his life that he had made some major life decisions. He finally seemed to know who he was and what he wanted. He finally had the confidence, independence, and maturity to go for it. I was just getting to know my cousin Ryan in a more personal way. He was developing new passions in his life such as wanting to meet a wife. I felt so honored that he was willing to share some of his deepest desires with me. Ryan's loss is so tragic and senseless. I will not only miss this man, but also what could have been in his life.

I thought I would look through the cards I kept because I knew Gregory Santos's letter was in the bag somewhere. It's a good letter to include with the others. As I am looking for it, I come across this poem. It puts my ideas of grieving in another perspective because this is my thinking; that I have to "get through it" and "push to the other side."

Grief
By Gwen Flowers

"I had my own notion of grief.
I thought it was the sad time
That followed the death of someone you love.
And you had to push through it
To get to the other side.
But I'm learning that there is no other side.
There is not pushing through.
But, rather,

There is absorption,
Adjustment
Acceptance.
And grief is not something you complete.
But, rather, you endure,
Grief is not a task to finish
And move on,
But an element of yourself-
An alteration of your being.
A new way of seeing.
A new definition of self."

So, that's what it is. I don't know if I can take this on. It is so draining and saps the energy right out of you. Sometimes, I can set aside these feelings and concentrate on other matters. This happens mostly when I am teaching. These moments lift me from a drained, sad, non-motivated state. I don't think I can endure a constant state of depression and grief.

CHAPTER 26

Yet another visit to the doctor in early February. I feel like I go see her once a month. My physician assistant prescribed another drug called Celexa which is citalopram, an antidepressant. For starters, I take a half a pill for a week to check for any side effects. She wants me on those after the trial as well, but one whole pill. I still don't want to be a zombie. I still don't sleep the full night.

Later in the day, going through a box, I find Donna's son's letter; Ryan's second cousin, Gregory Santos.

Dear Terri and Richard,

I am truly sorry about Ryan's death. I know that nothing I say will erase the pain you feel, but I want to share what I remember about him. Maybe that will help a little.

I first remember meeting him at our house when he came to stay for Thanksgiving. We played the board game Risk and talked about life in the Army. I liked playing with him because no one else in the family likes to play, so he was the first person I played with.

I remember we went and saw "Walk the Line", just the two of us. We sat in the first row, the first time I ever did that. On the way home, I forgot to tell him which one was our house, and we passed it right up. Everyone was outside doing something and started waving as we came closer. And kept waving after we drove past. We got endless grief from grandma and grandpa about that mishap.

I also remember when we drove to Austin in his convertible. We never stopped talking the whole hour and a half. We talked about you guys, how he liked Texas, the army, and his friends.

That is all the memories I have of Ryan. I didn't get to know him as much as I wanted to, but I knew him well enough to say he was a friend.

Death is both the end of life and the beginning of a legend.

Gregory

Recently, in an email I write about the fact I am feeling so stressed about this waiting and waiting. It's like torture. Work doesn't always help. I know I was born to teach. With all the changes at work, I'm glad I will retire. The passion is gone; the excitement is over. Sometimes I can make it through the day, but many times the car ride home is miserable.

But first, I have to think about the trial. I contact my union president to find out how I get days off for the trial. She advises me to talk to the Education Association's lawyer about the wording needed to use sick days. I told her I know I would be a basket case during the week of the trial if I couldn't go, and I don't know how I will be feeling the week after. It was fortunate I was able to make a doctor's appointment tomorrow.

I do call the lawyer and ask him to talk to my Physician Assistant to be sure the wording is right for me to have sick days used for the trial and the week after.

Rich gets the phone call in mid-February for which we have been waiting. "Mr. Schlack, hello. This is MAJ Michaels. How are you doing these days?"

Rich replies, "Oh, hello, MAJ Michaels. I am hoping you have some positive news for us."

"Actually, sir, I do. The trial date is set for May 4," the major responds. "I just don't think it will change anymore."

Rich asks, "Would it be any earlier?"

MAJ Michaels explains, "No, but it could be moved later. The defense has a reputation of being a real pro at finding ways to postpone a trial. But as I said, I don't think it will be postponed anymore."

I was elated when Rich told me this news. I prayed the major is correct, May being the month.

While coming home from work, I considered informing my cousins in the Netherlands. In my email to Nel and Wim, I ask about their well-being and the current weather. Then my email goes into the difficult time we are having with the trial always pushed to a later date. Adam's wedding is talked about and my plans to retire at the end of the school year. My sign-off is expressing what a great time we had visiting them and what a beautiful country The Netherlands is. We treasure all the pictures we took which are now in a photo album.

It's Valentine's Day. After two weeks of taking antidepressants, I haven't experienced any noticeable side effects. I can say I have no real happy feelings, kind of a monotone attitude with a few tears here and there.

I should reply to an email Michelle sent to answer a few questions she had.

2/14/2010 1:58PM
To: Michelle
From: Terri
Subject: Re: The trial

First, about Ryan's tours. His first tour of Iraq was Jan–Dec 2006. In 2007, he was stationed at Ft. Hood and came home for Christmas that December and ultimately my mother's funeral. His second tour was May 2008 until 2009. In June of that year, he drove home to visit with friends and family and stayed until July 16.

I do receive a pension after retirement. Apparently, a person gets one credit per year. I have twenty years teaching in Wisconsin. I am glad to know that I can participate in the reasonably priced health insurance.

The trial is May 4 or let's just say there is an actual date given rather than the answer of, "Oh, Mr. and Mrs. Schlack, I expect in four to six weeks." *That answer was getting old and worn out. We still don't know if we can sit in the courtroom during the trial. Not knowing is stressful for me. We are bringing Ann along. Jerry and Rita may be able to make it. We need someone to keep us informed if we can't go into court. The Army will fly Rich, Adam, and me (excluding Ann as she won't be speaking) to Fort Hood.*

Not much else to say.

Love, Terri

The evening after Valentine's Day, another bomb drops. Adam calls sobbing. I quickly put the phone on speaker for Rich to hear. "Mom, this is Adam," he begins.

I can tell by his voice something is not right. "Adam, what's wrong? What's wrong?" I ask in a slight panic.

"Mom, Ann broke up with me. She doesn't want to marry me," he whimpers. "I tried to talk to her, but she doesn't want to talk. I don't know what to do now."

"Oh, Adam, I am so very sorry. Where are you now?" I ask.

"I'm still here at the apartment. I don't know what to do. Why does she want this?" he asks.

"Adam, listen. I want you to come here for the night. Come home. Just bring what you need for tonight. We'll talk more, okay?" I respond, concerned. "Just come home now."

Rich says, "Adam, it is best for you to come home and stay here for a few days. Maybe she needs some space. Some time."

"I didn't do anything. This is so not right," Adam continues, sounding confused. "She gave me the ring back. How can she just turn it off?"

"Adam, please, we will talk more when you come home. Give her a little space like Dad says and let her rethink and be sure this is what she wants. It would be the best. You can go back and get more things tomorrow," I advise.

"Yeah, okay, I'll be there in a little bit," Adam says more calmly. "Bye, Mom."

Adam arrives in the evening and looks like he hasn't slept in a while. He keeps saying he doesn't know why and what can he do to fix this? We talk into the night, and it comes out that Adam and Ann's relationship was changing. Adam admitted they stayed together out of convenience. He believed marriage would improve things. He wanted to try to work it out. I assure him he can stay home as long as he needs. He should not try to fix what she must have been thinking about for a while.

Rich is kind enough to let me sleep until noon on weekends. He knows I am not sleeping well even after trying three or four suggestions from various friends. There were the ideas of drinking warm milk, taking melatonin, focusing on one part of my body and tell it to relax, and a few others.

CHAPTER 27

The Saturday after Valentines, members of our motorcycle group meet in Mt. Calvary to bowl. I plan to bowl one round, although I have no ambition to play. One guy talks me into bowling every other set in the second game. There is music in the background as I am preparing to bowl my first round. Isn't it a Nickelback tune?

It doesn't hit me until I am standing up, ready to throw the ball that the song was the one Ryan had on his MySpace.com page. The name of the song is "Gotta Be Somebody" by Nickelback. I lose it right there. I simply drop the ball, start crying and take off toward the bathroom. I cry so hard; it is tough catching my breath. I had the impression Ryan felt this way about his getting girls.

After a time, a good friend, Chris, comes into the bathroom. "How are you doing?" she asks. I am still crying and trying to calm myself.

Finally, I sob, "I knew I shouldn't have come. A song I have heard on Ryan's internet page unexpectedly played. It's getting too much and extremely nerve-wracking."

Chris keeps talking. She's really helpful in that way, helping me get a grip. I then tell her why I came crashing down. All through Ryan's school years, I worried about his lack of social skills. Really, how does a parent teach that? I was unsure of what to do while he was in high school. He had found a few friends and maybe that was enough for him. Their interests were the same. Gratefully, Chris had gotten me out of whatever I was feeling, but I just was not ready to go back to bowling.

Eventually, others from the group came to see how I was doing. It takes a bit of time, but I calm down enough to go find Rich.

"Rich, take me home. I can't do this," I whisper to him. He immediately puts his bowling ball back and turns in his shoes. We say goodbye to those near us and wave to the rest. Rich is hungry so we stop in Fond du Lac to eat, and then on to Pick n Save for ice cream, my comfort food.

I can increase alprazolam up to three times a day. I wonder if I should. As pointed out, I am not really happy, just evenly somber. Yeah, somber is a good word to describe me.

It's about two months away to the deadline date but Ryan's taxes need to be done, but the W-2 form said he earned $9,000+; now that can't be right. Active military personnel do not pay federal taxes while on deployment. Ryan was in-country for only six weeks last year. Rich calls the Army finance department at Fort Hood and when Rich asks why Ryan's taxable income was so high, the guy apparently floundered around and said he'd get back to Rich. Of course, he never did.

This makes Rich suspicious. So, Rich is trying to get ahold of the Inspector General but is being given a big runaround. He is persistent and finally, he talks to someone at Fort Hood who said they will look into it.

Rich and I finish selecting pictures for the trial photo album. Following that, I go to the basement to examine the stacked War Hammer and White Dwarf books. What am I going to do with all this? There's got to be a second-hand place for this kind of stuff. I think a place to start is Chimera in Fond du Lac and see if they could help me out. Rich thinks I am wasting my time.

Looking into more boxes, I find a huge box of books labeled "College books" which are Ryan's Fox Valley Technical College books. I start tossing books and loose papers in the trash and come across an empty journal book which could be useable. Well, I think it's empty until I see the second and third pages. It's Ryan's writing.

"What is it about my mind that it does not like things to be permanent? Every time I have brilliant thoughts, they disappear by the time I get a pencil."

Ryan and I have had a few talks about this. I am sure this is what got him into trouble at times. It is confirmed as I find counseling forms from his military superiors while going through papers. In typical military fashion, they didn't want to hear excuses, just see results.

Ryan also indicated he couldn't sleep. This was a common thing with him. I hoped he would see a doctor, get meds, and improve his focus and sleep. There were also the stomach problems so I was thinking ulcers, but the autopsy never mentioned anything.

It is time to look for a substitute when I am out for a few weeks due to the upcoming hysterectomy. Yes, my decision is to have it done before the trial. I couldn't get any of my favorites for subbing because they are booked already, and one is going on vacation. Asking other teachers in the school, I find out about one who subbed earlier this year in kindergarten when the teacher was on maternity leave. In my classroom I have a lot going on and will show her what I do, but in the end, she needs to feel like she can handle it and, let's face it, she is not getting an enormous amount of money. I arrange to meet her next week. She'll sub for me one day and I'll show her what I can.

When I met with the doctor who will do the hysterectomy, he said I need to be 100% ready mentally and physically, and he didn't feel I am ready for surgery. I think, "No. no, no, I will not accept that." Rich suggests I call and arrange it because he wants to do some motorcycle riding this summer. That plan works. I am doing the preliminary workup next week and surgery will be on March 9, just a couple of weeks away.

Now comes the planning and working on the six weeks of lesson plans for the sub and getting some grades on the report cards. How can I swing that because the principal said he would not let me do them? Who else will do the report cards? The last day of the trimester is March 9. Oh, then there's parent-teacher conferences with thirty sets of parents. Those fifteen-minute conferences need to be scheduled in between all this.

Another project is to put a dent in extracting my stuff from what belongs to the school. I am not sure how I will unload it. I spent hundreds and hundreds of hours on my math, my writing lessons, and reading plans and just can't toss it. Does anyone put blood, sweat and tears into their work and just toss it? Okay, I know one teacher who would enjoy receiving my writing lessons. Maybe Donna would like my reading lessons, but would that be insulting? Due to those in-services, Donna and I have the same math lessons we developed together, so maybe I will leave it for the next fourth grade teacher. I won't know if the new one will toss it or use it. I have come up with a good idea. On the final day of school, during the teacher's workday, I will set up a display in the room. Everyone is welcome to browse and take items.

More victim statements for the trial are arriving, and I am glad to see some of Ryan's friends contribute.

Ryan's long-time friend, Chuck Reynor:

Ryan has been one of my best friends since I was in 8th grade; since I was 13. During the last 17 years, me and Ryan have lived together and worked together at various times. My wife of two years has gotten to know Ryan well, and my oldest two children knew Ryan well, too. They enjoyed his visit and loved riding in his "cool" car. My kids miss his visits, and once in a while, they ask why he doesn't come to visit anymore. I lost a valuable and old friend.

Ryan was an avid gamer playing video games and tabletop hobby games of all sorts, and I enjoyed playing these games with him. I will no longer be able to play War Hammer against my challenging opponent or take a road trip with my buddy. When we were kids, we biked everywhere from Omro to Oshkosh which is eight miles away and once even to Appleton which is twenty-five miles away. As we grew older, our enjoyment of the road migrated to cars. We had a road trip planned to Florida after he finished his service to our country. Now that cannot occur. I have to tell my children why Ryan, who used to even play games with them, no longer can come to play video games. I can no longer enjoy the company of my great friend, no more road trips or all-night gaming sessions.

Maybe these are considered by many to be kid's activities, but Ryan was a big kid inside, and so am I. When we were younger men, 20-24, we used to enjoy going cruising the avenue looking for girls. And while I have no need of that anymore, I still enjoy going out and partying with Ryan. Ryan enjoyed doing everything, but his friends and family came before himself. My wife, my kids, and even my mom, who remembers Ryan fondly, will miss him greatly. Ryan's friendship and companionship are irreplaceable. I will miss my friend very much.

Chuck's wife, Carol:

There is so much I could say I don't even know where to start. I guess I will start at the beginning. I met Ryan when we were 16 and working at Burger King together. We weren't really friends to speak of, just co-workers to start off with. We didn't really become friends until I moved in with him and Chuck in Appleton, when we were 22-years-old. This is when our friendship really formed. We had next to nothing to speak of, but we had each other and that is what really mattered. I think that is why we became such good friends in the first place because even though we were hard pressed to say the least, he made sure we were all taken care of in our own ways. When we moved back to Oshkosh and Ryan told us he was going to go into the Army, I was so proud to call him my friend and scared of what may happen at the same time. The only thing I said to him was he had to come back so we could continue playing our games together. Ryan was a sweet, caring, goofy friend that I am gonna miss dearly. Chuck and I gave our youngest child a namesake for Ryan as his middle name because he meant that much to us.

So the long and short of it is I am proud to have called Ryan Schlack one of my best friends and even though his life ended far too soon, I wouldn't trade any of the moments that I did have with him for anything.

I am going to leave you with this quote because it fits in almost any situation, but it fits this scenario really well in my opinion. When I am missing him, I just think of this: "You are not alone. I am here." Thank you for your time and miss you, Ryan.

CHAPTER 28

Today is the hysterectomy surgery. Being early March, it is still chilly with a little snow.

As the nurses are prepping me, we are just making some small talk. One nurse asks, "Are you concerned about the upcoming procedure?"

I say confidently, "I am a bit nervous, but mentally, I am ready for this."

The two nurses are asking me general questions and then, "How many children do you have?"

"I have, ... I, ... I had two," I reply in a halting manner. The nurse raises her eyebrow which tells me she is wondering what I mean.

Trying to stifle my sobs, I say, "My..., my oldest son was murdered." Then, I panic. "Last year, in Texas. Oh, oh, no, the doctor says I should be in good spirits, or he won't do the surgery. You won't tell him, will you? I must have it now; I can't wait any longer. There is too much to do," and hear myself ramble on and on through my sobbing. The poor nurses are doing their best to console me and assure me the doctor will perform the surgery. Wiping off my face, I calm down and lay down on the bed to await the procedure.

It takes me a couple of weeks until I feel like going out in public. However, I am relieved this one thing is over. One less thing to think about to the point I make myself anxious.

While I am convalescing, Donna Vosters calls and says, "There is a contest offered by the Wisconsin Education Association called the 'WEAC's Weather Day' contest. All you have to do is to write about how attending a baseball game would further students' education. And, oh, by the way, it's due by noon. Terri, if anyone can write something, it is you." I laughed and said I'll take a crack at it. The prize is that The Wisconsin Education Association (WEA) will finance the bus and game tickets to send a class to Miller Park. They'll get to watch the Milwaukee Brewers on April 28, Wednesday. So, I sit and begin to write.

The theme I wrote begins with thanking them for this opportunity. Also stated is all who sent in a theme should go, but that is impossible. The Roberts Elementary fourth grade classes would love to be selected. The submission then goes into education and what children could learn. The architectural structure of Miller Park, the senses being bombarded, the teamwork needed to be successful and sportsmanship is discussed. Students at their first professional baseball game, comparing these semi-pros to the high school teams they watch, the science in the weather and how it effects batting, throwing, and pitching, and of course the math lessons covertly embedded into the game such as economics, operations and geometry. The comprehension by reading the billboards, scoreboards, and handouts is an important skill here. Learning rules and applying that to living in our society and the fact we see social studies close up. Don't forget the music so unique to the baseball world. I wish I had time to polish it, but it was 11:58AM when I emailed it. All we could do is hope for the best.

I shoot an email off to my brother in Texas. By telling him the date of the trial, I am hoping he will tell me definitely that his wife and he will come. I also tell him Adam's wedding has been called off, so Ann will not be coming with us. Adam moved back home and is staying in Ryan's room. This forces us to put things such as Ryan's dress uniform, military memorabilia in the wooden chest the army gave us. It took quite a bit of time for Rich to bring himself to do it, and I didn't push the issue. After all, there was no reason to move it until now.

More questions popped into our heads, so I send an email to MAJ Michaels. He responds the same day.

4/5/2010 10:32PM
To: Richard Schlack
From: MAJ Frank Michaels
Subject: Trial Details
Mr. and Mrs. Schlack:

I'm very sorry I have not been in touch with you in a while. Let me answer as many of your questions as I can.

1. The court date is still 4-7 May, and at this point, I doubt it will change. We actually have a preliminary hearing this Wednesday just to hammer out a few details and argue over some motions. As I said, I would be very surprised if the court date were moved at this point.

2. Unless the defense objects (possible, but not likely) you WILL be able to sit through the entire trial even if you do want to testify during the sentencing portion.

3. The trial is open to the public. Your brother in Austin can absolutely come. Please give me his name and we will do our best to reserve a seat for him.

4. I will speak with Ms. Hammons tomorrow and ask that she contact you ASAP.

5. One thing you, your husband and your son may want to work on is a victim's statement much like you are asking family members and Ryan's friends to write.

You can send those and the family and friends' letters with CPT Earhart when she visits.

I hope these answers help. Ma'am, I'm afraid I won't be able to come up to Wisconsin before the trial. We will have to do our interviews and trial prep over the phone, and then, of course, when you come down to Texas for the trial. I'm actually heading into the field for training from the 8-18 April, so I will not be reachable by phone and will have only limited e-mail access. I'm cc'ing Captain Meghan Earhart on this e-mail. She is my partner for this trial and will be able to answer any and all questions you may ask.

As always, Ma'am, please do not hesitate to call or e-mail at any time. Thank you!

CHAPTER 29

I am on sick leave for six weeks from school to recover from the surgery. Rich and I begin to pursue how to take care of the boxes of stuff in the basement. Adam tells us of the Media Exchange in Appleton that buys used games, and we'd get a pretty good price for it. Adam kind of directs us as to what this store might buy from us. So, one day, Rich and Adam load all games into boxes and we drive to Media Exchange. The boxes contain Play Stations systems, Gameboy systems, DVDs, strategy books, and I don't know what all. It really is a good idea, and we get rid of eight or nine boxes and take very few things back home.

Since that went well, I decide to try the Chimera Hobby Shop in Appleton. "Can I help you?" a young clerk asks.

"I would like to speak to the manager," I respond.

"I'm sure I can help you," the young lady persists.

"Okay. My son has recently died," I begin quietly. "He has War Hammer miniatures, and numerous other things that I have no idea what to do with. Perhaps some advice can point me in the right direction."

The clerk's expression tells me this is a request she hasn't heard before and she isn't sure what to do. Finally, she says, "I can pass this information on to the manager who could help you." I leave my name and phone number.

The manager, Mr. Kevins, calls later in the day. "Is this Mrs. Schlack? You were in the store earlier asking about what to do about miniatures."

"Hello, yes, this is she. I talked with one of the clerks about what I can do with the miniatures and whatever there is," I replied. "Some packages have not even been opened. Is it possible you can help me?"

"Can you bring them to the store so I can look them over?" Mr. Kevins asks.

"Mr. Kevins," I explain, "there is just too much of it, and I know it won't fit into my car." We make arrangements for him to come on Monday, April 12, in the evening.

4/6/2010 9:16AM
To: Rich and Terri Schlack
From: Sofia Hammons H CIV USA FORSCOM
Subject: Unclassified
Mrs. Schlack,
I am sorry that I have not been in touch lately either.

I will be making the flight, lodging, and car rental arrangements next week. (I might be able to do them sooner.) I am working on another court martial travel arrangements now and am almost finished with those arrangements. The dates of travel will be the 2 May and return on 8 May.

Are there any flight arrangements you would like (window, aisle, early morning, etc.)? I know that the closest airport is Appleton and am not sure how far that is from your home.

I understand that you will be needing 2 separate rooms. (One for you and your husband and one for Adam.)

I will be sending a subpoena for you for your work as well. Does Adam need one?

Please let me know if you have any questions.
Thanks.
Mrs. Sofia Hammons

4/6/2010 10:51AM
To: Mrs. Hammons
From: Terri Schlack
Subject: Re: Travel Arrangements for US v. Abadia (UNCLASSIFIED)
Mrs. Hammons,

Thank you for your communication. With the date of May 4 coming up quickly, you can understand our anxiety.

As for your questions - We would like to get on an early flight, sit in close proximity, but it doesn't matter window or aisle, but more importantly legroom. We are tall people with a need for legroom. The closest airport is Appleton and is only 1/2-hour drive away.

We would like two separate rooms. At first, I wanted a kitchenette, but having a microwave and refrigerator in the rooms would be enough. We would prefer a king bed and Adam a queen size. He is one big guy.

Since we are tall and need room, we are hoping a full-sized vehicle will be rented. We have no problem being billed for the upgrade.

Yes, please send a subpoena for Adam and me to our address. Please let me know what information you will need.

Thank you so much for your help. Contact us if you need to.
Terri Schlack

4/6/2010 9:22AM
To: Mr. and Mrs. Richard Schlack
From: Meghan Earhart, CPT MIL USA
Subject: Message from Fort Hood Prosecutors (UNCLASSIFIED)
Sir & Ma'am,

I am MAJ Michael's co-counsel, CPT Meghan Earhart. I am the senior prosecutor at Fort Hood, Texas, and have worked this case with MAJ Michaels since last summer.

I am going to handle the sentencing portion of the case. We would very much like to meet with you both in person before trial. I would fly up to Wisconsin, talk about the court-martial process, review your testimony for sentencing, and ask if we might be able to have some pictures of Ryan and your family. These will be used during the sentencing phase of trial.

If you are okay with me visiting, could you let me know how the dates of 22-23 April look? Also, what town do you live in and what is the closest airport? I will need to know to arrange travel and book a hotel.

I look forward to hearing from you at your convenience. You can reach me on email or call me on any of my phone numbers (government cell phone, office phone, personal cell phone, home phone)

Thank you and I look forward to hearing from you.
Meghan Earhart
CPT, JA
Senior Prosecutor
Fort Hood

The captain and I quickly set up a day she can come. I ask for a Friday or Saturday because Adam works until 1:30PM on Fridays. I suggest the Appleton airport. I am feeling somewhat relieved. My greatest concern is that we feel vindicated at the end. The feeling of closure may not hit for some time. The sense of loss is still fresh. Some days I still can't believe it. Like the poem says "Absorption", "Adjustment" then "Acceptance". I am still absorbing.

Mr. Kevins arrives at 4:00PM on Monday, the 12th of April. I take him downstairs where the boxes are piled by common themes. As he looks around the basement, he is shocked. "Wow! What a collection!" he exclaims.

"Look inside boxes to see if you're interested in items. Neither of us knows anything about what he has," I say, embarrassed.

While Mr. Kevins is in the basement, the owner of Chimera calls him and they talk. When Kevins gets off the phone, he says, "I think I will sort this all out at the store. Your son definitely has what we can sell. I will offer you one price for all the stuff."

"Are you at all interested in any of the strategy guides or other such books?" I question, hoping to get rid of more stuff.

"No, we don't sell that, but let me give you the names of a couple of places in Oshkosh that might very well be interested."

The manager and a helper carry things up and down the steps to load his van.

CHAPTER 30

The Victim/Witness Liaison Officer Mrs. Sofia Hammons sends orders, flight info, subpoenas and meal information. She sends directions and gives us step-by-step procedures. This is the first evidence that the trial will truly happen. There is no going back. I send a quick email back to her:

4/12/2010 5:28PM
To: Sofia Hammons
From: Terri Schlack
Subject: Re: Orders and light itinerary (Unclassified)
Yes, we did receive the email. I doubt it makes a lot of difference since I didn't see it on the actual flight itinerary, but one line of the travel order says, "You are invited to proceed from Oshkosh, Michigan...". Now, we have nothing against Michigan, but we live in Oshkosh, Wisconsin."

On the same day, a Monday, I email Jerry telling of details about when we arrive, how long the trial will be and when we will leave. Jerry also needs to know how to access the base and find the Judicial Center's location.

A couple days later, Rich hears from the powers-that-be regarding the error on Ryan's income. They finally figured it out and will send a new W-2 form. We already had Ryan's taxes done and mailed out April 1. In fact, we get his state tax refund, and they make it out to Ryan, not

Estate of Ryan. Now, we'll do another tax form. We will visit our accountant, ABC Associates before we leave if there is time.

The Comic Book Store accepts four boxes of Ryan's comics. After about an hour of going through them, the owner writes a check for $300. The owner is impressed with the condition of the books. The games are not as easy to find a buyer for, but a shop did buy most of them and gives me a check for $50. Mr. Kevins calls and offers $1500 for the War Hammer merchandise. This seems fine to me. Rich and I feel relieved and content with our actions. We save the money for a future memorial for Ryan.

After I hang up, I turn to Rich and say, "Wow! Who could imagine getting $1500!"

Rich chuckles and says, "Gee, and I was going to toss it all because I thought your idea was dumb."

I return to work on April 19. I've been consistently waking up at 5:00AM for a few days now. But tonight it is quite late before I fall asleep, then wake up at 3:30AM and that is it.

After three days, I have a long day teaching and cleaning my classroom. The other day a teacher friend asked me if I could talk to her college class, so I did a reading presentation at Marian University. I come home at around 9:00PM and feel drained. I ache all over as I go to bed.

Five days before the April 27 baseball game, Donna finds out we win the WEA contest and are going to a baseball game. She prepares parent permits while I make phone calls to WEA to advocate for two other deserving classes I teach. At the end of the day, the WEA agrees to pay for the transportation and baseball tickets for all three classes. Happy times!

Wednesday, I go to bed and Ryan is on my mind. He is always on my mind, especially at bedtime. But this time feelings of how I felt at the funeral come rushing upon me, and I begin to cry. I mean real loud, in frustration and anger and helplessness and inconsolable sorrow. Rich comes to bed, and I can feel his hand rubbing my arm. I can't control myself. It's so beyond consoling. Poor Rich. He feels helpless trying to comfort me. I know he wants to fix it, to take care of me. After several minutes, I am hyperventilating and know I need to breathe deeply.

I think I'd know when I would have to increase the anti-depressant pills. Today is the day. I am only taking one pill a day. Why do I have such an aversion to pills? I finally sleep, and I get up too soon for work.

I tell myself I can do this yet again. As I walk toward the school building, the tears start to flow. It isn't going to go well. My eyes are puffy and sunken in with big dark lines around the bottom. My mood shows on my face, and I know Zoey the school secretary can see this.

I don't stop in the office but go through to the teacher's lounge and sit down trying to pull myself together. A few minutes later, a fourth-grade teacher comes in.

"I have a confession to make, Terri," she says, grinning. "I borrowed your overhead yesterday, so I'm paying you off with a pistachio muffin." She puts it on the table in front of me and this makes me smile.

She looks squarely at me and knows something is wrong. She pulls me up and into her arms. "Oh, Terri, you need a hug. A bad day, huh? Is it because of Adam or Ryan? I heard the trial will be coming up." That is when a steady stream of tears come sliding down my cheeks.

I have another meltdown after she leaves. I won't work another day in this mood, although it's not as bad as at home. I have done so a couple times before and felt so useless teaching with my mind off in different directions.

Shortly after, a kindergarten teacher comes into the lounge and gives me a hug. Oh, that really did it. I have the phone in my hand ready to call Becca to see if she'll come in to sub for me. As I am sobbing on the teacher's shoulder, Zoey walks in.

"Shall I get a sub for you, Terri?" Zoey offers.

"I'm trying to get Becca on the phone right now," I murmur through the tears.

Zoey replies, "I'll take care of it," and walks back toward the front office.

I make it to the classroom to begin writing very sketchy lesson plans. Becca has a general idea of how I run my classroom because when Becca was Donna's student-teacher, she was in my classroom to observe, learn, then practice reading techniques. As I am writing, Becca comes in. I quickly write down the final plan and tell her at the same time. The kids are coming in, so I try to compose myself and leave as soon as I can.

CHAPTER 31

As planned, CPT Earhart and Sofia Hammons the liaison officer are visiting today. Because it is Saturday, I know Adam isn't working and call him to be sure he is here on time. I make sure I have ready what I want to share with them. Rich comes in and hands me his statement so I can update the copy saved on the computer. Adam had done his last weekend. I've been refining mine.

MY FIRST BORN
By Terri Schlack

Richard and I had two sons; our first-born was Ryan and then three and a half years later, Adam. As long as I can remember, we would plan our free time around family activities; there were road trips to see other cities and their parks, zoos, theme parks, and campgrounds. As the boys showed interest in sports or school functions, I was there. Ryan participated in scouting, Tae Kwon Do, wrestling, drama, and playing the drums in the high school band.

When Ryan was in his early teens, we took motorcycle trips as a family, but, at some point, it wasn't cool to hang with your parents anymore. He'd walk or ride his bike the eight miles most every weekend to meet with friends in another town.

A few years after high school, Ryan decided to join the army. My son took the tests and scored extremely well, thereby allowing him to choose most any job position.

He wanted to learn about computers and electronics. Attending technical college gave him a good start, so he knew what to expect. Ryan and I had talked a couple times about the life his father and I had because my husband made the military a career. To me, the traveling and experiences were unique opportunities that made life interesting. It is what you make it to be.

As any parent, we went to his completing basic training, graduating from school, and then visiting him in Ft. Hood. His phone calls were always the brightest spot in our day.

When Ryan was in Iraq the first time, we received letters, e-mails, and the occasional phone calls. The second time he was there, we figured out Skype, and that was THE best ever. During his leave, when he was home in the middle of the first Iraq tour, he visited my classroom and talked to the students about the war. He brought home their letters I had sent him about six weeks before and answered every question. Ryan was so amazing bringing why the US was there down to a 10-year-old level.

Along with others, I, too, could see how self-assured and confident he was becoming. I could see he was ready for his future and had a plan. Going on to school was part of his future. Ryan was such a bright young man and could do anything he set his mind to. He only needed to finish up the last two months of his military service.

As always, Ryan called us while on the road heading back to Texas. I talked to him that Friday morning. He said he crossed into Texas but was going to sleep a bit before finishing the trip to Ft. Hood. I told him to be safe. Yes, be safe.

My world caved in on July 18, 2009, when three soldiers knocked on our door. The news they brought seemed to suffocate me. What they were saying was so hard to believe; so impossible to accept. It just couldn't be true. He was in the US, safe, with friends, not in a war zone. How can this be? But it must be because every time I lifted my head and opened my eyes, there were the three soldiers. So incomprehensible, so senseless, so unfathomable.

A couple weeks later, Ryan's first shipment of personal items arrived which included his bike and his beloved red Mustang convertible. Then, a few weeks after that, his second shipment arrived; his belongings from Iraq. I still have not finished dealing with his things. Sometimes, it's just too overwhelming and painful.

I have been teaching for over 35 years and every morning the Pledge of Allegiance is said. Every morning I think of the brave men and women, and especially Ryan, and what they are doing for me, for our country, so we can continue to live in a free nation. When I went back to work in September, it was very difficult to say those words without fear of tears starting to fall. Sometimes I would step out into the hall to compose myself.

On Veterans Day, the students shared their stories about family members being in service. This year, one boy asked about Ryan, and another girl said her brother told her Ryan got shot. That was it. I tried my best, but tears began to fall, and I had to step out of the room.

September came, and Ryan should have been home.

As I said, I have been teaching a very long time. I had no plans to retire for years yet. It wasn't work to me. I loved my job spending many happy hours planning for my classes. I never in my life thought I would feel like I have over the course of this past year. Never. Now, my heart isn't in it. There's no excitement.

Holidays like Easter or Thanksgiving will not be the same where, every year we'd sit around the table having our hysterical conversations as to what to do with the hard-boiled eggs neither of the boys liked or all the leftover turkey. On Christmas Eves we would spend it watching "It's a Wonderful Life" or "The Christmas Story" as a family. I can't look at a Mustang out on the road without tearing up. I sold my Miata convertible because, well, it wasn't the same. When the radio plays some songs, I have to turn it off–from classical to patriotic-themed country songs and especially to old songs from my youth. You see, Ryan, Adam and I would sing along with those songs.

Recently I was bowling and a Nickelback song was playing. I realized it was one that was on Ryan's myspace.com and I had to go home right then and there. Music, I find, brings back lots of memories.

Then there's all the things I have saved to give to him when he had a family of his own. Things like his baby items that he would use with his children; grandchildren that we'll never have. The school projects of clay pots, artwork, writings, and Christmas ornaments. Ryan would have laughed at all the stuff I saved. I was so looking forward to our family life with my grown-up sons getting married, having children, and loving every minute of it. Now, everything and all chances to create memories with Ryan have been stolen.

My Big Brother
By Adam Schlack

Aside from my parents, Ryan was the only person I had known for my entire life. Extended family lived in other states when we were little because dad was in the Army. We moved a few times as kids, so friends changed, and towns changed, but there were always the four of us.

Like many siblings, Ryan and I didn't always get along when we were young. Through years of practice, he and I learned the delicate art of getting under each other's skin, fueling fights and arguments over the most trivial of things for days on end. This rivalry never completely went away.

Still, in spite of hating each other's guts, we were still very close. We played together almost every day. Sometimes video games, sometimes with our Ninja Turtles toys. We both became interested in a lot of the same things when we were kids, and that stayed true into adulthood. He would suggest a movie or song or game I may not have heard of and vice versa. Usually when we tried it, we were happy with it, whatever it may be. We knew each other very well and could easily predict what the other would or wouldn't like.

However, I was quite surprised when Ryan decided to join the Army. I did not see that coming. He never seemed the soldier type to me. He was always the kid who was maybe a little too quiet in unfamiliar situations for his own good. But if ever there was an example of taking the metaphorical bull by the horns and proving someone wrong, this would be it. He truly enjoyed being a soldier and acted like it was just something he had always done. There was still that guy inside who loved '80s pop culture and video games, but then there was this side of him that seemed to know exactly what he was doing and was proud of it.

We spoke as much as possible when he was away. No matter where I was or what I was doing, I always took his calls. On leave, we would spend a lot of time together. We would go for rides in his Mustang or catch movies. Ryan was home for his 30th birthday, and I made a point to find him that day and call him an old fogy. He chuckled and replied with an impolite remark. Two days later, he treated me to a movie. After it was done, we drove to my apartment and sat in the car talking about the film and others that were coming out soon. One movie coming out was based on a TV show I had never seen, but Ryan had the entire series. We agreed that when he came back, we would watch the show so I would know what I was looking at when we saw the movie. We shook hands and parted ways.

That weekend I was out-of-town visiting a friend when I got a phone call from my mom. All she could say was my name, "Adam, Adam." The pain in her voice was apparent. My first thought was that she had been injured somehow, and I wondered why she was calling me, not 911. Finally, she said, "Adam, where are you?" Now I thought that maybe they were trying to find me, but I was out of town so now that they had gotten a hold of me, everything would be fine. I told her where I was, and she said I had to come home right away. I asked what was wrong, but I couldn't get an answer.

The entire drive home, I thought that it had to be something to do with Ryan, since he had just left for Ft. Hood. During the ride, I hoped he had just been injured or something, but I tried to prepare myself for the worst. When I got home, an aunt and uncle were there, but I didn't know why. I came in and asked what was going on. My mom asked me to take a seat, and I knew Ryan was gone. She told me what had happened, and I tried not to cry. I knew my mother was going through the hardest thing in her life, and I wanted to be there for her. I hugged my mom then my dad. When my aunt hugged me, the tears came, and I couldn't stop them.

I thought about our entire life together. From as early as I could remember to right that moment. I knew I never hated him. I didn't even dislike him, even as a child. I loved my brother every day of my life. I still love him.

I knew that my parents would eventually leave us, and I always thought he would be there to help me through that. I wanted to see his wedding. I looked forward to being a biological uncle someday. If nothing else I always knew that no matter where I was or what was going on in my life, I would always have someone I could call. Now all I have of him is my memories, but when I think of them, I still don't know if I should smile or cry.

My Son
By Rich Schlack

For me, this nightmare started 18 July 2009. I was sitting in my living room at home when out of the corner of my eye, I saw through a window, a car drive by.

A moment later, it backed up and then turned into our driveway. As the car was turning, I could see there were three men in uniform in the car. I got up from my chair and walked over to the window. My wife asked who was out there. I had a cold feeling in my stomach. I looked at her but could not say anything. Then the doorbell rang. My wife and I opened the door and in front of us was an Army Chaplain. That's when I knew Ryan was dead.

I still have a hard time accepting the fact that after five years in the army, Ryan was deliberately killed for no reason. I knew that while Ryan was in Iraq, the Army made sure he had the means to defend himself. Ryan was trained to use a number of weapons and had body armor for protection. He had no defense the night he was killed.

Some days I feel like I'll wake up and this would have just been a big mistake. That Ryan is away in the army and just hasn't come home yet. Other times the phone will ring and for a split second I think it's Ryan calling. While Ryan was in Iraq, he would call home once or twice a week if he could. I just needed to know he was OK. I miss those calls.

When Ryan came home on leave from Iraq, he told me he was seriously considering reenlisting. That surprised me. He mentioned it two or three times while he was home. But once he left to go back, he never mentioned it again during any of his phone calls. Once he finished his tour in June 2009, he said he decided to get out of the army and go back to school at the University of Wisconsin, Oshkosh.

I think this was the time where I finally felt I could stop worrying about Ryan. He did his two tours and now it was time to come home and start a new chapter in his life.

I don't sleep through the night very often. I'll wake up and start thinking about Ryan and all that's happened. Then I'll find myself having to get up. This comes about most every night. I don't foresee the nightmare ever ending.

Ryan was a wonderful son. I think his friends will tell you he was smart, witty, and honest. Nothing meant more to Ryan than his friends and family.

CHAPTER 32

CPT Earhart and Mrs. Hammons arrive at 1:45PM. People never look like you'd expect, at least for me, it's true. The first thing to notice about CPT Earhart is her bright red hair pulled back in a low chignon. She is dressed in her military uniform, is petite in stature but moves in a self-assured way; not someone to mess with. Mrs. Hammons has brown hair, dressed comfortably, probably in her early 50s, but is also a no-nonsense person. You can't help but see these women are comfortable in what they have to tackle, and I like them right off. Rich said it best when he says 'they exude a confidence'. I offer some refreshments, but both decline. Rich, Adam, and I then sit at the kitchen table with them.

As she is sitting down, Mrs. Hammons is looking through the deck doors. She comments on the beautiful large evergreen trees we have in Wisconsin. Living in Texas for a number of years, I know what she is in awe of. The trees are one of the few things that are scrubby in Texas. The poor things seem too tired to grow many leaves.

Seated, CPT Earhart begins, "Let's start with any questions you have."

"Maybe as we talk, we'll have questions," I state. "Both Rich and I have been on a jury and assume a military courtroom is similar. Also, we have a binder with statements from our family and Ryan's friends. I'll show you the binder of pictures, too."

CPT Earhart says, "Great, I'll take them with me."

"What other things do you have that Ryan values or that he gave to you?" she asks. "I might take pictures of them."

Rich jumps in, "For Christmas a few years ago, Ryan gave us a shield and sword with supposedly our family crest. It is an interesting wall hanging. It's so heavy, we are trying to figure out how to hang it without the wall being damaged. Another item is his last miniature piece he was painting. I don't remember who told us that. Here, I'll show it to you."

Rich goes into the living room and opens the curio cabinet to take out the four-inch-high beastly character. "I think it may be from some game called WarHammer 40,000."

CPT Earhart takes it and examines it closely. "Did Ryan paint these kinds of things? How tiny and the detailing is fascinating," she exclaims. The creature she is holding is a warrior with features of an animal but stands on two hooves. His dragon teeth are clearly seen. In the left hand is a whip with something menacing on the end and in its right is an ornate medieval double headed battle axe. The creature is mostly red with white skeletons hanging on his backside. It has huge green wings with a span of six inches curling high over its head. The detailed painting is very remarkable.

She hands it back to Rich and turns her attention to the box I put on the table. "These are things I kept from his school years," I quietly say, hoping I don't burst into tears. "You know, all the neat things at school a child makes or certificates he earns and brings home as the school years go by."

As we are going through the box, CPT Earhart digs out a drawing of the Fort Hood Army base Ryan drew when he was very, very young. She can't help but notice Ryan's first gift from his father, now a well-worn beloved brown monkey.

"What do you think of carrying this down the aisle when you speak at the trial?" she asks.

"I, ... I am not sure," I say puzzled. I am wondering if she is serious.

Later, I pull Mrs. Hammons aside and tell her I don't like that idea. Ryan is a man, not a child, and I don't want him portrayed that way. Sofia agrees.

Mrs. Hammons then talks about compensations if we go over the week of the trial. We can make contacts to see what Wisconsin does to help. Some places to check are the Department of Justice website, Wisconsin Crime Victim Compensation, Victim Witness Liaison, and DOJ. Personally, I feel we are being treated very well, so doubt I will pursue this.

CPT Earhart becomes quiet and asks, "I want to hear from each of you what you think Abadia deserves if found guilty."

She looks at Rich and he says, "I want the death penalty. I want that piece of shit dead."

Adam then shares, "I agree with Dad. It is right to hope for the death penalty. Ryan was unarmed, not a threat to him, and gets shot."

I feel like I am not putting up a united front with what I was thinking, but I feel strongly about this. "I want Abadia to spend his whole life in prison, so he has to think about what he did every day of his life, every morning he wakes up. His actions affected so many people; you know, the ripple effect. Killing him would be too easy on him."

CPT Earhart clears her throat and says, "I would like to share some things with you. I also will be sending you a list of questions that I may ask you while you are on the stand for the sentencing portion. This way you will feel more or less prepared."

"Wait a minute," I say. "I want to jot this down."

Between Mrs. Hammons and CPT Earhart, we get quite a bit of information. We now know the name of the judge, the defense attorney who they see as a weasel, and two assigned military defense attorneys. Then there are the witnesses who were at the scene, names of investigators and police and the forensic specialists from both sides. Sometimes Mrs. Hammons throws in a comment or two. Other things they share with us:

- Abadia is pleading not guilty by reason of insanity.
- Defense will say the police coerced him into stating he did it so, the questioning tactics during interrogation will be under fire.
- Video exists of Abadia's interrogation; we might see six hours of interrogation depending how defense plays this, there may be a lot of

discussion about interviewing.

- Prosecution cannot call Ryan a victim or SGT because Abadia is presumed innocent and SGT was given posthumously.
- Abadia chose a panel of enlisted which means there will be 1/3 enlisted and the rest officers.
- Described the process to find a panel (jury)
- There are two parts to this trial. Abadia is sane or not and guilty of the crime(s) or not.
- Needs to have four of six panel members in agreement
- To determine actual sentencing, there needs to be five of six to agree
- S. Smith was in the cell next to Abadia; Abadia allegedly told Smith the whole incident; Smith is a jailbird and not reputable.
- SPC Spencer Vans is having difficulty dealing with Ryan's death; Still seeing a psychologist. He may or may not be called to the stand.
- We can get transcripts of the trial through the Freedom of Information Act, although it takes a few months.
- The most Abadia could get is life without parole; CPT Earhart and MAJ Michaels would think it was a loss if he got less than twenty years in prison.
- While in the sentencing portion, each of us will read our statements, then defense and our side can ask questions. The panel can ask questions, too.
- We will be notified whenever Abadia is up for parole. We must write back telling why he should not get out. We should send pictures, or better yet, show up at his hearings. We must write back telling why he should not get out every year that we get a notice.
- Keep a journal on how you feel on particular days.

At around 5:00PM, CPT Earhart and Mrs. Hammons pick up the Statements Binder, a few items of Ryan's and the binder with Ryan's photos and say their goodbyes. Rich, Adam, and I sit down and discuss what we heard. We are feeling good about having these two women working with us. We write down some questions and make sure we understand everything that was said.

Eileen Stanford from NBC26 News sends an email asking if Rich and I are related to Ryan. I reply yes, we are his parents. She expresses condolences and sympathy, but then asks if we are planning to go to the trial and would I be interested in speaking with NBC26?

I hope I am not making a horrendous mistake and reply to Ms. Stanford. She did treat the situation in a respectful manner on TV when she reported the story, so I feel comfortable with her.

4/26/2010 7:50PM
To: Eileen Stanford
From: Terri Schlack
Yes, we are flying to Texas this Sunday. I would like to talk to my husband and son about speaking to NBC26, so we will get back to you on that. I would think something will be on the AP once the trial begins. Our concern is that something we say would result in a mistrial. This has been a long, torturous several months and want closure.

I think I would like a copy of questions ahead of time since I don't think I would do very well "cold turkey". I tend to think about questions before I answer; even then I might be nervous. My husband is on the quiet side and my son may not say anything. There is the fear of saying something to cause a mistrial.

CHAPTER 33

4/27/2010 8:47PM
To: Terri
From: Meghan Earhart
Subject: Sentencing Direct Examination (Unclassified)
Here you go, Mrs. Schlack:

MRS. SCHLACK'S BACKGROUND
Where are you from?
When did you meet your husband?
When did you get married?
Before you were married, did you talk about having children?
How many children do you have?
When did you find out you were pregnant with your son Ryan?
What emotions did you experience when you found out you were pregnant with Ryan?

SGT SCHLACK'S CHILDHOOD
From a mother's perspective, what was Ryan like as a child?
Where did he go to school?
What sort of activities did he excel in?
What qualities were in him that made other people so fond of him?
Did he share his dreams and aspirations with you?
What were Ryan's hopes for his life?

SGT SCHLACK & THE ARMY

Why did your son want to join the army?

How did you feel about his decision?

As a mother, were you fearful for him during his deployment to Iraq?

Did your son share with you what he liked about being a soldier?

RYAN'S DEATH

Where were you when you found out about Ryan's murder?

Can you even describe the physical and emotional impact that news had on you?

How do you feel knowing that a fellow soldier was suspected of killing your son?

What actions did you take immediately after hearing that Ryan was shot?

How did your son's death affect your physical health?

How did the murder of your son affect your emotional health?

What was a typical day like for you in the days following Ryan's murder?

Can you even describe the emotions you felt when the lieutenant handed you the folded American flag?

What is the most troublesome part about not having Ryan in your life anymore?

Ryan's murder was almost 10 ½ months ago. Are the emotions you are feeling different from how you felt when you first were told of your son's murder?

At this time, do you feel that you will be able to recover from the physical, emotional, and mental pain this crime has caused you and your family?

Today is the day for the fourth graders to have a good time at a baseball game. The late April weather is cooperating, which means it isn't raining. The busses arrive at school early and seventy-six fourth graders climb on the bus for the two-hour ride to Miller Park. To say there is excitement in the air is an understatement. The seating where we are assigned is a good spot to see the game. Prior to the game starting, we get a lesson in meteorology.

There is the excitement in the air with all the hoopla of the players coming out of the pen, students calling out to their favorite players, and running to the bottom of the bleachers to touch the hands of any Brewers player. There are all kinds of characters walking around, including "the Sausages" who run a race. One or another comes around visiting the class and pictures galore are taken. Lots of things going on all around plus there is even an extra inning. It must have been open to many schools because everywhere you look, there are classes of students.

It is a unique school day. One I hope the kids will remember for a long time. I can say I am so tired I will sleep tonight. But I don't.

A couple days later, I receive an email from NBC26. Ms. Eileen Stanford states she would like to do the interview either Thursday or Friday. I already know I do not want to do this interview.

4/29/2010 1:07AM
To: Terri
From: Eileen
Subject: Talking with NBC26
The list of questions we might ask:
What type of person, son, friend, and soldier was Ryan?
What have the past 10 months been like for your family?
Most military parents feel fear when news like this comes from the battlefield, not on US soil. Do you believe more needs to be done at Ft. Hood to protect the soldiers?
What are your thoughts as you travel to Texas for the trial?
Can justice truly be served in this case?
How do you stay strong through such a heartbreaking and stressful ordeal?

A few days before we leave for Fort Hood, we receive a newsletter from the Military Veterans Museum (MVM) in Oshkosh called, "News From Home". In the newsletter, there is an ad asking if anyone would be interested in becoming the Gift Shop Manager for the museum. I call and get an interview, requesting the interview be in late June. Rich slips in that he'd like to go along, too, and we could both work in the gift shop. Really, the reason I am checking into this, even though I know nothing about managing a shop, is I know me. I have got to do something away from home or I will be one depressed and miserable person. Rich volunteering with me makes me so happy because all I see is that he sits all day in the Lazy Boy watching the television.

CHAPTER 34

The clock reads 5:30AM. Today, May 2, is the day we have been waiting for, going to Fort Hood for the trial. There's not a chance I will sleep anymore, so I get up and go on the computer. As usual, I check the mail first, but CPT Earhart's documents she said she would send from the psychologist never came through. Last night, Rich got a copy on his computer, so I will ask him to print it for me this morning. After I printed the report, I then e-mail a few friends and share with them about what had been the news from CPT Earhart which is this 32-page report on Abadia from the psychologist which I haven't read yet and how confident I feel about CPT Meghan Earhart and MAJ Frank Michaels.

It is about 7:00AM when I hear the bedroom TV and that's an indication that Rich is awake. I shuffle into the bedroom, and we talk a bit about the upcoming days while starting the morning. Adam rises at 7:50AM and we leave around 8:30AM. I put the psychologist's report in my big carry-on so I can read it later. We stop for breakfast at McDonald's and make a stop at Ryan's gravesite.

The three of us are in our own thoughts. Who would ever think that we would be standing here at our son's grave? I start to talk to Ryan in my head. "Oh, Ryan, this isn't happening, is it? You're never coming home again. There is so much yet you could have done with your life. How could this happen?

"I have such contempt for the person who did this. All I have now are memories of you. I wanted more. How could we know you would be so brave? I hate to admit I was so scared and insecure when I first found out I was pregnant. I had no one to talk to about this since we were in Germany, and it's not like nowadays that I can just pick up the phone anytime. I didn't feel I had the right stuff. But then you arrived, and I was going to give it my best. You made it easy.

"I remember your distinct sharp, high-pitched cry you had when you were first born. Everyone on the floor of the hospital knew who was crying. You were so difficult to try to feed. The nurse would try to rest you in my arms one way then another. She was ready to give up and bring a bottle, but I so wanted to do the whole mother thing. It was the second day when you and I figured to lay you next to me, no arms around you, no cuddling, just be next to me and there you were finally feeding all stretched out on the bed. At your 6-week checkup, the doctor thought he had the tape measure held wrong when he measured you - seven inches in six weeks! Remember the pair of pajamas I had to cut off you in the morning?

"God, we were so proud of how smart you were! You were 3 ½ years old when you pointed to the photo chemical bottle and read very carefully, "Stop Bath". Then said it again a bit faster. Your dad and I stopped talking and looked at each other in amazement. We turned to you and asked you to read it again. OMG!

"In kindergarten, I explained to the teacher you were reading third-grade material, but it was obvious she didn't believe me even though I had taught intermediate grade level for ten years by then. The parent teacher conference was a joke. My sweet boy, you didn't get phonics, so in the teacher's view you didn't do well in reading!

"Was it a bad move not to have you placed in a gifted and talented program in first grade after the school suggested we get you tested for it? I just felt you needed to be with other kids and learn social skills. This decision bothered me for a long time. You just seemed to be an outsider in a group, and I wanted so much for you to be happy and adjusted. You were placed in a second-grade reading class, though, which was a compromise.

"Ryan, I only wanted the best for you. I would not listen to the pediatrician about having you on ADHD pills. That is until third grade. Every year prior, I would share with your teachers research information about how to handle ADHD children in a classroom. I didn't expect them to follow every suggestion, but they could just try. The awful third grade teacher was an idiot. Talk about bringing down any self-esteem you had. Half-way through third grade, I had to say yes to the pills, or it would be more damaging to you in my estimation. The pediatrician said you'd have a happier life.

"You could not be on any drugs when you joined the Army, so you didn't take any ADHD meds for a couple of years, is my guess. Boot Camp must have been hell.

"You and I even talked about having friends. My response to you was to look for one or two that have the same interests as you. Then, when you get into middle school, there will be more kids that enjoy similar activities. In high school, even more kids will like what you like. You'll see. And I hoped.

"You were crazy about bike-riding and I wouldn't be surprised if you put on nearly a thousand miles by the time you joined the army. You never tired of it and continued riding into adulthood.

"And then came high school. I learned things about you I never knew. One of your strengths was math, as shown when your math teacher told me you could figure out a difficult problem and explain using another way than the teacher expected. Not that you brought a lot of art or anything else home, but I was so impressed at the huge five-foot drawing of you hanging from a tree limb, the bicycle done in pencil and the African mask. Oh, we had those things hanging in your room for a long time. I was amazed to be told as a high school junior, you walked into the music room and asked to audition for the high school band. To humor you, the music teacher let you try out, and he was impressed by how you could do what he threw at you. Then drama, oh, that was your favorite. In one play, you were in seventh heaven playing a tall, lanky, dressed-in-black creepy character. With how skinny you were and so tall, it was a good role for you, and you played it to the hilt!

"We hope we can convict this guy who murdered you. I am hoping for a long, long sentence. I know you once said you'd vote for the death penalty if there was no doubt the convicted person did it. I was surprised by that answer from you.

"We have to go now. I love you, my son."

By this time, I am crying and know I have to pull it together by the time we get to the Outagamie County Regional Airport in Appleton. No one spoke as the car made its way to the airport. Rich, Adam, and I arrive at 9:45AM. At the check-in, I show the attendant our orders, not the usual plane tickets. Her expression is a hint of surprise, probably due to the fact Rich and I were too old to be military, so why does this threesome have orders?

On the plane, Rich sat ahead of Adam; Adam was across from me, and we all had aisle seats. We weren't in a chatty mood so we just kind of waited this 45-minute ride out, each of us wondering what's next.

There is a brief moment when I think about when I talked to the school counselor at my school. "It would be best if you can please explain to my students about why I will be gone so long. I will leave it up to you on the approach but, I don't want them asking me questions upon my return. I know I would get emotional, and it may frustrate or make the students even more uncomfortable dealing with a crying teacher."

"I can sure do that for you," she assures me.

At the Minneapolis Airport to get to Concourse F, we take a tram. Then we walk to find F but pass an area food court. It seems like a good idea to grab a bite to eat so we head to Burger King. I have chicken salad while Rich and Adam have burgers. Immediately, Adam and Rich search for reading materials for the plane.

About 30 minutes before we are to leave at 2:40PM, there is an announcement over the PA system that the airline overbooked first class. They are offering $400 for someone to move. Between waiting for Delta to fix the problem and waiting to take off from the tarmac and get into the queue, we finally leave at 3:50PM. Rich is sitting in 37A, and Adam and I are behind him.

The attendant gets on the speaker to tell us this trip takes three hours. No way are we going to make the next connection. Now my blood pressure is rising. To help get this stress off my mind, I begin to read the psychologist Dr. Simon Barker's report. The government hired him to conduct their own inquiry into Abadia's mental capacity.

Dr. Barker has the distinction of being Board Certified in Adult, Child, and Adolescent Psychiatry, and is Assistant Professor of Psychiatry, Division of Psychiatry and the Law, Department of Psychiatry and Behavioral Sciences at the University of California, Davis Medical Center. CPT Earhart speaks very highly of him.

In the report, CPT Earhart posed three questions for Dr. Barker to answer which he restated in the cover letter:

- At the time of the alleged criminal conduct as set out in the attached charge, did the accused have a severe mental disease or defect which does not include an abnormality manifested only by repeated criminal or otherwise antisocial conduct, or minor disorders such as non-psychotic behavior disorders and personality defects?
- What is the clinical psychiatric diagnosis?
- Was the accused, at the time of the alleged criminal conduct and as a result of such severe mental disease or defect, unable to appreciate the nature and quality or wrongfulness of his conduct?

The interview report begins with the doctor introducing himself to Abadia, what he is hired to do, that his report will be given to the defense, the prosecution and made available to the panel. This doctor's report will be classified as non-confidential. Abadia asked questions like if the doctor will be fair, and that he understood what the doctor was going to do. There is a list in the document of twelve people and reports the doctor used to write his information.

A Summary of the Social History:
- Was a good student and had a good life
- After parents divorced, lived with his father until Father remarried
- Issues with Father's new wife
- Age 14, moved in with his mother and her new family
- Age 14, first tried alcohol; Thought it was "gross"
- Didn't like the bigger town, new school and didn't make friends
- Age 15, tried marijuana; Smoked it about six times during his teen years
- Age 16, things deteriorated dropping out of school after a fight in school
- Age 17, guessed he was drinking two beers every two weeks on average
- Passed a GED; Given a scholarship to a 2-year college but dropped out after about one year
- Met an Army recruiter and joined up. At first, it was not a good decision because he struggled with the training. Frequently disciplined; Afraid he'd disgrace his family
- Age 21, tried cocaine, but it was "gross"
- Improved when sent to Advanced Individual Training; Made friends but still concerned about his Army decision
- Started drinking every weekend with friends; Took eight drinks to get him drunk
- Once at Fort Hood, he drank off-duty as much as he could
- Was told he was an outstanding soldier because he did what he was told
- Felt depressed, alone, becoming more angry, volatile, and aggressive when drinking

- Once, while drunk, lit himself on fire
- In 2000, stabbed himself while drunk; Was arrested for running from the police; Denied he intended to hurt himself but told police he attempted suicide because he was depressed.
- Received an Article 15, where a commanding officer determines guilt or innocence and administers the punishment for a minor offense; Given extra duty so he could not drink; Went through alcohol withdrawals
- Went back to drinking after the two weeks
- After more issues, his commanding officer sent him to the Army Substance Abuse Program
- Feared going to Iraq; Couldn't drink there; Survived alcohol withdrawals and made friends
- Thought the mortar attacks were a rush
- When he left Iraq, was initially fearful with thoughts of mortar attacks or someone trying to harm him, but that settled after two months.
- Began drinking on weekends
- While home on leave, he purchased his first gun; Was always interested in weapons and admired his father's collection
- Took optional classes to qualify for a variety of guns
- Met a woman when on leave; Got married
- Was happy for the first few months, but missed the comradery with the soldiers
- After a few months, both began to drink.
- Argued frequently; Found out wife had a large debt and may have been cheating on him
- After six months, the marriage was annulled; His life began spiraling downward.
- Three months before his second deployment, he stored a gun in his car. Was not aware of no guns allowed on post; Was told to register the gun; Didn't know what that meant

- In 2008 went back to Iraq; Again sweated it out, but eventually felt like his old self
- He enjoyed the working long hours.
- Recalls a man who would not stop approaching the gate; Locked and loaded the gun to show he was serious; The man stopped and asked for medical care for his mother
- Pointed his gun at a vehicle until it stopped; Said the event was fun and not scary
- Felt he had a special ability to read the intentions of others
- Becoming more interested in his building a good physique "for the women", he began taking "testosterone" pills
- Was taken off guard duty; Others were accusing him of buying pills from Iraqis at the gate; He denies this.
- After Iraq, was back to feeling lonely and began drinking; Feeling on guard or paranoid
- Had a reoccurring dream of a moving box at the gate he was assigned to in Iraq
- Going on leave, he drank and had fun drinking with his brother-in-law
- Concerned about his future; maybe not reenlist; Go to college instead; but the Army was predictable
- Became moodier, depressed and difficult
- In 2007, he was arrested for driving under the influence of alcohol. He was placed on one year probation, installed a breathalyzer in his car and paid a fine of $2000/year for three years. He completed 30 hours of community service and enrolled in the Army Substance Abuse Program.
- In 2008, his mother asked him to see a doctor. Abadia went to a psychiatrist but did not share with the doctor about his depression or substance abuse.
- On the day he was to go back to Fort Hood from being on leave at home, he saw some of his gear was missing. His mother told

him a hobo stole the gear. He punched a hole in the wall but apologized to his mother.
- In 2009, once Abadia was arrested for this current alleged crime, he was put on suicide watch and put on medication for depression. After seven months, the anti-depressants were changed plus a sleeping aid was added. A psychiatrist would visit once a week and he felt better.
- After three months, he accepted his predicament and after five months his paranoia subsided; Felt better than he did before the tragedy
- Is currently in solitary confinement; Continues to take an antidepressant and a sleep aid

CHAPTER 35

Thinking about what I just read, his childhood years indicated a middle-class family. His teen years and moving out of his father's place seemed the start of his troubles. He maybe couldn't handle change. Reading that he was given a scholarship and then dropped out was interesting to me. A free ride for a good future. Did he not feel he could do well? Not sure of his purpose, he chose a new path by enlisting in the army to experience the world. But again, that would be a change in his life.

What is with this 2005 incident because he stated he did not intend to harm himself but was attempting suicide? He's contradicting himself and I wonder if he realizes it. I continue reading more about his family, and my view changes. Apparently, many of his relatives live in and around him and maybe had a strong influence on him. I read about uncles dying of alcoholism, one uncle drinks despite losing part of his face to cancer, and another relative who is a Vietnam Vet abuses heroin. His mother is on medication for depression. According to the Medical History, Abadia denied any medical problems. The statement says he had later repeated thoughts of wanting to hurt himself, but never acted on it. So, am I to believe he doesn't think he's an alcoholic?

I had to stop reading. I worry myself sick and couldn't do anything else but think that we will miss the beginning of the trial.

We arrive in Atlanta, Georgia, at 8:15PM. The plane is packed, so getting out of the plane is a feat in agility. We are instructed to go to the Travel Aid Counter on the other side of E-12.

"Follow me, Adam, so we can take care of this mess," I state firmly to hint we need to move it.

Adam and I are off the plane. "Where's Dad?" I ask.

Adam explains, "Dad's baggage had to go in an overhead a few bins behind where he sat. I think he is still on the plane trying to get at his carryon." Rich does find us once he deplaned.

There is a huge line to stand in, but I see on a kiosk machine that if you are booked on another flight that you can use this machine to change flights, so I have Adam run his ticket through. I glance at Adam's ticket and he flies out at 7:30AM. It will have to do. Sounds good, so Rich and I ran ours through. We also get vouchers for $6 off meals. Adam sees he is assigned to another hotel, so we need to see what to do to change this. But first, I sit down and try to call Sofia Hammons to update her on the change, but she doesn't answer, so I call CPT Meghan Earhart.

"Hello, Meghan. This is Terri," I begin.

In a surprised voice, Meghan says, "Hello, Terri. Are you in Killeen?"

I reply in as calm a voice as I can muster, "No, we are not. Our Minnesota flight was late in arriving, so we are in Atlanta, Georgia, and cannot get a flight until tomorrow."

"Oh, wow, well, okay. Let's see. What flight were you to take out of Atlanta?"

I look closely at the tickets and am shocked by what I see. We are on standby!

"Oh, Meghan, I didn't catch it until just now that Adam is to fly out at 7:30AM tomorrow and Rich and I fly out at 7:30PM tonight on standby!"

She sounds a little worried but says, "Now, now we can figure this out. I'll get ahold of Sofia. She is a wizard at getting this sort of thing fixed. Ya'll sit tight and wait for Sofia to call you."

Of course, I am thinking maybe I can work on something at my end, so I go back to the Delta Priority next to the kiosk machine. After a long wait in line, I explain the hotel situation. I try to get the woman to focus on getting us all into one hotel. She then explains one ticket is good for up to 4 people, so we should have no problem getting into the same hotel which is The Wesley Hotel. The flight attendant then asks for our tickets and starts trying to find us a way to Killeen. I know Sofia is working on it, but figure, why not? Better to be scheduled on more than one flight than none. She types on her keyboard for a while.

"The best I can find for you is for Adam to stay on that 7:30AM flight. The two of you can go on standby." She looks up expectantly.

I am not going to take this so easily, so I say, "You know we'll not get on because of overbooking."

"Oh," she scoffs. "You'd be surprised how many miss that flight on a Monday morning."

I reply, "No, I want a for-sure flight with all three of us going."

She's back on the computer. "How about this one? You all can get on a flight that goes to Austin but leaves at 4:00PM tomorrow. You'll then have to drive to Killeen which is maybe 70 miles from Austin."

Using that plan, we'll miss the first day of the trial. I'm thinking it could be worse. She gives us breakfast vouchers for tomorrow as well as three overnight shaving gear-type bags which have a t-shirt, toothbrush, paste, comb, and cleansing stuff in each of them.

I get a call from Meghan. She tells me Sofia is calling for emergency help and will get in touch with me. Hunger motivates us to find a restaurant by the name of TGI Fridays where we use our vouchers. Rich orders chicken fingers, Adam orders baby back ribs and I have a chicken quesadilla. None of us feel like talking, but we all agree food is what is needed.

We gather our things when we finish the meal. Good thing I insisted the guys pack a change of clothes and Rich's pills in the carry-on.

We walk out to the taxi/bus shuttle area and look for the Wesley bus.

Walking up to a Hyatt bus driver, I ask him, "Can you tell me where to meet the bus for the Wesley Hotel, please?"

He tells me as he points, "The bus should show up shortly and pulls in right there."

I thank him and we three stand and wait. A few minutes later, that Hyatt bus driver waves us toward him and calls to us, "Come on, I'll take you."

We are on the bus when Sofia calls me to tell me the confirmation numbers and flights on a Continental Airlines. Talk about relief to hear from her!

Thank goodness for that Hyatt bus driver. As Rich is waiting in line to get us rooms, a whole busload of people come in with the same problem of missing flights. It turns out that Rich is the last one to get rooms for us.

The hotel isn't top notch, in fact is on the dumpy side. The three little supply bags from Delta come in handy and we crawl into bed at 12:30AM. Getting up at 3:30AM to catch a 5:00AM shuttle back to the airport is what is next.

It's now Monday, May 3. I worry the room alarm clock wouldn't work and that Rich's travel alarm seemed low on power. But, no worries, I did wake up to blaring rap music.

Stepping out of the shower and toweling off, I say to Rich, "The shower is actually a tiled area. Very nice. The downside is when you turn on the water, it runs cool and takes forever to warm up."

"What did you do?" Rich asks.

"Oh, it finally warmed up at the very end. I'm glad because I am tired and don't want to start the day in an off mood."

When Rich came out of the shower, he calls, "Hey, the water is warm for me!"

Adam knocks on the door at around 4:30AM then we head to the lobby. The 5:00AM shuttle comes early. The trip to the airport takes 10 minutes.

As we walk through the airport, we have to find Continental. It takes maybe fifteen agonizing minutes for the attendant to cancel all our other flights and to get proper boarding passes for us on Continental. Then we go back to the tram to concourse D and find our gate. Rich and Adam take the Delta vouchers and get breakfast at Burger King. As they are getting breakfast, the attendant starts calling rows to board the plane. When Rich and Adam get back, I hustle down to get a croissant sandwich, tater tots and juice. We have to carry our breakfasts out to the plane and finish eating there.

At 8:05AM we arrive in Houston. We are hoping our luggage is sent to Killeen from Atlanta. The route to the Killeen flight strikes me as comedic. To get to A-8 gate, we must walk to Terminal B, then look for B-84T, which gets us on a tram to take us to A. Amazing that we found the right terminal. The flight is fine and when we arrive in Killeen, we deplane on the tarmac and head into the airport.

Inside the terminal, Sofia and her husband are standing in our path to go to the luggage carousal, but we are so intent on finding where our luggage may be, I walk right passed them.

"Terri?" I heard my name, did a quick look over my shoulder, but nothing registered in my head.

"Terri?" a little louder and here is Sofia walking toward me. I am turning around feeling a little embarrassed and say hello. Sofia and I wait for the carousal of luggage but held little hope our luggage got put on a Continental flight from a Delta who arranged it to go to Killeen. Sofia and I go to the Delta counter and the attendant informs us it'll come in at noon.

We all head to Bill and Sofia's car and head directly to the Justice Center on Ft. Hood. A bit of small talk occurs in the car. As we walk into the building, it is an unassuming place. A small entryway leads to a bit larger hallway that goes straight out from the entry. Another hallway is to the right.

Sofia points down the side hallway and says, "On the right down this hall is where the restrooms are. I want you to be aware that across from the restrooms are where Abadia's family will be staying. They have chosen not to be in the courtroom. I'm telling you just so it isn't a surprise should you run in to one of them."

We continue to walk down the hall and are shown a couple rooms on the left we can use for whatever reason, such as when there is a break-time or just to decompress. A gentleman opens the door into the courtroom. I've been in a few courtrooms, and this one looks plain. I really didn't know what to expect. Sofia has us sit in the back right set of seats next to the entry. Adam, Rich, and I file into the row which can seat six or eight people. The seats are old theater seats that can be pushed down for sitting. CPT Earhart's mother, who is sitting in front of Adam, turns around and introduces herself. Sofia gives me a little pat on the arm and takes a seat in front of me.

Before we get situated, CPT Earhart brings a military dressed man toward us. He's in his 30s, brown hair which recedes from his forehead, and exudes a very calm manner.

"Mr. and Mrs. Schlack and Adam, I want you to meet MAJ Frank Michaels who will be the Head Prosecutor. Major, this is Mr. and Mrs. Schlack and their son, Adam," CPT Earhart says quietly and gestures to us.

"Hello, so glad to finally meet you," MAJ Michaels whispers as he holds out his hand for each of us to shake. "I hope this will not be too difficult for you. We think we have a good case. CPT Earhart is an excellent prosecutor, so you are in good hands."

After settling in, I note the courtroom has three sections of seating, again like a theater. There are probably five rows in the side seating. A very plain medium brown table is the prosecutor's table sitting in front of our section. Nearby, a medium brown panel box faces left, allowing ample space to walk to the witness stand. At least the panel's chairs looked like office chairs that could swivel and lean back. The middle grouping of seats has more seating across the row and more seats in each row. A divider made of medium brown wood separates the visitors from the bench. Up front, the witness stand is attached to the side of the judge's desk, but at a lower level than where the judge sits. The court recorder and her equipment are a bit lower than the witness seat and her area is carved from the corner of the judge's bench. On the far side of the courtroom is another group of seats like our side and in front are the defendants' chairs and table. What surprises me is there is only a US Flag behind and to the left of the judge. No artwork on the back blond paneled wall. There was an air conditioner humming, but it was so loud, CPT Earhart asks the judge if it could be turned down or off since it is difficult to hear everything.

We had arrived at 11:00AM, about an hour late. I didn't know who he was at the time, but SPC Vans is answering questions, although I am confused about what I am hearing. On the stand, Vans appears visibly shaken and shy, and maybe a little confused. His frail body slinks back into the chair and he doesn't raise his voice, so is difficult to hear. The defense asks him a couple times to please speak up. He is about 5' 9" as he stands up to exit and heads to the door nearest where we sit.

He is walking out of the court area and has to pass us. I get up and need to hug him and talk to him. But what do I say?

"You can do this," I whisper into his ear and hold him. "Be strong and do your best. I know you will do well because this is for Ryan." He lingers in my arms. I feel so sad for him.

Before we are excused for lunch, there is some incoherent talking from the defense, but I understand enough to know defense is asking the judge about excusing us from being in the courtroom. This is where the three of us tense up and are at the edge of our seats. From our position, we can hear the judge quite clearly as he asks why but, apparently the lawyer had no good answer so the judge decreed we can stay. We are not witnesses and we were not present during the altercation. What a welcoming piece of news!

CHAPTER 36

The three of us grab a bite to eat. Then the Hammons give us a ride to pick up our luggage from the airport. We say our thanks and wave goodbye. We walk to the car rental check-in to get a silver Suzuki SUV. Rich makes sure he points out the burn hole in the front passenger seat to the car custodian.

The court started at 2:30. We are late once again and quietly settle in the back row of the courtroom, where I will begin to take copious notes. The person on the stand is talking about what happened after hearing gunshots saying that Abadia staggered to the car, then drove away very slowly.

Q–Was law enforcement contacted?
A–Yes.
Q–How much time between Abadia leaving vs. law enforcement arriving?
A–One hour.
Q - You gave a statement?
A–Yes. I am angry for allowing this to happen.
I can only conclude this was Jaks. The party was held at his house.
Agent Jirit is the Criminal Investigator. First, there were questions about his background.
Q–How was the evidence handled?
A - I was the responding agent. I gathered photos and evidence, searched the house and street, and found spent casings of 45 cal.

CPT Shannon Jones is one of three who represents Abadia. She does a recross with Jirit. She questions him about the credibility of the death scene and reviewed his actions. She questions Jirit regarding who handled the evidence prior to him.

PFC Evan Anderson is a friend of Ryan's and was at the party.

Q–What is your job? Your MOS?

A–MOS is 94 Fox which means I am a Computer/Detection Systems Repairer

Q–How do you know Abadia?

A - I worked in the same shop. We became friends in Iraq.

Q–Where did you live at the time of the altercation?

A - I lived in Montague Village, West Ft. Hood.

Q - Who was the least drunk?

A - Vans was the least drunk.

Q–What were you doing?

A–I was ordering pizza by computer. I then hear an argument between Owens and Abadia coming from the living room.

Q–What happened then?

A - Jaks told Abadia to go outside to the backyard. He told Vans to go with him. Owens walked to the wall and punches a hole in it, then goes out the front door because he was asked to. Owens went out to where Schlack was. I stay in the house but then hear a pop. Jaks came into the house to say Schlack was shot.

Q–Then what happened?

A - I look for my phone, then walk to the front door while talking on the phone. Jaks comes into the house with a gun. He holds the gun over the table; tries to clear it but couldn't do it. Jaks then puts the gun on the kitchen table with other things. As I walk to the window to look outside, Abadia barges in and asks where the weapon is. Abadia sees the weapon, grabs and swings it around. Abadia leaves and has the gun in his possession. I go outside only about 5 feet from the house. I grab Owens and see Schlack near the drain area lying on the ground crying and moaning. Owens looks "a mess" saying, "He's gonna die." I pull Owens into the living room to calm him down.

Special Agent Albright is a CID Agent.

Q–What is your part in this altercation?

A–I did the crime scene interview.

Q–When were you told of the incident?

A - The call came at 23:30. My job was to get information about the crime scene.

Henry Hanson is a police officer.

Q–Can you tell us what part you played in this altercation?

A–I brought a weapon to the CID. I also drove up to the crime scene telling them about a 45 I had found.

Officer Felicity Miller is a military police officer (MP) who was first on the scene.

Q–Tell us what you did on the night of July 18, 2009?

A–There was a call coming in at 23:26 that shots were fired. I look at the CAD which is in every police car that gives the location or address and I go for it. It took me about 3-4 minutes. I turn on lights so the recorder turns on.

Q–Then what happened?

A - "He's gone," someone says, referring to Abadia. I see quite a few people around Schlack on the ground on my right. Ryan is responsive moaning, "It hurts." I can't see any wound right away. People were saying he's shot on the side. I locate a hole, but there's not a lot of blood. I check for a pulse. Owens is nearby talking to Schlack as I check for an exit wound. Then I talk to Schlack. CPL Thompson shows up a few minutes later and takes over. Schlack answers but not in complete sentences. He throws up blood, so I tilt his head to his side to prevent choking. Thompson and I move Schlack to the sidewalk about 2 to 3 feet then I kneel at Ryan's head. Ryan throws up some more, and he appears to be fading or passing out.

Although the information given by the witnesses is interesting, the delivery is very matter-of-fact. It is just a question then an answer one right after the other. After the court dismisses us at about 4:00PM, we talk to CPT Earhart a bit about what happened today.

"Today is just a practice, so do they all have to repeat what was said today in front of the panel tomorrow?" Rich asks.

"Not necessarily," CPT Earhart replies. "It is to craft our questions better and know what the answers are before we ask them in front of the panel."

Off we go to Popeye's Chicken for dinner. The dinner conversation was recalling what has happened today. Next, a quick visit to the Post Exchange for junk food and drinks to take back to the hotel. After that, it is still light enough to drive to Ovnand Street to see where this terrible event happened. Ovnand Street is in West Fort Hood which is several miles from the main base where the hospital is located, so we were given incorrect information earlier.

Like older military base housing on West Fort Hood, the house is a one story, white wood-clabbered home and about 1500 square feet with 2 bedrooms and one bath. Two large shrubs grow on either side of a small porch with an overhang across the entire front of the house. A small storage shed is set a bit back from the house with a portico for one car. There are mature trees easily seen along the back of the house and one good-sized tree in front. The sidewalk is abutted right next to the black-topped road. Houses are spaced about ten feet apart.

The three of us park across the street and stare at the house, imagining the sequence of events the night Ryan died. No one says a word. There is no need. Adam took a couple of pictures. After about ten minutes, we pull slowly away from the house.

We head back to our hotel where I plan to iron and check email before bedtime. Adam heads to his room next to ours. Our room has two queen beds that are calling to us. With having a full kitchen, it is a welcome place to decompress–if that's possible. I set the alarm for 6:30AM. Rich turns on the television, as is his habit, and settles himself into bed. With my short tasks complete, I crawl next to him.

CHAPTER 37

We get up at 6:30AM on Tuesday, call Adam so I know he is up, then get ready. In the hotel's restaurant, the three of us eat a breakfast of eggs and hash browns. While eating, Jerry calls.

"Hello, Terri. It's Jerry. Rita and I are at Denny's Restaurant in Killeen. I want to be sure we go to the right building. Can you give us directions?"

"That is a task for Rich, Jerry. He knows his way around the base, so I'll hand the phone to him." Rich takes the phone and gives the best route to get where we will meet them.

Rich drives us to the Magistrates Court and we meet up outside the building with Jerry and Rita around 9:00AM. This is what our family has been waiting for. The "real" trial begins. First, Jerry and Rita enter, and then we take our seats in the same row as yesterday. This is the first time we will see Abadia in person as the defense team appears. Three attorneys are now seated at the table. The civil attorney hired by Abadia's family is George Janis. CPT Shannon Jones and MAJ Gary Branson are the other two appointed military attorneys.

Barto Abadia seems average height when comparing him to the two soldiers bringing him into the courtroom. Dark hair, round face, of Hispanic descent and a hangdog look.

George Janis, the hired attorney, is in his mid-60's, a medium build with gray hair, wearing a nice neutral colored suit. Being military, CPT Jones and MAJ Branson are impeccably dressed and physically fit. The hair coloring on MAJ Branson is brown and CPT Jones has a lighter, almost blond, shade.

Seated in his role as judge, Judge Gil Andrews appears comfortable. His hair is dark brown, is physically fit, is about late 30s or early 40s, and since I can't see his features and is seated, there isn't much to say except he wears glasses.

Every trial starts with voir dire. About twelve prospective jury members are being asked questions by the judge. The first question is if there is a military job-related reason anyone cannot serve on this panel. A few tell the judge they have an important appointment such as preparing to "go to the field" or "already in field exercises". They are dismissed, as declared by the judge. The remaining questions pertain to health or the defendant's relationship. A question or two is also asked by the prosecution and defense.

The judge sends the remaining individuals to a back waiting room and now calls out one person at a time for more personal questions. Two people reported deaths in their family.

One Sergeant Major reported that someone shot and killed his first wife during a convenience store robbery approximately 22 years ago.

The judge asks, "Sergeant Major, considering what happened to your first wife 22 years ago, do you think that will play any part in your serving as a panel member in this case?"

"I don't think so, sir. It's—you never forget something like that, but—I mean, I think about it, but it doesn't influence my judgment on different things. I think I've been in the Army long enough and seen and heard of other people overcoming stuff, so I don't think it will," the Sergeant Major replies.

George Janis challenges the judge. The military judge denies the defendant's challenge for cause based on implied bias ruling. Judge Andrews stated, "The Sergeant Major also stated that he's been in the Army long enough to know that you overcome things and drive on. He said that human nature dictates that he will think about it, and it has already caused him to think about it. He was asked, which is likely the reason. However, he did indicate that it would have no effect on him whatsoever in this situation. Even considering the liberal grant mandate, the defense's challenge of the Sergeant Major is denied."

In a second individual questioning of a candidate, a female officer stated that six years ago one of her cousins goaded his brother into a

"Russian-roulette type of thing" which resulted in the brother's death. She stated she was close to both cousins.

Judge Andrews asks, "Major, with the experience you had with your cousins, do you think that is going to affect your impartiality at all in this case?"

The Major replies, "At this point, I don't believe so."

The judge continues, "Okay. Do you think that you're going to be able to separate this case from your cousin's case…"

"Yes," the Major replies.

"—and decide this case solely on what you hear in this courtroom and the instructions that I give you?"

"Yes, sir."

Judge Andrews again denied the defendant's implied bias challenge for cause against the Major. In response to the defense challenge for cause, the judge stated, "She can separate what happened with her cousins from this case. She said that she was geographically well-separated from her cousins when that incident happened. She didn't attend the trial. She still speaks regularly with the person who—the remaining cousin, the one who lived, who was responsible. Again, she said that she can actually separate it and it won't affect her in any way in this case. So, the government feels that even with the liberal grant mandate, there is no appearance of bias in this case."

Finally, the judge calls all the perspective soldiers to come out and announces the names of those he is excusing. I am shocked when a command sergeant major's name is called to be excused, and he does an arm pull and with a loud whisper says, "Yes!" with a grin and clear relief on his face.

The judge, along with many in the courtroom, is startled by this behavior and the judge severely reprimands the command sergeant major who instantly apologizes. I silently applaud the judge for correcting this insulting behavior and throw a hateful glare at the commander's back as he bounds out of the courtroom. Adam did not understand ranks, but he still thought it was inappropriate. Rich felt disgusted.

Two females and four males are selected. As the panel is seated, Rich identifies for me the ranks of the six. The highest-ranking member is the panel foreperson, so that would be the colonel.

(back row) Command Sergeant Major/ Command Sergeant Major/First Sergeant

(front row) Major (female) / Colonel (female) / Command SGT Major

CPT Meghan Earhart for the Prosecution gives an opening statement basically reviewing what occurred, the details of the wound, and what the charges are.

CPT Shannon Jones for the Defense gives an opening statement by telling of an incident occurring on Oct. 8 when Abadia perceived a threat at the entry gate in Iraq. She relays that Abadia did know he had an argument at the party. He was aware he was very drunk. That he slowly goes to his car, gets the gun from the car but can't remember firing the gun.

Never having met Greg Owens or seen a photo of him, I pictured Greg to be very short so was surprised he's probably 5'10" but only about 130 pounds. With his light brown hair and eyes and dressed in his military uniform, he is a good-looking guy in his early 20s. Ryan and Greg used to run a lot, so he is physically fit but thin.

THE PROSECUTOR AND SPECIALIST (SPC) GREG OWENS-

Q: Specialist Owens, tell us about your background and your job in the army.

A: I am from a small town in northern Minnesota. Ryan was from Wisconsin, so we became friends very quickly. I joined the army after high school graduation and my job is 92Y, which translated is in supply. I met Ryan in March 2007 at Fort Hood.

Q: Explain what a company's "block leave" is.

A: It happens after returning from a tour of duty overseas. The whole company goes on leave or has free time. Most soldiers go home for a month. This block leave was to end on July 20.

A poster resting on a tripod is displayed of the aerial view of the neighborhood. Owens identifies Jak's military housing. Another poster displays a floor-plan of the living room interior with furniture, window and door placements.

Q: On this first poster you see a simple drawing of an aerial view of the neighborhood. The second one is the floorplan of the living room interior. Tell what happened. Come up and point to what area you are referring to.

A: Abadia and I were in the living room. I told Abadia to stop drinking. Abadia became angry. I moved to the window, but Abadia pushed me into the living room wall. Jaks told Vans to walk Abadia out to the backyard. Schlack took me to the front yard, but before I left the living room, I punched a hole in the wall.

A third poster of the outdoor property is displayed on a tripod.

Q: What happened outside of the house?

A: Schlack and I were in the front yard by a tree for about 10 minutes when Abadia and Vans walked down the driveway and toward the road. But instead of going to the car with Abadia, Vans turned and headed to where the two of us were standing.

Q: What happens next?

Using the posters, Owens continues showing the areas of concern.

A: Abadia went to his car across the street. Vans, Schlack, and I were standing here. Schlack is 5 to 10 feet from Abadia when shots were fired. I grabbed the weapon from Abadia, gave it to Jaks and told him to call 911. I held Schlack until the MPs came. I estimated the MPs took about 10–15 minutes while I sat with Schlack.

THE DEFENSE AND SPC GREG OWENS –

The defense asks Owens to clarify.

Q: Did Abadia hurt you? Didn't Jaks take car keys from everyone?

A: No, Abadia didn't hurt me that night. And everyone was told to put their car keys on the table if they were going to drink. It goes without saying that the guys will stay until morning.

CHAPTER 38

Anderson looks younger than Owens with a boyish look. He has a solid build, and I think likes to have a good time. Jaks and he initiated the party idea at the residence where they live. Anderson lives with Ethan Jaks because Anderson was going through a divorce. Since the divorce was not final, the Army would not issue a place for Anderson to stay, and Anderson could not afford a place by himself.

THE PROSECUTION AND PRIVATE FIRST CLASS (PFC) EVAN ANDERSON-

Q: Tell us how the party got started.

A: I decided to call some friends to get together that day. I called Dannon, Owens, Vans, Dale, and Schlack. There was drinking. There were designated drivers, but they didn't stay long.

A poster of the house plan is again displayed on a tripod.

Q: What happened?

A: I heard Abadia and Owens scuffle and saw Abadia pushed Owens. I told Abadia and Vans to go outside through the back door. I then told Schlack and Owens to go out through the front door. As I ordered pizza, I heard a pop.

A poster of the outside home is shown.

Q: What happened next?

A: I walked to the front door and was told Schlack's been shot. I looked for my cell phone. Jaks came in holding a gun and he's on the phone to 911. Jaks and I walked to the kitchen table to try to clear the gun, but it's jammed. I put it on the table. Abadia ran through the front door and proceeded to rampage through the house looking for the gun.

Abadia shouted in an irritated voice, "Where the fuck is my weapon?" Neither of us replied. Abadia finally saw his weapon and grabbed it off the table, swung the gun around and aimed it at Jaks and me. Abadia left the house. I grabbed Owens and brought him inside. I saw Schlack on the ground.

Q: How did Abadia drive off?

The answer is mumbled, so I can't understand what Anderson says.

A: I heard Owens saying that he blames himself. Eventually, a CID agent came to get statements.

THE DEFENSE AND PFC EVAN ANDERSON–

Q: When did CID ask for statements?

A: A few days later. I heard all conversations of questions by CID, but only Vans was pulled aside. The group agreed there was heavy drinking.

Q: What's your reaction as to how Abadia is when he is drunk?

A: He gets meaner and out of control.

Ethan Jaks is built similar to Anderson and in his mid-20s. The impression I have of him based on how he is handling himself as he walks up to the bench is he is a bit more serious and responsible.

PROSECUTION AND SPECIALIST (SPC) ETHAN JAKS–

Q: There was a mention of designated drivers. Who were they?

A: Thomas Dale and Ed Dannon were the designated drivers, so they didn't drink alcohol.

A poster of the house plan is shown.

Q: Tell us what happened.

A: Abadia and Owens are in the living room arguing when Abadia pushed Owens. I got between them. Abadia was asked to go out the back door and Owens to go out the front door. I glanced outside to see Owens and Schlack in the front yard.

An outside map is displayed.

Q: What happened next?

A: Abadia said, "Fuck this shit. I'm going home." I went to the backyard to possibly stop Abadia since he was drunk. By this time, Abadia was in the front area, but was walking up from the street.

A neighborhood map poster is placed on the tripod.

Q: What happened next?

A: I heard a kind of a lock and load sound. I saw a muzzle flash at the end of the yard and heard one pop. Owens yelled 'Schlack is shot'. Someone gave me the gun, so I ran into the house and put the gun on the table. Abadia came into the house and yelled, "Give me the fucking gun!" He found it soon enough then waved the gun around and says, "I'm going to kill you." Abadia put the gun in his pants then walked outside. Anderson shouted, "Police are on the way! Get away from here." I ran to try to get the license as Abadia drove off.

THE DEFENSE AND SPC ETHAN JAKS-

Q: Was everyone drinking?

A: Yes. The designated drivers had left so all the guys would spend the night.

Q: Please tell us about Abadia's actions and behavior while drunk.

A: Well, no one was acting aggressively toward Abadia. When Abadia does get upset, it is short-lived.

Q: Can you tell us more?

A: When Abadia was asked if he knows what he did, Abadia said, "You're messing with me." Owens took the gun out of Abadia's hands. He wasn't fighting it. I took the gun from Owens and took it to the kitchen table. I couldn't get the magazine out. Vans handed me a neighbor's phone to talk to police. I say he never left Ryan's side.

REDIRECT–

Q: How was everyone acting?

Suddenly, I was caught off-guard because Sofia turns around and hands me a note. It's from Meghan and it says, "Just so you know, we are not showing any autopsy photos in court. I just wanted to let you know, so you didn't have to worry about it or become unnecessarily anxious about something that is not even going to happen."

A panel member asks a question. In a military court, a panel member may ask a question but has a procedure to follow. S/he would write the question on a paper, hand it to the bailiff who shares it with the prosecution and the defense and then to the judge. The judge reads the question out loud.

Q: How did Abadia act in Iraq deprived of alcohol?
A: We couldn't drink at all, so we never saw him drunk.
Q: Were all the keys collected?
A: All car keys were kept on the table.

PROSECUTION AND SERGEANT (SGT) KEN CARSON–

An aerial neighborhood map is set up.

Q: Where did you live at the time, SGT Carson?
A: I lived here on the corner of the street. (He points out the location on the map.)
Q: Tell us about the visibility on the street. What could you see?
A: There are, of course, the streetlights and many porch lights were on. I can't say if the moon helped at all.
Q: What happened?
A: I heard what I thought was a firecracker about 23:00, so went outside and looked up the street. I saw Abadia in the front yard of Jaks's house. Abadia had the gun at his side. After dialing 911, I heard shots fired, so I go outside again. This time, I saw Schlack on the ground and Abadia with a gun. Abadia then walked back to his car, and I think he's

thirty feet away at one point. I saw Abadia get in the car, sit for a minute then pulled around my truck to leave.

DEFENSE AND SGT KEN CARSON–

The defense reviews with asking questions about the description of Abadia and seeing an article in the newspaper about Abadia a couple days later. Carson describes Abadia and admits he read something about it.

PROSECUTION AND SPECIALIST (SPC) ASTON JANSEN–

The aerial map of the street is on display.

Q: Where did you live, SPC Jansen? Show us on the map.

A: I lived on Ovnand Street which is located right here.

Q: Tell us what happened.

A: I heard a noise like a firecracker. My wife asked me to move her Civic from the road. As I was backing my van, a soldier ran up and asked to use a phone. I gave it to him. Later I found out it was Jaks who asked. I saw a crowd around a soldier in a ditch, so I walked over and saw Schlack. I went to get another phone and a flashlight. The MPs showed up, so I waited at my house to give a statement.

DEFENSE AND SPC ASTON JANSEN -

Defense reviewed the same material with their questions.

The panel had a question. Jansen pointed to the top left corner of the enlarged inset map, causing confusion as to why he pointed so far left and up on the map. The portion of the map is explained, so it is understood it was an inset map.

PROSECUTION AND PRIVATE FIRST CLASS (PFC) FELICITY MILLER–

Q: Tell us your job and what happened that night.

A: I was with the military police since February 2009. I got a call of a possible shooting at 23:26. Using the CAD in the police vehicle, I could acquire maps and get a house number. I can also track other police vehicles, as well. It took 3-4 minutes to arrive driving at a significant rate. While en route, it was confirmed that a weapon was drawn, and the shooter is on the scene. When I arrived, I assessed the situation. The shooter is gone, but I saw Schlack on the ground with a few people around.

Schlack was responsive, saying, "It hurts."

I asked, "Where? Show me. Explain it." I asked people to back away, then looked for a wound. Schlack was still talking. I moved his shirt and saw a hole above the hip with a significant amount of blood. I applied pressure but couldn't find an exit wound.

Corporal Thompson arrived. Now Schlack was making moaning sounds. Thompson cut the pants to get a better view. Schlack began to foam at the mouth and threw up. Both Thompson and myself moved Ryan to the sidewalk.

Today in court, Felicity Miller is seven months pregnant and seems very nervous as she gets on the stand. She somehow asked CPT Earhart for a moment to talk to me after her questioning.

I follow her out as instructed. We are offered a small room in which to talk. "This whole ordeal has been haunting me," she says quietly. "I was only a few months with the MPs. I ran to Ryan and told everyone to back off. I knelt down to try to comfort him. I thought you'd want to know his last words to me were, 'Help me, please. Help me, please'. Tears were falling down his face. I hoped the ambulance would come soon. I'm sorry."

"Thank you very much for sharing," is all that came from me, as I brush tears away. I wonder what she was feeling again, having to remember it all for this trial.

PROSECUTION AND SPECIALIST (SPC) SPENCER VANS -

Q: What is your MOS or job? How long did you know Schlack?

A: My MOS is 94 Echo which is a radio and communications security repairer. I worked with Schlack for two years.

Q: Tell us your experiences that night.

A: I arrived at the party about 7:00PM. I was in the front yard smoking. Then I went inside to see what was happening. I tried to talk to Abadia about the fact that he should stop drinking. Owens and Abadia got into a fight. Jaks separated them. Abadia and I exited the house and went to the back yard. Owens was still in the living room. I heard a sound inside the residence and peeked inside. I saw a hole in the wall. I estimate I spent about 10 minutes outside with Abadia. Abadia then began to walk down the driveway and seemed to be leaving.

An outside yard map and a street map are displayed.

Q: What happened next?

A: I followed Abadia, but at a certain point turned and walked toward Schlack and Owens. I believed Abadia was leaving.

Q: Where were you and the others? What happened next?

A: In the front yard were Owens, Schlack, and me. About fifteen feet from us, we all heard two cocks then a gunshot. Schlack fell and was grabbing Owens. Schlack fell to the ground. Schlack was sweating and going into shock. By now, everyone went to render first aid. I also saw Abadia go into the house and, several minutes later, came out with a weapon. Abadia got into his car and drove away.

DEFENSE AND SPC SPENCER VANS–

Q: How many times have you reviewed this crime scene?

A: A few times, I guess.

Q: Your story has changed. It seems every time you tell it.

A: I'm trying to recall it to the best of my ability.

It was known that Schlack had a measuring cup of alcohol and the defense continued with lots of questions about who drank how much.

It seems obvious that Vans is confused and becomes very nervous on the stand. To me, the defense seems to badger him with differences in his testimony to CID during the defense meeting, and what he's saying now. Then Defense changes direction.

Q: When did you have contact with Abadia?

A: Early in the morning on the next day, Abadia called me. I told him what happened. Then Abadia cried, 'I'll go to hell!' I said to him that you should turn yourself in. It will go better for you.

I suspected Abadia was having suicidal thoughts. Abadia called me several times. CID told me not to talk to Abadia, but I talked to Abadia once more. I did turn over my cell and video to CID.

Q: On a drunk scale 1 to 10, how drunk was Abadia?

A: Abadia was 8 on the scale that night.

REDIRECT–

Vans says he went to CID. He also arranged for Abadia to turn himself in. All the soldiers went to CID after the incident. Vans revealed he saw the gun but said nothing. Officer Burnett talked to Vans about Abadia, saying to Ryan, "I didn't shoot you."

PROSECUTION REDIRECT–

The prosecution asks questions for clarifying purposes.

CHAPTER 39

The five of us leave the courtroom at 6:30PM. Rita and Jerry leave for their hotel while the three of us take a journey down memory lane at the Copperas Cove Mobile Home Park where we lived for the last eight years of Rich's military career. It is sad to see it has become a dump, not that it was a top-notch place to begin with, although, originally, when we checked it out, it wasn't dirty or rundown. It was considered to be the best mobile home park back then in the area.

We come across an old Jack-in-the-Box and make a quick stop for burgers and fries. On our way back to Killeen, we stop at an H.E.B. and pick up soda.

At the hotel, I iron and write what has become a daily email to family and friends about our day. Recalling Dr. Barker's report that he interviewed some of these guys on the stand, I flip to the pages to read and compare the information with what they were saying today. I notice some of the testimony written in here is from the Article 32(b) judicial proceeding back in 2009. I remember Rich telling me that this is like a preliminary hearing in a civilian court. It may lead to dismissal of the charges or a court martial.

Article 32(b) testimony from SPC Gregory Owens:
"Spencer Vans and I told Barto Abadia to stop drinking and cut off for a little while. Abadia had slurred speech, he was incoherent, and he was being a little verbal with all of us. I proceeded to the living room to listen to music and then, all of a sudden, I was shoved against the wall

by Abadia. Prior to Abadia shoving me, there had not been a verbal argument between Abadia and I. There is nothing I said to him that in my opinion would have set him off...I remember seeing Abadia walk back to the front and proceed to his car...All of a sudden, I heard Ryan Schlack say, 'Owens, watch out!' and pushed me out of the way, and then I heard a shot and Schlack fell to the ground. Then I turned around and saw the gun in Abadia's hands and I grabbed the gun from Abadia and I told him that he shot Schlack...I then remember seeing Abadia go into the house, but I don't know what happened in the house. That was the last time I saw Abadia. I have seen Abadia with a bad temper after he drinks on several occasions. He becomes pushy and very verbal...I believe Abadia was the most intoxicated at the party... He has been verbally aggressive toward me in the past; he's wanted to fight, he would say fighting words to me...On this night in question, he pushed me and he said that I was a horrible battle buddy...After they separated us, it was roughly 5 minutes that the shooting took place...When I said to him, 'You shot Schlack!' he replied, 'Oh, I did?'...After two of us got up from the ground, Abadia said to Schlack, 'Get up you baby, you're not hit!' He said it more than once. Schlack didn't respond. I don't believe Abadia was surprised. I would say he was mocking Schlack. Prior to that shooting, I didn't see anything that Abadia said or did that made me believe he would end up doing that in the evening..."

Article 32(b) testimony from SPC Ethan Jaks:

"...At some point there was an altercation between Greg Owens and Barto Abadia, and I separated them. I told Abadia to go out back and Owens to go out front...I heard Abadia say he was leaving...and I saw him walking back up the driveway.

That's when I heard a weapon lock and load...I didn't see a weapon, but I heard it...Then I heard the weapon go off, but I still didn't see it. Schlack said that he had been hit and fell to the ground...Abadia was not in the street, he was more like on the sidewalk. Owens was with him, took the weapon from Abadia and was asking him 'What did you do?' ... Abadia walked back in my house, picked up his weapon, waved it in the air, and said that he would kill us all...he walked out to leave. He wasn't driving erratically...Everyone had been drinking except Dannon and Dale...because they were going to be designated drivers. Later in the evening they left because I thought that everyone was going to spend the night and therefore not need designated drivers...Abadia brought a case of beer. I considered him heavily intoxicated when I saw that he could barely stand up and that took place about 30 minutes before his altercation with Owens...Owens asked him if he knew what he had just done, and Abadia kept saying that he didn't do it in disbelief...when he came back in the house to get the weapon back, he could barely stand...When I took the weapon from Owens, I walked back in the house. Then Abadia came back into the house after me and said, 'Give me my fucking weapon.'"

Summary of Telephone interview with SPC Spencer Vans on April 10:

"Spencer Vans met Barto Abadia at Ft. Hood before his second deployment, and they deployed together to Iraq as part of Bravo Company. They worked on the same gate but different shifts. In Iraq, they played X-Box and ate meals together often. According to Vans, Abadia did not appear to be struggling in any way... When they returned home, Vans saw Abadia two weeks before Abadia left to go home on leave. During those two weeks, he did not appear bizarre, incoherent, anxious, paranoid, or depressed.

On the day of the alleged offense, they played X-box together for four hours. Vans could not recall the games they played that afternoon. He observed Abadia to be friendly and happy. Abadia did not appear agitated, tense, or anxious. He was not aggressive. Abadia did not express fear of others following him or trying to harm him. They did not drink alcohol. Vans did not recall Abadia discussing Iraq... Later that evening, at the party, Abadia appeared to be having fun. He appeared happy. He did not appear fearful. Abadia did not speak incoherently, nor did he speak of others wanting to harm him. He did not appear tense. He was laughing and having fun. Abadia said that it was a 'fun get together' until Abadia had the verbal altercation with Owens about not being a 'good battle buddy.' Vans said that a good battle buddy was 'Army talk for a good friend.' Vans had observed Abadia interact with Owens in Iraq, and they were always friendly."

Article 32(b) testimony from SPC Spencer Vans:
"...We were all just having a good time. Barto Abadia and I were outside smoking, and I felt Abadia needed to be cut off at the time from the alcohol. He was swearing and slurring words, so I talked to him for about 30 minutes...I believe it was Abadia who pushed Greg Owens first. Abadia was telling Owens that he was not a good battle buddy and pushed Owens into the corner. Then I talked to Abadia into going outside to smoke again...We just basically kept each other company for a few minutes...Abadia pulled out the weapon, he charged 2 rounds, pointed, aimed and shot...I believe Abadia was trying to aim the weapon at Owens, since they had that previous altercation, but I don't know. I saw him pull the trigger, and he kept pulling the trigger, but the weapon jammed... I didn't know at first that he'd been hit... and Schlack said to Abadia: 'Why did you shoot me, why would you shoot me?' and Abadia said something like 'I did not shoot you, I did not hit you...Stop being a pussy.' After I saw Schlack's wound...it wasn't bleeding. Abadia said something like 'I didn't hit you, that barely glazed you'... I am not sure who grabbed the weapon from Abadia, but he was standing still, watching us, saying 'I didn't shoot you, it's just a wound...stop being a pussy'...I did see that he had a gun, waved it in the air again and said, 'If you walk toward me I'm going to shoot you,' and went towards his car again. He drove away, but he was not swerving. A previous phone call, a couple weeks before the incident, he called me and left a voicemail asking me if I was Tobar and he was asking me for cocaine, which he later stated was for a friend... I also received a phone call from Abadia the day after the shooting at about 20-30 minutes after I had

gotten to my house. He said that he knew he shot Schlack, and he asked me what happened… Abadia broke down immediately. He actually said he was going to hell for this…When I saw Abadia walking back to the car, he said not to come after him or he would shoot us…When Abadia called me that morning… He was uncertain as to what had happened after…when I pulled Schlack's shirt up, that's when he saw the wound and that's when he knew that he had shot Schlack. From Abadia's reaction, he didn't seem surprised that he shot the weapon."

It is not clear if questions are asked at an Article 32. If so, I don't believe the same questions were asked at the Article 32(b).

CHAPTER 40

We must be in court at 8:00AM today. Rich, Adam, and I get up at 5:30AM and have cereal and I have a bagel.

There are many Criminal Investigative Division personnel (CIDs) including the head of the division in the courtroom this morning. Some will testify, while others want to observe a real-time murder trial. You just don't hear of any murders on a military base. I am not saying it has never happened, but it is a unique event.

PROSECUTION AND MS. SAMANTHA DAY –

Q: How are you involved with what occurred, Ms. Day?

A: I am the Criminal Investigator as well as a Firearms Examiner. I did the forensics. I can testify the bullets match the gun. CID gave me six cartridges, a pistol, and a fired bullet. After firing the bullets into a water tank, I compared the two cartridges.

THE DEFENSE AND MS. SAMANTHA DAY –

Q: The gun doesn't always function. Why wouldn't a weapon fire?

A: The lab followed protocol to the best of my knowledge. There are ejected rounds and no evidence of misfire.

I can tell Day is not going to make a definite statement as to why that weapon didn't fire by her vague response. It could be due to being thrown out a window or that a vehicle might have run over it. Clearly, the defense is trying to make a case for the weapon being dropped out of a vehicle.

Meghan hands a note to Sofia who hands it to me. It reads, "After CPT Towns, the ER doctor, testifies, if you'd like to speak with her, she said she would be glad to meet with you and talk with you. Just follow her out after her testimony."

I respond to Meghan with a question, "Who follows CPT Towns for testimony? Will we miss someone's testimony?" Terri

Meghan's note back to me says, "Just the firearms examiner; pretty dry testimony." I wonder if whatever will be going on while I am gone, she doesn't want me to hear or see.

REDIRECT-
Q: If the gun is dropped, the bullets coming from the gun which is run over by a vehicle doesn't change it, does it?
A: No.

PROSECUTION AND CAPTAIN (CPT) HELEN TOWNS-
Q: Tell us your MOS and how you were a part of the incident.
A: I am the medic in the Emergency Department at Darnell Hospital.

I received a call from CPR Trauma. The patient, Ryan, was pale, cold, cyanotic, blue, with no sign of life. There was little bleeding out, but there was blood in the stomach.

Atropine and epinephrine IV fluids were administered. The decision was made for no blood transfusion. At 12:06AM Ryan was pronounced dead. Ryan's wallet identified him.

After her testimony, CPT Towns and I go into a small room next to the room where Abadia's parents and sister are waiting. I feel a bit like I am invading their area, but of course there are doors and walls between us.

Towns leans forward and in a low voice she begins with, "Ryan couldn't feel the internal wounds, just where the bullet entered. Ryan was so badly injured not even a team of doctors could have saved him if they were right there on the spot. He didn't suffer long before he passed out."

"I wondered about that," I reply. "If the call came around 11:35PM and he was still talking when the MP joined him, it would appear as 15 minutes of pain. For Ryan, it would have felt like hours."

"The bullet went through the left hip, through two large arteries and lodged in the other hip. No exit wound," she tells me.

As she speaks, tears are forming. I know I need to listen and understand whatever she tells me and hold it together. I realize she didn't really confirm or deny my comment about how long Ryan suffered.

Prior to going back into the courtroom, I detour into the bathroom. There is a woman of Spanish descent standing by the sink fixing her hair. I only glance at her and feel it is best not to say a word. Talk about an awkward moment to go to the bathroom when someone I feel so uncomfortable with was outside the stall. I am thinking she is Abadia's mother. Only after she leaves can I take care of business. Getting out of the bathroom as soon as I could, I walk back to the courtroom.

PROSECUTION AND SPECIAL AGENT MICAH RUSSELL–

The interior house floor plan is shown along with the street layout.

Q: Tell us your part in the crime scene.

A: I show up at 2:30PM and I make note of the condition of the crime scene. This includes taking pictures of the whole residence, crime scene, and of cups placed to mark where the 45 cal cartridge rounds were found. I have the photos with me today.

There's sudden movement in the courtroom. There is no indication why at that moment, but the judge orders the panel to be sent out. The defense wishes to view the pictures. There are photos of the doorway leading to the kitchen, a view of a countertop, a table in the dining room and a close up of a kitchen table. Also, a photo is shown of an actual fired round and the shirt Ryan was wearing. The conversation among the lawyers and the judge could not be heard, but the photos were not shown to the panel when they returned.

PROSECUTION AND OFFICER HENRY HANSON –

Q: Officer Hanson, how were you involved in this crime?

A: I heard radio traffic at 23:20. I heard that shots were fired, a rifle was involved, and a car description. I went to the scene where I saw a patrol dog being used to search for the accused. I decided to go patrol the southeast area of housing and then went west to south to look for the rifle used. I caught sight of a pistol in the road, a pit bull pistol. At the time, I didn't realize it was the weapon used in another crime that night. I also discovered it was not registered on Fort Hood.

THE DEFENSE AND OFFICER HENRY HANSON –

The defense asks questions about running over the pistol with his tire. Hanson is adamant he did not run it over.

PROSECUTION AND SPECIALIST (SPC) GREG OWENS –

Photos are brought to the witness chair where Owens is seated.

Q: Specialist Owens, can you identify the people in these photos?

A: The first one is a photo of Schlack. The other is a photo of Abadia and Schlack taken the day of the party.

Prior to the next testimony, CPT Earhart sends me a note telling me of the pictures and specifically of Ryan's wound. She is clear that it is very close up and will not show Ryan's face. So, I should be prepared, right?

PROSECUTION AND LIEUTENENT COLONEL (LT COL) FABIAN JONES –

Q: Lieutenant Colonel Jones, tell us about your role in the aftermath of the shooting.

A: I am an Air Force Pathologist from Lackland Air Force Base, Texas. While working the autopsy, I was shown a picture of Ryan for the purpose of making sure to understand the circumstances of background framework. I opened the body to look inside. I use a microscope to look at the external markings such as the scrape on the elbow and the gunshot to the hip.

I am not prepared for what happens next. How can anybody be prepared? I cannot wrap my head around what I am seeing. A male anatomy outline poster is shown with a marked trail of where the bullet went through arteries, one called the internal iliac artery. A photograph shows the wound on Ryan's body and a third photo of the bullet.

I can barely breathe. I can't look at Rich to my right nor the guard at my left. Frozen in place, my heart breaking in two, I cannot stop the tears. I just can't. It didn't take long to show the photos, but it is enough. I bump Rich and ask for his handkerchief. Sofia, sitting in front of me, hands me a box of Kleenex.

Adam told me later that when he saw the photos, he became more depressed this had happened to Ryan. He remembered the funeral day again.

DEFENSE AND LT COL FABIAN JONES –

Q: Relying on your experiences, LT COL Jones, how are deaths categorized?

A: I have had about 800 gunshot/death experiences. The causes of death fall into the following categories: natural, homicide, suicide, undetermined and accidental. 'Natural' is when the body itself fails with no external causation. 'Homicide' is an external trauma done by another person causing death. 'Suicide' is self-imposed harm leading to death. 'Undetermined' is exactly that. There is no evidence of how death occurred. And finally, 'accidental' is a no-fault situation where the death is caused by an occurrence that was unintentional.

PROSECUTION AND ABADIA'S MOTHER–

Abadia's mother is from Santa Fe, New Mexico. She confirms a receipt for a gun and verifies both her ex-husband and her purchased the gun.

PROSECUTION AND SPECIALIST (SPC) ORLANDO NORTH–

Q: Tell us about yourself and your involvement.

A: I am from Wasilla, California. I recently got out of the army. I had lived with Abadia and two other soldiers since June 2009.

About 9:00AM, I woke up hearing Abadia come into the house. Abadia asked me, 'Did the police come?' This was such a strange thing to ask that I started asking Abadia questions. Abadia said he shot somebody and talked about 30 minutes more. He was nervous and upset when talking. Suddenly, Abadia's phone rang. He broke down as he hung up the phone. He was saying things like, 'How am I going to explain this to my family?' and 'What am I going to do?' and 'I accidently shot someone.' Abadia talked about options which Abadia decided are to turn himself in, run to another state, or commit suicide. I ended up taking Abadia to the Main Gates entering Ft. Hood.

DEFENSE AND SPC ORLANDO NORTH–

The defense basically reviewed what was said and retold the timeline. They brought up Abadia's drinking behavior; sometimes it would be fine and another time he would get angry.

PROSECUTION AND CAPTAIN (CPT) GENE DOMINIC–

CPT Dominic is introduced as the replacement taking over the company commander's position. He also reviewed the Ft. Hood laws on concealed weapons regulations.

It is late afternoon and the prosecution rests. The defense questions the charges having to do with not having the level of proof for 2 of the 3 charges that Abadia is on trial for. There are unbecoming behavior questions. The judge says he will reserve judgment. The premeditated charge is not off the table. The insanity plea never comes up. The defense claims the prosecution did not put on enough evidence of that threat.

Later on, Rich is handed a typed folded paper from a possible investigator who quickly walks by us. It reads:

"The housing area was on West Fort Hood, not McNair or whatever the newspaper said which means it was further from the hospital than originally thought.

The gun was a 45 cal.

After shooting Ryan, Abadia was using foul language and sneered at Ryan to get up; that he was only fooling around. That is when Owens took the gun away from him. Abadia followed Jaks into the house and Abadia threatened to kill everybody if Jaks didn't give him the gun.

Somehow, Abadia got the gun away and left. Abadia went down the road a couple miles and threw the gun out the window.

He turned himself in according to one newspaper account, but another said he was stopped at the West gate the next morning.

The bullet went through Ryan's hip and through both femoral arteries which means he never had a chance."

CHAPTER 41

The trial ends around 4:00PM. As we walk out the door of the court building, we run into Anderson, Jaks, Vans, Dale, and Dannon. It is the first time since the start of the trial we encounter them.

"Hello, guys," Rich and I say.

Rich begins with, "We thank each of you for whatever you could do to help Ryan and hope you can keep the memories of your good times with Ryan."

I give each man a hug and whisper 'thank you'. In Owen's ear, I whisper, "You have been given more time on earth and this gives you more time to do something more and worthwhile."

As Rich, Adam, and I are walking toward the car, I say hesitantly, "I think I said something to Owens that was not the right thing to say. After all, I hardly know the guy." Then I told them what I whispered to Owens. Neither of them responded.

"Is he strong enough to take it on? Have I put more pressure on him? Oh, geez, what a screw-up I can be," I say with frustration.

"What's done is done, Terri," replies Rich as he puts an arm around my shoulder. Recalling what I said makes me feel a bit depressed about the incident.

At Clothing Sales, we buy a tarp and pens because I am on my third pen. Adam finds Sergeant pins and a Fallen Soldier's sticker for his car. We also look for a coin display case for Ryan's commanders' coins, but no luck.

We eat at Ryan's Restaurant, a buffet, come back to the hotel so I can iron and eat junk food. I begin to rewrite my courtroom scribbles and reread what I wrote the previous days. It now hits me that each soldier's description of what occurred is told a bit differently. How will that affect the trial? The lawyers must have caught this. I hear about people seeing the same accident, but the retelling is different. It is happening right here and now. Does the panel depend on the investigators' findings? Will they be able to determine who has the correct version of what happened? Will they remember almost a year has passed and may have forgotten some of what happened?

Today, Barto Abadia's roommate was on the stand and I looked to see if he is mentioned in Dr. Barker's report.

Article 32(b) Testimony from SPC Orlando North:
"…I remember seeing Abadia at around 0900hrs. I was sitting on the couch when he walked in the door. He was nervous and was asking if the police were in the apartment. He was wearing a white t-shirt and jeans. Then he began to explain what happened. He was extremely nervous, and he told me that he shot his friend accidentally. He didn't go into detail very much. I didn't understand the severity of the situation. He was crying and cursing himself. He was a nervous wreck. I was concerned that he would hurt himself, and I was trying to calm him down. He kept on asking what he should do, but since he said that it was an accident, I told him to turn himself in…When he got off the phone, he said that he was going to turn himself in, and that he needed a ride…Abadia kept telling me the story, but it kept changing because he wasn't sure of where he had shot his friend…When he first explained to me what happened, he knew he fired a shot, but I don't know if he knew that he had hit anybody…At one point, he picked up a knife from the kitchen, and he said: 'I don't know if I should just kill myself or take off running'…During the phone call is when he found out that Schlack had died, and then he had collapsed on the couch…"

Summary of Telephone Interview with Specialist Orlando North on April 28, 2010

"Specialist North said that he was assigned to live with Specialist Abadia in temporary barracks for two weeks after SPC Abadia's second deployment to Iraq. He did not appear bizarre, and he did not speak of others wanting to harm him. He spoke of his guard duty in a limited fashion. He did not speak incoherently when he was sober. On the first night, Abadia showed him a weapon, but he did not tell him why he had the weapon or where he intended to store it. SPC North observed SPC Abadia become angry when intoxicated. After the first week, North went to a bar with Abadia. Abadia became enraged at a woman who called him a name. He yelled at her, and 'called her out to fight'. She was angry and continued to exchange words. North had to escort him out of the bar. North decided he never wanted to drink with him again.

On the day of the alleged offense, North observed Abadia became extremely upset after he received a phone call from a SPC Vans. He asked North to not turn him in. North said that Abadia was in a state of panic. He was not sure if Abadia was intoxicated. Abadia did not express fears that were not reality based. He did not speak of seeing or hearing anything not present in reality. Abadia was not speaking of anything related to Iraq."

CHAPTER 42

Back to the courthouse by 8:00AM. We are early, so we head to a gas station to get a soda for Adam and a cappuccino for me.

I am feeling a pressure, a weight so heavy it physically hurts, and it is constant. I can't relax even if I will it. This trial is taking a toll on me, and it's only day four. Is Rich and Adam feeling as uptight and not able to stop to take a breath? I am tired and maybe that's why I sometimes forget to take notes. Will we finish by Friday?

There are others who take the stand and a couple who are recalled to the stand. The two designated drivers are asked about what they observed and when they left the party. SPC Jaks shows a video and pictures of everyone drinking and said Ryan came about 23:00. A forensic chemist for firearms and gunshot residue instructs us about the process used on the bullets, and a forensic latent print examiner says he looks at characteristics on skin and talks about the tools used. Another forensic chemist takes residue from around the area once a gun is fired, so he explains about finding particles on Abadia's outer shirt and undershirt, but not on the hands and clothing.

When the defense was re-questioning SPC Spencer Vans, he talks about Absinthe, a kind of liquor they all drank, shows videos and answers questions about the next day and the phone calls with Abadia. Vans states to the prosecution that he was on the phone with Abadia two times and at 8:03AM Abadia calls him and they talk.

Anderson is called again by the defense and answers some of the same questions asked before. Pictures belonging to him are shown on a television screen of the kitchen table and coffee table.

When the prosecution is up, CPT Earhart reminds Anderson that he told CID that Abadia was a 6, but 8 is Abadia's normal "drunk" using a scale of 1 to 10. He also thinks Abadia was there three hours before the shooting.

Sofia turns around and alerts me the next witness is one of the psychologists the defense is relying on to help with the case.

DEFENSE AND DR. RHONDA STEMS–

Q: Dr. Stems, what is your medical background and tell about interacting with SPC Abadia?

A: I am from Georgetown, Texas, and my field is staff psychologist, triage, and clinical psychologist. I first met Abadia on Aug. 9 and thereafter met 18-20 times for 45 minutes each. I would determine if he needed therapy to deal with issues. Initially, I think it is adjustment disorder and depression. Then, it seemed to have progressed to post traumatic stress disorder.

PROSECUTION AND DR. STEMS–

Q: Please define Post-Traumatic Stress Disorder.

A: SPC Abadia had a tough time with his second deployment and it's not necessarily one event that can trigger stress. Being at a front gate is a huge job. Injured people would come to gain access. He must decide who to let in the gate. Is he in danger? Is someone else in danger? Is this a life-threatening event?

A second issue is re-experiencing events such as a cardboard box near the gate or smells or sights. Abadia hears men in uniform talking about deployment. He prefers to avoid this.

A third is he feels detached from the family. He's drinking excessively and has no interest in doing anything.

A fourth criteria is hyper-vigilance. This would be a direct impact and drinking was his therapy for dealing with it. The others who work with him said he did not talk to commanders.

Q: Can you tell me if malingering was possible?

A: I rely on the patient bringing it to me. If no one brings this up, I do not follow up. However, I do listen for cues and didn't see Abadia as malingering.

Q: Can you tell us about any forensic evaluation done?

A: No, I never was asked to find if he is competent to stand trial.

DEFENSE AND DR. STEMS REDIRECT–

Q: This is a hypothetical question. Say there is a friend who is killed in a car accident. As a result, the one who survives begins to drink heavily. This is very stressful. He caused his friend to die. What could he have done? He can't redeem himself.

A: Abadia wants to switch places with Ryan.

Q: Where does Abadia score on a scale when evaluated for PTSD?

A: PTSD can be chronic or acute. It is a clinical judgment as to why he cried about murder vs. why he cried about Iraq stress.

DEFENSE AND DAVID ABADIA –

Q: Mr. Abadia, tell us about your son. Gives us a little history.

A: We lived in New Mexico. I still do. Barto lived with me until he was 14 years old. At 17 years old, I again spent time with Barto. When Barto was 14, he was easygoing, impressionable, respectful, smiling. He was liked and protected his niece, nephew and cousin.

In 2004, my son joined the military and was deployed for 14-15 months. On leave, Barto spent quite a bit of time visiting on and off. I noticed Barto didn't smile and didn't visit as much. He would spend time with his grandparents before but didn't visit them as much. He drank more and seemed angrier.

After his second deployment, my son spent even less time with the family. He was quick to anger and was hard to calm down. He didn't visit relatives much at all nor did he display any sense of humor. It was bizarre behavior. He even seemed angrier.

PROSECUTION AND DAVID ABADIA-
The prosecution asks Mr. Abadia to clarify some things that he said.

DEFENSE AND DAVID ABADIA REDIRECT-
Q: What actions were taken regarding SPC Abadia?
A: I guess you want to know I told Abadia to talk to his uncle who has PTSD. The same uncle told me to sign the papers so Abadia can go into the army.

After Mr. Abadia steps down off the stand, Sofia turns around and cups her hand, so I lean forward. "Next up is the other psychologist the defense uses. It seems the defense is pinning their case on what this doctor says."

DEFENSE AND DR. DERRICK JOHNSON-
Q: Dr. Johnson, what field of study are you qualified in? What did you do when you interacted with SPC Abadia?
A: I am an adult psychologist and have a degree in Forensic Psychiatry. I reviewed the court order requesting a sanity board, the legal motion requesting the sanity board, the Article 32, CID case file along with the video tape of the interrogation, and Abadia's medical records that were available. I spent over 15 hours reviewing all the materials. Regarding my meetings with Abadia, I met with SPC Abadia on five occasions between 17 November 2009 and 8 January 2010, for a total of almost 8 hours.

I gave the Psychological Assessment and Inventory (PAI) and MMPI 2 which gives an overall impression of an individual in terms of providing relevant clinical information, in addition to also having some measures of validity in terms of whether somebody is answering questions forthrightly or not. The diagnosis I determined is "alcohol intoxication, alcohol dependent, adjustment disorder with mixed disturbance of emotions and conduct, and nicotine dependence."

Q: Have you had the occasion to form an opinion about SPC Abadia's ability to appreciate the nature and quality or wrongfulness of his conduct at the time of the alleged offenses?

A: Yes, I did. My opinion is that SPC Abadia did not have the ability to understand the nature, quality, and wrongfulness of his actions.

Q: …in this case, his intoxication rose to the level to cause him to be a severe, in your opinion, severe mental disease or defect? …And as a result… he was unable to appreciate the nature and quality or wrongfulness of his conduct?

A: Affirmative.

PROSECUTION AND DR. JOHNSON–

Q: Dr. Johnson, can you please clarify, from a forensic psychiatric point of view, to not be able to appreciate the nature and quality or wrongfulness of one's conduct?

A: I have an opinion, but it may be different from opinions among other colleagues.

Q: Please share with us your opinion.

A: My opinion is that…he was so intoxicated that he did not know what he was doing throughout much of the evening and into the subsequent morning.

Q: Sir, you were charged with the duty of making a forensic psychiatric determination for this court and these proceeding as to whether this soldier understood the nature and quality or wrongfulness of his conduct…What does "nature", "quality" and "wrongfulness" mean?

A: Well, the "nature" is what; did he know what the actions were that he did. The "quality" is, …

Q: So, it's his own opinion of whether he himself knew, is what I'm hearing?

A: It's an understanding of what he seemed to have known at the time.

Q: Do you rely solely on Abadia telling you he believes what he was doing was wrong or if he could even remember?

A: I do not. I reviewed the sworn statements from those at the party.

Q: Well, let me… let me take a step back because I think we're still not quite there. If I understand what you're saying, you're telling me that "nature", "quality", or "wrongfulness", in order for one to appreciate that, is just whether SPC Abadia believed whether he could appreciate; whether he knew what he was doing was wrong; is that right?

The exchange between CPT Earhart and Dr. Johnson continues in this vein with the doctor insisting Abadia did not even know he had a gun at times due to his level of intoxication.

CHAPTER 43

Q: Let's consider severe mental disease or defect. You had diagnosed Abadia with alcohol intoxication and dependence, nicotine dependence and adjustment disorder.

A: I believe the alcohol intoxication and dependence were the etiologic factors at hand.

Q: Give us the meaning of "severe", in other words, how severe must this disease be in order for someone to have no idea what he is doing? I did confirm that you called the hospital attorney at Fort Hood and discussed this. I will share what the attorney stated, '…just because somebody is voluntarily intoxicated, it does not mean that he or she is not responsible for his own actions….'

A: I must state for the record this is not exactly what the attorney told me. He told me that, at least according to his understanding of current military law, when someone is involuntarily intoxicated, it does not excuse them from bearing some responsibility for whatever incident occurred. Then I asked because the accused had been charged with premeditated murder, how is that addressed legally? The hospital attorney said, his understanding is, and he gave me assertion or a PAN, which I have now, since I'm maybe a little out of date, but from what I understand, 'It's still fairly accurate in terms of instruction that may be given by a judge to a court in regard to a situation which somebody is charged with a crime when they are involuntarily intoxicated.'

Q: You believe that the accused, given the state of his excessive intoxication at the time, does not appear to have acted in a premeditated manner.

A: Correct.

Q: May I remind you, Doctor, you were not charged to make a determination in regard to the charge of premeditation. Did those mental diseases or defects have a bearing on whether he could appreciate the nature and quality or wrongfulness of his conduct? I mean, that is what you were charged with, but it seems your report is more concerned with whether he had the intent to form the intent to kill. Would that be fair, sir?

A: One of the questions is, in premeditation, is one of intent. Do you intend to do something? And if you intend to do something, what is it? SPC Abadia was so intoxicated that he didn't seem to have the ability to really know what he was doing.

Q: What constitutes severe mental illness?

A: It is something that could hinder somebody significantly in terms of their general, social, occupational, and other human functions.

Q: What determines severity?

A: Many psychiatrists would agree that there are certain illnesses that are very severe such as having a thought disorder, major depression, having a substance abuse difficulty and maybe an anxiety disorder. An example is of the Jack Nicholson character in "As Good As It Gets" with the excessive-compulsive disorder.

Q: Can you give a couple more examples of severe mental illnesses?

A: Somebody who has a severe depression that they're so depressed that they're no longer able to go to work or take care of their family. They're at the point of losing their job. Now, you can take that even a step further by adding that they have a psychotic process on top of their major depressive ailments.

Q: What is a psychotic process?

A: This is where a person is holding beliefs, delusions and often hallucinations that are not correct. An example is of someone who believes his body is rotting from the inside out.

The questioning now focuses on the severity of the severe mental diseases and defects that the psychologist diagnosed Abadia with on the night of the crime that being alcohol intoxication and alcohol dependence. Although the doctor did not discuss that July night, he skirts around it by talking about other times.

CPT Earhart seems to slow down a bit verbally as she sets up her question.

Q: Well, let's just kind of break it down a bit further. DUI's, driving under the influence, how do you bounce that?... If someone is drinking to excess, gets in a car behind the wheel, speeds away and runs someone over and kills them, how is that any different from what SPC Abadia did when he drank on the 17th of July 2009 and fired a .45 caliber round into his friend? What is it about SPC Abadia that makes him different from everybody else in the world? What is it about inside of his head? If you pry his head open, what makes him not mentally responsible? That's what I'm trying to figure out.

A: In both situations that you give, due to the amount of alcohol, presumably, the person who's driving the car and SPC Abadia took away the ability to rationally not engage in those activities or behaviors.

Q: But, sir, you were talking about the amount of alcohol. I'm asking you, from a forensic psychiatric point of view, what is it about the inside of Abadia's head that makes him any different or any less culpable than any other human being who would've done the same thing? I could've drunk that night, got into my console, pulled out a gun, and shot somebody. If I had drank the same amount as Abadia, what's the difference? What makes him so unique or so psychiatrically absurd for you to determine that he had no idea what he was doing? He couldn't understand the basic building of wrongfulness? I got it. I understand that he was drinking, but what is it?

A: Well, if you were to be in that situation as he, both of you would not understand what you were doing. But it sounds like what you are getting at is a legal question.

Q: That's what you were charged to do, though, sir. You were charged to come back to this legal environment to make a determination as to mental responsibility based on nature and quality or wrongfulness. I mean, we could go through what SPC Abadia reported to you that would point to the fact that he actually did understand the nature, quality, and wrongfulness. The first thing he said when he got to his apartment the morning after he shot his friend, 'Are the cops here?'

A: Abadia had time to sober up a bit.

Earhart tries a few different ways to talk more about this time frame, but each time the defense objects and the judge sustains. Her next line of questioning deals with PTSD.

Q: I understand you considered PTSD. Could you tell us whether Abadia was suffering from PTSD on July 17?

A: In my forensic evaluation, I tried to do a very thorough evaluation. And particularly for someone who is a returning combat veteran, some individuals do develop PTSD. Now, while PTSD may be a significant difficulty, it may even be a severe mental disorder, generally, it is not viewed as a disorder that could exonerate someone in having done some action that they, therefore, lose their ability to rationally know what they were doing. I evaluated Abadia at length in regard to his having PTSD and, while, yes, he did have some symptoms of anxiety, PTSD, being an anxiety-type disorder, he did not meet the criteria for having PTSD. At points, I think he became a little insulted with me–with my asking those questions, although my intentions were certainly not to insult or upset him but to do a thorough evaluation. Sometimes maybe those factors might be mitigating in terms of better understanding an individual's situation.

Q: Why did you specifically rule out PTSD in regard to SPC Abadia?

A: Because he didn't have that as a diagnosis in my opinion. SPC Abadia told me many things that were upsetting to him but was not upset to the point of warranting PTSD, in my opinion.

Q: The criteria is that he must have witnessed some kind of traumatic event first, correct?

A: That's the criteria.

Q: And then would have to experience some kind of re-traumatizing from the event or of the event?

A: Yes.

Q: And then he would start feeling differently or want to avoid talking about it, correct?

A: That would be one of the criteria.

Q: And then he would start, perhaps, behaving differently, acting in ways that he would not have acted before the traumatizing event, correct?

A: Possibly.

Q: And then, finally, it would have to have some kind of monumental impact on his life such that his life would become much different from what it was before the traumatizing event. Is that a fair summation of the criteria for PTSD?

A: That's, I guess, a summation, but it's somewhat of a complex diagnosis. Somebody can have many of the symptoms of PTSD, but yet, not have a full enough or enough of the symptoms to meet the criteria for having frantic PTSD.

Q: So what is the case with SPC Abadia?

A: SPC Abadia did have some symptoms of severe anxiety or anxiety-type symptoms. He did have some symptoms of depression. He was also not engaging in behaviors as best he could, and that is why I gave him the diagnosis of having adjustment disorder with mixed emotional features because he did not; that is not to say he did not have some of those difficulties. That is why it seemed, although not the best choice, to be one of the aspects in which he decided to carry a gun. Unfortunately, apparently a fair number of our soldiers do, upon returning home from combat, even though asked not to do so by the rules and regulations.

Q: What about the possibility of malingering?

A: The fact is I did not specifically test for malingering outside those questions that are incorporated into the PAI. In terms of what I observed from what SPC Abadia told me and the 6-plus hour CID investigation DVD, as well as his own sworn statement, he seemed to be pretty consistent in terms of all the things that he said in all of those formats.

Q: Please confirm for us what Abadia conveyed to you in terms of him not remembering anything in his account, anything that happened between when he was firing the gun on the front lawn or in the kitchen, as he says, and waking up the next morning.

A: That is not correct. If I may elaborate, he told me that much of his loss of memory, I believe, and to be most accurate I would need to review my report, but from reviewing it this morning, I believe that his memory, in terms of particulars, left him largely after SGT Schlack arrived at the party. He then begins to have some memory again when he sees himself in the kitchen of Jak's home. Schlack is on the ground; and I believe someone said that Schlack has been shot, and he doesn't believe. He believes that it's sort of a game and wonders why Schlack is laughing, when, probably, Schlack is in pain. And believes that he made some comment of, 'Get up. Stop'…

Q: I believe it's 'Get up, you pussy, you're not hurt?'

A: Something like that, yes. In terms of his memory, he then does have a loss of memory. One of the very interesting things about how he recounted everything is that he actually went out of his way to not say, 'Gee, I don't remember,' as though he was trying to avoid having a memory. It's more that he couldn't remember and so he didn't know how to make sense of much of what apparently happened to him.

Q: Because of the large volumes of alcohol that is consumed by anybody, on some level, has some kind of impairment when we drink.

A: Yes.

Q: Did you, Doctor, do a live interview with anyone who was at the party?

A: I did not. I relied on the soldiers' sworn statements.

Q: What was the reason for the gun in the car?

A: It is because he did not feel protected due to his combat tours and other incidents that took place in his life.

Q: What did he tell you when inside SPC Jaks's house that made him not feel safe to the point that he had to go retrieve his weapon? What happened inside that party that all of a sudden, he was not feeling safe or feels the need to get the gun?

A: From what I was told, it seemed as though he had no idea of why he went to get the weapon nor that he felt unnecessarily unsafe. What exactly was in his mind is unclear.

Q: He didn't tell you about a confrontation that he got into with one of the soldiers at the party?

A: He told me that he did get into a confrontation, but his knowledge of the confrontation sounded as though that was secondary to information that he had learned from others who were telling him about the party.

Q: So, he only recalls there was a confrontation because other people told him there was?

A: It sounded as though it was somewhat murky to him.

Q: What did he say was his rationale for running into Jak's house after he shot Schlack, to retrieve his gun? Why didn't he just run away if he didn't know what he was doing or was too drunk? What made him consciously go into the house to get his weapon?

A: He didn't completely remember going and retrieving the weapon or exactly what was going on at the time and what had happened.

Q: Let's look at 'wrongfulness.' It has been verified that Abadia did drive back to the scene of the crime, had seen the paramedic's gloves and some pillows. That SPC Abadia reported to you that something bad has happened, but he believed that it involved a bad incident, an ambulance and SPC Schlack being taken away.

A: He reported that something bad had happened and, I believe, had some sense of realization that he had some involvement, although he didn't seem quite sure what had happened.

Q: Whether or not he knew, the facts are the facts. He fled. He left the scene after SPC Schlack was shot. He didn't stay. ...He threw his gun out the car window. I know he doesn't remember that he did, but he did, and when he got to his apartment, he asked if the cops were there.

A: Yes.

Q: Are the following actions I will list in a moment be indicative of wrongfulness? Were they rational actions? For example, when SPC Abadia saw the gloves, when he didn't want to go back into Jaks's house because he thought that the guys were going to jump him, spoke to his roommate about being charged with murder; maybe he could just be charged with involuntary manslaughter, Abadia leaving his ID at home and didn't want to drive his car because he knew the car would be impounded after being taken into custody.

A: These actions you speak of were not reported to me.

It is evident that the counselor softens her approach.

Q: Dr. Johnson, if all of these things that we just went through are indicative of wrongfulness, just about 13 hours after pulling the trigger, what was the severe mental disease or defect at the time he pulled the trigger? I'm not talking about voluntary intoxication. Are you saying his alcohol dependence was so severe that it caused psychosis? I mean, he wasn't delusional, was he?

The defense immediately objects to counsel asking many questions. The judge rules to let the doctor answer the question.

Q: I will ask again. Was Abadia suffering from psychosis when he pulled the trigger?

A: When he pulled the trigger due to his being so severely intoxicated, he was not in his right mind.

Q: Would you say that about anyone who commits a crime while they're under the influence of alcohol?

A: That would depend on how intoxicated they are.

Q: If everyone was as intoxicated as the Specialist reported to you he was that evening, and committed a crime, would you believe that they are not mentally responsible based on the level of intoxication?

A: If they lacked the ability to plan and lacked adequate judgment at that time.

I know I am not the only one who thinks the psychiatrist is talking in circles. Some of the counselor's questions were not answered in my opinion. Next is Defense's turn to question. Because the psychiatrist was hired for their side, it will be interesting to hear the types of questions and directions they will go. Surprisingly, I am more alert than I thought I could manage.

CHAPTER 44

DEFENSE AND DR. JOHNSON REDIRECT–

Q: Dr. Johnson, if, in your professional opinion, did SPC Abadia's level of intoxication rise to the level of lack of mental responsibility?

A: It rose to the level of his not knowing what he was doing.

Other questions had to do with the doctor consulting other collateral sources and using other statements from the case file indicating others believed that Abadia didn't know what he was doing.

Q: I want to talk to you about the difference between a clinical diagnosis and a severe mental disease or defect and doing a forensic type of evaluation. In terms of that person being subjected to a forensic diagnosis or forensic evaluation would undertake everything, that person is obviously aware of your role in reporting to the court. …How does your approach with him differ from if you were going to be engaging in a treatment or therapeutic type of treatment?

A: Primarily, my role is to try to assess as best I can in understanding of what the nature of his mind was at the time of the offense, but not to engage in what… to be objective about what I've been asked to evaluate.

Q: He might be less likely to open up to you in that type of objective environment that he might in a more treatment type of environment, fair to say?

A: I can concur with that.

The interaction continues with the justification for the doctor going outside the basic questions on the order received from the court, but the doctor couldn't remember the order in terms of what other questions may have been asked. The information about Abadia's actions after about 13 hours was information Abadia found out about after the alleged crime.

Q: What about the malingering theory?

A: One has an index of suspicion that somebody is malingering. Abadia was so consistent in the various formats of telling his version. He didn't act schizophrenic or bipolar or hearing voices and things of that nature.

Q: What about someone Abadia told you about was attempting to get him to malinger? Can you tell us more?

A: It was someone in jail and Abadia told me that this sort of freaked him out a little; made him a little paranoid, but not as though his every move was being monitored or anything like that.

PROSECUTION AND DR. JOHNSON RECROSS -

Q: Dr. Johnson, did you consider the fact that SPC Abadia was charged with premeditated murder into your decision or your assessment of whether Abadia may be malingering because of the severity of the crime?

A: I want to clarify I would have if I could have seen that he was trying to malinger but all I conclude is here is somebody who does have significant difficulties with the use of alcohol, who got significantly drunk and did something he wished he didn't do. Also, that he cannot see where he was malingering other than that he could not remember.

Q: Your main concern here was his report to you of his level of intoxication; that the level was so high he could not remember what he did.

A: He did not report anything in such a way to suggest that he was feigning taking responsibility for what he did. He later turned himself in. He did ask that a friend go with him. It sounded like for moral support; it may be an appropriate thing to have done.

Q: Well, then, Doctor, wouldn't that indicate to you that he knew then the wrongfulness of his conduct?

A: But that was after he became sober.

Q: But not too long after. And you just said, 'After he became sober.' There's a difference between sobriety, becoming sober and becoming free of this severe mental disease or defect, is there not?

A: It sounds as though, when he's sober, he was free of the defect or the difficulty of the severe intoxication.

Q: So you are asking this panel to find SPC Abadia mentally...

"Objection, Your Honor. Argumentative," one of the defense team calls out.

Q: You told me in a pretrial interview that, let's say he was guilty of murder. If the case went to court, that you wouldn't say he was not mentally responsible. Isn't it true that you're more concerned with his intent to kill more than anything if this was not premeditated murder?

A: My concern is the intent is being able to make a decision, make a judgment. And how does one tease that out of having a nature and quality of understanding of what they did?

Q: But the criteria is not judgment. It is nature and quality, is it not?

A: But doesn't judgment figure in similarly?

CPT Earhart states, "That is why you're the forensic psychiatrist and I'm not."

The judge asks everyone if there are any questions. The court takes a 20-minute recess. Adam and Anderson are walking out to the building and joke about the psychiatrist. Walking out, the psychiatrist held the door. It's impossible that the doctor didn't hear what was said. Once through the door, the jokes kept coming. Adam found this to be the most entertaining.

At 3:00PM the panel is brought in and the judge informs us the defense is going to show a video interview of the accused by CID that could take four and a half hours. After one hour nineteen minutes, the tape is paused. There is a short break, and the video is played for another two hours.

The sets are mostly of Abadia on the floor writhing and mumbling; Showing so much footage of Abadia wallowing on the floor...What is the defense wanting us to think? At first, I didn't see how it helps. They are supposed to have an interrogation expert but didn't use him.

As I sit and watch the video, it dawns on me what this is all about. It is to get the panel's sympathy. The defense suspects Abadia will be found guilty. Is this better than any documents I sent or pictures of Ryan or all those people writing about how Ryan's death affected them? Does the panel even take the time to read any of it? Many people rather watch information unfold rather than read about it.

At one point, the colonel suggests a dinner break, and the judge agrees. We are back at viewing the video around 7:00PM.

At 8:20PM, I feel my phone vibrate. I could have sworn it is off. There is no ringing, just a vibrating, but I get confused, so I push the button thinking I am turning it off but, guess what, it goes on making all the noises it does to wake up. I panic and look at the judge who is looking at me. I jump out of my seat, falling over the legs of the seated bailiff and race out of the courtroom. I let myself fall into the opposite wall from the courtroom door and just hold myself against the wall.

Every bit of me is shaking, and I can't stop it. I have enough sense to turn the vibrator off on the phone. It took every fiber of me to compose myself and go back into that courtroom. Right then, I knew I had to hang on and watch my every action. The strain and the pressure is getting the best of me. I have got to hang on. He will be found guilty. He will go to prison. He has got to. That's all there is to it. Total video shown today is five hours, and we are excused at 9:00PM.

What a long day. Rita and Jerry say goodbye and head toward their car. We will see each other in the morning. Rich, Adam, and I are too tired to go anywhere to eat. None of us are really hungry. We decide to just munch on the snacks in our room.

CHAPTER 45

We are in court by 8:00AM. There is a discussion among the judge, the defense, and the prosecution about a Mr. Smith. Mr. Smith's conviction records were difficult to get, apparently. According to the discussion, both sides were debating if the videotaped interview with Smith is relevant. Defense wants time to talk to Smith and review his arrest records.

I lean over and very softly whisper in Sofia's ear, "Who is this Smith person they are talking about?"

"He was the cell mate of Abadia's. Supposedly, he told Smith what he did. Abadia also asked him how he could beat this."

I recall a Mr. Smith in Dr. Barker's report but am too tired to read anything tonight.

An internal investigator is the first witness. Absinthe and its effects are discussed, but it was not tested.

PROSECUTION AND STAFF SERGEANT (SSGT) BLANEY-

Q: SSGT Blaney, tell us about how concerns are handled when in the gate tower?

A: I was the control point/visitor supervisor at the gate in Iraq. We train the guards extensively prior to assigning someone to the gate tower. This includes verbal communication with a possible visitor, using proper radio communication with the sergeant in charge, and what steps are unquestionably followed. If someone approached the gate, one thing that occurs is a runner would inform the upper ranks or those in charge of what was happening at the gate tower's entry point.

DEFENSE AND SSGT BLANEY–

Defense pointed out that he was not physically there and Blaney agrees.

PROSECUTION AND SSGT BLANEY REDIRECT–

Blaney is asked to clarify. He explains that the guards are not alone, so Abadia couldn't shoot without him finding out.

PROSECUTION AND FIRST SERGEANT (1SGT) GENE CORONE –

Q: 1SGT Corone, you were the 1SGT for Bravo Company in Iraq. Tell us the steps a guard would follow when confronted with a potential visitor.

A: When the visitor was still relatively far from the gate entrance, the guard would call out, "Halt!" or "Stop!". If the visitor does not stop and continues walking forward, the guard is to call louder, "Halt!". The guard would call out a third time but also says he will fire a weapon. By this time, a runner has gone to find the higher ranked soldier in charge to come and assess the situation. A round cannot be fired unless he had permission from the soldier in charge. You never want to get to that point of firing a gun.

PROSECUTION AND DR. SIMON BARKER–

Q: You are a forensic psychiatrist, Dr. Barker, is that correct? What are your qualifications? Tell us about what you did in testing Abadia?

A: Yes, I am a forensic psychiatrist from California but currently teaching in Boston. I have a Bachelor of Science in Chemistry, a medical degree, and child psychiatry. I have studied malingering in adults and children. There are written exams and interviews to detect malingering.

I used forensic exams on Abadia, saw the videos and read reports. I talked to Owens and Vans and had Abadia talk about his childhood.

Dr. Barker is repeating approximately what his report stated that I have in my possession. The defense would object quite a bit during the Prosecution's questioning of Dr. Barker because the doctor would continue to talk about malingering. I must have missed something, but it is brought out that Dr. Barker is not allowed to define "nature", "quality" or "wrongfulness" during his time on the stand.

The defense stated the doctor was defining the three words yet again, and they had made an objection three times, so the defense quickly asks for a mistrial. The opinion is to use "able to appreciate". This can be admitted. The judge overruled.

The prosecutor instructs Dr. Barker not to define these three words and just stick to answering the questions. From then on, the doctor uses carefully selected words, but makes occasional errors.

DEFENSE AND DR. BARKER–

The defense bombards Dr. Barker with questions such as:
How much money are you making for this?
Can you give more details about your background?
Let's discuss the time the incident happened versus when you talked to Abadia.
Did you examine Article 32, the CID video, the psych records, the autopsy report, and charge sheet?
Please clarify what you focused on when working with Abadia.
The defense questions the diagnosis.

During a break, we're in a side room. Dr. Barker peeks around the corner and says, "How are you two holding up, Mr. and Mrs. Schlack? I am so, so sorry about this all. During the questioning, I would look over at you and feel so bad about what you are going through." After a brief conversation with Earhart and Michaels, he says his goodbyes and leaves.

CPT Earhart asks, "Is being here any help at all? Is this helpful?"

I reply, "Yes, oh, my yes, of course. We wanted to be here. We never would forgive ourselves if we didn't attend."

"How are you doing?" MAJ Michaels asks in a concerned voice.

I look at each and say, "A person has to compartmentalize as best she can."

Final closing statements are made by both defense and prosecutors. CPT Shannon Jones is first and the gist of her presentation reflected Abadia's problems with intoxication, his suffering PTSD possibly set off with Abadia's encounter at the entry gate tower with a decision about firing a gun at a civilian and dealing with pressures that spiraled into insanity.

CPT Megan Earhart's statements focused on refuting what Jones had said by reminding the panel the gun should not have been on post, the entry gate tower incident could not have happened and there was no sign of killing due to any kind of insanity. She spent time taking points from Dr. Johnson's testimony and basically gives reasons his responses do not hold up.

After the prosecution and defense rests, we are told there will be three hours off for preparations of instructions for the panel.

We leave to eat an early lunch at a Mexican restaurant Ryan took us to a couple years ago. The décor of the restaurant is very festive and colorful as you would expect. The atmosphere was light and comfortable. The group consisted of Jerry, Rita, Evan Anderson and the three of us. We ordered tacos, burritos, enchiladas, and drinks which tasted very good.

"Where are you all from?" Evan Anderson asks.

Jerry replies, "Well, Rita and I live in Texas near Austin. However, we were both born and raised in Wisconsin. These three live in Oshkosh, Wisconsin, which is on the east side of the state on the Lake Winnebago shores. How about you?"

"I come from Georgia on the west side, a small little town called Cave Spring. The closest big city would be Atlanta," Evan answers. The small talk continues during the meal.

After lunch, Adam takes off with Anderson and the rest of us head to the Post Exchange (PX). The PX is like a department store for anyone in the military or retired. The cost of items is a bit less than Walmart most times, but no sales tax is charged. The four of us look around at the furniture and appliances. Rita and I look more closely at items and make comments while the two guys talk about whatever guys talk about roaming around a store. We spend about forty-minutes looking around. Making it back to court by 1:30PM, we are instructed to wait.

Meanwhile, Adam tells us he drove around the base with Anderson, and they talked about Anderson's relationship with Ryan being a great friend, about what Adam is doing and things they have in common. Adam also got a quick tour of Anderson's barracks which he thought was a really nice setup. Anderson gets Adam back in time for the afternoon session.

We are all sitting in one of the rooms designated as a break room for our group. Needing something to do, I dig into my big bag and pull out Dr. Barker's report. Towards the end of the report is a section called "Opinion", which seems to be a summary of testing and interviews, but more importantly, clearly states Dr. Barker's answers to the three questions posed by CPT Earhart.

Q. At the time of the alleged criminal conduct as set out in the attached charge, did the accused have a severe mental disease or defect which does not include an abnormality manifested only by repeated criminal or otherwise antisocial conduct or minor disorders such as non-psychotic behavior disorders and personality defects?

A: With reasonable medical certainty, Abadia was not suffering from a severe mental disease or defect at the time of the alleged criminal conduct. Diagnoses from other testing results fundamentally indicate the cause was by Abadia's voluntary ingestion of alcohol and does not constitute a severe mental disease or defect. Dr. Barker continued with the following points regarding Abadia:

- Went to work without difficulty on the day of the offense
- Enjoyed playing video games for four hours with a friend, Vans
- Vans did not recall Abadia being sad, in fact consoled Vans about his wife cheating on him.
- He enjoyed a workout at the gym and felt pumped.
- Was taking pride in self-care and body-image
- No evidence of impairment in his grooming, social or occupational functioning–all factors that deteriorate if presence of severe mental illness.
- Appeared unaffected by his reported severe depressive symptoms when he attended a party
- Brought a case of beer to the party
- In fact, was having fun with friends
- Reasoned his tolerance to alcohol would be better at a lower altitude due to lower air pressure
- Does not recall arguing with others
- Enjoyed exchanging stories of his deployment
- Appeared jovial until he became intoxicated and had a verbal altercation with Owens
- Based on all Abadia's behaviors during the day, the late-night agitation was more related to alcohol intoxication and not representative of an alcohol-induced mood disorder.
- Abadia exhibited the signs of severe alcohol intoxication such as slurring of speech, ataxia and talkativeness, but did not feel or appear depressed.
- He chose to drink excessively but not suffering from a severe mental disease or defect.

CHAPTER 46

Q. What is the clinical psychiatric diagnosis?

A: With reasonable medical certainty, in my opinion, SPC Abadia meets Diagnostic and Statistical Manual of Mental Disorders IV edition-Text Revision (DSM-IV TR) criteria at the time of the alleged criminal conduct for the following psychiatric diagnoses: Alcohol Dependency, With Psychological Dependence. Evidence supporting this opinion includes:

- Engaged in a maladaptive pattern of alcohol abuse, leading to clinically significant impairment and distress
- Between the ages of 17-years-old and 22-years-old, Abadia needed markedly increased amounts of alcohol to achieve intoxication. He began drinking 2 beers every 2 weeks, but this escalated to 12 drinks a night to achieve the desired effect.
- When he did not drink alcohol, he experienced withdrawal symptoms such as tremors, depression, sweating and fatigue.
- Had periods where he drank every day and for entire weekends. He spent all his time outside of his required military duties drinking alcohol.
- Stopped associating with anyone that did not drink alcohol. He stopped seeking new social relationships because of his alcohol abuse. His divorce was negatively influenced by his alcohol abuse.
- Continued to drink alcohol despite his arrest for driving under the influence of alcohol, depression, and the knowledge that two of his uncles died from alcohol abuse

- Has met no criteria for alcohol dependence or abuse for at least the past month because he was in jail and does not have access to alcohol.

With reasonable medical certainty, in my opinion, SPC Abadia meets DSM-IV TR criteria for Alcohol Intoxication. Evidence supporting this opinion includes:
- Ingested a large amount of alcohol on the night of the offense
- Shortly after Abadia's ingestion of alcohol, he acted inappropriately in an aggressive manner
- Demonstrated slurred speech and incoordination
- Had an unsteady gait and reported impairment in memory while intoxicated

With reasonable medical certainty, in my opinion, SPC Abadia meets DSM-IV TR criteria for Alcohol-Induced Mood Disorder, With Depressive Features, With Onset During Intoxication. Evidence supporting this opinion includes:
- Experienced a depressive mood or diminished pleasure in almost all activities (except the party on the night of the alleged offense)
- The depression developed during heavy and daily alcohol intoxication.
- Depressive symptoms did not precede the onset of the substance abuse. It began after Abadia began drinking heavily.
- The depressive symptoms caused him to feel lonely and not seek new relationships. He was angry and volatile when intoxicated.
- I considered whether Abadia met criteria for other disorders, even PTSD.
- He reported hypervigilance, anxiety, and irritability following his return from Iraq which were suggestive of PTSD but did not meet the full criteria for the disorder.
- Most importantly, SPC Abadia's response to traumatic events during deployment was excitement. He enjoyed these brief moments of danger. He opined that other soldiers were exaggerating their fear

during one attack. His response did not involve intense fear, helplessness, or horror. He spoke with his friends about his deployments and considered remaining in the Army rather than avoiding another deployment. On the night of the alleged offense, he felt he was among friends and did not re-experience painful combat-related memories that night.

I carefully considered whether SPC Abadia met the DSM-IV TR criteria for substance-induced psychotic disorder, caused by alcohol, cocaine or the over-the-counter Methyl 1-D XL pills. However, prominent hallucinations and delusions are the predominant symptoms in this disorder. Abadia never experienced hallucinations. His report of Iraqis or someone following him was delusional, but this idea did not appear fixed or developed, rather it was vague paranoia. These symptoms occurred exclusively following his deployments, but not during deployments even though he was taking the Methyl 1-D XL pill for six months during his second deployment. Abadia's sense of reality was never an issue to his friends. In my opinion, SPC Abadia did not suffer from a substance-induced psychotic disorder which was solidified by the fact that his self-reported paranoia subsided after five months in jail. If he was suffering from a substance-induced psychotic disorder, the paranoia would have subsided within days, or several weeks at most.

With reasonable medical certainty, in my opinion, SPC Abadia meets DSM-IV TR criteria for Depressive Disorder Not Otherwise Specified, In Full Remission. Evidence supporting this opinion includes:
- Reported depressive symptoms following his second deployment to Iraq
- The depression developed during heavy and daily alcohol intoxication.
- Did not experience depression during his deployments when he did not ingest alcohol

- Depressive symptoms did not precede the onset of the substance abuse. Symptoms began after Abadia began drinking alcohol daily.
- When Abadia was incarcerated in the Bell County Jail, he continued to report feeling depressed and was placed on suicide watch. These depressive symptoms lasted several months, beyond the more typically described one month following the cessation of alcohol ingestion in an alcohol-induced mood disorder.
- Given the suicide thoughts and severity of depressive symptoms, his initial month of depression in the jail was likely more severe than an adjustment disorder, and more related to his alcohol dependence.
- I am unable to determine if the depression that he experienced in the following months in the jail, after his withdrawal from alcohol, was primary, an ongoing substance-induced mood disorder, or reflective of a poor adjustment to incarceration.
- During the past two months, no significant signs or symptoms of depression have been present.

With reasonable certainty, in my opinion, SPC Abadia meets Diagnostic and Statistical Manual of Mental Disorders IV edition-Text Revision criteria for the Malingering. Evidence supporting this opinion includes:

- The essential feature of malingering is the intentional production of false or grossly exaggerated psychological symptoms, motivated by external incentives. In my opinion, Abadia is exaggerating his purported memory impairment regarding the night of the alleged offense.
- Is motivated by two primary incentives: evading criminal prosecution and evading responsibility to his family. Abadia was aware of the difference between involuntary manslaughter and premeditated murder on the morning following the alleged offense and continues to correctly define involuntary manslaughter. In my opinion, Abadia is motivated to purport to not recall the offense because he wants to limit

his intent on that night and avoid responsibility for the premeditation to murder. While that is a significant inventive, in my opinion, Abadia is equally motivated by evading responsibility to his family. He admires and honors his family. He considered dropping out of Basic Training but didn't want to dishonor his family, becoming emotional during a CID interview each time his family was mentioned, the same reaction during my interviews and even more than his feelings for the alleged victim. He became angry and swore when I questioned if he told his mother about his Iraq experiences. He is clearly extremely protective of their feelings and he feels ashamed that he perceives he has disappointed them.

- In my opinion, Abadia is exaggerating his lack of memory of the alleged criminal conduct because he is trying to evade prosecution and he does not want to admit to his family responsibility for his actions.
- In my opinion, it is more acceptable to Abadia to blame his alleged actions on alcohol intoxication rather than face the possibility that he may have formed more conscious intent than what he wants or can admit to his family.
- In my opinion, Abadia already moved beyond guilt for his alleged offense when he explained that he felt better than before this tragedy. He also expressed his appreciation for learning to accept what he can't change. However, he is still ashamed of his family's feelings.

SPC Abadia's estimated intelligence is above average. At 23 years old, with such intelligence, he should not struggle to recall simple objects as he did during the Mini-Mental State Examination (MMSE) and Test of Memory Malingering (TOMM). He performed significantly below his expected capacities.

According to Sam Smith, SPC Abadia engaged in a blatant fabrication of psychiatric symptoms during his sanity board. I considered the validity of Smith's statements, but I am impressed that he came to CID of his own volition and knew numerous facts of the case that could not have been known unless he spoke extensively to

Abadia. To my knowledge, Smith has not gained anything by making his report.

SPC Abadia frequently referenced his paranoia and fear of others during my interview.

When questioned, these fears were vague to me and his psychologist. He did not speak of these vague fears to the CID agent (instead he discussed some local robberies), nor to his friends. In my opinion, these reported symptoms now appear an attempt to create a notion of psychosis or PTSD. Yet, he never appeared frankly psychotic to anyone, and he never met criteria for PTSD, including the most fundamental responses: intense fear, helplessness, or horror. SPC Abadia confronted traumatic events during his deployment in Iraq, but he only spoke of how excited he was by these events. It is hard to reconcile his attempt at creating a sense of hypervigilance with his excitement that he experienced during these witnessed traumas. Furthermore, this paranoia resolved after five months in jail. In my opinion, these symptoms are fabricated, and perhaps the remnant of Mr. Smith's coaching.

During my interview, Abadia did not recall retrieving his weapon or returning to his car after the alleged shooting until he woke up in his car. About 12 hours after the alleged offense, he told CID that he remembered retrieving his weapon and running to his car after he pulled the trigger. To a psychologist, he said he vaguely remembered walking to his car. Abadia remembered Schlack lying on the ground in front of the porch, but he told CID that Schlack was lying on the linoleum tile. He told varying versions of where he drove. He first said he drove to Austin, but later said that he went to West Fort Hood. During my interview, Abadia could not recall anything until he awoke in his car on the side of the road.

These story variations could have been due to the passage of time, but in one instance, Abadia exposed his fabrication by saying he did not have any memory between pulling the trigger and waking up in his car on the side of the road. He later recalled returning to his apartment and talking to his roommate. As he recounted his feelings very coherently, he revealed he considered suicide, and said, "I started regretting that I threw my gun out." I questioned what he said. In response, he stammered, and said that because his car window was open, he figured he threw his weapon out. This reasoning further contrasted his denial of the weapon disposal during a CID interview.

The TOMM and the Structured Inventory of Malingered Symptomatology (SIMS) results suggested that SPC Abadia was malingering his presentation.

CHAPTER 47

Q. Was the accused, at the time of the alleged criminal conduct and as a result of such severe mental disease or defect, unable to appreciate the nature and quality or wrongfulness of his conduct?

A: No. Foremost, as stated, it is my opinion that SPC Abadia was not suffering from a severe mental disease or defect at the time of the alleged criminal conduct. Despite the lack of severe mental disease, I carefully considered Abadia's ability to appreciate the nature and quality or wrongfulness of his conduct. It is my opinion, with reasonable medical certainty, that SPC Abadia was able to appreciate the nature and quality or wrongfulness of his conduct. Evidence supporting this includes:

- Was raised around guns. He enjoyed hunting and admired his father's gun collection.
- Sought optional, countless hours of weapons training; Was qualified by the Army to use multiple weapons; Was highly trained in the safety and proper use of guns. This evidences SPC Abadia's understanding the use of a gun and that a gun could cause bodily harm.
- Knew that he was in violation of Texas's concealed weapons law
- Pointed his weapon at Iraqis when deployed because he wanted them to stop approaching his assigned gate.
- On one occasion, he cocked and loaded a weapon to show an Iraqi man that he was "serious". He was aware of the effect of cocking and loading his weapon and pointing a weapon at a person.

- Drank heavily on the night of the offense, but reasoned that his tolerance would be better at Fort Hood than New Mexico because it was at a lower elevation with a lower air pressure
- Told the CID agent that he knew he shot Schlack when he saw him lying on the ground and bleeding; He appreciated that a gunshot could make someone drop to the ground and bleed.
- Had a history of prior altercations with SPC Owens when intoxicated and allegedly retrieved his weapon from his car after another verbal altercation with him on the night of the offense
- Knew that he shot the weapon once because he heard one boom
- Owens said that SPC Abadia told Schlack to get up because he had not been shot, thus illustrating his appreciation that a person would be hurt and potentially not able to walk if shot.
- After pulling the trigger, SPC Abadia immediately returned to the house to retrieve his gun. He appreciated that he was the owner of the gun that had shot Schlack.
- Allegedly waved the gun in the house threatening to kill others with the weapon
- Kept a gun loaded in his car in case he needed to defend himself quickly. He appreciated guns were used to defend and potentially harm someone if needed.
- Returned to the scene of the alleged crime and saw a latex glove that led him to conclude Schlack had been attended to by an ambulance.

Evidence supporting SPC Abadia's appreciation of the wrongfulness of his conduct includes:
- Said that he fled the scene immediately after he determined Schlack had been hit
- Asked his roommate, North, if police were at their apartment on the day of the offense
- Allegedly disposed of the weapon .8 miles from the scene of the crime, suggesting an attempt to avoid justice

- Did not stop at Jak's home when he returned in the morning of the alleged offense because he feared the other guys would jump him because they would be angry he killed Schlack
- Told the CID agent that he wouldn't blame his friends who wanted to kill him for what he did
- Appeared nervous and distraught when he entered the apartment on the morning of the alleged offense.
- Cried loudly when he was told that he shot Schlack
- Said that he would go to hell for shooting Schlack
- Looked for himself on the news because he knew a murder was newsworthy
- Worried about the reaction of his family to his conduct
- Was considering his intent behind the criminal conduct approximately 8 hours after it occurred, and strategized that he would pursue involuntary manslaughter
- Turned himself in to police
- Immediately admitted to killing Schlack
- Left his ID card at home because he realized he would lose it if he was locked up by police
- Did not drive his car to the police because he did not want it impounded
- Lied to Vans when he told him that he was in Austin to have an additional hour to consider his options

This was a lot of information to take in. Now we know where CPT Earhart got some of her ideas for the closing statement.

We are finally called into the courtroom for the instructions to be read. The judge clarifies what is accepted from the instructions sent in from the defense and the prosecution.

1. Premeditated
2. Involuntary manslaughter
3. Negligence homicide
4. Culpable negligence

The charges against Abadia:

Charge 1 - Violating a general regulation - Certain laws to follow while on post
- Duty to observe laws
- Violated transport of weapon
- Conduct unbecoming a soldier

Charge 2 - Premeditated murder -
- Schlack is dead
- Cause is the act of the accused
- Premeditated was designed to kill Owens or Schlack

Will consider "Unpremeditated murder"
- Convinced Schlack is dead
- Did shoot him
- Intended to kill Owens or Schlack
- Intoxication by itself is not a crime
- Will not include "Premed" or to inflict harm

Will consider "Involuntary manslaughter"
- Schlack died
- Act of accused made
- Culpable negligence meaning "Failure to act followed by careless act of accused"
- Doesn't require having intent to kill
- Unlawful act
- This does not require having "intent to kill"

Will consider "Negligent homicide"
- Schlack died
- Result of accused act
- Unlawful act
- Simple negligence
- Discredits armed forces
- Simply doesn't care

Charge 3 - Communicates an offense - Language used such as "I will kill you!"
- Communicated to Jaks

    Was a threat
    Wrongful
    Discredit to the Army
    Injure another now or in the future
"Pre-meditated" or "Unpremeditated"
    Sane/impairment to understand act
    Determine mental disease
    Consider intoxication, but doesn't mean he couldn't premeditate;
    Consider blackouts
"Accident"–Premeditated or Meditated
    Accused in death not planned
    Not negligence
    Death unintentional
"Simple Negligence" is neither pre-meditated nor meditated homicide.
    "Sane" or "Insane"
    Appreciate the nature of his actions
    Was not mentally capable
    Clear and convincing evidence

At about 4:30PM, a recess is called. It's a short one, and soon the judge has us reconvene.

As a courtesy, the judge asks if the panel is ready to deliberate. To everyone's surprise, the colonel speaking for the panel, states, "No, we'll continue on Monday." According to military court rules, the judge really didn't have a choice; he had to concur.

I am furious that the prosecution makes final arguments and then the panel decides not to go into deliberations. My family expresses that sentiment as we walk down the hall to the exit. How will anyone remember the panel's discussions, especially after a weekend? We all felt annoyed at this turn of events.

Also, our family will sit around in this town all weekend, stressed from the trial, stressed from not knowing the verdict, and oh, how inconsiderate the head of the panel is. I feel she had it figured out how she is going to vote without another thought given.

At 6:00PM we meet with COL Stone 27th BSB Battalion. The current 1SGT is also here.

"COL Stone, is it possible for you to investigate giving the 'Soldier's Medal' to Ryan?" Rich asks. The "Soldier's Medal" is given to a soldier who saves someone's life.

"Mr. Schlack, I can certainly investigate it. There needs to be clear statements describing what Ryan actually did in the reports."

"Yes, sir, I know," Rich replies humbly, "but we would appreciate being kept apprised of your findings."

"I will let you know anything that is discovered," responds the Colonel. "Again, you have our sympathies. It is good to meet Ryan's family. Goodbye." We all shake hands and leave.

At 7:00PM we have dinner with Greg Owens, Ethan Jaks and his wife and daughter, Evan Anderson and Thomas Dale. At first, the conversation was awkward. But once we started talking about Ryan, the stories began to flow. They each talk about the fun they had with Ryan.

"One time he was driving his Mustang past everyone who already was in formation. Ryan looked with shock at the unit realizing he must be in trouble and snapped his head straight ahead and stepped on the gas to get out of there," Tom laughed, recalling it all.

"Okay, I got one." Evan giggles and begins. "I was feeling down because of my divorce and things just not going right. I went into Ryan's room for no reason, really. Ryan was cutting his toenails. His nails were like claws, so long and sharp. I can't understand how his boots fit on his feet. He looks at me and as calmly as can he says, 'I guess I should cut my toenails before I go home on leave. My mom, she wouldn't like me going bare feet with these.' The way he said it, I laughed so hard and forgot why I was feeling down."

"We did a lot of running at night. I don't care what time it was, but I would call him or he would call me and we would run a couple miles," Greg shared. "His steps were so long, I had to run twice as fast to keep up with him. It was like for one of his steps, I had to take two."

Evan Anderson made a comment about the car being a three-seater because Ryan had his seat pushed back so far no one could sit behind him.

Then everyone jumped in when the group started talking about the trip to New Orleans and what a fantastic time they had. Ryan drove because, of course, he had the cool car. No one really had a lot of money and they figured pooling the funds would be best.

They sure sound like a tight group. Before leaving the restaurant, we exchange phone numbers and Facebook addresses. As a parting thought, Rich said, "Ryan looked upon you all as his second family, and he thought very highly of you."

Adam, Rich, and I go back to the hotel exhausted. Adam called work to let them know he would have to extend his vacation even though he used it all up. There is a concern he might be fired as he was talking to his boss. His boss snickered at the suggestion Adam made and said Adam shouldn't worry about it and to see him on Wednesday. Sofia already has called Rich and told him that the hotel stay is extending, and the car and flights are changed for Tuesday.

CHAPTER 48

Dr. Barker's report does have a very interesting account from Sam Smith. I am hoping it isn't long because I am tired, but the more I read, the more I can't stop.

According to the Sworn Statement by Sam Smith, dated Feb. 3, 2010:

Barto Abadia told me that he was back from Iraq about a month and he got invited to a party. He was drinking a little, but he wasn't drunk. He said that he had a high tolerance for liquor…He said that the guy he killed was mouthing off and being a smart ass and embarrassing him in front of his friends, so Abadia told him that he had something for him. Then Abadia left and went to his vehicle to retrieve his sidearm. I told him that I thought only officers were allowed to carry firearms, and he said that it is his own personal weapon. He told me that he owned lots of guns. Abadia told me he went back to the party and cocked the gun three times. I then told him that he must have been drunk because he didn't need to cock the gun three times, but he told me that he wasn't drunk because he wanted to scare the guy a little bit. I said that I guess he wasn't scared then, and Abadia said, "No, he wasn't, that's why I shot him." I told him that was kind of a fucked-up reason, and Abadia said that wasn't the only reason. Abadia said he shot him to hurt him and try to get out of the military. He said it was a win-win situation. I told him that it was fucked up because he died and now he will also be in prison and he said that he really didn't give a fuck either way. I told him prison was bad…Abadia said after he shot him, he got back in his vehicle and drove away and started drinking a little more and fell asleep in his car because he was afraid to go to his apartment because the cops would be looking for him. Abadia received a phone call that morning and woke him up, and it was the owner of the house saying that he shot the guy, and he was told the police are looking for him and that the guy died. Abadia then went to turn himself in. I told Abadia that it sounded weird and that it wasn't an accident. I told him it sounded like he could get himself in a better position by using PTSD thing as a defense. I told him to talk to his lawyer about using the PTSD thing. He asked me questions about how he could use it. I told him because he was in a war a couple times and killing people and blowing buildings and stuff. He told me that he didn't really go to an action zone, and he just did a lot of walking and patrolling. There were no fire fights or shooting. He asked if he could still use the PTSD as a defense, and I said yeah, he could still use it…Abadia got really excited about that and said that he was going to try it.

Later, Abadia said he was going on Thursdays and Fridays to see his doctors. So, the following week after he saw the doctor, we were talking again, and he told me that it looks like the doctor is going to buy the story. Abadia said the story was he was out of his mind, that he was suffering from PTSD, that he was belligerently drunk, and that he didn't remember what happened that night. He told the doctors that he only remembers the next day when he got the phone call that the guy died. That went on for a month and a half and every week he would have more news about how close he was getting to being found insane. He told me that it was really working now and his lawyer told him that they found him incompetent and that he should be going to a hospital real soon. I told him that it wasn't over yet and that it was just getting started. Abadia got real sad and thought that it was over and he would be going into a hospital as being insane. We talked every day about his day and I coached him on what to say to the doctors before he would go to see them…Then he finally mentioned that the guy he murdered was a very good friend of his. The reason that he told me that was because he was making a joke about an incident the guy was involved in...

I would write a letter to the best of my ability then I would send the rough draft over to him, and he would correct it and then send it back to me so I could send it to my family. I would send him a nine-page letter that took me 3 or 4 hours to write, and he would send it back to me in a few minutes, completely rewritten.

He also had about 22 books in his room. He gets about 3 or 4 books a week. He would finish a 900-page book in about a week or so. The books were about real history, conspiracy history going back to 10,000 BC. They were like textbook kind of books. He speaks well, sleeps well, and has good eating habits.

There was a section of reports from other psychologists, and I wonder if it would contain anything that the cell mate suggested to Abadia. I believe I found some evidence.

From a Clinical Psychologist on July 28, 2009
Barto Abadia (BA) denied that he was arguing with other party members, however vaguely recalls walking over to his vehicle. BA stated he has "no memory of anything else". He then reported, "I woke up in a field the next day."...BA stated that "I couldn't believe what I was hearing but immediately knew that he had to turn himself in"... BA became agitated and despondent when talking about certain memories in second deployment. He talked about feeling "horrible and helpless" when he had to turn away civilians who were in clear need of medical attention...BA then spoke about first deployment, which "was so much worse". He spoke about one of his friends dying and remembering seeing one soldier going into a fetal position on the ground, not knowing whether he was going to survive mortar attacks...

BA also addressed remorse for killing his friend...BA expressed a lot of feelings of shame and is greatly concerned about his family...BA also stated that "things make me jump" and provided an example how "popping balloons" scared him...He began to drink heavily prior to deployment following a death of friend (car accident, non-combat related). BA stated that today is the first time he has ever openly spoken about intrusive memories, suicidal thoughts, and other anxiety symptoms. BA stated that he wanted to learn about himself so that he could provide more concrete and clearer answers to family when they ask him "Why?"

From a Clinical Psychologist on August 3, 2009
BA continued to present w/extremely depressed mood, expressing much remorse at the death of his friend. BA was very tearful, agitated at times, expressing great shame and guilt. He spent much time talking about disappointing and shaming his parents. BA also spoke about owning a gun because "I never felt safe around anyone." BA couldn't elaborate as to what he meant by this, only repeated, "I just didn't feel safe. I can't explain it, but I just didn't feel safe."

From a Clinical Psychologist on August 7, 2009
He had an especially hard time with his second deployment where he was responsible for the front gate and having to tell desperate people that they couldn't gain entry, some dying, or seriously ill…

From a Clinical Psychologist on October 1, 2009
Today he talked a lot about Iraq, which started from a discussion about a recurring dream he keeps having about his second deployment. He experienced several life-threatening incidents during the first deployment, and he also recounted some stories of brotherhood.

CHAPTER 49

From about 1:30AM to 8:30AM, I didn't sleep well. Rich and I get up and start our day. The first issue is to find out why our shower water is cold. I run the shower for 10-15 minutes to get the water at a temperature I can handle to wash my hair and shower.

The three of us have a chance for an egg and bacon breakfast in the restaurant because we usually had to leave before the restaurant opened. Rich and Adam take the Suzuki SUV back to the Dollar Rental to extend the contract. After that, they go to an HEB Grocery Store to buy junk food and to Army Surplus because Rich loves to wander around places like that. It brings back his days in the army; I am sure.

Meanwhile, I separate the laundry, run down to get quarters, and start on that. I do three loads. None of us have enough clothes to last the extra days, so this is a necessary task. I have the housekeepers change sheets and bring fresh towels and creamer. Even when the guys come back, I am still at it. The dryer doesn't always cooperate, so there are lots of clothes draping over the chairs and bed.

When I finally do finish, we go to play putt-putt golf. I win! Wow! That never happens to me. I get a score of 46 and those two get 54.

Rich suggested we go tour Killeen. Eventually, we ride to our first apartment building on Gray Street in Killeen. It was the first place Rich and I lived when we arrived here in 1975. It is in the shape of a square, but only three sides had apartments. The light-colored brick building has a hint of Spanish design with the entry ways. The front side has a brick wall to enclose the swimming pool. Adam couldn't fathom us living in the dumpy place.

At 3:00PM we are to call Greg Owens to make dinner plans. After I make the call, Rich and I walk over to the Gold Wing Road Riders Rally and briefly roam the parking area looking at motorcycles. GWRRA was the group we rode motorcycles with for 15 years now. For the fun of it, we walk in. It is 3:30 or so and are told closing ceremonies will be at 4:30, so we figure things are packed away.

At Boston's Bar and Grill, we meet up with Greg Owens and Evan Anderson. Greg talks about that night, incidences with Ryan, and we ask about his family.

"My parents live seven hours north of St. Paul even beyond International Falls, Minnesota. My sister is moving home because her marriage is not working out. I have a year to go before my enlistment is up. Then maybe get out and go to school."

It is tearful, but a memorable time this evening with the guys Ryan hung with.

The three of us drive back to our hotel. I write in my journal but at 8:45PM we go to K-Mart to buy lipstick, then to add a bright spot in the day, we head to Dairy Queen for a cone. Rich and I call it a night, but Adam has plans with the guys at 9:30PM.

Adam went to the movies with Evan and Greg. He had bought tickets earlier in the day. Realizing he bought an extra ticket, he went outside of the theater and started saying loudly that he had a ticket, and someone can have it for free. He wasn't scalping the ticket or anything like that. Someone did walk up to him and took the extra ticket. "Ironman 2" was the movie the guys wanted to see.

Back at the hotel, I am thinking about what role this Agent Andrews, the agent responsible for interviewing the witnesses, plays in this, so I return to Barker's report. And there it was.

According to the Charge Sheet

Preliminary investigation revealed SPC Abadia and SPC Greg Owens...became involved in a verbal altercation while at a party...SPC Abadia went to his vehicle, which was parked across the street, and retrieved a handgun which was unregistered and unlawfully concealed. Abadia walked back to the front yard of the residence, chambered a round in the pistol, and discharged the firearm. The bullet struck SPC

Schlack in the left hip and Abadia fled the scene. Individuals at the residence performed first aid on Schlack until emergency medical services arrived on the scene. EMS performed advanced life-saving measures and transported Schlack to Darnell Army Medical Center…

A military police officer discovered a handgun approximately .8 miles from the residence while he was conducting a search of the area. The handgun was a 45 caliber Thompson "Pit Bull" that appeared to be the same caliber as the shell casing found at the residence, and it generally matched the description of the handgun provided by witnesses.

On 18 Jul 09, Abadia was apprehended without incident. Abadia was advised of his rights and stated he pointed his loaded pistol at Schlack and fired it, which caused Schlack to fall to the ground. Abadia stated he fled the scene and discarded the pistol somewhere on West Fort Hood. Alcohol was a contributing factor in this incident…

It is Sunday, Mother's Day. We go get our free breakfast of eggs and meat. My brother Jerry lives a bit more than an hour from Fort Hood. We head out to Jerry's place arriving about noon. We visit and eat cheeseburgers, potato salad and beans.

Sitting out on this beautiful day, we compare notes about what we know about our brothers and sister. Then share what is going on in our own families. Rita and Jerry's youngest daughter visits with her two children so it is a nice surprise since we don't get together due to distance and living our separate lives. There is catching up on what her children are majoring in college, and places she has gone on her motorcycle. She is an enthusiast rider so we talk about places we've been and still want to go. It is a nice break from hanging out at the hotel. We get back to Killeen about 7:00PM.

I tackle ironing all the clothes I have washed. Rich buys us popcorn and we try to relax by watching television.

CHAPTER 50

It is Monday and we do the usual getting-ready stuff. The trial continues at 8:00 today.

Jerry and Rita call and tell us they are coming a bit later. The judge gives instructions as to what the convictions are and how this should be handled. For instance, there is no discrepancy in rank, discussions should be held, vote by secret ballot, and vote on specifications. The judge talked so fast that I give up writing. After the judge finishes, he calls a recess.

At 11:49AM, we are called back into the courtroom. The panel deliberated for 3 ½ hours. One of the defense lawyers is running late, so we wait some more.

The results are:
1. Carrying a loaded weapon on Ft. Hood. It was not registered.- Guilty
2. Unpremeditated murder – Guilty
3. Threat/Convey a threat to SPC Jaks – Guilty

At 1:42PM, the defense has finished reviewing what was brought as support for the sentencing portion like the binder with Ryan's pictures, Ryan's letters to us, and the binder with other people's statements. The defense did not want Greg Owen's letter to us shared, so it was taken out of the binder. They also object to the music "Band of Brothers" playing with the video of all photos of Ryan's pictures while in the military.

Adam says he feels vindicated. He is not concerned it would turn out the way he wanted, but the verdict was what he was hoping for. Guilty on all counts. Rich and I feel the same way.

Now begins the sentencing portion. The prosecution goes first. We all have the opportunity to get on the stand and say what we want about how Ryan's death affects us.

SFC Ken Carson, a neighbor of Jaks, is called first. He responds, "My family has since moved out of the neighborhood to secure safety for my wife and child. I once felt living on a secured base would be the safest place to live. It turns out not to be that secure. The attitude of the neighbors had changed dramatically during the time that I got back from Iraq."

"Sir, can you give a few examples, please?" asks CPT Earhart.

SFC Carson replies, "No one talked to each other, and nobody took care of their houses."

The trial counsel asks about his actions on that night. "I think if the MPs would have been more forceful, it could have been stopped."

SPC Greg Owens is the next person called to the stand. He states, "I knew Ryan for about 3 years. I am from northern Minnesota and with Ryan being from Wisconsin, there was a lot in common to talk about."

CPT Earhart asks, "What are your thoughts on that night holding Ryan while he was bleeding?"

Greg answers, "I was just ..., I don't think that I've ever been that big of a wreck in my life. My biggest concern wasn't my safety, but the concern for me was my friend. Nothing else mattered to me at that moment but Ryan, his life and his well-being. It's something that I think about the first thing when I wake up. It's the last thing that goes through my mind when I go to bed. I have dreams about it. I just wish that I had an opportunity to thank Ryan for saving my life. It's something that I can't do. I wish that I could reach out and talk to him, but I can't. I just miss him..."

"But it's been ten months since this happened. Do you still think about it every day?"

"Yes, every day, Ma'am."

"If you could talk to your friend today, what would you say to him?"

"I would just give him a hug and thank him and that I really…, everything's so generic without him here. He was kind of like my older brother, like I say, "a gentle giant", and he always had a different way of doing things. You know, people maybe thought that he was misunderstood or an outsider, but I never, … I heard that term that it's great to be misunderstood, and I never believed that until I met Ryan. He always had a way of doing things that always made sense. That was always my voice of reason, like 'Greg, don't do that'. Or he would just, … he was just someone that I could talk to when I was feeling down. Right now, I don't have that guidance and the mentorship that I had from Ryan, and that's what I really miss."

"Greg, tell us about the letter you wrote to Ryan's parents and what it said. Did you have a chance to talk to Ryan's parents during this time? What about the photos that were shown?" the counselor questions.

Greg explains, "My letter contained my thoughts on that night and about what Ryan meant as a friend. We were told not to contact the parents at all right after the incident. The photo was taken toward the end of the last deployment."

Next on the stand is SPC Spencer Vans. "Tell us about your thoughts about what happened," CPT Earhart asks.

Vans begins, "I was being helped by Ryan when we were in Iraq when my wife was asking for a divorce. I admit I had a lot of restless nights sleeping, anxiety and depression. There was an incident when I was pulled off the rifle range due to having a panic attack and my heart racing when I heard gunfire."

The counselor continues, "Do you feel there were changes in yourself after Ryan's death?"

Vans quietly answers, "I have withdrawn from a lot of my friends. I get confused at times. I am getting help."

Adam is next. MAJ Michaels asks, "Adam, what was it like growing up? Did you and Ryan experience typical sibling rivalry?"

"My dad was in the military for 20 years, so we lived a couple different places. Ryan and I were over three years apart in age, so for the early years, we had nothing in common. During our school years, we did play together, but not exclusively. It probably was when Dad retired from the army and moved to Wisconsin, Ryan and I became close since we discovered similar interests in movies, video games and friends. I do admit that many times we were at each other's throats," Adam shares.

"Are there or were there family members in the military?" wonders MAJ Michaels.

Adam says, "There is my dad, my grandfather, several uncles and a few cousins."

The counselor follows up with, "What did you know about Ryan's thoughts and plans for the future?"

"I wasn't ever clear about what Ryan's intentions were. Sometimes he'd talk about re-enlisting because it wasn't such a bad thing to be doing. He was less than a year before he would be out, so then he would talk about getting out and going to school. Maybe set up an electronics shop for selling the latest technical stuff or for repairs or something on that order."

The prosecutor asks, "Did your brother ever share any experiences with you about being a soldier, about deployments or things of that nature?"

Adam replies, "Occasionally. Because we would talk on the phone when he was in Iraq and you're generally supposed to assume that someone might be listening because it's possible, I generally tried not to talk about anything too specific. But I remember one time when he wasn't deployed, I asked him, 'What is a mortar attack like?' He said to me in the calmest voice imaginable, 'Oh, it's not that bad.' That actually made me chuckle, just with the notion that somebody launching a bomb at you, you know. 'Whatever. I slept through it a couple of times.'"

Then the question I was dreading they ask him, but I knew it had to be. The prosecutor asks, "Where were you when you found out about your brother's death?"

"I was actually out of town at the time, visiting some friends. I was friends with these people in high school and they lived 100 miles away or so, and I went to visit them for the weekend. …I was at a Burger King getting like a shake or something, and I got a phone call from my mom."

Adam shows a lot of emotion to the point of stifling crying. I think this whole experience was pent up in him for a while. I know he couldn't help himself, but it still hurt so badly to see him like that. He continues through sobs about our phone conversation until he asks for his dad.

I begin to cry and rock back and forth in the chair. I keep repeating, "Oh, my God, oh, my God." Sofia turns around and hands me some Kleenex.

Adam continues, "I knew that Ryan had just left, so I knew that it had to be something with him, and I was trying to prepare myself for the thought that Ryan may have been killed in a car accident or something because he was a crazy driver sometimes.

"I got home and my aunt's and uncle's car is in the driveway, but still I had no idea of why. I was just hoping that Ryan was okay, but I was trying to mentally prepare myself in case that I was told that he had died. My mom meets me in the kitchen and tells me that I should sit down, and I knew that, as soon as she told me to sit down, he was dead. She sat me down and told me that he had been shot. I thought, 'That's impossible. I'd just seen him two days ago.' The five of us spent time together, just talking about how he'd just left and collecting our thoughts. I had to leave after spending hours with my family. I called my friend back and informed him why I had left. Then, I had to go and inform all of Ryan's friends that he was murdered last night. Those are the words I had to say."

"Adam, what emotional or even physical impact from the news of your brother's death have on you?" asked MAJ Michaels.

"I just felt sick, like I wanted to throw up. I wanted to stay, I guess, like a strong example, to try because I knew that whatever I was going through, my parents were going through worse. I was certain of that. I knew that I had to be there for them. I tried to bottle everything in, at first, for minutes, which is about as long as it lasted. I hugged my parents and, by the time I got around to hugging my aunt and uncle, I just started crying. I couldn't stop. I had to take a week off of work after that. I was... I'd never been in any sort of depression before, but I was constantly tired and sleeping and not doing anything, for the entire remainder of the week."

Adam is asked what was going through his mind when he found out it was a fellow soldier who was suspected of his brother's death. He replied that it was unreal.

He is asked how it has been since then. "It hasn't been easy. Another acquaintance of mine committed suicide about one month after the burial, and there's some part that makes me think that maybe he somehow saw the attention that everything was getting and giving to Ryan and maybe somehow that fueled his thoughts. Occasionally, I still run into people who I haven't seen in a while and they say, 'Oh, so, what's been new in your life?' and I have to explain to them and it's still very difficult to talk about it and bring it back up.

"Really, the burial was the end of my denial. We got to go to the airport and they let us go out on the airstrip where they actually unloaded the coffin with the flag over it, and we had an escort back to Oshkosh, where we made it to the funeral home and the director arranged the body because it shuffled around in transport. The day before the funeral, we got to go in and actually see him lying there. I was... um, squeezing my girlfriend's hand as hard as I could. Then I knew that it was real and that he was lying in a casket, not moving. We had many, many people come to the actual funeral and burial, old friends and family members and we received flowers from one of the Senators and another one sent from a representative. At the burial itself, it was surreal because I know that Ryan told me something about dealing with practicing funerals early in his career. I just remembered him talking about training, about doing things like that. I watched the woman give my mom the flag from off of the casket. The gun salute was startling, but I knew that it was coming. I couldn't stand to turn around to look for it. I cried a lot, similar to right now, during that."

Adam was thinking at one point to say, "Abadia would go home to his family when Ryan can't." He stopped himself because he didn't think it was appropriate.

"Ryan and I shared so many similar experiences and silly recollections or insider jokes that only Ryan would get."

"And what about now?"

Adam is reflective, then says, "My emotions are still up front, and it's still very hard. That I'd come across a picture taken at Christmastime or being dressed up in suits and ties for Grandma's funeral. We never dressed up. I treasure that photo now. I don't anticipate my feelings changing much, especially when it comes time to bury my parents."

"I have one more question, Adam. Would it make more sense if Ryan was killed in combat, to help what you're experiencing right now?"

"Yeah, but that is somebody who is actively trying to kill him. This was somebody that he was supposed to trust, in a place where he was supposed to be safe. I mean, there's a movie that came out a couple of years ago and there's a line in it that I've been thinking about several times since the day I found out. The movie is 'Iron Man' and in there, there is sort of a background; there's supposed to be a physical joke going on at the time, but, in the background, there's a soldier who's speaking and the line that he's saying is, 'Every morning when I wake up and I put on this uniform and I look in the mirror, I know that everyone else that has this uniform on has got my back.' I think about that a lot, because he was supposed to help Ryan; supposed to keep him safe, but he didn't. He killed him for no good reason. For doing everything right, Ryan died."

When Adam walks back to where we are seated, I am still weepy, but give him a big hug and tell him he did a great job. Rich, too, hugs him and says he did very well.

I quickly recall on one icy day, I was volunteering at the Military Museum with two other volunteers, Ben and Bob. The guys were talking about Ben's son-in-law, who is mid-60s, has cancer and is not expected to live long. I am not ready for Ben's reply.

Ben said, "Geez, it is so sad to have your children die before you do. Nobody wants that."

Thank goodness I was not in the room, but just outside of the door, so when tears started rolling, I could get to the back office to calm down.

CHAPTER 51

It is my turn. I approach the stand, trying to compose myself. CPT Meghan Earhart already told us not to look at the defense table; to just look at her.

"Mrs. Schlack, where did you meet your husband, Rich?" she begins.

"Rich and I attended the same grade school, but we never crossed paths. His family was very transient. Rich did attend the Little Chute High School for a couple years. During my college years, I worked the night shift at a local restaurant in the summers, and he came in with another girl to eat. I was their waitress, so he asked if I was Terri Huber. The story went from there."

"How would you describe your marriage to Rich?" the captain asks.

"We've been married for 35 years, and I think we will hang together," I quip.

"What was your life like when Rich was in the army?" she continues.

My response is, "It is not easy with your husband being gone for weeks or deployed for a year. Life is different from what you'd expect with more responsibilities and with no family around to pitch in. I saw it as a bit of an adventure because I never would have lived in different places and experienced so much."

"How did you feel when you found out you were pregnant?"

I thought for a second or two and explained, "Rich and I wanted to plan our life carefully. We wanted to be established in our careers before children came."

"What was Ryan like as a child and in his growing years?"

"He was such an easy baby to care for. I believe he had a happy childhood. The shock came when he read words to Rich and me when he was only three and a half. I knew he loved books, but by kindergarten, he was reading to me. Ryan was diagnosed with Attention Deficit Disorder with hyperactivity, so this was a constant issue in school. But he got through those years. Ryan was funny, smart, excelled in math and loved high school drama."

Then, I talk about Thursday and Ryan's leaving and Friday morning's conversation. Her questions move to what we were doing on the day we found out. I recount how everything occurred right up to being told how Ryan was killed.

By this point in my story, I am crying but trying so hard to keep it in control. Placing three binders in front of me, CPT Earhart asks me about them. One is full of pictures of Ryan from baby to adult, a second binder is of statements from people, and a third is of communications from Ryan to us. I touch each gently and more tears flow.

CPT Earhart hands me a toy monkey and a picture of Ft. Hood drawn by a very, very young Ryan. I know the monkey was going to be given to me but did not know about the Ft. Hood drawing. I have to admit I feel embarrassed at this because Ryan is a man, and why are we sharing with this group what Ryan was when he was a young child? We had plenty of great photos of Ryan in the "Ryan Album" when he was a kid. Rich took beautiful photos. Of course, by this time I cannot speak clearly without gasps. During this, the stenographer hands me a box of Kleenex. There are many other recounting and memories she asks about.

The final questions were about how I felt about Ryan's choice to join the army and what I miss about him. "I was thrilled he finally got a career going instead of mundane jobs. What I miss about Ryan is his humor, his point of view and Ryan being Ryan."

As I get off the stand, I have to walk toward the panel then turn right to get to my seat. Walking toward the panel, I glance up at them. I slow my steps because I can't believe what I am seeing. The Command

Sergeant Major in the bottom row farthest to the right has his eyes closed! Is he sleeping? What to hell? Does anyone else see this? I hesitate, but I have no clue how long, and just angrily stare at him. There is a second when I think I should say something. Or do I point at him? If I say something at any time, will a mistrial be called? I quickly scan the other panel members and everyone else on the panel is looking straight ahead with no expression on their faces. I may have glanced back at the judge. I then glance at Meghan and hope she sees what I see and will do something. But she is smiling with hands folded in front of her watching me. It takes everything I have to walk past that piece of shit without leaning over the divider between us and loudly saying something to him.

Evan Anderson got up and left. He later told Adam he sat through Adam's and my statements but could not bear another person crying when he knew Dad was going up next.

Rich's first questions from CPT Earhart deal with his own military career, Ryan growing up, character traits of Ryan, Ryan's aspiration, and Ryan's joining the army.

"How did you feel about Ryan going into service?" CPT Earhart asks.

"I was somewhat excited about it," Rich answers. "I wanted to go with him down to the Recruiting Station, but he decided that he wanted to go on his own. ...One thing that the army offered was a bonus. They offered him a particular job that he wanted, as long as his aptitude tests were high enough, and he got very excited about that. So, we talked, and he decided that would be a good career choice for him and I supported him 100 percent."

"How did you feel when your son was deployed to Iraq on both deployments?" asks CPT Earhart.

"I was more apprehensive, I think, on the first deployment because I didn't know what he was going to expect when being there. I discussed with him his feelings on deploying and whether his concerns were in a fashion in which, you know, he was scared to go. He didn't really mention any real fear in going. He had talked to enough NCOs and people who had already been to Iraq, and that put his mind at ease, I think, to where he wasn't concerned. In telling me this, he kind of put my mind at ease as well.

"The second time he went over there, he had no concerns about danger at all, since he'd already been there on one tour. He felt that this would be just about like the first one. So, I had no problem with it.

"He called home on a regular basis and it was important to talk to him just to get a sense that he was okay and he never seemed depressed or anything. He was a very upbeat guy and as long as he had his friends with him, he was good to go."

Rich is asked about when he heard the news and his version is the same as mine. The next question had to do with what made it so difficult to believe this happened on the post.

"After being in the military for over 20 years myself, I always felt that I had two families. I've got my own personal family and then I had my unit, the other family. We took care of each other. To hear that another soldier had shot my son, it just didn't seem real. It couldn't happen.

"…If he had died in a combat zone, it would have made more sense. My son and I talked about the possibility of him getting injured or even dying. We both came to the conclusion if it happens, it happens. There's nothing we can do about it. But the fact that he got killed on Fort Hood, I mean, this was my home for almost nine years. That's like somebody killing you in your own home. It just couldn't happen."

"What were the days and weeks like after Ryan's murder?"

"When I woke up in the morning, that was the first thing I thought of. When I went to bed at night, that was the last thing that I was thinking of. I think about it all day long. It got to the point I got physically ill. I had to go to a doctor, and he put me on tranquilizers. To this day, I still have a difficult time trying to sleep through the night."

"Are there days you still think that he's coming back?"

"Yes, I'll hear the phone ring and I'll think, 'There's Ryan,' just for a split second. Then, obviously, reality hits real quick. Or I'll go out to get the mail and I think, 'Maybe there will be a letter' and it's just so unreal. It's hard to accept."

"What does the road ahead look like for you and your family?"

"It's going to be difficult. I don't foresee this pain ever going away. I mean, on the day I die, I'll still feel this. My wife decided to retire, so I think our whole life is going to change somewhat. It has changed so much, just in the last ten months. A lot of things that we used to enjoy; it's hard to enjoy life anymore, knowing that somebody deliberately took something like your own child."

The last question for Rich is, "What would you tell your son now?"

"I am extremely proud of him. He did a great job; he touched a lot of friends' and families' lives and we couldn't be more proud of him."

There were no questions from the panel, the defense, or the judge. To wrap up, the prosecution plays a video of assorted pictures of Ryan during his army days.

CHAPTER 52

Now, the defense has their turn having Abadia's dad, mom and a stepsister speak. During their time on the stand, they tell of a happy, friendly, bright, and helpful child.

The father shared, "I did have concerns about Barto joining the army, but my son was adamant about it. His mother and I were worried about him for both deployments. You may know he had a stop-loss, so had to stay in the army another year. We did recognize his alcohol problem. We even seriously considered getting him psychological help even if it is for the rest of his life. Barto had a dream of going back to college and working in Syndia Lab in New Mexico.

I cannot begin to know what the Schlack Family is going through. I wish to extend my condolences, but it would be best if Barto came home which is the best place for him now."

The Captain on the defense team now asks, "How did the events of the past year impact Barto and your family?"

Mr. Abadia spoke slowly, "It has had a big impact. Again, never knowing, I mean, a lot of times, you're eating at the table and you're wondering, 'What is he doing?' You know, you have the freedom to go here, to go to certain places, and you wonder what is he doing. That weighs heavily on you. It weighs heavily on your mind, for sometimes you can't even eat because you start thinking about things like that."

Barto's father ends his time on the stand with a message to the panel. "I would like to tell the jury today that I want to plead mercy for my son. I want you to give him that opportunity, because he has his whole life ahead of him, has future plans, and I know that some of those plans will have to be put on hold. However, he is a proud soldier. He spent five years in the Army. He's that kind of person; very honorable, very respectful, and that's the way we see him. I hope that you got to see a lot of that during this process."

Barto's mother is questioned about her thoughts on being in this situation and how the past year has been.

She replies, "This is a nightmare for me. I work at a place that has counselors, and I have gone to them and talked. They've helped me with the anxiety and prescribed sleeping pills. I am on anti-depressants. I would go to pray and light candles and wouldn't watch the news when Barto was deployed. Please, please, send my only son back home with me."

The panel had a question. The judge reads, "What are your thoughts about your son's drinking problem?"

His mother explains, "I did send him to see doctors about it, but they can do nothing if he denies it. I did not know it was so bad because I have never seen him as drunk as described."

His half-sister talks about their growing-up years and how happy Barto was. "Our lives were good even after our parents divorced. I did see drastic changes in him after joining the army and after going on deployments which concerned me. I will do what it takes to get him the help he needs. I see him helping other soldiers who are struggling and need help. Barto is very good at this type of thing."

Finally, Barto Abadia takes the stand. The defense counsel hands him things, and he describes family letters, awards he received when younger, and photographs.

Then he reads his statement.

"Never in my whole life could I have predicted this day. Up to ten months ago, I thought my future was planned and clear. I never thought it possible, in one severely tragic moment, that the lives of many could be so drastically altered. I'm so sorry for the great pain and suffering of the family and friends of SGT Ryan Schlack. I have dishonored the Army, my unit, and this country that I love. My family has been devastated, as well, by this tragedy. There are not enough words to describe how remorseful I am. God knows that a simple, 'I'm sorry' wouldn't alleviate the anguish that I've caused you. I apologize for everything, although I could never ask you to forgive. I will always remember Schlack as a big, gentle giant. He would stick out wherever he was. I'd first seen him around when I was reassigned to Bravo Company, 704th, in September 2005. I didn't really get to know him until our year-long deployment in November of that year. I remember the first time we spoke was when he and I were tasked with burning old manuals in the burn pit. We had started talking about video games and Star Wars and all different sorts of similar things. I took an instant liking to him because he was a person who wouldn't try to be someone he was not. Schlack was just that. He showed me that I should embrace all things that I found interesting, whether other people did or not. We came back home from deployment as good friends and battle-buddies. Schlack and I were two individuals who found our past times to be drinking and socializing. We would set up trips to Austin and end up drinking the whole weekend away. This is how it would go on until our second deployment.

"On that deployment, Schlack and I were assigned to the Entry Gate Control Point Guard. Schlack was usually assigned to the overview tower, while I was at the front gate, tasked with searching vehicles. When we first got there, we were on duty for twelve hours a day, seven days a week, in full body armor in 120-degree weather. I remember us at the beginning of our tour being very hyper-vigilant and treating every Iraqi that approached us as the enemy. We'd have our weapons locked and loaded ready to neutralize any hostile acts. After a while, we started to ease up a little, although we never got complacent. Schlack stayed on the tower overhead, ensuring that adequate firepower was available if necessary. There was a certain trust that we gave him for this reason.

"When we were redeploying home, Schlack was on the flight scheduled for a week ahead of me. When I got back, I had no means of transportation or civilian attire. I called Schlack up and he picked me up from my barracks room and took me to the PX to shop for clothing. No one else would have helped me the way that he did. I just hope that, wherever he is, he can find it in his spirit to forgive me."

His speech continues with his life story, and that once in the military, he indeed did drink all the time.

"Then July 17 happened. I was suicidal, crying and sleeping all the time, in a cell with only my thoughts of that day to think about. From here, I will eventually go to college, get a good job, and not drink because I see in my own extended family what it can do to a life.

"I know there is nothing that I can say that can bring Ryan Schlack back, but I want you to know that, with the tragedy of his death, lives have been saved. I have never seen life as precious and fragile as I do this very day. He saved not only everyone there that night, but me, too. For this, he will always be regarded as a hero, not only to his country but to his friends and family. I hope that the soldiers there that night can remember what kind of person I was and know that alcohol is not the answer to any problem. I hope it is a wake-up call to find help and to not be ashamed of what other soldiers think of them."

I am sitting in my seat in total disbelief. What twisted thinking is he handing out? Does he think I am supposed to be comforted by these words? I shake my head and quiet my sobs as he is allowed to continue to talk. I can feel Rich tense up next to me and worry he might get out of his seat. Now, I hear Abadia addressing us.

"To the family of Ryan Schlack, I will always be indebted to you. I would ask, if you please, that you exchange information with my family after this, so that I can keep in touch with you and show you how I have progressed to live my life for both me and Sergeant Ryan Schlack.

"I would like to conclude with a quote that a wise man who I am proud to have called my grandfather once told me: Life was never meant to be a straight road, but a route of many twists and turns. There are no dead-ends on this road, but we must remember to turn. Thank you."

Adam is thinking what an amazingly ridiculous thing to say about his parents and my parents becoming pen pals. Just the thought of getting together with Abadia's family was an absurd suggestion. Were we going to sit around at a picnic? Meet each other for dinner?

I am stunned by the suggestion as well. It was so weird to think Abadia would put such an idea out there. I wonder if his family is as uncomfortable with the suggestion as I am.

After Abadia is seated, the judge makes sure everyone has said and done what they had planned and now instructions will be prepared which will take about 20 minutes. He asks if the panel would like a short recess or a lunch break. After a short conference among the panel members, the colonel states a short recess is fine. The panel is excused and after a short conversation with both defense and prosecution counsels, a recess is ordered.

Rich gets up to climb over me to walk out of our row first. The aisle is narrow, and the bailiff was still seated next to our row. While I am waiting my turn to get up, I see two MPs walk Abadia toward us. The MPs talk to Sofia who is already standing and seems to be preparing for some action. MPs lead Abadia to Rich, who is now standing in the aisle waiting to get out the door.

Abadia is hanging his head and continually apologizes in a quiet tone. Rich is shaking his head, saying angrily, "No, no!" Rich moves quickly out of the door.

Adam got up to follow his father, but because Rich is struggling to get passed Abadia and to the exit door, Adam had to stop. Abadia is now apologizing to Adam but Adam replies in a dismissive tone, "Okay," and keeps moving toward the exit. He didn't know what to do with this situation. Adam said he thinks the defense was sure he'd get a guilty verdict but wanted to minimize his sentence by pulling every trick in his book.

Abadia steps into my path and probably says the same to me. I stifle my crying quietly and briefly look at him. He doesn't look at me. Not at all. Should I say something? What do I say? I just am so done in. I do not want to be standing in front of him now. Sofia must have seen this in my face because she steps between Abadia and me and firmly says, "Get him out of here!" And the MPs do just that.

After a 20-minute break in which I basically fall apart–jittery, crying out loud - we were called back.

At 5:13PM, CPT Earhart speaks to the panel reviewing the aggravation and the past. After she finishes, the defense lawyer, George Janis, speaks about Abadia and his future. Finally, the judge gives instructions then the panel goes into their chambers.

Some of Ryan's friends who were witnesses and our group go to one of the small conference rooms. Sofia asks if anyone is hungry and the guys say yes. She can see no one wants to leave just in case the panel comes back, so she orders from Pizza Hut. Three large pizzas arrive along with two liters of soda. Sofia finds cups and plates.

At 8:00PM we are called back to court. The panel met for a little over two hours. Abadia's sentence is announced.

Abadia's rank will be reduced to E1.

There will be forfeiture of pay and benefits.

Abadia will receive a Bad Conduct Discharge.

Abadia is sentenced to Leavenworth Penitentiary for 20 years.

The court is adjourned at 8:10PM.

CHAPTER 53

Adam is disappointed because Abadia is getting only 20 years. He feels slighted and thought the court-marshal would be worse for Abadia. He expected more. A bad conduct is way too nice.

We are beyond shocked by the results. A bad conduct discharge is for menial offenses. It should have been a dishonorable discharge. Unpremeditated murder is serious. A mere twenty years is hardly a just sentence.

An inkling of something I read pushes its way into my head slowly as it takes its time to develop. If I'm understanding my recollections, I read somewhere that in a courtroom, the criminal intention is punished, or was it the guilty mind? The phrase is:

'…the act does not create guilt unless the mind is also guilty.' That supports the fact that children are not usually convicted, and neither are schizophrenics and drunks… 'These groups are not capable of deciding to commit their crimes with a true understanding of the significance of their actions.'

Children, schizophrenics, and drunks. Am I to understand that the military panel looked the other way because Abadia had too much to drink? The sentence they imposed certainly reflects a slap on the wrist for this worthless piece of being. Drinking is a choice. No one was forcing Abadia to drink beyond the point of him not making rational decisions. There was no hazing going on. Will someone not see that a human life was taken and all the panel says is, Abadia will get a lighter sentence because he was drinking? So what if his commander put him in a program to do something about this. It was not successful and more pressure should have been put on Abadia or discharge him because his job had to do with handling guns. This is a responsibility, not something to be taken lightly.

When Rich was in the Army in the 1970s and 1980s, if a soldier was caught in a DWI, that soldier could figure he'll be kicked out of the Army. It didn't seem the panel even considered this offense. Yes, I know he wasn't accused of DWI, but he did kill someone while inebriated.

We had to bury a son because Abadia knowingly brought a weapon on the post. He went back to his car to retrieve it. He pointed it at human beings, as well as pulled the trigger to shoot someone. I believe Abadia's target was to be Owens, but instead shot Ryan who was hoping to save his friend from harm.

They didn't really take a serious look at the fact Abadia carried a gun onto the base. Did the sleeping sergeant major have a say even though who knows how long he slept through things?

After the court adjourned, Jerry, Rita, Greg Owens, and the three of us go into another one of the small conference rooms. We are all sharing our disbelief of the sentence.

A while later, CPT Earhart and MAJ Michaels come to express their disappointment in it. They did say this panel is usually light on their sentencing. Meanwhile, in another room, the judge is discussing with the panel how they came to their conclusions. CPT Earhart and MAJ Michaels leave us so they can meet with the judge and defense to discuss the trial.

A short while later, as we are still sitting in the small room, the Colonel from the panel steps in and says, "I am so very sorry this happened to your son. I offer my condolences. I have children, too. I just can't imagine what you are going through."

Jerry asks, "Why is the sentence so light? Why just a bad conduct discharge?"

She replies, "The panel talked about a number of ways to sentence, but I can't talk about what went on during deliberation and sentencing." I interpret this as she didn't want to get into a discussion with Jerry.

Soon Anderson, Owens and Vans hug us goodbye. The other two friends are waiting in the hall. Jerry and Rita leave, too, and Rich needs to go back to the hotel to get his pills. Adam and I sit silently for a while. A paralegal brings in the binders as they are being copied. Sofia sits with us. Our two lawyers return eventually to say their goodbyes. I thank them again.

For a short while, I am left alone. I kind of take an inventory as to how I am feeling and tell myself it's all over. I close my eyes and begin to decompress, if that's a word for what I am doing. It all slowly washing out of me and I'm talking to myself. "Okay, now we have to go on. We have to. It won't ever be the same. Remember the poem? I don't have to 'push through to get to the other side'. There is absorption, adjustment and acceptance, but nothing will be like you want it to be."

The door opens and I think it's Rich, but it is the Colonel again.

She says, "I just came to say, well, you know this incident was one big sorry mistake, don't you? A terrible, terrible mistake."

I am not comprehending what she is saying. I am interpreting her words as "Yes, the court's sentencing is a terrible mistake." I feel my head is imperceptibly shaking yes. But wait, she said "incident". Does she mean the outcome of the trial is the incident? She can't mean how Ryan was killed, can she? Did she?

The Colonel keeps saying, "I know it's a terrible thing that happened." She might have said more but I am trying to focus and do not realize when she leaves.

Rich, Adam and I leave the Magistrate's Building about 9:30PM. As we are walking to our cars with Meghan and Sofia, Judge Andrews drives up. He gets out of his car, walks over and shakes our hands.

"Thank you for allowing us to be in the courtroom," I say gratefully. "We have learned how little involvement a military judge actually has. I couldn't believe the panel could tell you to hold the trial over until Monday or actually specify what the sentence will be." Jerry began discussing something with the judge, so I left them alone.

In the car, not a word was said. What is there to say? We will pack tonight and be ready to leave tomorrow. We are all truly exhausted.

I don't know why I wanted to read this part from Dr. Barker's report before we leave for home.

Specialist Abadia Account of the Alleged Offense

Returned to Ft. Hood from leave in New Mexico one day before the alleged offense. He said that he drank alcohol with his roommate the night before. Abadia said they talked about leave and had a good time together. However, he also said that he felt on guard and concerned that someone would steal from his car because a hobo allegedly stole something from his gear on his last day in New Mexico. Abadia was also upset about the lost gear because he would have to pay for it.

On the day of, he went to work for an hour and was invited to a BBQ later at Jak's house. After formation, Abadia returned home with Vans. They played games and Vans told Abadia about his wife cheating on him. Abadia said he tried to comfort his friend.

Abadia went to the gym and felt pumped. Also continued to feel vaguely paranoid. Asked to explain, he said he felt watchful, on guard, and tense.

Returned home and drank two beers because he believed that would thin out his blood. Allowing the subsequent ingestions of protein shake to go faster to his muscles. Abadia realized this is unlikely, but it was a practice he had heard about during deployment. He also took 5 GNC Methyl 1-D pills.

At about 7:00PM, Abadia purchased a case of beer and drove to Jaks's house. Abadia began to drink heavily. He said he was drinking mixed drinks and beers "double-fisted". He tried two shots of Absinthe. Abadia didn't recall how many drinks he had, but it was many, perhaps as high as twenty. Abadia said he reasoned his tolerance would be better at Ft. Hood than in New Mexico because it was at a lower elevation with a lower air pressure. He smoked cigarettes but did not use any illicit drugs. Abadia recalled the party was very fun. He particularly enjoyed spending time with Vans. They talked about 'Hao 3' and stories regarding their time in Iraq. He said that they exchanged stories about their gate duties and deployments. Abadia said he was not concerned, paranoid, or guarded that night because he was with friends. He did not recollect any arguments or fights with anyone at the party. He did not recall anything that night that reminded him of events in Iraq. "It was just old friends."

At about 11:00PM, Abadia said that he welcomed Schlack to the party in a loud and animated fashion. Abadia reported that he did not have any further memory of the night until he later sees himself inside Jaks's kitchen, with his back to the counter. The refrigerator was to his left, and the stove was to his right. He recalled feeling "woozy" and seeing two lights when he looked at the kitchen light. Abadia said that he had his .45 weapon in his hand that he normally stored in the car. He was spinning the weapon on his finger. Abadia said that he did not know why or how he had the gun. He said he kept the gun loaded in case he had to react quickly. Abadia then thought to "put a shot" out the front door for an unknown reason. He said that he cocked the weapon, spun it once on his finger, and fired the gun. Abadia said that Schlack hit the ground, landing in front of the porch on the ground. Abadia said that he could not remember what happened, why Schlack hit the ground, or if Schlack had been hit. He recalls someone said, "Schlack has been hit.", but did not remember what he considered this statement to mean or if it had any relation to him firing the gun. He observed Schlack lying on the ground, and his mouth was open with his head jerking. Abadia could not determine if he was "laughing or crying". Abadia could not recall any thoughts or feelings he may have had at the time of seeing Schlack on the ground. He could not recall if he considered Schlack had been shot or why he was on the ground.

Abadia said his next memory was waking up in his car on the right side of a road by a field. He did not recall getting into his car, driving his car, or parking his car. He said that he checked his car's arm compartment where he normally stored his personal weapon, but it was gone. He checked his phone, and saw that he had new voicemails, but did not listen to them. Abadia recollected Schlack hitting the ground, and decided he wanted to find out what happened to him.

At about 8:30AM he drove to Jaks's house. He observed latex gloves in the street and pillows in the yard. He assumed the latex gloves meant an ambulance had come by to check on Schlack or to take him. Abadia said something told him "Something bad has happened, so I decided not to stop." He said that he feared if he stopped at the home, his friends may have jumped him because they would be angry he shot Schlack. Abadia said that he did not know what happened but felt something bad had happened. He said that he believed he had shot Schlack because he couldn't find his weapon and "my memory recollection told me I did."

Abadia said that he wanted to get his "thoughts straight," and returned to his apartment. He listened to his voicemail and heard a message from a CID agent who told him he was in serious trouble and to turn himself in. He said that he contemplated what to do and entered his apartment to speak to his roommate. Abadia told his roommate that he thought he had shot out the front porch but hit his friend. Abadia thought he hit Schlack in his leg, side, or stomach.

Abadia tried to call Vans, but he did not answer the phone. He said that he was extremely worried and anxious about what happened. His roommate told him to turn himself in. Abadia called Vans again and asked him what happened. Vans told him that he shot Schlack. Abadia asked him if he was okay. Vans responded that Schlack died. Abadia began to panic and weep loudly. He told Vans that he would go to hell. Vans told him it would be okay because he did not understand what happened. Abadia felt some relief that at least Vans knew he did not do it on purpose. Vans told Abadia that the other guys were angry and would try to kill him; thus, it would be better to turn himself in. Abadia asked to meet the police and Vans at the mall, but Vans convinced him to meet at the Visitor's Center. Abadia told Vans that it would require an hour because he was in Austin. Abadia was not in Austin, but he said that he wanted some extra time to figure out what to do.

Abadia considered running to Mexico, but worried he would never see his family. He thought about killing himself and grabbed a dull kitchen knife, but he couldn't harm himself. Abadia then said, "I started regretting that I threw my gun out." When queried about this statement, he explained he "figured" he threw it out because his car window was open, and he couldn't find his weapon. He clarified again that he regretted throwing his weapon out because he could have committed suicide. Abadia said further that his roommate was educating him about involuntary manslaughter, and that the penalty was not as harsh. Abadia decided that it was the "right thing" to turn himself in and not kill himself. He decided he would "try for involuntary manslaughter". Abadia defined involuntary manslaughter as taking a life without intent. He then considered what he would tell his family. He watched the news to see if his face was on the TV. He chose to not drive his car because he did not want it to get impounded or put in a place his family couldn't find it. He was then arrested. Abadia said that he told the CID agent he was doing cowboy tricks with his gun.

CHAPTER 54

On Tuesday, I wake up early. Since Saturday morning we have been showering in cold water. On Sunday, I had a moment of warmth. Monday's water was chilly.

Today, I get experimental. I run the water from the faucet and it turns tepid. So, I shampoo my hair under the faucet and then turn on the showerhead for a quick shower. Rich is taking cold showers every morning. He tells me he would tell the desk clerk every day. When we pay the bill, we get 25% off our bill, thereby saving the government a few bucks.

We have the free egg breakfast, drive to the airport, drop off the car, and board the plane and assigned to row 12. No one wants to talk, so I seek out something to read. I have copies of the letters from friends and family and realize I didn't read all of them. So, during the flight home, I read statements.

From Ryan's friend, Grant Rassmussen:
I've known Ryan since April 2000. We met each other while working at a crap job building United Postal Service totes. As soon as we met, we became friends. He had a kind heart and a soft head, but that's what you've got to love about the guy. He was a good friend who always enjoyed hanging out and attempting to teach us new games that only made sense if you were fluent in dork.

Ryan was living with me before he left for the army. It was tense counting down the time until he left. My friends and I knew he was going to war after boot camp. Our group of friends used to joke about how he was going to get booted out of the army before he ever got a chance to go. However, deep inside, we all knew he was going to do fine. When he ended up in Iraq, we all talked about him and asked who had all heard from him so we could make sure he was alright. Then the last time he came home, we all felt a sigh of relief; he made it through his trip to Iraq. He was coming home for good in just a few short months, and I was excited about it.

When I was first told about Ryan's murder, someone robbed me of that feeling. I didn't want to believe it. My first reaction was anger; I thought it was some sick joke because I had just seen my friend a couple days earlier. He was home on leave, and he had to go back to his military base in Texas. He had to go back to a military base, where he should have been as safe as if he was in his mother's arms. Now he is gone, and the world has lost a unique individual. To make matters worse, now all I have are memories of the plans I made together with Ryan. Following through with all these plans now is a moot point.

I don't know what kind of older man or father Ryan would have been, but he enjoyed showing my son how to play video games which I never had patience for, or listening to them babble on about whatever. He would have made a great father, and as a father, I know he missed out on the great experiences of being one. Ryan was a kind spirit that will be missed.

From Ryan's friend, Lewis Zane:

I see Ryan riding through town. It's summer, but he's still wearing that long-sleeved plaid shirt and narrow jeans. He biked everywhere almost, as long as there wasn't ice. He regularly biked seven miles to Omro from Oshkosh to visit a friend. Tall. A head taller than most and skinny. He wasn't mousy, just didn't talk a lot until he knew you or felt the need to speak.

And it's what he said at the last cast party for our high school theatre department that sticks out the most. At the end of the night, the seniors *started giving farewell speeches. Most were nice rambling things I've forgotten any details of, but Ryan's I remember.*

He mentioned having a good time, but also admitted not always sure where he fit in. At some point, we were all wondering the same thing about ourselves, but he actually said it.

Years later, more of us know less where we fit in than we thought we did back then. But Ryan had a plan.

He joined the army. He told me that afterward he was planning to use the training he received to open an electronics repair shop.

I'm not saying that Ryan was just serious. What I liked most about him was that he didn't take himself too seriously. More than once, we made home movies just for fun.

But Ryan had direction, and when the time came to do the right thing, Ryan did.

From Ryan's friend, Paul Channing:

Three months ago, someone asked me to write a letter about how my life has changed since Ryan's death. I have concluded that there is no way to answer that question. Because of this person, I will never know what it would have been like to grow old with my friend of fourteen years. I can never hang out and play games or have him annoy me until I agree to play War Hammer again. We no longer can go pointlessly driving around just talking and having fun all night or go out drinking and trying to find a girl.

I will never know how great it would have been to have him standing up there while I got married this past fall. Instead, all I had posted was a sign commemorating one of my best friends. Also, once my wife and I have children, he will not be there for that. I will never get to see the happiness on his face when he is standing up getting married, or becoming a father himself, or raising our kids together.

This person robbed all of us of the opportunity to see the man Ryan was becoming, the great things he could have accomplished, and the many lives he would have touched if he were still here.

So, how has my life changed? In a word, it's worse. The world is now worse because of losing the most kindhearted, loving person I have ever met. Ryan was a genuine hero in many ways. My life and everyone he came in contact with is better because they knew him, and the world is worse off without Ryan.

From Paul's wife, Penny Channing:

Ryan was a great friend. There are so many wonderful memories of the past eight years I have known him. My husband Paul introduced me to Ryan when he was living in Appleton with Chuck. I remember going to visit their apartment almost every weekend to play games and hang out. When he decided to join the military, I considered him a hero. Every time he came back home, our group would get together and do something fun to celebrate Ryan being here. On October 3, 2009, Chris and I hoped that Ryan could be part of our wedding. My sister-in-law and one of my friends made a sign in memory of Ryan, and we displayed it at our wedding.

Ryan was looking forward to returning from military life and coming home to his friends and family. Even though Ryan always loved his video games, he was still an adventure kind of guy. He loved driving his awesome car, and he loved to hang out and have fun. But now poor Ryan will not even get the chance to get married or have children. I think Ryan would have made a wonderful husband and father. He was always there for his friends and family. I will miss him.

What wonderful things that are said about Ryan. These kids nailed it.

At 3:15 CST we are in Atlanta, Georgia, waiting for our Delta flight to Appleton. It isn't long before the Appleton flight calls people to board. Each of us dozed a bit on this flight. Our intention is to retreat home, avoiding the world temporarily.

Already the media has its hands on our story. On the NBC26 station, the title is, "Killer Sentenced for Oshkosh Soldier's Murder" and the WFRV station states "Soldier's mother disappointed with sentence." The Oshkosh Northwestern has an article with the photo of Ryan in his uniform with a helmet on and the heading, "Slain soldier's mother disappointed: Wanted stronger penalty for son's killer". You bet I did. Sofia sent me clippings from the Killeen Daily Herald.

Adam tells me he saw things on u-Tube and the media covered it well. This is a good thing to know because I hate misinformation out there.

CHAPTER 55

Adam comes home quickly to move into his new apartment and filling it with furniture and whatever. This move will put him closer to work and rent is manageable.

The thought of going back to work is daunting. Can I pull it off for the last few weeks of school? No one can do the report cards or separate my teaching stuff from the school's materials. There are a hundred other things that need to be done before the school calls it the end of the year.

Shortly after my return to the classroom, a student lingered after the others went out for recess. She comes to my desk and asks shyly, "Is the reason you would step out in the hallway after the pledge is because you were crying? I mean, you would come in with a red face."

I pause a couple of seconds before answering. "Well, yes, sometimes it is difficult to say the pledge because then I think of all the people in the military who are defending our country. This leads me to think of my son."

"Hmm, I kind of thought it was something like that," she whispered then walked out the door.

When I am at school, I do what I need to do and go through the motions. Managing the emotions is my focus and do as well as can be expected. Pulling it together is my way of life at school. Compartmentalize, trying to leave my personal life at home. When at home, I try to take one day at a time. Rich is still in the chair and Adam goes to work. That is our life now.

It is near the end of May on a weekend that Rich and I take the pop-up camper to Westward Ho Campground in Glenbulah, Wisconsin, for the motorcycle group's Dust Off. Dust Off implies "dusting off" your Gold Wing motorcycles and get together with other riders in a camping atmosphere for the weekend. We didn't bring the motorcycles this time, so we hang around just to visit and have a good time with friends. It is one way not to be at home to think about our lives. Rich and I were obviously more somber than usual, but there were moments and a few pranks that made us smile.

We rarely attend the Oshkosh Memorial Day activities, but this year is different. Rows of chairs and a portable stage are set up in the cemetery near the burial sites of the veterans. The mayor and the AMVETS Commander give speeches, a re-enactor reads the 1868 speech by Commander-in-Chief John A. Logan, and someone leads the singing of the patriotic songs.

The AMVETS Commander picked up a few roses from a stand after his presentation. He calls individuals to the front and present each with a rose. Unexpectedly, he says, "There is someone here who lost a son last year. Her son served two years in Iraq and I would like to recognize her. Terri Schlack, will you come to the front, please?"

I hesitate, not sure I heard it right. I get up to walk to the stage as I start with the tears. A 'thank you' tries to make it through my raspy voice. Turning back to the audience, a few women come to give me a hug. Feeling embarrassed, I ask Rich to take me home after the presentation.

May 27, 2010
To: Terri and Rich
From: Jerry
Subject: Here's a thought.
Dear Rich and Terri,
Do you recognize the defense lawyer in this news article photo? He got the trial postponed four months.

Recently I heard Jake Silverstein speak. He is the editor of Texas Monthly, a magazine that does in-depth articles. I wondered if you and he are interested in Ryan's story. The story, I think, is how does an Army win wars if it has so little respect for itself that it does not dishonorably discharge one convicted of murder of a fellow soldier unprovoked?

Think about it and contact him if you wish. I am reading his book (he autographed it) "Nothing Happened and Then It Did". He writes somewhat in the Michener style. Writes well.

Take care. We plan to visit some of Rita's siblings June 26 and 27. Maybe we will see you too. Time will be short.

Love ya, Jerry

There is a retirement party for another teacher and me, which is being held at the Fond du Lac Yacht Club. I keep telling myself I will not be a Debbie Downer. Rich and Adam are also attending. One of the desserts in the catered meal is mint chocolate bars, which Zoey makes and happens to be a personal favorite of mine. Zoey delivers an enormous piece to me. Although I ask her for the recipe, I know it will never be as good.

I write poetry for various events and the staff surprised me with their attempt. And a noble attempt it is! A small group gets in front of the crowd and sings "Glorious, glorious retirement!" to the tune of "Glory, Glory Hallelujah". I am very touched by this gesture. I have already prepped Claire to stand up with me to say our goodbyes in poetic form. Rich, Adam, and I enjoyed ourselves. I can admit the whole party is a moment to step away from the turmoil that is my life. My parting gift is a concrete bird bath that still stands prominently in the front yard. We will treasure the concrete bird bath.

Two days later, the entire school is outside enjoying the time left of the last school day. Finally, there it is, the ringing of the bell. The strangest feeling comes over me. I feel this strong, what's a good word, relief? I now know what it is like to be high. One fifth-grade teacher runs to me and hugs me, and I hug him right back. What a welcoming emotion. I laugh. Yes, I do. I laugh and giggle like a kid.

The next day is closing up the room, giving away teaching materials, and saying farewell to other teachers. Loading up the last few things of mine in the classroom, I walk out the door and drive home.

Time to get into the "being at home every day" mode. I think seriously about Jerry's suggestion. The thought is appealing. Testing the waters, I email one of my favorite television presenters, John Stossel. I knew of his libertarian views but still agree with some of his positions. I will give it time to see if anything happens. It occurred to me that this was not the way to go about it, but still there is a chance.

June 15, 2010
To: Sofia Hammons
From: Terri
Subject: How do we find out about…
Hello Sofia,

We hope this finds you and Meghan well. Busy, I am sure, but well. I retired from teaching for the Fond du Lac School District, and Rich and I are making plans as to what to do this summer. I feel a great sense of weight off my shoulders- one less thing to take me away from my family. Of course, I really don't think I can get out of teaching, so I am checking into teaching for a university; just one class for now and see what happens from there.

Rich and Adam are going to Germany in July. I see it as a father/son thing; good for them both. I know where they are going and have been there enough times to suit me. I think sometimes Rich needs to get away from all this a while and a different scenery can be the ticket.

The reason I am e-mailing you is that you told us at some point we can ask for Ryan's personal effects CID has in their possession and the video of the party that night. Is this still a possibility? We are in touch with SPC Ethan Jaks, and he says he did not receive his videotape back yet. How do we find out about receiving these items back? Is there a certain amount of time that must pass? Thank you for any assistance you can give us with this.

We still have a hard time with the sentencing–the bad conduct discharge is still unbelievable. The 20 years is well, I think not enough for the THREE charges against him. I still recall the panel member in the lower right of the panel dozing as I was speaking. I stared at him in disbelief, like I wasn't important enough to keep his attention. It took all I had not to say something to him. The thought running through my furious self was if I say something, there might be a mistrial.

The moment Abadia came up to talk to me–I was so rattled I wish I could have asked him all the questions I wanted to ask him but couldn't gather my thoughts. It is better I did not continue a conversation. He may have seen it as a bit of forgiveness. I am not there yet.

I think about the unfair advantage given when the panel wouldn't continue after closing arguments. The three and a half-hour interrogation video we all watched had nothing to do with coercion, I believe, but had to do with the panel seeing how distraught Abadia was and played upon the panel's emotions that way.

There was an article in the local newspaper on May 13 entitled "Slain soldier's mother disappointed: Wanted stronger penalty for son's killer". The author had called to see if he could interview one of us and I told him as long as he gets the facts straight. The screwed-up stuff the news put out there was frustrating. Ah, well,…

Say hello to your hubby for us. Tell Meghan and MAJ Michaels I know they worked hard. We appreciate their hard work.

Hope to hear from you soon.

Terri and Rich

Early on a Thursday morning in mid-June, we start a busy, busy day. We get out of the house to go to Wal-Mart to look around. First, I have a doctor's appointment with a podiatrist. She is a bit more suspicious of the symptoms I tell her about. Luckily, I need bloodwork done for my PA, so after setting up an appointment to get a new foot insert, I go to get blood drawn for both the podiatrist and the PA.

After that, I stop at my neighbor Kathy's house and borrow her brown stone necklace I used during the trial. Meanwhile, Rich went to get his hair cut and the car washed. I finish the laundry so packing can begin.

> June 20, 2010
> To: Terri and Rich
> From: Sofia Hammons
> Subject: Re: How do we find out about...
> Terri,
> I will find out about the personal effects the CID has. Usually, the CID does not release items that are in evidence until all the appeals are completed. But I will ask.
> The videos of the party should be part of the record of trial. I am going to send you the address where you can ask for it under the Freedom of Information Act. However, the record of trial is not yet complete, and it will take some time to finish. I will let you know when it is so that you can request the record of trial.
> Meghan is doing okay. Her grandmother passed away, so she went home for the funeral.
> It is clear how upset you and your family are over the sentence. It was unbelievable. I was upset about the bad conduct discharge, as well. That did not make sense to anyone in the courtroom. I am not sure what was going through the panel's mind about anything.
> You know my house is always open to you all. I would be thrilled to see you all again.
> I have heard nothing about the Soldier's Medal awards ceremony. Has anyone made the contact yet with you about that?
> I will tell Meghan that you were asking about her.
> Sofia

I am tackling my personal teaching materials which have been in our garage since I brought them home. I clear out a corner shelving unit in the basement to store it all. There are hundreds of children's books I can give to my nieces' and nephews' children or sell at a garage sale along with my adult novels. I also pulled my binders of lessons and teacher's guides from boxes. Why am I saving them? What will I do with it all? Good questions. I just feel I want them. I have the option to toss them when I reach that point.

CHAPTER 56

Rich and I are on our way to Pittsburgh, Pennsylvania, to a nephew's wedding. Rich drives the whole time, and it takes two days to get there arriving at 4:30PM on Friday. Once there, we were busy with walking to a paddle boat, walking around some place called The Square, and peaking into a beautiful train station turned into a restaurant which was very upscale.

On the wedding day, Rich and I get up early and walk along the river, not sure if it is the Allegheny or the Monagahela River. On our walk, we run into Jerry, Rita, and a couple of their kids and take a ride on a tram up a steep incline. Coming down and sitting at the front of the tram is quite an experience and a hoot. It is soon time to get to the church.

The church was enormous, and the ceremony was lovely. After church, we are wondering what to do because it's now about 3:30PM and the dinner begins at 6:00PM.

Donna's daughter calls us and invites us to a family gathering in room 1414. Two boys had a good time pushing buttons on the elevator because we had a ten-minute ride up and down stopping at different floors. They serve wine at the gathering in the room, so I decide to have a peach wine while Rich opts for a beer.

I have never seen such a layout served at a wedding. First served is soup with spicy meat and chicken pieces followed by a spinach salad. Next a sorbet then filet mignon, mashed potatoes, and three veggies. They serve the wedding cake with strawberries dipped in chocolate.

Later, huge trays are filled with dozens of different cookies. I am told the custom is to have relatives bake and bring cookies. All those cookies could feed an army battalion.

However, the best part is at the reception when there is dancing. I love to dance, so I head to the dance floor. My dancing partner Rita and I are talking between segments.

"I envy that you two can travel to so many countries. How wonderful! Rich and I travel in the US and have managed a couple of times to go to Europe. There are a few places we would like to tour before we get too old."

Rita exclaims, "Yes, there are a couple of countries we still want to see. We've never been to Ireland or Scotland. I'd love to go see what there is to see."

"Oh, my! Rich and I are kicking around the idea of going there next year!"

Rita excitedly suggests, "Why not go together? It will be fun!"

Still on the dance floor waiting for the next song, Mary joins us.

"What are you two so giddy about?" she laughs.

Rita and I both say, "We are going to Scotland and Ireland next year!"

Before the song is over, the three of us decide that our husbands and we are going to travel together to Great Britain.

We spend Father's Day in Pittsburgh then on to stops at Hershey and Gettysburg before heading for home.

Thinking about what I should find to do further down the road, I email the Education Department chairperson from Marion University in Fond du Lac to tell her I am interested in teaching one class this fall. Hopefully, we can meet for the interview soon.

To follow through with volunteering for the Military Veterans Museum & Education Center (MVMEC), one day in late June, Rich and I meet with the MVMEC President at Becks Restaurant along the river. After introductions and pleasantries, we get to the business.

The President clears his throat and states, "I want to be upfront with you, so you know what is going on. There is nothing to do now but take inventory. This way you will know what we sell and find other things to add to our merchandise. Some well-intentioned members are hauling things to sell at events, not telling anyone what they take or when they need it. I'm going to put a stop to that so we can run it efficiently.

"We were asked to leave our storefront in the City Center a couple months ago, so we temporarily stored everything in a county garage. Most of our artifacts and all the store merchandise are boxed up and sitting on shelves.

"For you to have access, the secretary can get you keys to the garage storage rooms. I think my wife and I will help you with inventory and arranging things in a useful order. Do you have any questions?"

Rich and I ponder the question, then I ask, "After inventorying, what do I see myself doing if there is no museum or place to show your artifacts?"

"Right now, a few of the members go to military events or some armed forces meeting and bring a box or two of merchandise to sell. We hope you can take over and keep a closer eye on what we sell. You can work with the guys to learn what they do and where they go. We have every hope of having a building where there will be a PX Gift Shop. You will be the manager."

It seems this will not be so tough. Rich and I are told we can have the position. I hear nothing from anybody for a month. In the meantime, I get things organized to take to any upcoming events I find out about.

Every day, every hour, I think about Ryan gone. There is nothing I can do. It is the most helpless feeling ever. I remember how he lay there in the coffin. It doesn't seem right to remember anyone that way. I don't think of anyone else who is dead in that way.

There is too much time to think about the trial, about when Abadia walked up to me to apologize right there in court. We heard about him trying to outsmart the psychologist and act like he was not mentally competent; about how he went for the PTSD due to what he experienced in Iraq; about how he claimed he couldn't remember some parts, but at another time during the trial, he remembered. Then there is how he said he wanted to show his friends the gun. He had it for a couple months, I understand, so why not show it to his friends when he first gets it? Why that night? Could there ever be answers?

When Ryan fell to the ground with the gunshot, how was it for him? For how long was he in so much pain? Despite all efforts, they couldn't have saved him. Did he hold out hope of being taken care of or did he know this was fatal?

Being on medication for depression and anxiety does not seem to help me.

CHAPTER 57

July 12, 2010. It is Ryan's birthday. He would have been 31, out of the army, into school, and going out on dates or hanging with his buddies. I'm wondering when the happy pills will kick in. Because Rich and Adam are gone to Germany, I keep myself busy. I am so hoping this Father/Son trip will be a good thing, but I didn't have any desire to go.

Today, it all falls to pieces when I sit in the dentist's chair for teeth cleaning. There is a moment when I sit and wait. This is not good. The music is somber, the technician talks about summer, my retirement, and will I miss teaching. What can I say? I retired because I have trouble dealing with my life. The stress of new expectations at work and Ryan are gone. I start to tear up and try to think of other things. All I need is teeth cleaning. The tech leaves the room. I can't sit here anymore trying not to let tears fall.

The technician comes in and I slide out of the chair, saying, "I think I'll schedule for another day." Grabbing my purse, I walk past the two secretaries and through my whimpers, say that I'll schedule for another day.

By the time I get to the car, the waterworks have started. I go home and sit for a while trying to get my act together. Keeping busy, I realize, is the thing to do. This morning from the get-go, I stayed busy until sitting in the dentist's chair.

I am home maybe fifteen minutes when the dental secretary calls.

"Terri, is everything all right?" she asks.

"No, it is just me having a bad day," I reply.

"Is it an anniversary of some day?" she hinted but didn't want to ask outright.

"Yes, it is. I'll call in a day or two to set up a teeth cleaning. I am sorry, but I could not do it," I say as I hold my sobbing.

After looking at mail, writing checks to pay bills, and a few other things, I do grocery shopping. Maybe not a good idea because since I have been home, all I do is eat.

Should I go to the gravesite? All I see myself doing is standing there crying. Ryan always got frazzled when I cried, like when he'd have to go to Iraq or came back to Ft. Hood. I feel torn. Tomorrow, when I have it together, I'll go visit the gravesite.

I drive to the cemetery. I stand and talk to Ryan in my head, and, of course, cry the whole time. The things I think about when at the gravesite is how the trial so infuriates me and could we have done more? Should I have brought up the sleeping panel member? Should I have said something to Abadia when he came to apologize? I know I am driving myself crazy with questions. Questions I can do nothing about. Sitting in my car, I have to wipe the tears away and drive home. It seems a difficult task.

I recognize I need to do something. There is no kidding myself. I need to make a future for myself, like Adam. His fiancé did a good thing to call off the wedding because Adam thought about what his future would be like. He sees now there is no chance for advancement or pay increases at this job. I think he sees he needs a career, not a job.

Adam and Rich are home by now. Rich and I go to visit Ryan's grave. We notice that the plastic flowers have faded, so we go get something new to replace them. First, we go to Steins and find a pretty arrangement of plastic red roses with white baby breath in it. We put a flag in the back to bring out the colors and it looks nice. We take out the old and put in the new. Then we stand, each of us in our own thoughts.

Sam Mathers and Adam get together on the day Rich and Adam get home from Germany. Sam and Adam are friends from high school. The two toasted to Ryan and talked about memories of him. Due to a medical injury, Sam was dismissed from the Army.

I cry because I miss him, because I feel we didn't do enough, because Abadia got a bad conduct discharge and not dishonorable discharge, because Abadia didn't man-up but used all the tricks he could to get out of it. What makes a drunk person even consider harming friends? To carry a gun to a party knowing he'd be drinking and knowing he gets "stupid" when he drinks. What was his intent of going to the car for the gun if not to harm? I can't believe for one minute it wasn't premeditated since he walked to the car to get the gun. He wanted to shoot Owens. No one will ever convince me of anything else. I cry because Ryan had a life ahead of him and we won't know what an impact he would make on others. The letters and notes we received support the fact that he was a gentle, caring person. Because I wouldn't ever get to know this man that would come home after being gone for five years. Abadia robbed us of that. We never discussed how he wanted to be interred when he died. I wish I knew what he wanted, but he was in the states and would have been home in September. He was out of danger, wasn't he?

Rich pulls me out of my thoughts when he says angrily, "It's just wasn't fair." And walks back to the car. No, it wasn't. But how do we cope? What can we do now?

As we drive back to the house, Rich is still angry and says, "Once Abadia is out, I'm going to post an ad in the paper in the place he'll reside informing the public of the murderer in their presence." I knew he would not follow through but will think of some action he can do to make Abadia's life miserable. Maybe as time goes by, Rich will reconsider.

I see on Facebook my niece and sister make a comment about the one-year anniversary. We get a few cards from a couple of groups set up to let us know they are thinking of us.

It is early August as we pack the motorcycles and leave early to meet up with others for a trip around Lake Superior. There are twelve of us on eight motorcycles. We have been talking about this for a while because we know some of the back roads are so picturesque. Along the way, we know we want to stop at Porcupine Mountain to walk along the rivers and see waterfalls and walk over a suspension bridge.

By Sunday we are in Superior, Wisconsin. Near Duluth there are the Lower and the Upper Falls in a Minnesota State Park. The group makes it to Thunder Bay, Ontario, Canada, but Jill gets sick. We are thinking dehydration so we stop so Jill can get rested. After an hour, she says she is better.

On Tuesday, we see the waterfalls that are the second largest next to Niagara Falls. Later we view a gorge which is stunning. The rain starts and dampens our travel. We get out of the rain.

We have slow-going over the bridge in Saulte Ste. Marie, Michigan. It is now humid, so we turn the engines off and glide down the slope when we can. I am the last going through the Customs Gate.

As I pull through the gate, I see most of the group surrounding Dave's bike. Jill is on the ground with people pouring water on her. My mind jumps to an awful thought and hope I am wrong. You hear things come in threes and there are a few seconds when I am afraid to go see what's going on. But it's Jill laying on the road and something tells me this isn't the time to think; it's time to act.

As I pull up, I see Bob getting an umbrella from his bike and hold it over Jill for shade.

Dave yells to Customs, "Call 911!"

Jill is rallying enough to holler back, "No!"

I have an idea. "Let's get a car and get her to a hotel."

"Good thought, Terri," Dave replies.

The Customs Officer then speaks up saying, "You can take my car."

All of us are thanking her profusely and a few of the men get Jill into the car. Dawn rides with Jill, and we find a hotel for the night. Thank goodness for the generosity of the Custom official.

In the evening, I visit to see how Jill is doing. Carrying a bag of a favorite snack of hers, I tease, "Now if you aren't up to eating a little, I can keep it until you are ready."

"Oh, Terri, how sweet. It is just what I need," she whispers as I hand her the M&M's. That puts a smile on her face, although she is looking a little pale to me.

In the morning, Dave and Jill, along with Yvonne and Curt, leave early so they can ride in the cool of the day. The rest of us leave about 7:00AM but only ride until 3:00PM because of the heat. To this day, I do not know how they got the car back to the Customs Officer.

On Saturday, we meet up with Dave at his parent's home in Marinette, Wisconsin. He headed there to ensure that Jill could be taken home in Dave's dad's car with air conditioning. Dave looked up Jill's condition and tells us it's heat exhaustion.

I call Jill and Dave every other day until I hear Jill is doing fine.

For most months, the Military Veterans Museum Board Meetings are the fourth Wednesday of the month. At this August meeting of the Board of Directors, I have to give a summary about what is going on with the PX Gift Shop. I tell about what sold at the July's Experimental Aircraft Association (EAA) AirVenture event in Oshkosh and about a future event in Little Chute called "Nick's Ride to Remember".

When I talk about who Nick was, a young man from Little Chute killed in a helicopter crash in Afghanistan in August 2009, I become overwhelmed and my voice breaks. My eyes tear up and my voice wavers. Thank goodness, Rich knew it is becoming difficult for me and picks up where I left off. I got a grip, but it is embarrassing to falter like that especially in front of strangers.

CHAPTER 58

At September's doctor appointment, I tell her the citalopram pills aren't working.

"I still cry most every day. It is at night when I have time to think before going to sleep," I tell her.

She replies, "Increase the pills by 10 mg for a week to get past any side effects, and then see if the pills help. I advised you that you can do that at our last meeting."

"I don't recall you saying anything like that. I could take alprazolam when needed, but I didn't think I could take both."

"Now take alprazolam when you need it and let's jack up the citalopram to 30 mg. Call me in a month to let me know how you are doing."

In my whole adult life, September meant school. In some ways, I miss school and in some ways I don't. Replace some of what I missed with one semester of teaching college students twice a week seems like a good idea. I love to teach and interact with students.

Will I visit Roberts? I do not miss the new techniques being imposed for behavioral purposes-PBIS- because there are so many exceptions not addressed. It is an acronym that stands for Positive Behavioral Interventions and Supports. I do not miss the meetings, paperwork, the committees, some of the new strategies to teach math that I wasn't comfortable doing because I didn't see the point, the reading class with no help to address the various abilities of students, and a principal I used to respect and, toward the end, well, maybe he had pressure from the upper administration, but he changed. It was all too much and on top of that to handle coping.

I wish the museum didn't take up quite so much time, but it is all just getting started. I feel it will only get better once we get it organized sensibly in our eyes. We just want it to work out.

Today Rich and I are doing inventory of items to sell for the Fields of Honor Military Veterans Museum. The thought occurred to me I enjoy doing something for the soldiers. I find this keeps my mind occupied in a constructive way.

While inventorying, Rich and I come upon some key chains with bullets attached. He is telling me the names of each when I say, "Wait. You said a 45 caliber?"

"Yes, I did," he says as he stands up.

"This is a 45 cal. It's the same caliber that killed Ryan, isn't it?" I ask, dreading the answer. "I didn't know what to picture in my mind when they were talking about the 45 cal in court. It's bigger than I thought." Tears come as I imagine that size of an object going through Ryan's flesh. It takes my breath away. I stop for a while and sit and sob. Rich gets up and leaves me alone. He has a difficult time dealing with me crying.

A day or two later, CPT Meghan Earhart calls. Meghan begins, "I am leaving for Iraq tonight. I wanted to call to say goodbye. I think of you often and carry a picture of Ryan with me." Imagine, of all the things she has to do, and still she remembers to call us.

Rich inquires, "Have you read in the Army Times about PFC Donnie Stevens, Jr. being convicted of unpremeditated murder involving 20-year-old SPC David Middlebrooks? Stevens is sentenced to life in prison and dishonorably discharged. This happened in November 2009. The report says on September 3, witnesses saw Middlebrooks hit two women, one who was pregnant, before he and Stevens fought following a night of drinking. Both soldiers returned from Iraq in June 2009. I think it is the same unit as Ryan."

Meg replies, "There is nothing I can do except be frustrated that the same thing occurred with Ryan and the sentences are so different."

"What can I do?" Rich asks.

She pauses and says, "Get ahold of your congressional representative and point out that there are no guidelines in the military courts. There are guidelines in place for state and the federal levels, but not the military. This may take going in front of Congress and telling our story and show the injustice of it all."

After a bit of talking about other things, I take the phone from Rich. "Meghan, have a good tour, a wonderful time. Well, I mean, have a safe tour."

I figure she will send us her e-mail address. She will have Sofia Hammons send us the "Result of Trial" on both this case and Ryan's so we can share an intelligent conversation with a congressional representative. She is crying when I said goodbye. I have a special spot in my heart for her.

On another day, the mailman comes to the door. As I walk to the front door, I say, "Rich, that can't be the 'Result of Trial' from CPT Earhart, could it?"

I open the door as I call back to Rich, "Oh, it is from Ft. Hood. From CID".

The mail carrier says, "That is what I like about mail. It is always about them coming home."

I look at him and quietly say, "No, this one is the other way."

"Yes, it's about them coming home," he said. I figure he still doesn't understand, so I try one more time as I was signing for the package.

"You have no idea how I wish this was for coming home." But no reaction from him, so I give up, thank him for the package and close the door.

I head to the kitchen drawer to get a knife as Rich comes into the kitchen. Inside we find Ryan's dog tags and chain, his watch, his cell phone, and coins. We take one thing out at a time and inspect each item. He never seemed to carry much in money. I get emotional. He wore his watch and dog tags and carried his phone everywhere. Adam might like the watch.

Rich looks for a cord that might fit the phone so he can recharge it. Finding one in the box of cords we keep downstairs, Rich plays with the phone to figure if there are messages, photos, videos, or anything. He is not successful.

When our housekeeper arrives the next day, she helps Rich find the photos. There are a variety of things, people, and animals. We see a couple videos of guys being hit with pies, big ugly spiders, a foot with six toes, and two Iraqis who are translators when he was at the gate. Later in the evening we hear Ryan's not-so-tasteful message for those who want to leave a message. Since the package came, some of the old pain comes, too.

It's October and the leaves are going straight to yellow which means it won't be a pretty fall, my favorite season. My email to Sofia is if she can get paperwork called a "result of trial" for us to approach our congressional representative about our concerns about the vast difference in the sentencing of Abadia and PFC Donnie Stevens. Explaining that Meghan said to contact our congressional representative, our focus will be on why there are no guidelines in our military judicial system. I tell her the congressional representative's assistant gave us the brushoff, so we figured we need documentation.

Sofia promptly responded, stating her hope for potential action in future cases. Unfortunately, she does not know if that would happen because the military seems to hold tight to not having mandatory sentences in the military. She asks that we keep her posted on approaching our congressional representative. Sofia included some good information, so we are a bit more knowledgeable. Thanks to our Texas friend, we get copies of the "Results of Trial" on Ryan and for Middlebrooks.

CHAPTER 59

A news article caught Rich's eye in the Army Times. I call it up on the computer and find it on myfoxden.com.

Fort Hood Soldier
Gets Life for Party Murder

"Belton, Texas–A jury in Belton has ordered life sentence in prison for a Fort Hood soldier convicted in the shooting death of a homeless man.

Jurors late Tuesday decided the penalty for 23-year-old SPC Jared Lee Bottorff.

The case involves the August 2009 slaying of 36-year-old Dan Smith, Jr., after a party at Bottorff's house in Killeen. Investigators say Smith had hitched a ride with Bottorff.

Attorneys for Bottorff claimed the shooting was self-defense. The jury convicted Bottorff of murder early Saturday.

Authorities charged Bottorff's roommate, SPC James Thomas, with tampering with physical evidence.

This case has a few differences from Ryan's but supports our opposition to the leniency of the panel in the murder of Ryan. I hope we find more out about this case."

11/9/2010
To: Terri & Rich
From: Meghan Earhart
Subject: Hello

Just dropping a line to say hello and see how you are. It's hard to believe I've been in Iraq for over a month already. The time slowly goes by here and it feels like when we last spoke–the evening I deployed -was so long ago! I have a picture of your dear Ryan here on my desk among photos of friends and family. Knowing how lovely you and your son Adam are, I feel such deep sadness that I only got to know him through the nightmare of his untimely death; senseless at that.

I think of you so often (as does my mom, who so enjoyed meeting you) and I hope each passing day continues to bring you healing and recovery. Please let me know if I can do anything–ever. I also would be grateful if you can keep me posted on Ryan's Soldier's Medal progress. If I am home, I would not miss the ceremony that bestows this most deserving honor on your son and my brother-in-arms.

With much love,
Meghan
Please give my regards to Adam.

Around Thanksgiving, I email Evan Anderson's mother and Greg Owens's mother because I wonder if it is a good idea to continue Facebook or is it time to end communications with their sons. As goes for all of Ryan's Ft. Hood friends, I think of them and hope they are healing.

Both mothers agree the contact is important even if it is just Facebook. Both men thought very highly of Ryan and figured there was going to be a lifelong friendship.

Evan's mother shared, 'Evan thought meeting you was great and hated having to meet under such circumstances.' Greg's mother wrote,

'Greg is feeling very guilty that he is the one that lived and in keeping in touch, he'd feel a part of Ryan's family; that keeping in touch keeps him grounded.'

Right after Thanksgiving, a package of goodies from us is sent to CPT Earhart's address but didn't hear from her about it, so I thought I would check if I had the address right. In my email to her, I ask how her work is going and is it different from what she dealt with at Fort Hood. Did she have a nice Thanksgiving? I know the dining facilities put out a great spread on Thanksgiving and Christmas for the soldiers. Weather in Wisconsin is talked about and what our tasks are concerning the Military Museum's gift shop which is overhauling and reorganizing merchandise.

My email continues with the news I will finish teaching a college course in mid-December. In the beginning I found it exciting and knew I had something to offer, but lost interest, so won't teach second semester.

There are a couple weeks that we go south because Rich's arthritis is getting worse, and the cold really affects his hands. I wrapped it up with hoping she received the cookies.

11/30/2010 7:42AM
To: Richard Schlack
From: Sofia Hammons
Terri,

I am so sorry, but I thought your family was put onto the form. I had to get a copy from the court reporter. It is actually a Form 2704. I have attached one. If you, Richard, and Adam would please initial in the YES block then I will make sure that it gets to Fort Leavenworth and to the DA. You will then all be notified of Abadia's status. I am not sure why you were not put on the form because you all testified. I am sure that CPT Earhart did not see the form because MAJ Michaels is the one that signed it, and she would have made sure that your names were there. I put Adam's address as your own, so if you or he wants his new address, just write the one out and put the good one in.

Has Adam gotten any counseling? That might help. I would think that it would be very hard for him to talk with you and Richard because he probably does not want to cause you anymore pain (even though I think the pain never goes away).

I am glad that you all are doing fine. If you decide to come down here, just let us know. We have plenty of room as long as you do not mind two dogs that LOVE people!

Take care and let me know if you need anything.

Sofia

CPT Meghan Earhart sent an email the last day of November saying her thank-you card was returned and wondered if we thought the box didn't arrive. The treats were a big hit at the office.

She says the number of court-martials is fairly high in Iraq. She does get to see her husband, but he is busy trying to transfer the main detention facility back to the Iraqis, but there are some very bad men there, so it is a delicate situation.

Since she does half a tour, she is looking forward to her time to leave because she misses the hair dryers and indoor plumbing.

CHAPTER 60

One piece of news we receive is from Spencer Vans. I am so relieved by his letter tone that he is doing better. He was such a mess when the trial occurred. I worried about him so much.

To keep in touch with Ryan's Ft. Hood friends is kind of keeping a watch on them. Ryan's death affected all of them. Those now in Iraq since September are now under a different pressure, which I hope doesn't add to stress levels.

12/2/2010 8:35PM
To: Richard Schlack
From: Spencer Vans
Subject: Greetings

Yea, God has been really helping in my life lately. Anyway, I have been doing legal work for the company lately because I am on rear detachment. I want you to be the first to hear this. I went to JAG and I'm going to try getting another trial for you. I think that is why I have PTSD and the sleep issues, also I'm more withdrawn and bitter about the shooting. At the 32 hearing, I was a basket case at the court-martial. I let the defense bully me and didn't fight back like I did at the grand jury. I don't mean to bring it all back for you guys on the shooting and I'm sorry for that, but it's not fair to Ryan, your family, and the friends of Ryan. I'm going to talk to MAJ Michaels, but he's now overseas. I'm praying for you guys. I know the holidays must be hard for you. Ryan gave his heart to his friends and helped me deal with my ex with what she did. She got *knocked up while I was in Iraq. I know he isn't on earth anymore, but I see him looking down at us every day having a blast in heaven probably making gaming models and playing video games. God bless you guys. Keep me in your prayers and I'll do the same.*

Spencer

Every year my brothers and sister and whoever of their children gather for a Family Christmas Get-Together in early December. Since it is my turn, I take down my Thanksgiving décor and work on putting up the fake Christmas tree.

"So, you are thinking of putting up the tree? That's good. It gives a little Christmas feeling around here," Rich exclaims.

Getting out the Christmas ornaments, I come upon the one with Ryan's photo in it. He's in his uniform with the USA emblem on top. I start to cry. Rich sees me and walks toward me. We hold each other and calm each other. After a time, Rich whispers to me, "It never gets any better." Rich is not one to express his feelings, so when a simple line like that is said, I know he is still hurting more than I'll know.

The holiday home decorations have toned down due to no help at home. Now, I am the only one who hauls it out, puts it up and takes it down. Besides the Christmas tree, the fireplace mantel has four stockings hanging off the edge and four-inch ceramic white angels we got long ago when we lived in Germany. Each angel is holding a different instrument and posing different ways. With angel hair at their feet, it looks like it's floating around them. It is a favorite decoration of mine.

The coffee table holds a pretty candle holder with three red candles. Of course, pictures of Santa and the boys, the faux electric candles in the windows, and the three-foot German nutcracker standing near the door are about as much that get used now. The lovely smell of cinnamon and apple potpourri adds to the room.

It is just right to have some kind of Christmas decoration that's more meaningful near Ryan's gravestone at this point. So, Rich and I go to Stein's Garden and Gifts to see if we can find a wreath, a little Christmas tree, or a little something to put near Ryan's gravestone.

"So, what are you looking for? Do you have any idea?" Rich asks me.

"I'm looking around here. If I see it, I'll know it," I say as I stroll through the aisles. Looking around the store, I see nothing that is what I imagine.

"Rich, look at this plain wreath and here are some little ornaments. I am getting an idea in my head."

Rich comes closer and whispers, "I just don't think the store will help you." I head to the flower counter and explain what I imagine. She said to give her some time.

When I return in half an hour, she had put together a beautiful wreath. She found little cubical ornaments shaped as different colored presents, a round bulb with Ryan's name on it, a ribbon interwoven in the wreath and sprigs of white for a little accent.

"I love it!" I exclaim and grab Rich to see what he thinks.

"Yeah, that is great," he comments.

We go to the cemetery to put the wreath on a tripod next to Ryan's grave. The US flags are down on all the gravesites for the veterans, so people place other things near their loved ones.

Why is it I feel like Ryan can see this happening?

It is snowing and Christmas is two weeks away. It is the first snow of the season that may stay on the ground. As I am shoveling our sidewalk outside after dinner, a thought of Ryan jumps in my head. I can see his reaction to snow on sidewalks. He would walk like a skittish calf on ice until he was sure it wasn't slippery. When asked to shovel, you knew by his body language he didn't want to. He wouldn't complain but would just go out to get it done.

Something not right is going on with me. Lately, my heart begins to pound so badly I sometimes have to work to get air. Sometimes there is dizziness. I figure I will wait and see if it gets worse or happens more often before I do something about it.

It is Christmas Day, and we are visiting Ryan's grave. Today makes it much harder to do than any other day, but I expect that. I want Ryan to feel we think of him and yet I know he doesn't feel. Guess I should think of him in heaven, and it will make it easier.

Having fun on Christmas Day meant watching the boys open their gifts especially when we hit upon a great idea for a present and was totally unexpected by the receiver. Now, Adam is given money because we aren't sure what he needs. He says that's fine with him. There are still silly things, though, he finds in his stocking hanging from the mantel.

CHAPTER 61

2011

It's time to take Christmas decorations down. Who cares if we take a few days? A few years ago, in our decorating frenzy, our house used to take a week to decorate. This was largely due to the Department 56 Alpine Village Series all laid out on tables in our huge living room with raised platforms and bowls underneath cotton sheeting to create a mountainous Austrian topography. Oh, I loved it! To add detail, there were little evergreen trees placed strategically with two large, molded plastic mountains. There was a need for a lot of flat area because there were thirty buildings to lay out. They all lit up and were surrounded by tiny characters corresponding to the purpose of the building throughout the display. The collection started as a whim to remind us of our life and times in Germany, and because Ryan was born in Germany. We thought we would pass the display on when Ryan had a family. The collection is all now tucked away on basement shelves and hasn't seen the light of day in several years. One day I'll sell them or get rid of them somehow.

The Christmas tree was set up in front of one living room window, the four stockings hung from Santa's feet off the fireplace mantel and the three-foot nutcracker stood at attention nearby. On top of the mantel rest the angels. We bought the nutcracker and angels because I just had to have them, and our second child would have something from Germany, as well. Christmas cards covered the French doors between the living room and dining area. It was always such a beautiful room in the evening when each building had their lights on; the fireplace was lit, and Christmas songs played softly. The fragrance of holiday potpourri wafted through the house.

I was especially fond of the garland carefully tied to the wooden railing of the stairs. There were white fluffy bears with red scarves around their necks snuggling the corner of every other step. You could see it from outside and how cozy it looked.

The front of the house still has four huge wreaths on the four pillars of our Georgian Colonial Home. Rich had spotlights on each wreath and we placed faux candles in each window. Each year, I would go outside and cross the street just to look at our home. We did get compliments on it.

It's after Christmas and Rich decides to go to a gun show this afternoon to check out what is sold there; maybe get ideas for the MVM Gift Shop. I stay home because of my clumsy accident falling into the six-foot potted tree. This morning, I am reaching behind the two Lazy Boys to get a decoration off the window. I feel myself losing my balance as I am leaning forward. The tree and I take a fall. I end up going face down and get nasty carpet burns on my face. Getting out from between the Lazy Boys and the bank of windows is not the easiest and certainly not graceful. Rather than a gun show, I would rather work on packing things up into boxes. On one of the living room tables, I grab the Christmas pictures of Baby Ryan with Santa and another of Ryan and Baby Adam with Santa. Another breakdown. Clutching the pictures to my chest, I look up and say through clenched teeth, "Why? Just tell me why?"

Suddenly, I feel I am about to burst with anger. Screaming into my hands, I feel I am losing it. There's not a damn thing I can do. Sobbing and gasping, I could not focus on anything but how grief-stricken I feel. The same phrases came out of my mouth. It doesn't sound like me, but I can hear myself sobbing and trying to control the torture when I sink into this feeling of despair and helplessness. There is nowhere to go when the loss hits you like this.

My brain goes back to someone who went back to his car to get a damn gun to do what? Show he's macho? Get the upper hand? No one was attacking him. He walked up to the three guys and raised his gun. He wanted to do harm. They were NOT on a battlefield protected with body armor and weapons in hand. And because of this, how many lives were screwed up? Ryan pushed the intended victim out of the way, a hero in the eyes of those there and those who hear his story. I miss him so much, it's too "effing" hard.

Rich returns from the gun show. "How was it?" I ask.

"Well, you know, guns all over," he shrugs. I am so glad he is back with me.

Upping the Citalopram to 40 mg a day over the holiday season didn't really do the trick.

Today is a physician assistant's appointment. As soon as she walks into the room, I confess, "Okay, I have to tell you what I did. You told me I can raise the Citalopram up when I needed to. I find myself not always wanting to get out of bed, but about 9:30AM, I talk to myself in my head and convince myself to get up to start the day. For a few days over Christmas, I jacked Citalopram up to 60 mg but realized I was shaking so badly, that must not be good, so I drop back."

She thinks a minute then recommends, "Something different may be warranted. You first have to slow the process by being weaned off of one kind and then go on to another."

"We will be heading southwest next week. I am excited we'll be roaming around in Arizona for the winter," I lie thinking I do not want to go.

"Let's wait until you return and put you on the different meds," she decides.

My brother Jerry sends us an article from statesman.com entitled "Ignoring red flags brings disgrace to nation". The article basically says that there were enough concerning indicators flagging MAJ Nidal Hasan that he should have been kicked out of the Army, but no, and as a result he ends up killing thirteen people in November 2009. The article refers to people in the federal government who investigated this topic.

Jerry also sent his response to The Statesman. "This is a comment on your 'Ignoring red flags brings disgrace to nation'."

> "In July 2009, my nephew, SGT Ryan Schlack, was shot and killed by a fellow soldier. They had worked together in Iraq. He took a bullet intended for a third buddy while trying to protect him. This defendant's attorney is the same one who is representing Army Major Nidal Hasan convicted of murder. But then the panel decided to not Dishonorably Discharge the killer. Does our Army have so little respect for itself as to not Dishonorably Discharge someone who walked back across the street and lawn, shot at a defenseless man at close range and left him on the ground? Just as the Army let the Major continue his path to a massacre, there is something wrong with the Army."

I think about what Jerry had written. The feeling of pride flows over me as I read what my brother points out. It makes me want to take up the fight again. A renewal of strength to shake up the men and women of congress to what is such a clear wrong. There has got to be a serious look at taking the sentencing out of the hands of the panel and putting more responsibility in the hands of the judge. There has got to be guidelines in sentencing. Our country has the right to ask for justice when a man's life has ended.

Since Christmas, my heart is racing, sometimes having to take deep breaths, and I'd often feel faint to the point I'd have to pause with my hand on the wall to support myself. It doesn't happen very often, so I think old age is creeping in. The week before leaving for the Southwest, it happens more and more often until every time I head up the stairs, my heart pounds hard. The pounding and breathlessness are so bad I have to sit on the bed for a while and wait for it to stop. I am concerned but hate to screw up leaving on Saturday. Then again, I don't want to die in the middle of nowhere.

I don't know why I am fighting the thought of calling the PA and telling her about it. Finally, I do just that. The PA advises, "Drop the Citalopram to 20 mg and go into the emergency now."

Wow! I spend the afternoon with EKGs, X-rays and monitors. I am sent home with a monitor for my heart for 48 hours. Then I call to make arrangements to see my doctor on Monday.

Dr. House, my regular physician, is reluctant but in a concerned manner, says, "You can go on the trip if you take it easy especially in higher altitudes. If something is wrong with test results, I will call your cell, or you should call me if something is a concern." Rich and I are already packed, so we leave about noon. This trip is a get-away we need.

The weather doesn't cooperate as we drive south and have to stop due to icy highways and cars in ditches. Rich decides to head south as far as Amarillo, Texas, then turn west. We begin to find things of interest such as the Grand Canyon Sky Walk and Hoover Dam, and we let our relatives in California know we will be visiting.

But on Wednesday, since I didn't hear anything, I decide I should call the doctor to inquire about my tests even though we are hundreds of miles away. Unfortunately, the results showed some issues and am told to come home. We adjust our trip differently than planned and purposefully drive to the home where Ryan was shot on Fort Hood. Finding out we have to wait a day to meet with CPT Cotton to find out about Ryan's Soldier's Medal status, we instead leave a note.

A week later, we get safely home at 8:30PM on Wednesday, February 11. I now am on Venlafaxine 75 mg two times a day. Other testing is scheduled. Oh, geez, am I in that bad of shape?

Now that we are home, I can't find the address and all the information to get a copy of the detailed transcripts of the trial, so I email Sofia. Sofia sends an address to request the transcripts of the trial. We find out that the lawyer, George Janis, hasn't read it or turned it in with an okay so we can get it. I can't stand the man.

There is a phone call from CPT Stone, Ryan's commander at the time of the murder. He has been in Iraq since September. His call is in relation to the Soldier's Medal that Rich requested him to pursue.

When Rich came home from the doctor, I begin, "I got a call today from Stone; you know, Ryan's commander. He's been in Iraq since September."

"Oh, yeah. Is this about Ryan's Soldier's Medal? What did he say?" Rich asks hopefully.

"Stone told me it has been turned down. Why does that not surprise me?" I respond.

Rich sits down in his Lazy Boy and doesn't say a word for a moment. Then he angrily says, "I'm not done. I can go to a congressional representative and go that angle."

It is best to leave Rich alone for a while when he gets angry. He eventually did make a call to the office where all requests would have had to go through. There was never any such case turned in to them. This says a lot about that lying commander.

It is a good time for a Father/Son getaway. I am not up to doing anything at all, so Adam and Rich take a trip to Washington, DC. They take in the Pentagon Memorial, the Washington Monument, and, of course, the Capitol.

Adam tells me about something that happened near The Mall. Protestors had set up tents. Adam, who loves a good debate, went into one of the tents. He thought he would ask a few questions he thought were pretty basic. Questions such as "What do you want to accomplish? What is it you are trying to change? How is what you are doing now making this change come about? If magically everything did change to your liking and you can just go home, how is this new world different from the pre-protesting world? Why should I care what you are doing?"

Not surprisingly, Adam reports not a single one could give an answer. It was abundantly clear there was no goal, no direction or plan of action. Oh, to have been a little fly on the wall!

CHAPTER 62

Ryan's bed still has piles of papers. I would start to go through them, but then can't decide what Rich would want to keep. I seem to look at the piles of papers and notebooks for a couple minutes every time I go into the room.

About three months ago, I propose to Rich, "Let's go through the papers in Ryan's room. It isn't in anyone's way, but maybe we can get something done."

Rich flatly says, "No." I don't want to upset him, but my thought process is maybe this is a way to bring — what — closure? Not that everything we wanted to investigate is done.

So, I try again to see if he is up to going through Ryan's papers. Rich responds with impatience in his voice. "No, I don't know why you are in such a hurry to do something with the papers. It isn't in anyone's way. I'm not sure we are finished with them. Just leave it alone."

The anti-depression pills make me sleepy. I sleep late every day and have little energy, so there's a feeling of being worn and aging fast. Rich and Adam are doing okay, it seems, but who knows? Reading either of those two is not something I do well.

One day, Rich and I go to the cemetery. The snow is gone. The Christmas wreath is faded, but it is better than nothing. There are more gravestones nearby. I still feel the phrase, "Blessed are the Peacemakers" on Ryan's stone tells a lot. The ironic thing is Ryan was never an aggressor.

I'm checking e-mail and Facebook in the converted bedroom, now my office, and suddenly hear Rich downstairs. I listen more carefully and realize he is crying. This is good and I am glad he is finally getting emotions out. I recall my reaction putting away the Christmas pictures of the boys. Building pain up inside you is such an awful thing to allow to happen. You're a volcano that must erupt. A person can hold it in just so long. Better to let emotions come out than internalize it and possibly do something very unlike your personality.

I go downstairs and he has his laptop in his hands sitting in his Lazy Boy. When I walk into the living room, I quietly ask, "What's wrong?"

Rich sits stiffly and doesn't say a word as he closes the laptop.

I ask again, "Rich, please tell me what's wrong. Talk to me."

"I'm just looking at pictures," Rich says with a tremor in his voice.

I pull him awkwardly toward me and hug him. The need to be strong for him left me and I start to tear up, too, because it hurts me to see him sad. It can't be fixed. It can't be undone. No words will take it away. Feeling so helpless, feeling so sad.

Another crippling event occurs. My brother, Gib's birthday is today on the 28 of April. He will bury his 17-year-old grandson tomorrow. Gib and Mary's grandson committed suicide, not intentionally. Mixed feelings of sadness and loss rush back to me. All I think of on the day of the funeral is the hopeless feelings that the parents are going through. What a hell they are facing and will face for quite a while. I want to talk with my nephew and his wife, but don't want to push myself on them. They have close family ties who are there for them, I am sure. It is all so difficult to understand.

Letting a month pass, I call my nephew and his wife each once. "Aunt Terri, if I would like to talk with you, I will call, okay?" she kindly says.

My nephew is a little more hesitant to say anything, but then asks, "What can I do for you?" Maybe jumping to another subject helps him not to "go there". I learn the family is going to counseling, and they put a little memorial in the back yard; buried some of their son's ashes there. I think of the one remaining son which makes me think of my one remaining Adam.

I cry for Adam, too, since there is no sibling for him, no one who would know his past and know his experiences. It is good to say he is out seriously looking for a woman. When one doesn't work out, he is back on the computer programs that allow meeting other potential partners. When Rich and I knew we were going to marry, I said in no uncertain terms that if I ever got pregnant, I want at least two so they can be there for each other throughout their lives. Rich knew he had no choice in this matter.

It is starting again. The crying at night when I go to bed. Maybe because it is June and July is near. In my mind, I hash over things that really make me angry or, again, obsessively wonder about. I am on all these meds, but still I cry. I may have to stay on anti-depressants longer, and I don't want to.

July 12 is a waterworks day. Today Ryan would celebrate his 32nd birthday. I am in Rich's arms all night. He gets emotional, too. I feel frustration, anger, and helplessness.

I post the following on the Ryan Schlack Family and Friends Support Facebook page:

> Your friends are all coming back from Iraq safe and sound. Only Greg yet and he'll be stateside in September. It's been two years, my son, and how I wonder what life for you would be like now. I know you were ready to settle a bit and were making good choices about what you were going to do with your life. You had goals and direction and that wasn't always easy to figure out.
>
> I treasure when you came back and gave me a second kiss and hug before you left. You've never done that before. I think about the phone call to let me know where you were on the road that Friday morning. I remember telling you it was a

good idea to sleep a bit at the wayside since you were driving all night.

Thank you for all the together times of fun and laughter and singing. I still sing to "Horse with No Name" and can listen to the Nickelback song now without always crying.

I get a card from "Heaven's Heroes". I put the card on the living room coffee table and think who would have ever dreamed we'd have a table dedicated to the death of Ryan? I become overwhelmed.

CHAPTER 63

The mid-August day has finally arrived. Six of us are on our way to Ireland and Scotland for eight days of touring. If I say so myself, it is a well-planned, very busy agenda. Jerry and Rita, Gib and Mary, and Rich and I have never traveled together before. So let the adventures begin.

The days are packed with a variety of experiences. A few of the cities and places we tour include Glasgow, Edinburgh, Loch Lomond, Loch Ness, Ayrshire, Belfast, and Dublin. Then there is Blarney Castle where I had to be on my back and lay far back off the floor to get my head out onto the walls to kiss the stone. I thought I would fall! The countryside is so beautiful and different from what is in the US.

We sample a quality single malt whiskey, tour Edinburgh Castle, have our first taste of haggis, the national dish of Scotland. Haggis is a type of pudding composed of minced liver, heart, and lungs of a sheep, mixed with beef or mutton suet (hard white fat on kidneys or loins), oatmeal and other spices. The mixture is packed into a sheep's stomach and boiled. We are entertained with Scottish and Irish dancing and music, with the Military Tattoo that has music and entertainment from all around the world. Let's not forget drinking Guinness beer at the factory where one building is shaped like a beer glass. What an experience to see the strangest thirteen different kinds of sheep and an amazing sheep dog showing his skill in herding. And then there are more visits to pubs along the way. We eat dinner one evening in a castle like the medieval royalty with entertainment of music and a skit. The ten days are very memorable.

Back in our real world, I write a letter, but also send a copy to Sofia Hammons to see if I am clear on my request. My letter is requesting the transcripts of the trial US v. Barto Abadia.

Finally, after almost two months, a letter arrives from the Department of the Army, Director of Human Resources.

September 20, 2011
Dear Mrs. Schlack,
This responds to your Freedom of Information Act (FOLA) request dated July 21, 2011, in which you requested a copy of the transcripts of the May 2010 trial involving United States versus SPC Abadia, Barto R., B Company, 27th Brigade Support. Battalion, 4th Brigade Combat Team, 1st Cavalry Division.

While processing your request, we have determined that the requested information falls under the purview of the US Army Health Care Acquisition Activity. This office is not the releasing authority for the documents; thus your request has been referred to the following agency for appropriate action and direct response to you.

US Army Crime Records
ATTN: CICR-FP
6010 6th St. Bldg 1465
Fort Belvoir, VA. 22060

If you have further questions about your FOIC request, please contact the undersigned at 987-065-4321 or hood.dhr.foia@conus.army.mil.

Sincerely,
 Lily Jacquard
 Freedom of Information Act Officer

Jacquard also attached a copy of a Memorandum for the Crime Records Center and a copy of my letter to her. I feel a bit defeated.

An appointment with the cardiologist is today. He confronts me. "Tell me about the meds and how they are affecting your moods." I tear up and he says, "Okay, let's try something else."

Rich suggests, "Hey, what do you think about getting shirts with Ryan's name on it? It can be a sort of memorial." Rich, Adam, and I order long-sleeved button-down cotton shirts with "In Memory of SGT Ryan R. Schlack, July 12, 1979–July 18, 2009" with the kneeling soldier next to the rifle, helmet, and boots, called "The Soldier's Cross", embroidered on the left chest. Adam chose red with black embroidery; I chose pink with grey embroidery and Rich chose a navy blue with white embroidery. Rich and I also order sweatshirts with that graphic; mine on a teal sweatshirt and Rich's on a red sweatshirt.

The weather is turning cooler, and the trees are telling me autumn is on the way. In the beginning, I feel okay with taking nadolol but as time went on, I'd cry even more, almost every day. Now, I am on something else. I have been on it for 5 days and today I just start crying in the car coming home from a movie.

I think about how I raised my first born. Did I do enough hugging, kissing, holding, and spending time with Ryan so that he knew he was loved? With Rich gone to Korea in 1983, and Adam a practical newborn, I made sure I spent time with Ryan alone every day, so he received my undivided attention, too.

Another day it is thoughts of Ryan joining the army. This time he didn't follow his best buddy Chuck to another job as was his usual move. This Army thing was his decision. In letters to him, I would write and tell him how proud we were of him. I could write positive things about what he'd tell us. I secretly knew the ADHD that he still suffered from had to affect his work, but I never brought it up.

Ryan and I did have a heart-to-heart talk when he was home in 2009.

Ryan divulged, "I hated being home during high school because of you and Dad getting on my case for not having a decent job or a plan for the future."

"When you said you wanted to go to school, Dad and I were very glad you decided for something better. We tried to encourage you. Then you joined the army and had to go to school. You had told me you were off all meds for a year before you joined because you can't have any medications show up in your system. I know it must be frustrating not remembering, but now that it is okay because meds will help you stay more focused. Use that kind of help. You are bright enough to tackle anything you want. When you get out of the army, you can see a doctor and get help when you go back to school."

In the conversation, I admitted, 'Ryan, you are my first born. I did what I thought was best. I hope you know that. You didn't come with a set of instructions to guide me. Of course, I am sure you think I've made mistakes.'

After all was said, I felt he knew I loved him and wanted only the best for him. Oh, God, how it hurts to think I won't have that anymore.

In early October, I receive an email from the Freedom of Information Act (FOIA) Officer/Records Manager Lily Jacquard. She explains that they have received our request and due to the large volume of pages in the trial transcripts, this will exceed the 20-day limit of FOIA. She will keep us updated on the progress of our request and move as quickly as possible to complete it. Didn't she just send a letter telling me I sent my request to the wrong place?

More and more when I go visit the gravesite, I don't cry as much or at all. Am I adjusting?

And then on another day, I am driving back from getting a haircut and the song that Ryan had playing on one of his computer accounts is playing a Nickelback song entitled "Gotta Be Somebody". I was balling so hard I had to pull the car over and compose myself.

CHAPTER 64

We receive a notice from the Clemency and Parole Board informing us that Abadia is eligible to be "considered for restoration and clemency" on Nov. 22 of this year. Needless to say, it is a shock.

And what is this "restoration"? What needs to be restored? I needed to do a little research. I find that a Board must see if the accused has not had any rights violated. This includes:

- Retaining his/her civil and firearms rights and impose collateral consequences
- Sees to it the accused can pursue pardons
- If the accused is pardoned, there is ground for an expungement of all arrest records, or the sealing of records
- Dealing with a criminal record in employment and licensing

Abadia has been in only about two years. Rich decides to see if we can attend, so we send off a registered letter today. The letter states we have been informed by the Victim/Witness Assistance Coordinator at Fort Leavenworth about a board meeting for Abadia's Restoration and Clemency Board. We would like to attend and make a Victim Impact Statement personally.

Today I read some good news about Ryan's friends. Ethan Jaks is expected to graduate in December with an Emergency Medical Team license. He plans to go on for a PA. I think he lives in Florida. Evan Anderson got out of the army in mid-September and went back to

Virginia to go to school. Thomas Dale is out of the army and working for Schlumberge, a technology company, in Midland, Texas. He got married in late 2009. Spencer Vans is still in the army. He is trying to get disability for PTSD. Haven't seen him on Facebook in a very long time. Greg Owens has been back from Iraq since September.

Found on Facebook on 10/25/2011 from Greg Owens.–

> I got about one year left of the Army life. I know one thing is for sure, that when I get out, I'm moving back up to Northern Minnesota. I'm taking that $80,000 that I get for college and going to U of Minnesota and unleashing my brainpower on the sub-standard teaching methods of today! lol I won't give up marathon running though. Lol

That idiot, Lily Jacquard, has not been working on the transcripts. A gentleman, Scott Bailey calls us, "Is this Richard Schlack's residence?"

"Yes, it is. Who am I talking to?" I ask.

Mr. Bailey explains, "I am calling about the transcripts you requested. I work in an office in Ft. Belvoir, Virginia. I don't know why I receive your request. I assure you I can get you a copy of the transcripts next week."

Relieved and surprised I am hearing this, I reply, "Oh, you can? Oh, that would be great! Thank you so very much, Mr. Bailey. I was given an address from somebody who should know what we're supposed to do, and they send me another address which I imagine is yours."

"I looked over the transcript. I am shocked to hear Abadia got 20 years for murder."

"Yeah, we are angry about that," I admit. We disconnect and I feel good something is happening that is a positive step.

I think I'll write to Lily Jacquard and tell her I hope she enjoyed jerking us around like that. I am so angry with the whole trial panel who heard Ryan's case. I do the "If I would have…." Or "I should have…." I can't change anything or go back. It is so very frustrating. The incompetence is mind-boggling.

We find out the letter we receive from the Service Parole and Clemency Board is just a notification. I talk with two people whose names are on the form letter and they assure me that the hearings are the first Thursday of the month and Abadia is not scheduled for November or December. It is their job to notify us when an actual date is set.

I come upon Facebook entries from Greg Owens with a photo of Ryan and Greg.

> GO - My best friend Ryan and I the day before he flew back to the states... and a month later he was shot and killed. I'm still trying to get over it. Life without your best friend is empty. I guess God has plans for everyone. That's a comfort for me. I know Ryan is in heaven playing all the War Hammer he can. lol I can only wish to be as polite and helpful as Ryan one day. I miss you, buddy!
> JM - I miss him too. I think we all do.
> WP - It's sad that it happened, all we can do is keep his memory alive by remembering him.
> MK - I think about him all the time too... he was a great soldier and missed.
> GO - He sure was a great friend and person! I am so glad for the photos. It's good to have memories.

November 18, 2011
To: Lily Jacquard
From: Richard Schlack
Subject: Re: Followup of transcript request
Cc: Sofia Hammons
Ms. Jacquard,

I am requesting an update. On October 5 you sent an email that our request was "in progress". This tells me you started on it. You also indicated it would take over 20 days. You said you "will continue to update [us] on the progress and move as quickly as possible to complete the request".

It is now 43 days since the Oct. 5 communique. I have not heard from you once. Don't make statements you have no intention of keeping. I can't tell you what anxiety and the feeling of falling more into despair words like that can do to a person. If there were more steps involved, I assume you would have told us. Why wouldn't you? Wouldn't you want us to feel confident everything was being done? Now, I know a part of my anger is toward the panel that gave the killer less than 20 years for three major crimes. Part of me is exasperated because I don't know how long this hurt will permeate my life since it seems there is always something. Lately we are dealing with having been alerted to the killer's request for a clemency board. On the other hand, I had moments I felt consoled by the strong thoughtful decisions from the judge, the team of lawyers that worked on our case, and one who helped me through this ordeal. Still, I feel like I have been dragged through a wringer and slapped about and thrown down like a rag.

I say this because I got a call from Scott Bailey in Ft. Belvoir, Virginia, who called us to ask if we requested transcripts. After more conversations with my husband, this gentleman said he would have the transcripts to us by next week in CD form. Now, why is that, Ms. Jacquard? Where are these transcripts? Why don't you have them? Why didn't you tell me the process? I am sure you can tell my faith in you is gone.

A word of advice. Put yourself in the victim's parents/ wife's/ husband's place. Feel empathy for those going through an unimaginable ordeal. If you face this every day, I realize you have to put space between you and the work, but don't let your heart grow so cold you forget our feelings are very fragile. If you don't know what you are doing, ask questions to confirm.

May life be good to you.

Terri Schlack, Ryan Schlack's mother

On the same day we receive an apology from Ms. Jacquard and asks permission to send out a partial shipment. We reply yes, please do.

Eleven days later Ms. Jacquard gives us an update to tell us the transcripts are at the legal office for review to view the purposed redactions. Once finalized, they will be mailed to us.

Meanwhile, in the mail we received Scott Bailey's CD-ROM of the transcripts.

CHAPTER 65

It's early December and Liz Curtis, the person in charge of setting up dates for the Parole and Clemency Board, calls.

"Mrs. Schlack, the Board has sent the formal request form for the Clemency and Parole Board meeting and is tentatively set for February 2. Is that date okay for you both?"

"Ms. Curtis, I am surprised we have any choice in the matter. To be honest, March 1 would be better because we will be out of the state in February."

She didn't seem to mind and said okay, she will send out the paperwork and information we need.

I have been having episodes again of being out of breath when I get to the top of the stairs or walk from the car to inside a store. I have been doctoring with this since January. My heart would pound and race, so I doctored with it and that is under control. I thought the breathing was, too, but it started up again. My cardiologist says I need to check into the cause being my lungs. Now, I am setting up appointments with a pulmonary specialist.

What now? The last few days I have not had one breathing problem. Now it is muscles in the legs. Whatever is jumping around in my body needs to stop. This is getting old, and I am tired of it. I am explaining this because a nurse friend asks if I ever discussed anxiety with the doctor with all that is going on. Oh, boy, another cause to research. I am curious to see if health issues pop up due to the Abadia Parole/Clemency Board appearance.

Back in November we received an Open House Reception Invitation. On Thursday, December 8, Rich and I decide to go more out of curiosity than anything. Scott and Tonette Walker are the current Governor and his wife, so we are able to see a bit of the Executive Residence. As we walk in, our eyes take in the swags, wreaths and ribbons adorning a double grand staircase. Those who attend are asked to sign a book and receive a candle in a container etched with Open House December 2011.

As we walk through the heavily Christmas decorated rooms, there are trimmed trees from different businesses around Wisconsin complete with theme names for each one. The dining room tree is called the "Enchanted Forest" because of its birds, sugar-encrusted grapes, frosted flowers and snowflakes. The "Tribute to the Troops" graces the reception room with ornaments provided by military families and embellished patriotic décor. Everyone is asked to be sure their son's or daughter's name is on an ornament hanging on the special tree. Then there are the themes of "Timeless Elegance", "The Glow of Christmas Past", and "Santa's Workshop". All the trees are colorful, beautifully trimmed, and spectacular! There is an ensemble playing various Christmas melodies next to a huge lit fireplace in a chamber room. The potpourri filtered through the rooms. The hors d'oeuvres spread was very impressive.

This is a once-and-done kind of thing. We both feel a little out of our element. It will be a very memorable event. Funny coming from a guy who insisted we go to every Army's Spring and Christmas Balls.

I contact Sofia Hammons to keep her updated and ask a few questions including asking for Meghan's stateside address. I feel good about the Christmas cards to family and friends being finished and now mailed, figuring where we will stop on our upcoming trip, the receiving of the CD from Ft. Belvoir, and Jacquard telling us they are at the redacting stage.

Embarrassed to bring this up to Sofia, Rich wants me to ask what happens to items such as videos and photos that were presented at trial. Rich would like copies of the video showing Ryan partaking in a drinking contest. Ryan and one or two others were standing with a drink in hand. There seems to be talk of Ryan and his favorite flaming drink and how fast he can gulp it down.

A letter comes from Liz Curtis, Parole Assistant from the Army regarding what the Army Clemency and Parole Board is all about. This is very explicit.

December 9, 2011
Dear Mrs. Schlack,

Your appearance before the Army Clemency and Parole Board Hearing (ACPB) regarding Mr. Barto Abadia is scheduled for March 1, 2012. The Board proceedings will take place at Crystal Mall 4, 1901 South Bell Street, Arlington, Virginia. The phone number is 987-654-3210. We are located directly across from the Crystal City Marriott Hotel and the Crystal City Metro Station. You will be required to check in prior to 8:15AM with a security guard (call the office number and someone will come to escort you). Please be sure to bring a picture form of identification and allow ample time to park. Additionally, we ask you that you confirm your attendance with us five days prior to board date.

The ACPB is an administrative board composed of five members, the Chairman and four active-duty field grade officers or career civilian service employees at or above civilian pay grade GS-13. It is important to note the ACPB is not a statutory board, cannot retry the case, and is not bound by rules of evidence. Witness statements may be sworn or unsworn. In addition to any information you may provide, the Board bases its decision on the seriousness of the offense, progress in confinement, prior military/civilian record, proposed parole plan and recommendations made by the staff and Commander of the military confinement facility and any other documentation that may be submitted to the Board, including victim impact statements.

Your comments should be designed to advise the Board of information that is not already contained in the documents at its disposal. Three witnesses are authorized to appear; however, one spokesperson should be designated to speak to the Board. In the interest *of fairness to all parties appearing before the Board, please limit your remarks to 10 minutes. The Board begins deliberations at 9:00AM and typically lasts three to four hours. The time of your appearance and the order of presentation, your wait may be lengthy and for that reason, we strongly discourage children from attending.*

Sincerely,
Liz Curtis
Parole Assistant
Army Clemency and Parole Board

Rich, Adam, and I go to Ryan's grave to put the Christmas wreath next to it. It is done so well; I don't think I'll ever find another like it.

In a text message I find out Owens, Anderson, Vans, and Jaks get the impression somewhere that Abadia is asking for a retrial. So, I send an email to whom I have email addresses for and cc Adam, Sofia and Meghan.

Date: December 16, 2011
To: Evan Anderson, Ethan Jaks, Greg Owens, Spencer Vans
From: Richard Schlack
Hello,

You guys have given me the opportunity to follow your lives on Facebook and, for that, I thank you. However, in the same breath, if you feel you need to detach yourselves from us, then no one will think less of you. I want very much for all of you to heal in your own way. I know I can say there isn't one of us who thought we knew what this was going to be like.

However, you feel, here is what I know. Read on if you wish.

There has been information going around among some of you about Abadia, and I can set the record straight. I received a letter from the Army Clemency and Parole Board on 9 December 2011. An Army Clemency and Parole Board regarding Abadia is scheduled for 1 March 2011 in Arlington, VA. ...

The email continues copying the description of what the Army Clemency and Parole Board is all about from Ms. Curtis's letter. I explain Rich, Adam, and I will be going, and we can speak for ten minutes.

Then my email continues:

I am again asking for all of you to consider writing a short paragraph if you can to describe what you have been through and/or what you have done that you may not have due to losing a friend, and/or what you still may be going through due to being a witness to Ryan's death and the incident itself. Greg, you had something on Facebook about you missing Ryan. I would like permission to use that in my statements, please.

I know what I am asking is hard to do. I know it hurts, and it's upsetting. But, Guys, I don't want that murderer out any earlier than his last possible day. I know you don't either. You and I know Abadia will try his best to con the board. At the trial, he tried to use blown-out-of-proportion defense and lies to get out of what he did. To me, one thing that the panel didn't hear or ignored was Abadia went back and got his gun. He wanted to hurt or kill somebody. No one can convince me otherwise. Rich, Adam, and I ran into the judge after the trial as we were walking to our cars. I could tell he was in disbelief over the verdict. Everyone seemed to be. A similar incident happened a year or so later at Hood and the killer got life.

As much as I want you to help out again, I will also respect you if you can't bring yourself to pen your lives to strangers. You probably figured out I will ask you each time a parole and clemency board comes up. We will not give up. We will fight for Ryan because he needs a voice to speak for him.

So, there it is. I thank you ever so much for your help if you decide to write a short paragraph. We have only ten minutes but I will use all I can to help this board realize, not only is Abadia up for murder, but threatening your lives, Evan and Ethan, and break a Ft. Hood law of carrying weapons on post. Is this less-than-the-20 he was handed, really all Ryan's life is worth?

I will email you all again to let you know what was decided. I won't be able to recall everything. One of you already asked me only to give the end result. Details are just too upsetting. I understand.

Thank you again for letting me know how things are going via Facebook. It really is comforting in a weird sort of way I cannot describe.

Terri Schlack

I know, I know, Mrs. Schlack to you.

I am thinking how Ryan's death has affected so many lives, just like the ripple effect. If Ryan's friends are still struggling with it, is Adam in a lot of pain yet? Does he talk to anyone about it? I hope so. He never has initiated with me although after the funeral, I have asked him how he is doing, and he knew why I was asking. I stopped asking because maybe not talking is better. I am rethinking that in light of what the guys on Facebook are saying.

March 1 – That is the next hurdle. How many more will we jump over?

CHAPTER 66

Yesterday we received part of the transcript of trial. Of course, I begin to read it. I also have been thinking about what I will say at the board hearing. Rich already says he would prefer if I did the speaking.

On a very chilly early morning, the alarm rings. Why the alarm is set, I don't know. I actually sleep fairly well with using the Breathe Right. This is Day 5 and the tape on the nose works a bit better.

My mind goes to what do I talk about at the meeting in Crystal City. I get out a notepad and at least start on it.

- Abadia's Military Occupational Specialty (MOS) was with a rear detachment, not on the front lines. Hmmm, PTSD from guarding the front gate. He had a partner with him. It is not his decision to fire a weapon at those moving toward the gate.
- His relatives all in New Mexico vs. our family scattered all over the Midwest and CA; Advantage to Ryan; he was welcome to stay anywhere.
- Speaking of relatives, on Christmases past, the house would be quiet while my husband and I enjoy the coffee. We knew Ryan and Adam and sometimes a girlfriend arriving would change all that, and what a welcome chaos. On holidays now, as hard as each of us tries, there is a somber feeling adrift and always, always the missing of Ryan.
- I used to bake favorite cookies and make Christmas candies and the boys might help. I don't anymore and hope my family understands.

- His mother on anti-depressants vs. my health issues including anxiety which caused physical problems such as eczema, loss of breath, fast heart rate, legs aching. I see some doctor at least once a month. Between December 2011 and January 2012, it is six times.
- His light sentence vs. Ryan's life sentence
- My constant, constant thoughts about my son's life having less value shown by the 20 years sentence; Try getting over that.
- Abadia and how he planned to avoid a stiff penalty. I have so many questions to which I know his lame answer is, "I don't know."
- Why did he try to figure another angle at the trial? PTSD and blackout of the evening's events, wanting to show the gun to his friends. Why then, knowing bringing a weapon on post is not tolerated?

An incident from the trial pops into my head. When CPT Earhart was talking straight to the panel, she held a picture of some of Ryan's friends with him just standing in a line ready for a picture to be taken. The photo was used because the prosecutor wanted the panel to imagine that where Ryan was shot in the hips would be in the vicinity of Greg's mid-back. Maybe I can use the idea of showing pictures somehow in my presentation.

A Christmas Day Brunch seems like a good idea today and afterward sit in the living room to watch "A Christmas Story", an annual tradition. Adam takes his own car as we pile into ours and drive to the cemetery to spend time with our son and brother. After that, Adam goes off to hang out with friends while Rich and I drive to Jim and Ellen's house and spend some time visiting.

I feel like I need to do more so at 2:30AM, I send an email to every brother, sister, niece, and nephew I can. I put a little cc in for Adam to ask that he share this with Ryan's Oshkosh friends from high school through present day. I ask Jerry, to please forward this to his daughter, Donna and her son, Gregory.

December 27, 2011
To: Family
From: Rich and Terri
Subject: Letting You Know
Dear Family,

Just when I think I have a grip on my life, something comes along to kick me in the teeth. Barto Abadia, Ryan's murderer, has asked to go in front of the Parole and Clemency Board. I guess he has a right to do that this early in his sentence. The Board date is set for March 1, 2011, near Arlington, Virginia, and the three of us are going. This is copied from the letter I received.:

The board is "not a statutory board,.." and I continue on with the copy from Ms. Curtis.

Next I write:

"The victim impact statements" are you.

I want to thank those who wrote letters for the trial. Now, I am asking again, and including all family members. Those who wrote before should not include anything you have written in your previous letter that was for the trial. The theme or topic is for you to describe how has your life been affected by Ryan's death during the past year, what you have seen or changes you have seen in you, your family, or our family due to Ryan's death, or how you are toward the Schlack Family.

I found out through copies of the trial and maybe I wasn't supposed to get this information is that 19 of Abadia's aunts, uncles, cousins, grandparents, you name it had written statements on his behalf. His whole relation must live in New Mexico where he's from.

Our families, on the other hand, are spread out, and the fact that Rich and I were gone from the area for so many years makes it tough. I will also ask Ryan's Oshkosh friends, army buddies, and anyone else I can think of to do the same.

Terri and Rich

Included in the email is the news of our receiving the copy of the trial, Rich's pursuit of Ryan's Soldier's Medal and the plan to put in front of congress members a need to regulate guidelines for a military panel.

We truly hope we are ready for the next year.

CHAPTER 67

2012

Thinking about my health, the upcoming January Snowbird Trip isn't a real concern. My lungs are great. Dr. Reiser gave me pills to control my heart rate (but the pills take care of the symptoms, not the cause), my PA checked my thyroid and arthritis so no real scare there. It is narrowed down to anxiety, so I get pills for that; the same kind I have taken before.

We decide to use smaller luggage pieces due to hauling and sometimes not needing everything. In our basement, we find the luggage pieces we think will work. We want to spend a few weeks out of the Wisconsin cold winter and have to consider the warmer winter the farther south we go.

"We've been talking about where we want to go, but we should get some kind of plan to what the route will be to get there. Don't you think?" Rich asks. "Let's get out the US map book and check it out." As we look at the maps, we know our Winter Get-A-Way is to the Southwest and a possible swing through Texas.

"Let's first plan a route to Tucson, Arizona," I suggest. "I know you want to see that huge airplane boneyard."

"Yeah, that's a good start. I am sure it's called Pima Air and Space Museum," Rich says enthusiastically. "My thought is to head south and get out of the cold as soon as we can."

"That sounds fine," I agree. "I just hope we don't have to leave in the snow."

"Let's do this. If it is snowing on the day we plan to leave, then we will wait for a day. It isn't like we are on a schedule."

"Good idea," I say. "Okay, back to the route. It makes sense to go through New Mexico and on to Texas to visit your niece in Amarillo and then head to the Fort Hood area. Would you mind if we drop in at Sofia's house?"

"I don't mind but wait before you call her because I am not sure on what dates we'll be in the area," Rich says firmly.

We planned the route and estimate the time we will spend in each place. We pack very carefully, mindful of the difference in temperatures. Of course, I have more bags than Rich does.

We leave on a snowy day but it's not a heavy snow nor windy. I have my books to read while Rich prefers to drive most of the day. Rich is more himself when we get away from home and maybe changes me some, too. With the sleeping issues I have, usually an hour after I am in the car, I sleep for an hour or two. Then, in the early afternoon, another short nap. As a result, I can't fall asleep when I go to bed.

Sometimes I try very hard to stay awake. But then, I am still up all hours of the night. How weird is that! How do I control something like this? It isn't like I haven't tried any suggestion offered to me.

Rich was looking forward to touring the airplane site near Tucson, Arizona. We walk through the huge museum, but my legs begin to ache so badly I can't walk without pain. I am also sick with flu-like symptoms when we are at the High Sierra in Ruidoso, New Mexico, so I am in bed for two days. We leave for Amarillo, Texas, to visit with Rich's niece and her family. Our next stop is Copperas Cove and Killeen, Texas, which is near Fort Hood. We are very comfortable around this area, so we look around the towns. We even meet up with Ryan's friend, Ethan Jaks and his family for dinner. Jaks confides to me that when he thinks of that night, his whole rest of the day is shot. I can understand that because many of my days are shot. We also get with Greg Owens for dinner. Our conversations are about what is going on in their lives and the Hearing in Crystal City.

Rich and I make a point of visiting Sofia and her husband in Harker Heights. I grew to be very fond of her and this is something I want to do. We talk about lots of things kind of skirting around the trial itself, but certainly catch up on Meghan.

Sofia tells me about Meghan's mishap. Apparently, Meghan was carrying too much gear coming off the back of a military transport plane. They landed at Al Asad Air Base in Iraq on the way home to Fort Hood, and she badly sprained her ankle when she tripped over the lip of the ramp onto the tarmac. What a way to start a new job at a new place!

It is time to move on and secretly hope we can visit again. We stop in Branson, Missouri, to window shop, but my legs give out, so we head for home.

I hit the ground running because two days after we get home, the American Veterans Organization (AMVETS) is having a dartball tournament in the new museum building, and I have to run the PX Gift Shop for two days. Prior to leaving for the winter getaway, I packed all the merchandise away, including new signs and a couple of new items that arrived before I left. My thinking is that it will be kept clean and the signs fresh. Due to being a one-man operation, I arrange the merchandise as best I can, and add whatever cutesy stuff to draw attention. Also, I am curious about what is happening on the committees I am on, so emails and phone calls are a priority on the To-Do List.

> Date: February 26, 2012
> To: Meghan Earhart
> From: Terri Schlack
> Subject: Checkin' In
> Hello Meghan,
> If it's all the same to you, I believe we can be on a first name basis except when you're at work.
> We did receive your email dated 1/25/12. Thank you for replying. When we were in Texas in February, we did visit Sofia and her husband.

They seem to be doing well. You were right about the Department 56 villages she has collected. Amazing! And yes, I am a bit envious however do not have the room to display them all year 'round like Sofia.

We are now home from our winter vacation and are focusing on the Board Hearing we are invited to attend in Crystal City, Virginia, and getting ready to depart. I guess I am nervous about this Clemency and Parole Board Hearing which is on March 1. How can someone be prepared to defend a position when one doesn't know what the position of Abadia is? However, Sofia did say Abadia might be asking to be moved to a federal prison so he can be closer to home. We never thought of that angle. This is another new world.

What are your thoughts? I will bring the recent letters some of the families have written and put it in a binder like I did for the trial. I will include Greg Owens's letter that we had in the original book of letters for the trial but was taken out. Remember? Do they receive copies of all photos and letters we had at the trial? I have kept a journal as Sofia suggested and will bring a copy along. Sofie didn't know it, but I find journaling comforting somehow. It is typed and I will make copies of all I take.

We will have the computer along, so feel free to answer if you ever get to this. I know you are busy. I just need reassurance. Hope you are fully recovered from your little incident coming off the plane in Kuwait.

Take care,
Terri and Rich

CHAPTER 68

Adam, Rich and I leave on February 28 about 8:00AM for Arlington, Virginia. We plan to take two days travel time then do the presentation on the 1st. Adam sits upfront with Rich to talk while I sleep or read in the back seat. Staying on the interstates, we save time and head directly to Crystal City.

It is clear the three of us are nervous about the unknown. We talk about what we are expecting during this presentation in front of the Clemency and Parole Board. The major question is what will Abadia ask for after only such a short time in prison? Will they tell us? How many are on this Board? How long will this take; all morning? Will there be questions from the Board? Can we ask questions? What is the background of these people on the Board? Can we know what their recommendation is for Abadia? Does any other committee have to take a look at the data? At this point, we are only guessing the answers.

Our first night is spent in Strongsville, Ohio. Sometimes our GPS would not work, so Adam gets out his phone and navigates. Doing 510 miles today, we will do 400 miles tomorrow to end up in Georgetown.

About 4:00PM we arrive at the Holiday Inn in Georgetown which is your average-Joe's hotel, so the inside is nothing out of the ordinary, but it is orderly and clean which is important to us. After finding our rooms and hanging up our clothes, we are anxious to take a look where 1901 S. Bell Street is located in Crystal City so we know what we will be facing in the morning. No one wanted any surprises. It's early evening, so we have plenty of time before it gets dark.

Old 2-3 story buildings surround us as we are walking along the streets busy with cars. The fumes of the cars' exhausts linger in the air. That could be why there aren't many people on the sidewalk. There is a bit of trash about, but the perception is it is an older part of town.

As the three of us are walking to the multi-level building, I complain to Rich, "This is odd, but my feet and legs are getting so sore. Slow down and let me hold your arm as we walk."

"Okay, Old Lady, I'll take your arm. Let me know if I go too fast," Rich jokes. We hike to the Bell Street address, but it takes us longer because it isn't the couple of blocks we are led to believe and my legs are getting more sore by the minute.

The three of us continue down the blocks in the shade of the buildings until, at the end, it opens up onto a complex of two very similar tall buildings lit with the brightness of the sun. Each building seems to be spread out more than those we walked past, so the difference is noticeable. We mosey into the interior of the light concrete-block building with a lot of glass panes on the right. With all the glitz, it sort of reminds me of the entry to a bank or small lobby of a fancy hotel, minus any furniture. In the middle of the room is the elevator shaft which has the entry on the opposite side. The thing about it is there is nothing, absolutely nothing except a phone and this elevator shaft. I imagine I could almost expect to hear an echo if a word is said. The room dimensions are probably 60' by 60' with the walls covered with shiny gold square metal panels. Above the wall-mounted phone there is a letter encased in a plastic frame directing to call a certain number and someone will be down to escort you. We step out and over to the nearby building, but there is nothing to see. There is no place to go but back to the hotel.

The trip back for me is more painful and slower as I try very hard to keep up, but I am gritting my teeth and holding onto Rich's arm so tight, he must be having a tough time walking and dragging me along. Adam excuses himself to say he really needs to get back to the room and starts jogging to the hotel.

There are no words to describe the shooting pain in my feet and legs. I make Rich stop every five minutes or so. Tears well up in my eyes as we slowly shuffle to the hotel elevators.

"Rich," I say as I rub my legs, "I am hoping we find another way to get there. There is no way I can walk back that far if my legs and feet feel this bad tomorrow. We may need to find a wheelchair."

"Let me see what I can find out," Rich replies.

While I rest on the bed, Rich goes back downstairs and talks to the desk clerk. The clerk happily states, "It so happens a hotel shuttle runs right to a Metro Stop and you only need to walk a block."

I can only hope this pain goes away before morning. To help make my legs feel better, I take as many acetaminophens as I can, but before I call it a day, one more thing needs to be done.

Adam comes to our room later. I read Rich and Adam the draft of what I thought I would say. Together, we fine-tune it. We will be as ready for that 9:00AM meeting as we can be. We treat ourselves to snacks and call it a night.

"Oh, my god, Rich!" I exclaim. "It's unbelievable that my legs and feet are not nearly as sore as last night. This takes a little pressure off." How amazing, and I am so grateful.

"That's good, Terri," he responds as he gathers the items we need for the meeting. Getting on the Metro, we enjoy the little ride. Heading straight to the building we visited last evening, we enter and I head to the phone and reread the posting. While on the phone, the response is simple. Someone will come for us soon. While waiting, we point out and discuss certain interesting things about the structure such as the box-like room we are in, the shiny gold-colored panels all the way to the top, and the starkness of the room in which we are standing.

About ten minutes later, a well-dressed middle-aged woman dressed in blue who is not in a uniform walks toward us. She introduces herself then takes us up the elevator. Stepping off the elevator, a table is immediately to our left and each of us shows an ID, gets a body scan, signs in, and receives a badge that reads "VISITOR- ESCORT

REQUIRED" with our name on it. We are escorted to a point and get handed off to another woman.

This neatly dressed woman in a gray suit takes us to a huge conference room maybe 40 feet in length with a long beautiful inlaid table with chairs all around stretching right down the middle. Huge television sets are hung all around; I have never seen such huge sets not even in stores. My guess is the televisions are 100-inches or more in diameter. The conference table can easily handle thirty people, so we feel like we are in the wrong room. We are asked if we'd like water or coffee, but decline.

A third woman, in her early 50s, comes in and sits across from us. She introduces herself as Liz Curtis and says that she will walk us through what to expect. It is a very thorough briefing, and she answers all questions that we ask. As Ms. Curtis is saying she'll be back to get us, I mention I need to use the restroom.

Ms. Curtis sends in a woman to escort me to the ladies' room. We walk about twenty feet to the restroom. On the way there, I am thinking I can't take care of my business if she is coming into the restroom with me. I just can't.

"Did you have a good trip here?" she asks to fill the quiet.

"Oh, yes, we took two days so as not to be in a rush," I reply. Thankfully, she waits outside in the hall and now I am thinking this better be worth it.

I am then led to a room where the panel will sit on one long courtroom-like desk which is elevated and located in the front of the room. There are five chairs and a computer at each station that is receded into the table. Rich and Adam are already seated. Rich and I sit at a table for two. Adam sits behind us along the wall, which is really a step or two behind us. At a table to the left of us sits Ms. Curtis.

Trying to appear calm while I am shaking inside, I remind myself to read slowly and clearly. I miss the names of the panel members but did catch that the first man is a lawyer, the next three are colonels and finally the chairman whose credentials are impressive. Each of them say they had read my journal and express condolences.

"Welcome, Mr. and Mrs. Schlack and Adam," the chairman begins. "Sorry to meet you under such circumstances. We understand it is difficult to be here and want you to know we are very appreciative. Let me tell you a bit about myself. I was a warden at Leavenworth and did this type of job with the Navy/Marines." He goes on talking, but I lose track of his accomplishments. I pick up on a change in tempo and hear him say, "You will be videotaped, and anything given to the panel today will be sent on to Leavenworth. It will be up to them to agree with today's decision or not."

I am sworn in because I will be speaking. The first thing I do is hold up an 8X10 picture of Ryan in uniform and say, "I want you to meet Ryan." For the first half of my speech, I hold up the picture as I talk to them.

Then, at a critical point, I switch to an 8X10 picture of Ryan's gravestone. I was vaguely aware Rich was sniffling. Adam is sitting behind us and grabs a Kleenex from the table in which Rich and I are sitting.

CHAPTER 69

CLEMENCY AND PAROLE BOARD - 2012
By Terri Schlack, Mother of Ryan Schlack

Three soldiers in uniform came to our door one Saturday afternoon. Looking for Ryan, maybe? But then I saw my husband's face turn pale when he opened the door. I knew what one chaplain and two soldiers meant. Our lives are forever changed.

Adam was not home when the soldiers arrive and had to be called. He wanted to know why. I couldn't tell him this news of his only brother over the phone. During the two-hour drive home, he knew it was about Ryan and thought about all the ways Ryan could have gotten hurt. When he arrived home, I asked him to sit down, and Adam knew when I asked him to sit; he knew it was going to be bad. After quite some time, Adam went to look at the family portrait taken in 2005 hanging above the fireplace. He stared at it a long time, thinking now and forever, it will be just the three of us.

Contacting family, funeral arrangements, headstone design, and waiting for the latest news on when Ryan's body will arrive via airplane and picking him up with the hearse are what is dealt with. The casual assistant officer meetings, forms to fill out, questions to answer, and problems to solve need to be dealt with. Then the day of the funeral itself. You think, okay, I can pull myself together. We as a family can help each other through this day.

You think things would wind down, but the casualty officer still has things he says needed taking care of and this stretched out for a month. One thing to deal with is Ryan's personal belongings and what to do with his beloved red Mustang convertible. I cried then when I would see one on the road and now his car is home. My husband and I decided to sell it, but not to anyone in the area.

There was so much that belonged to Ryan that things were placed in the basement and sat there for a few months until we knew we had to do something with it. Slowly, we dealt with his things, but it was hard to part with because it was just another confirmation that Ryan wouldn't be returning.

Meanwhile, I couldn't find the excitement in teaching anymore. It was difficult to get up to go and put on a happy face for those 4th graders. I had been teaching for 35 years. A lot of time was spent thinking of Richard and Adam. Because Rich was retired, he was home alone. He felt an all-consuming emptiness and there was nothing to ease his pain.

Ryan's bedroom is still full of items, but of a different sort. There is a wooden chest to hold his uniform, medals, all the letters and emails he sent to us, pictures of him, and an album of cards and letters sent to us when Ryan died. Then there are some of his artworks we had framed because they were so good, and the Schlack crest on a huge shield with an accompanying sword that Ryan was so proud to come home with and present to us as a Christmas gift.

There are firsts of everything that have to do with family. Since we were a military family, you simply depend on each other more. Everything we did, we made memories and didn't take time together for granted. The first year after Ryan's death, holidays were spent reminiscing Labor Day parades and picnics, Halloween when Ryan really created some interesting creatures, Thanksgiving, Christmas Day which was always just the 4-of-us kind of day. After a couple of days, my side of the family would go "tree-hopping", which means going to all my siblings' houses for food and exchanging gifts. Rich's side does the same thing, and these are all-day events. Then there's the 4th of July, followed by Ryan's birthday on July 12. You think you can manage now, but then the trial transcripts arrive and the notification of a Parole and Clemency Board hearing. Life is forever changed.

There is no way to describe how life changes when your oldest son dies. Oh, not by his own doing, but by a fellow soldier who shot him. Actually, Barto Abadia's target seemed to be another soldier whom he recently had a quarrel with. Ryan just happened to push Owens out of the way and took the 45 caliber into one hip and it then lodged into the other hip. The damage done was too much for anyone to save Ryan's life.

As I write this, I think of all the advantages given to Barto Abadia and then think about Ryan.

Abadia's relatives knew him since childhood vs. Ryan's relatives not knowing him during his younger years.

Barto Abadia has lots of relatives living around him in New Mexico. The Schlack family was away from relatives due to Rich's career in the army. Ryan's father and a couple of uncles were military career men.

My side of the family's jobs took them to California, Texas, Michigan and throughout the Midwest, so interacting with relatives was difficult. When Rich retired from the army in 1990, we wanted our two boys to experience the traditions of our families, so we moved to Wisconsin, where many of our relatives live today. When Ryan went into the army, he began spending time with family members in Texas when time permitted.

Now, our families will not get to know Ryan. Now, those family get-togethers, as hard as we all try, carry a somber feeling in the air and the ever-present thought that Ryan is missing.

Barto Abadia's relatives can jump in a vehicle to see their son vs. my family jumping into a vehicle to, oh, Ryan isn't here on earth anymore.

Abadia's family can share thoughts and feelings with him vs. there is no sharing with Ryan anymore.

Abadia's family can use phrases such as "in the future" or "next year" when referring to Barto vs. Ryan's what?

Abadia's family can see Barto's face, touch him, hug him vs. the Schlack family having to see a cold, granite gravestone.

Abadia's conviction of three major crimes and given only a twenty-year sentence vs. Ryan's sentence.

A constant, constant thought of mine is about my son's life having less value; It is difficult to accept. Let me explain. Abadia's 20 years vs. SPC Jared Lee Bottorff who killed a man after a party at his house and received a life sentence. Abadia's 20 years vs. PVT Donnie K. Stevens who stabbed a man at a party soon after an altercation and received a life sentence and dishonorable discharge.

I have so many questions. Abadia played a non-combat role in his duties in Iraq and was not in the front lines. Why play the PTSD card? Why did he knowingly bring a loaded gun onto the post? He said he wanted to show it to his friends, but there are rules. Good soldiers obey the rules set by the military. He must know how aggressive he gets when drinking because people don't want him around when he drinks.

And the one that tears at my heart. The one I can't get out of my thoughts—Why did he decide to go back to the car for his gun? Why did he decide to go back to the car and get the damn gun? This nagging question in which only he knows the answer.

In my opinion, after the altercation with Owens, he wanted to settle it in a way that gave him the upper hand. Owens was the target, but Ryan pushed Owens out of the way because friends cover each other's backs.

So let's think about this. Bringing a gun on post, threatening another soldier, and killing my son - A bad conduct discharge? This is incomprehensible. In the Soldier's Code it says something like "I will treat others with dignity and respect and expect others to do the same."

In the Army Values the definition of loyalty is "Bear true faith and allegiance to the US Constitution, the Army, your unit and other soldiers." AND OTHER SOLDIERS.

"Respect: Treat people as they should be treated". A person begins to wonder if some of these phrases might be words to spout off when requested.

Honor: Live up to all the Army Values.

Thank you for your time.

I also give them copies of letters of "victim impact statements" from Jerry, Shirley, Mary & Gib, Michelle, Greg Owens and from Ethan Jaks. The panel each expresses sympathy. A couple make comments.

"What happens next is we will meet and make a decision and then hand off the videotape we are currently recording and all documents you have given us to Leavenworth. They will come to a decision and then you will be notified," explains the colonel.

"We appreciate you coming to Washington to share your impact statements. Thank you for your time. I hope you will heal from this tragedy at some point," adds another panel member.

Then we are escorted out. As we leave, we are told we should hear from Mr. Holland in a few weeks. That is it. Fifteen, twenty minutes tops.

Adam describes the event as something very serious and a very important thing to do. He admits he was anxious but not overly so.

Prior to going to the meeting, we were not sure how long this whole thing would take, consequently now we have the rest of the day, so we visit the Pentagon, the Holocaust Museum, the Post Office Tower, the Reflecting Pool, and the Capitol.

CHAPTER 70

The weather is dreary as we head for home. I reread the copies of the Victim Impact Statements for this hearing.

Jerry Huber, Ryan Schlack's Uncle:
It was not that the jury gave Barto Abadia such a light sentence, which they did, but it is that I do not get an answer to the question I ask others, particularly veterans. My question is, how do we win wars with an army that has so little respect for itself as to not give Barto Abadia a dishonorable discharge?

Shirley Moore, Ryan Schlack's Aunt:
I am writing this on behalf of Ryan Schlack, my nephew, whose life was taken at the hands of Barto Abadia on July 18, 2009.
Ryan was a healthy young man of integrity and held great promise for an outstanding future. He faithfully served two tours in Iraq before his life was suddenly snuffed out by a fellow comrade only weeks before he was to be released from the military. Mr. Abadia gave no thought to the repercussions of his actions. He only sought to satisfy his own anger in a violent manner that affected hundreds of other lives.
Ryan has not only left a lifeless hole in the hearts of his immediate family, but his extended family and friends as well. Family gatherings and holidays are not the same without him. No one can fill the void of another person. Unless one experiences first-hand the pain of losing a

loved one, words are not adequate to express how it grips at our very soul. It is like cutting out a part of our innermost gut.

The joy and life that Ryan brought to all of us will never, ever be experienced again. There is no price that one can put on a life that was cut short so abruptly and was not given the opportunity to live out the future he had for himself.

I see the pain and suffering that Ryan's parents and sibling are going through. This pain will forever be with them. They cannot ever look forward to his return home. They cannot share in his life's dreams. Imagine not being able to talk to your own child again. Or ever hear his voice again. Unlike Mr. Abadia, Ryan is gone from this earth, never to experience life again.

I think about what my sister and husband have been through. Writing this took a lot of courage. Shirley and Dick are no strangers to this pain due to losing a son to melanoma. Their son also left a young wife with three babies behind.

Gib and Mary Huber, Ryan Schlack's Uncle and Aunt:

"Forever" certainly doesn't appear to be forever when it comes to the sentencing and prison term of Barto Abadia who so carelessly murdered our nephew, Ryan Schlack, in the summer of 2009. We have been informed that Mr. Abadia is eligible to appear before the Parole and Clemency Board on March 1, 2010. Not even two years after taking Ryan's life, Mr. Abadia could possibly be back to his own life. That's a travesty! Mr. Abadia is a convicted criminal. According to the dictionary, clemency means "mercy, leniency, forgiveness, compassion", etc. Mr. Abadia took Ryan's life without mercy, without compassion. It is difficult to understand how the Board could consider clemency for Mr. Abadia when there is no future at all for Ryan.

We are forever denied the opportunity to have Ryan be part of our lives. Every holiday, every birthday, every family event is different without Ryan's presence. We will never know who Ryan would have been as he aged and matured. We are denied knowing him, his wife, his children. His parents, our sister and brother-in-law, will never know *what contribution Ryan might have made to society. They are denied hearing the voices of any grandchildren Ryan might have produced. They are forever denied hearing Ryan say "I love you" or say to Ryan, "I love you".*

If awarded clemency, Mr. Abadia can go right back to his extended family-his parents, grandparents, uncles, aunts, cousins, brothers, sisters. Our extended family is forever changed. We look for Ryan at family gatherings, and he is not there. We look for him at holidays and he is not there. There is no going back for the Schlack family who went from a family of four to three. Ryan's brother, Adam lost his best friend. He lost his brother and there will never be another brother in his life. No one will ever fix that. We lost our nephew, a kind considerate young man who obviously would have and did anything he could for other people.

Releasing Mr. Abadia from the full length of his sentence is unfair to Ryan's memory and the selfless act that he performed in saving the life of a fellow soldier.

There are no questions about Mr. Abadia's conviction and the critical evidence that was presented during his prosecution. We request that you deny clemency to Barto Abadia and keep him interned until the full completion of his sentence.

Gib and Mary have two sons in the Air Force, both pilots, and they must feel anxious, just as we did with Ryan, when they are out of the country. I am sure they are counting the days when each has finished his career in the service. I wonder if Ryan's death gets them to think differently or are more fearful for their sons. To me, there has been a sort of special connection between Gib and Mary's family and us because of our children serving this country.

Michelle, Ryan's Cousin:
Ryan has been gone for over two years now. For myself, I had limited interaction with Ryan for much of his life because he lived a great distance from me.

However, it was actually the last two years of his life that we developed a friendship via the Internet while he was serving his second tour in Iraq. It was during this time he had come to make some very important decisions about the direction of his life. He had come to the crossroads of his goals and dreams, and he met the challenge by making decisions and plans for the path he was going to take.

One of my favorite memories of Ryan was that he and I conversed via Skype/email on how to best meet single women on the Internet. He was taking assertive steps as he started to settle down in his life. And as he proceeded forward with his new laid plans, suddenly all of it was stolen away in one abrupt, terrible moment in time.

As he started to head towards his new life goals, I could see the confidence and drive rise up in him. And I think now, "What would Ryan's life look like now?" He had begun plans for a career and a family. Ryan was such a caring and gentle man. He was the kind of guy that was never the center of attention. In fact, he could easily hide at family events because of his quiet demeanor.

However, it is this gentle and quiet spirit, and his humble persona that made him such a giant of a man. Certainly, this was exemplified in his death as he fearlessly attempted to break up an argument and laid down his life to do it. The fact that his life was taken by Barto Abadia, a fellow serviceman, only magnifies this senseless tragedy. Ultimately Ryan's very life was robbed, but with the loss of Ryan's life were the loss of future career, his future as a father and grandfather, and the loss of presence and influence in his family, in his friendships and in his community.

At Christmas, I was able to spend some time together with Ryan's family including my Aunt Terri, my Uncle Rich and my cousin, Adam. You could see how difficult it was for them to try to celebrate this holiday, this holiday among so many, without Ryan being part of it with us. They work so hard to "keep it together", but managing the deep pain and loss with which they must constantly contend is very difficult for them to handle continually. The negative effects of Ryan's untimely and harrowing death have taken a toll on their physical health, in their occupations, in their social lives, and in their emotional state. Ryan's family is notably very close. They have a deep love and respect for one another. And they are left to struggle with Ryan's murder, and to try to enjoy one another again, to laugh with each other again, and to be the family they once were. But yet they are only left with memories and insatiable aching. Ryan is deeply missed. We not only miss this man, but also all the potential and stolen opportunities for his life.

Evan Anderson, Ryan's Friend:

I still feel some guilt for the events that took place that night. Had I not thrown a party, had everyone not been drinking? Why didn't I die? Abadia put the gun to my head. Why didn't he pull the trigger? Why was I allowed to live? I can't say that the events that took place have caused me to act differently or do things differently. However, I can say that I can't see a red Mustang without catching my breath. It can be weeks or days that I go without thinking of that night, and without fail, every time a Mustang convertible shows up, everything comes back. The musicians or comedians that Ryan and I used to go see don't seem as enjoyable anymore. I feel awful that I have yet to visit his grave. I do hope that one day I will have the opportunity to come visit. I do hope we can all get together during a visit to Texas next year. As I said before, I would like to know the outcome of this hearing, not the intricate details, even if I ask. I get too worked up, and I let it consume me. I agree Abadia should not receive anything less than what his sentence permits. Personally, I think he should have received the death penalty, but I guess that wasn't an option. I heard all kinds of stories about how Abadia cried and sought the presence of his religious figure. I thought that he might have some remorse. It is apparent that he has none, that he cares nothing of the life he took, and the ones he impacted. At the beginning of his article 32 hearing, his family approached me and told me how sorry they were that all of this had happened. A week later, I learned that they had also paid for the assistance of an outside attorney. That lets me know that they were not sorry that their son took a life, but they were sorry that he got in trouble.

In a separate note not given to the Board, Evan writes:

I hope that everyone is able to have a good Christmas this year. I hope this letter helps things somewhat. I will always be around if any of you need anything. Rich, I know at some point you were asking if I had any copies of videos or anymore pictures. Unfortunately, the hard drive that everything was stored on went out over the summer and I lost everything. I'm sorry. Terri, in your letter you mentioned comments that were left on Ryan's Facebook page. I don't know if it helps, but his page is still up and can see all the comments that we've left. If you do a screen shot, you should be able to print all of it out.

I think about the panel and wonder if what I said makes a difference. The chairman asks for a copy of my speech, and I hand him the copy from which I read. I can't find a word to describe what I am feeling. I believe I am coming to terms with Ryan's death. In the poem "Grief" by Flowers, the words "Absorption, Adjustment, Acceptance" are stages. I think I am past absorption, although with parole boards being maybe a yearly thing, I may fall back into that. Adjustment may be the phase I am in.

We stop in Perrysburg, Ohio, for the night and the next day the sun is shining. Adam has just finished reading the Hunger Games and hands it to me.

CHAPTER 71

I go to the library a lot, reading through one book after another. I love the Oshkosh library. I'm reading "No Second Chance" by Harlan Coben, and come across something that reveals grief in its true form.

> "What gets me-what gives me that surprise wham-is the way grief seems to relish in catching you unawares. Grief, when spotted, can be, if not handled, somewhat manipulated, finessed, concealed. But grief likes to hide behind bushes. It enjoys leaping out of nowhere, startling you, mocking you, stripping away your pretense of normalcy. Grief lulls you to sleep, thus making that blindside hit all the more jarring." (Page 70)
>
> "Like grief, hope hides and pounces and taunts and never leaves. I am not sure which of the two is the crueler mistress." (Page 71)

Grief was like that for the first year. I can't say it doesn't happen anymore, just not as much. The hope, well, my hope is that Abadia will spend every one of the 20 years with no privileges. I know three years have already been cut, but I still hope he does not get his way.

We have not heard from Mr. Holland, so we decide to contact him. This is what Mr. Holland relays to us. "Abadia asked for ten years to be cut from his sentence. He was denied."

I wonder if Abadia's strategy is to ask for the same thing each year until they are tired of it and say yes. I am shocked when I hear what he asks for. The nerve; the balls of that guy! I emailed Owens and Anderson. Their sentiments are like mine. Everyone we tell, and there are many who keep us in their prayers, is also caught in disbelief.

Now maybe I can relax–until next year. Relax is not the word; maybe better wording is not ponder and worry over it so much. But about a year from now, this may occur again. The fact Abadia can do this every year, and we do it all again and again. It grinds on a person.

Family and friends have been asking about the Parole and Clemency Board. When I tell them Abadia asked for ten years off his sentence, I was not surprised at the number of people replying, "He has no remorse." Or "It shows he has no remorse and feels he is not responsible." These comments support our feelings about it. At least it is a logical reason because I cannot come up with a reason why he would ask for ten years off his sentence. Desperation?

In early spring, Rich asks, "I need for you to do something for me, Terri. Can you go through the trial transcripts and gather evidence and copies of letters to support getting Ryan the Soldier's Medal? It has to refer specifically to Ryan pushing Greg out of the way of the bullet. I think I heard it said at some point in the trial but can't recall who or when."

"Okay," I slowly agree. "This will take a long time although I don't have to read every page. The testimonies to look for are from any of the guys who were at the party."

"There has to be two people who have stated this incident," Rich adds. I don't know what he can do but go to the congressman, but maybe he has another way in mind.

Meanwhile, I hope to find how to get ahold of an investigative reporter of a high caliber to research and make known that the military justice system has no guidelines. I need to do that, or I will always wonder, for future similar incidences.

It is the end of May. It is 12:45AM and what am I doing? I am lying in bed and begin to weep. This is now the second night although last night I had cried a lot harder and longer.

I have not finished reading the record of trial but have a strong feeling I have found all the evidence I am going to regarding the facts. I give what I found to Rich.

I explain, "Only Owens heard Ryan say something and pushed him. Vans never stated on record that he heard Ryan speak to Owens. I hope this is good enough to get a reaction from whomever deals with this."

Next year's Parole and Clemency Board weighs on my mind. What am I going to say? I do think some people have accepted Ryan's death. It is hard to ask anyone else to write a statement about how Ryan's death is affecting his or her life. I just need to make the panel see although twenty years is the sentence, Abadia has to serve all twenty and not get out doing only ten or twelve years. I can't do anything about that now but will fight to keep Abadia in the whole twenty if I can because others who kill a fellow soldier on post get life.

What would Ryan be doing now? Would he be in school yet or finishing his courses for computers or electronics? If he went to a technical school, he'd be graduating this year. Would he be dating? After talking to Michelle, I think he was ready to settle. By his myspace and OKCupid pages, he wasn't bashful to say he was looking, but I have no doubt, when confronted, he would be shy.

I still write his birthday on the calendar. I don't know if I'll ever not do that. I have one son now and will try harder to make sure he feels important to me–because he is. I couldn't live if something happened to him, too. I just couldn't bear it. Why am I thinking in this direction?

This is what I put on Facebook on July 18, 2012:

> It is now three years. Tears still come often when I think about Ryan. Not every day, but most days. There are days that sometimes go into weeks when I am feeling his absence more than usual. Ryan's memory never completely leaves, nor will it, I believe. I know I wouldn't want it to.

> Life is forever changed. The family dynamics have changed. My youngest son is now the only son. Adam says not to worry about him, but how can I not? The future has been changed. Don't ever say to someone to "get on with life" or "it is time to put it behind you". The future Rich and I anticipated is no more. I am still working on accepting this change.

I bought an album by Nickelback some time back because it was on Ryan's myspace and it was a favorite group of his among many. I like some of their stuff, too.

Thank you to whomever put the geraniums by his gravestone. When I visit, I water it with a gallon of water and there are still blossoms on it. Tough flower. There can never be enough times to say "I Love You". It's just great to hear.

My journal entries are becoming less and less. From June into July, I was experiencing "the blues". I cannot say anything different about that.

There's way too much time thinking about the next parole hearing. What will I say? What would be different? Two points I need to remember–Abadia's asking for ten years off his sentence seems he isn't remorseful or sees he did anything wrong. The family dynamics have changed in that Adam is the one to take on all that comes with parents getting older and no one who has been there from the start and will be there with him through it all.

Autumn in Wisconsin still has very warm weather on most days. In September there is definitely a change, sometimes gradually, sometimes with such force. This time of year is my favorite and has always made me happy. I love everything about autumn. But who am I kidding? The Zoloft just isn't doing its job. There are many days of moping around. The anxiety attacks are frequent lately. I can understand how people can go mad trying to still the emotion. Maybe it is what causes some to become alcoholics. I have entertained the idea of having a bottle of something handy to help keep the edge off.

Rich has been purchasing things on the internet; something he never does. I ask him about it. "I am making a display, well, more like the Battlefield Cross or sometimes it's called the Soldier's Cross," he explains. "You've seen it a lot of times. It's the rifle up on its end with a helmet on top and boots straddling the rifle."

"Oh, yeah, I know what you are talking about," I say. "I hope the gun isn't real."

Rich laughingly says, "No. It's a fake gun with bayonet I ordered online. I am going to use Ryan's boots and helmet. Then I'm making or buying a case for all his medals."

"Sounds very nice, but where will you put it, or how will you use it?" I ask.

"I haven't thought of many places, but remember we heard about some Memory Walk in early October? It's for anyone who would like to display something in memory of a soldier who died."

"At least you have a couple months to work on this," I state.

In the mail today, we receive a notice from the Victim/Witness Assistance Coordinator, Ronny Holland. It is not a notice for the next Clemency and Parole Board meeting, though. It's too early to get that yet. Rich, Adam, and I have talked about attending the Board every year. Adam, of course, may not be able to go every time due to his job.

This time I read the "Victim/Witness Notification of Inmate Status" more closely. On the notification, it states in "Section II–Inmate Status":

#5 Minimum Release Date: 2026/01/19
#6 Maximum Release Date: 2029/07/17

My heart takes a giant leap and my hopes shoot through the roof. I jump up off the chair and run to find Rich shouting, "Look at this! Look at this! Am I reading this right? Is this really going to happen? Why is Abadia going to the Parole and Clemency Board if he can't get out until 2026?"

"Terri, I already told you Abadia may only do ten or twelve years," Rich calmly explains.

"I really didn't notice it on the previous forms. I should look at the first-year form we got." Hope that I am right is building in me.

"Rich, look at this. The form goes on to say Abadia will go in front of a Service Clemency and Parole Board for restoration and clemency on Nov. 20, 2012. We just went in March. Did they change it? I know he can go only once a year!" I state firmly. "This is something that needs to be clarified for us."

On Memorial Day this year, Rich is ready for his "Ryan Display" to be set up in the veterans' area of the cemetery. Included with the Soldier's Cross is a large photo of Ryan and a Ryan's medal shadowbox. Rich goes early to set up his display; a display that he will set up every year next to Ryan's gravestone. We both sit under a tree close to the gravestone. Many people walk up to it and stop to look.

CHAPTER 72

"You know we still haven't done anything with the Tree and Shrubbery Shop gift card we received from my brothers and sister," I say cautiously, in case the idea isn't something he'll want to do.

"Yeah, I know. But we sometimes talk about moving to a smaller place like a condo, so I don't have to do yardwork," Rich responds. "I'm not sure yet what to do with the gift card from the nursery."

"Well, I've been thinking about that on and off. I think I have a solution. Not now, but when we are sure the Military Veterans Museum will make a go of it and it is certain where the addition will eventually go, we could donate the tree or trees to the museum. We can give the trees in memory of Ryan. Maybe get a little sign stating that. There's not one tree in the front area and it has no greenery like plants or shrubs. And it sure would be a permanent place. What do you think?" I ask becoming more confident.

There was a pause for a moment. "Hmmm, I could go along with that idea. It will give us time to think more about this idea or come up with something better," Rich remarks.

I see the doctor and am going to ask about increasing my Zoloft. I am not happy. Is it because the weather is getting colder, and winter is coming? It's early October, though. Thinking about Ryan brings instant tears. I thought I was getting better control, but now I doubt that. I can't stand to be like this. It's like in the beginning when I refused to go to the doctor about depression. After about six months, I couldn't stand the daily constant miserable feeling.

I tell my doctor of my slipping into a funk which started around June, four months ago. She upped my Zoloft. I hope it helps. I hate the whole miserable feeling. The crying has got to stop. I also had higher numbers on my triglycerides and cholesterol, so I am back on meds for that. I figured that would happen, but just didn't give a damn about anything.

Today is the Memorial Walk at Menominee Park in Oshkosh. The Rachel Bosveld Memorial Walk offers to have parents of fallen soldiers set up displays or memorials along the path. Rich brought the Soldier's Cross. The dog tags were made on the museum's machine. It will be very sharp to have the Soldier's Cross, the flag/medals display case, dog tags and an enlarged photo of Ryan.

There are several displays to honor local fallen soldiers. How creative some are. I am proud of what Rich arranged. I learn today that the Walk is to raise money for a Memorial for Wisconsin Female Soldiers who died in war. Rachel's mother, whom I met at Ryan's funeral, has a couple of events planned, so I wish her luck in her endeavors.

Last night I woke up every hour on the hour. I took sleeping pills for the last month and they work most nights. I try sleeping without, but I guess I need to shop for something to take again.

Happy Birthday, Marines! Happy Veterans Day tomorrow! Rich and I attend a variety of presentations over the course of the week entitled "Eyewitnesses, Combatants and America's Newest Veterans: the Iraq War in Retrospect" at the University of Wisconsin-Oshkosh. I am hoping it will be worthwhile.

On Wednesday was a film and talkback about female soldiers in Iraq. The film was called "Lioness". On Thursday was a film "Valley of Elah" and a short discussion. I couldn't help but shed tears due to the depiction of a retired Sergeant Major's son who returned from a war only to be brutally killed. That hit too close to home.

The professor who appears to be in charge saunters over to us after the film and asks what brought us to these events since he'd seen us the previous night. I end up telling him about Ryan. I think I manage that quite well. Only in the beginning were tears which I somewhat control, but I do not break down.

Today is a daylong of different programs relating to those in the military. As we get into the car to head to the university, Rich hands me a couple pages of something and says, "Here." He had run off Owen's letter.

I look at him, confused, and ask, "What do you want me to do with this?"

"I don't know, but I can't read it."

"Should I read it? And to whom?"

"I don't know."

That little conversation scared me. What is he thinking?

Wayne Midlands, the Patriot Guard Commander of this area, came up to me at the introduction session and says he stops at my son's grave for a short while most every time he is in town. Another person affected by Ryan's death. On top of that, I never knew the man until Ryan's funeral.

Rich and I go to one program with five professors each speaking about things to consider about this war. Its focus is on the "Politics of War and America's Grand Strategy in Iraq".

The next 90 minutes we are listening to four officers answering questions from the moderator and is called "The Shifting Strategies and Roles of the US Military in Iraq."

Over lunch we listen to Dexter Filkins who is a reporter for The New Yorker and did other articles for NY Times, Washington Post and Time magazine. He was in Iraq and Afghanistan four times. His presentation is mostly of photos taken there and talks about his experiences as a reporter with a photographer.

The afternoon begins with "The Soldiers' Experiences of War" which has eight veterans talk about going into service, preparing their families for their tours to Iraq, how they are treated, how they feel now that they are back, and most of them still do what they call weird things for safety such as checking the tops of buildings for snipers, never driving over an item in the road, and not feeling settled-in yet.

The afternoon ends with "Hidden Injuries: The Iraq War's Impact on Military Spouses and Families". One Gold Star Spouse, one each of a father and a mother who lost a child, and one who had a twin son terribly injured in Iraq. It makes me wonder if I can tell our story and not break down.

Back home, I happen to look on the Facebook and see an entry from Greg Owens. I can tell he is lost or searching for something. Ryan's death is still heavy on his mind. He has said on Facebook that he plans to go to school (not to be a teacher like he once told me) but something else, although he never says.

Then I wonder about Adam and Rich. How is Adam doing? He never says anything even though I used to ask him. I wonder if Rich is healing. He recently bought a jacket and had embroidered "In Memory of SGT Ryan R. Schlack, July 12, 1979–July 18. 2009" on it. It also has the "Soldier's Cross". Maybe this is Rich's way of handling it.

Rich and I have occasional dinners with Adam. Every time we do get-togethers for dinners at the house or a restaurant, I feel a void. I feel we are such a small family now. Something is missing or incomplete. I know the answer. Will that feeling continue to be so powerful? Rich and I accepted being empty nesters long ago, but this feeling is different. Not a good kind of different.

We put Ryan's Christmas wreath by his gravesite in early December. On Christmas Day, we visit Ryan for a while and check over his stone to see that it is clean and no debris on it. We keep the tradition of watching a Christmas video, "A Christmas Story" while snacking on Christmas goodies.

CHAPTER 73

2013

On New Year's Day, Rich and I go to his sister Ellen's house.

Her daughter Jodi asks, "How is Ryan doing?"

She didn't realize what she said until I said, "Well, Adam is doing very well and has lost 80 pounds."

As soon as I say "Adam", she has a look of horror on her face and apologizes again and again. I tell her it's okay. Some people call Ryan by Adam's name and vice versa. I used to; more than I care to admit. I have not made that mistake since Ryan is gone.

Rich's arthritis is too painful in the cold Wisconsin weather. In January, he says he would like to go to the southern states for a few weeks. So, we planned a route, and in a week, we leave.

We look over the house one more time to be sure it is set for our being gone a long time and put luggage in our Hybrid Fusion. Visiting friends and stopping at the well-known and not-so-well-known sites, we head toward the North Carolina coast then into Florida. Next, we make our way to Georgia and home again. You can bet every military base and military museum site was on our radar.

We return from our winter trip in late February because the Parole and Clemency Board is coming up, and I still have to write something to say in front of the board. I ask Adam to do the same since he wouldn't be able to go. We arrange to fly this time and schedule it with plans to arrive late Wednesday and leave DC around 1:00PM on Thursday. Tight, but I think it could work.

I will not ask Ryan's friends or our family members to write anything. I know how they feel. During the holidays when we are with our siblings, we know there is a feeling of Ryan not here with us. I wonder if by being among them, the three of us make the family feel uncomfortable. Maybe not the right word. I don't belabor the thought, but it crosses my mind.

The morning of the day we are to leave, I get a text saying the flight from Detroit to Washington, DC, is cancelled due to snowstorms.

Ms. Curtis calls. "Hello, Mrs. Schlack. Well, I don't know about there, but we are having a bad snowstorm."

"Same here, Ms. Curtis," I reply. "In fact, I just got a text saying the flight from Detroit to Washington is cancelled. What is done in such a situation?"

Ms. Curtis answers, "We can reschedule or we can do a conference call if that's easier."

We will have to do a conference call because I have a knee replacement happening on March 11."

And that's how it is done. I read my statement and Adam's statement. Gee, Adam has quite a flare for writing. I am always impressed with his vocabulary both verbal and written.

FOR THE CLEMENCY AND PAROLE BOARD
March 7, 2013
By Terri Schlack

I was reading "no second chance" by Harlan Coben and came across a paragraph that truly sums up our sorrow.

"What gets me-what gives me that surprise wham-is the way grief seems to relish in catching you unawares. Grief, when spotted, can be - if not handled - somewhat manipulated, finessed, concealed. But Grief likes to hide behind bushes. It enjoys leaping out of nowhere, startling you, mocking you, stripping away your pretense of normalcy. Grief lulls you to sleep, thus making that blindside hit all the more jarring."

One year ago, I sat in front of a Clemency and Parole Board for the first time. In that speech, I described what our lives were like, beginning with the painful news of Ryan's death and what Barto Abadia's relatives' lives are like versus our lives. I spoke of how I struggle with the thought that two other convicted soldiers got life and Abadia got 20 years as well as only a "Bad Conduct" discharge. I still shake my head in disgust knowing there aren't guidelines for panels to follow in guilty trials.

I am sure it isn't in the minutes, but one panel member fell asleep for quite a long time on the last day. Talk about an insult! We feel if the judge had sentenced Abadia, Abadia would have gotten life and a Dishonorable Discharge. The panel did not have the background in law to know what a crime like this should warrant. We have a difficult time understanding how the panel concluded this murderous crime was not premeditated. The panel could not even anticipate what Abadia is thinking? I do not buy that.

In the Soldiers' Code, "I will treat others with dignity and respect and expect others to do the same." Does that apply to those who died for this country?

One year ago, I did bring in letters from relatives about how Ryan's death and the manner in which he died impacted them. I didn't this time because I can feel the sorrow in the room when our families gather. Coming into a room would be Rich, Adam, and me, and then the realization shows in their faces that Ryan isn't following behind. I believe with every get-together, there will always be a feeling that Ryan is not with us.

As for Ryan's army friends- Greg Owens, Spencer Vans, Evan Anderson, Ethan Jaks-Facebook is our way to keep in touch. At one point I asked Greg's mother (Greg is the one the bullet was meant for) if I should continue this contact with him or does this upset him. She emphasized to me how Greg needs contact and thought it was one way of keeping him in check. But there are times of depression that come through so clearly in Greg's Facebook comments. I believe he is trying, though, to move on as relayed in this email. This is an entry of Greg's:

"At times I think my life is a painting with dark colors of black, gray and all brownish tones. Then I think of great friends… and my wonderful family back home in Minnesota. That dark, lonely painting becomes a colorful masterpiece with all the bright colors that heaven will allow."

From time to time, I wonder how Spencer is really doing. Spencer was such an emotional wreck at the trial. He did get help for his depression and when I read his Facebook entries, his comments were more optimistic as time went on. But I haven't heard from him in about six months. Last I heard he's getting married, so maybe contact with us via Facebook was too much for him and he broke the ties.

Evan and Ethan have families now and it seems they are doing okay. Not one of them re-enlisted in the army. My take on it is they experienced enough with two or three deployments and the final straw was what happened to our son, Ryan. Ryan was to be the first of his group of friends to get out. Ryan had two months to go.

All of those guys know we talked with a Clemency and Parole Board last year. Owens and Jaks shared with me what they thought would happen at this board. I had to correct the hearsay. They all stated they did not want to know details, just the outcome because of how angry it makes them feel and it is difficult for them to get beyond that anger.

In 2012, when I did let Ryan's friends know that Abadia was asking for ten years off his sentence, comments were:

"He doesn't get it. He doesn't seem to think he's done anything wrong."

"He sure doesn't sound like he is remorseful. He's just thinking of himself."

On rare occasions, I allow myself to ponder what Ryan would be doing now. Shortly before he came home on block leave, he told his cousin he planned to go to technical school and learn more about computers. I wondered if he'd miss his battle buddies and re-enlist.

I miss Ryan because we would have finally had a good, solid mom/son relationship. I was so much looking forward to Ryan being home that September. During his teen years, he thought I was unfair and hard on him. When he was home in 2009, we had such a good talk. His whole demeanor toward me changed. This was confirmed to me when, on the day he was going back to Ft. Hood, he hugged and kissed me goodbye. He threw his last bag in the car and turned, looked at me, then walked back to where I was standing and kissed me again. Never, ever before had he done that. I can't tell you how I treasure that moment and how I ache for him to be with us.

It is painfully obvious that when Adam comes over for dinner, there is the fourth spot that is empty at the table. We don't talk about it, but I sense that Rich and Adam are feeling the way I do. We are not complete. It is definitely not like when Ryan was in Iraq or couldn't be home for the holidays because we would have talked to him or Skyped.

Why do I still write his birthday on the calendar? There is really no sensible reason, but I don't care. Maybe, deep in my heart, it is a way to remember him in yet another way. He was born in July and died in July. July is a tough month for this family.

When Adam turned 30 years old and 8 days (the same age as Ryan was when he died) Adam made a comment that he wondered if it was fate that this day was also Veterans Day. I am sure he thought a lot about the day he equaled Ryan's age and what it would be like. I just think that he would.

Thinking about this last year, I had bouts of sleeplessness. I'd finally decided I couldn't beat it by myself, so started using sleeping pills. I still do. I have had to increase my anti-depression meds as much as I hate the thought of that. But I have frequent episodes of anxiety attacks. I can understand how people can go mad trying to still this emotion by themselves. On top of that, I now have developed eczema. These quarter-sized or larger spots are extremely itchy and seem to be increasing in number. Funny thing is, it increased in December and in June. Is it because of the Clemency and Parole Meetings or anticipating the month of Ryan's death? Thankfully, I did notice a couple kind of fade away but never disappear completely.

Rich put together the symbolic gun, helmet and boots. Along with other families of fallen soldiers, we display it at Rachel Bosveld's Memorial Walk. Also displayed are Ryan's medals in a shadow box. It is now standing in Rich's office, but I no longer just think of Ryan when I see it, but of all those who have served and died in this war.

I would like to finish with a poem in which I wholeheartedly can relate. I finish my speech with "Grief" by Gwen Flowers.

FOR THE CLEMENCY AND PAROLE BOARD
March 2013
By Adam Schlack

This past year something happened that part of me had feared for a few years now. It was a milestone that I cannot ever come back from. On November 11th, 2012, I became exactly 30 years and six days old, one day older than my big brother got to be. I had actually done the math a couple years in advance, and I knew it was coming. But, despite my objections, the day came and went. From now on, I know that I have breathed more breaths and seen more days than Ryan ever got to. The days themselves aren't what is important, but rather the opportunities that come with each of them. The number of breaths is inconsequential; it's about the experiences we have while breathing them.

Ryan was proud to be a soldier, but after serving his five years in the Army, he was obviously looking forward to getting out. He always enjoyed electronics, and he intended to expand his education in that direction. He talked to me about how he wanted to spend his free time in the years after his discharge hanging out with his friends and chasing girls. The latter of which he did with mixed success, but with a soldier's determination. He mentioned once or twice about opening some kind of electronics repair shop when he got older and his education was complete, but that was long term planning. I know he eventually wanted a wife. I can only assume he'd want kids of his own. But that's where his life was—assumptions about where it could have gone. I think about that a lot.

I think about what he would be doing now. We talked often about movies or video games that were going to come out in the next few years. I wish I could talk to him about them like we used to. Sometimes things will happen that bring back memories of our childhoods together that are so specific that only he and I could appreciate them. On rare occasions, I will find a video online or a funny cover version of a song and my first impulse will be that I have to show this to Ryan, but that goes away quickly because I know that I can't. I do often wonder what he would think of my physical transformation. He always made fun of me for being overweight. I knew he was doing it to encourage me to better myself. Now, I have. I've lost 80 pounds and I'm physically fit, but he doesn't get to see it.

Thirty years and six days was not enough time for Ryan to meet all the goals he had for himself. I don't think it's enough time for anyone to do all they want to do in this life. He spent 5 years in the Army and served two tours in Iraq, but his life was cut short by doing the bravest thing I can imagine. He put himself in harm's way for his friend. He died on the front lawn of his buddy's house less than a week after his birthday because he did everything right. On November 11th, 2012, I was forced to surpass Ryan's age. November 11, 2012, was last Veterans Day.

Now is the waiting. The wondering what Abadia asked for. I can't even think that the Board would allow his request. But we wait.

CHAPTER 74

With a chill still in the air, ready or not, knee replacement number one, here I come. I get prepped, am put under with anesthesia and wake up with my left knee all bandaged up. There's no lying around because as soon as I am able, the nurses make me move. I have issues with breathing, so I am to stay overnight just to be sure things are good to go. Recovery is determined by how my physical therapy goes.

After a week or so, my physical therapist says I am doing beautifully. This seems like the best news in years to me. Some good news for once.

I am at home convalescing and Adam calls me. He tells me to go on a certain social page and read what is there. It took me by surprise that after all this time something is on it. So, I write on it, too.

> AM – Hey remember when we all went to Austin and got wasted lol
>
> Greg Owens – I remember it like it was yesterday haha he was such a gentle giant…we sure did laugh.
>
> Terri Schlack – Thinking of you. Glad to see u will go to see someone about your depression. Here's something to think about:
>
> A psychologist walked around the room while teaching stress management to an audience. As she raised a glass of water, everyone expected they'd be asked the "half empty, half full"

question. Instead, with a smile on her face, she inquired, "How heavy is this glass of water?"

Answers called out ranged from 8 ounces to 20 ounces. She replied, "It doesn't matter. It depends upon how long I hold it. If I hold it for a minute, it's not a problem. If I hold it for an hour, I'll have an ache in my arms. If I hold it for a day, my arm will feel numb and paralyzed. In each case, the weight of the glass doesn't change, but the longer I hold it, the heavier it becomes." She continues, "The stresses and worries in life are like that glass of water. Think about them for a while and nothing happens. Think about them a bit longer and they begin to hurt. And if you think about them all day long, you will be paralyzed; incapable of doing anything."

It's important to remember to let go of your stresses. As early in the evening as you can, put all your burdens down. Don't carry them through the evening and into the night. Remember to put the glass down.

Greg, I don't know who wrote this or if they have ever experienced a death of someone that is special to them. This is not easy, but it needs to be done so we don't become paralyzed and affect everyone around us, because it will. I know it will take time.

Greg Owens – But Abadia ruined my life and I can't get it back.

Because I am concerned, I reach out to Owens's mother on email.

Hello Mrs. Owens, I see on FB that Greg is going through a rough time. He isn't home either. Is there a reason he's in Louisiana? I also am glad to see he is getting help. I think of him often. What are his future plans?

Mrs. Owens – He is staying with friends down there, Terri. He isn't doing good at all. I think he is down there because he feels more accepted there and doesn't have to worry about us knowing what he is doing. He did go through treatment when he returned from his second deployment, but I know he lied thru it. He has many issues, including his eating disorder, depression, and alcohol. He is supposed to be going through treatment at the VA down there, but so far he hasn't. If he doesn't, I will contact his doctors and tell them everything... I am worried about him and it is so hard to do anything from here but pray. Hope your recovery is going well.

It's 12:30AM and I can't sleep. So, what else is new? I am worrying about Greg. He is having such a hard time. The Facebook entries from him concern me. I reach out to his mother and she is at a loss as well. It isn't right that Owens burdens himself with things he cannot change. He says he's getting help for PTSD, but his mom says he isn't being open or always up front. In a way, I hope alcohol and not drugs are his temporary fix-it. Of course, I wish he'd cut out the drinking. I don't think he'll get into drugs. I think he is drifting and has no goals or focus. It has been 3 years, 8 months. I know Ryan's death has changed our lives. I hope that with Greg not being in the army surroundings, he could cope. Is it even okay to keep in touch with him? Maybe not. Maybe I am the one who has to let go of him.

It's early April and by now, we should have heard from Mr. Holland. On the 10th, Mr. Ronny Holland calls and leaves a message, so I call him back.

"Mr. Holland, this is Terri Schlack, and you left a message to call you. We hope the news is good," I begin. "Are you able to tell us what Abadia asked for and if it is denied or not?"

Mr. Holland replies, "Well, hello, Mrs. Schlack. As you know, this is not something I should be doing, but I can't imagine living through all the wondering each time. Abadia asked for three years off his sentence and to change his discharge from a Bad Conduct to a General Discharge. It was denied."

Exhaling my breath, I gratefully state, "Thank you so much for the call. It is another small victory." I feel relief that Abadia's request is denied. Now I do not have it eat at me for six months or so; then it will start again.

My sister-in-law once told me, "It would be great to have the old Terri back with us." Gee, and I think I am outwardly doing okay.

I want to get Sofia's thoughts on something we found out. The quickest way is to send an email, so I sit down and write one to her. After asking about her and her husband's health, I talk about our health. Health issues such as my knee surgeries on March 11 and April 29 and Rich's high blood pressure, heart fibrillation, high cholesterol, and his need for rotator cuff surgery. Getting older has its negative side. The future plans of going to Italy in August are also shared with her.

Then I tell her about Adam and his driving truck and being in a community play. He is really very good. A great thing is he lost 80 pounds. I tell Sofia he is my idol now. Finally, I get down to the reason I am writing. My email continues:

Anyway, there has been something on our minds for the last couple of weeks. We had heard in the news that a court of appeals increased the sentence on a terrorist (from seven to twenty years) and now Lynne Stewarts also had a change in her sentence meaning it was increased. We would like to talk to a military lawyer about the possibility of pursuing something like this in Abadia's case.

I then tell her about the yearly Clemency and Parole Board hearings and what Abadia has been asking for. Yes, Wisconsin has one base here, Fort McCoy, but we do not feel confident we will be taken seriously. We can find someone in Chicago's Naval Station Great Lakes, but we first want to see if we can get ahold of Meghan and /or MAJ Michaels since they were part of the trial. If that is not possible, then can she get us the names of some military lawyers who could find the time to actually find out if it is possible for us to go through a process with a court of appeals?

Telling her my sister and I will be in Texas in September or October is an afterthought. Winter weather is always interesting to those who have never lived in it, so I describe the snow and freezing April we are having.

Sofia writes back the same day. Topics include Bob's declining health, her fairly good health and the fact they are in the midst of retiring. Bob retired in October and she will on May 2. This takes me by surprise, but she explains she had a rough year and in January she got sick but still went back to work. She just couldn't finish the day and someone asked, "Well, who's going to do the work?" She actually said she decided right then and there that they could take her job and put it where the sun don't shine. You gotta love her! Traveling is also on her agenda and tells me of many places both in the US and outside of it that she and Bob have been.

She has not heard anything about these changes I tell her about, but she will get in touch with Meghan. She does not know where MAJ Michaels is. At the end, Sofia gives me her personal phone number, email address and Meghan's new email address.

Armed with Meghan's email address, I begin one to her. My email begins the usual "How are you doing?" questions and goes into what is going on with our family. I mention to her that Adam has lost 80 pounds and now wears contact lenses. He is looking more like Ryan. But the shocker was when he was in a community play. He turned sideways and my heart skipped a beat. The resemblance was uncanny. I pretty much copy and paste the whole part about what we are wondering about from Sofia's letter. One point that is added is that I read The Army Times, and I have found two cases that are similar to what happened to Ryan and have them to refer to if needed. This is something we will definitely pursue if we understand it correctly. Other news at the end that is added is what I know about Ryan's Army friends.

CHAPTER 75

4/16/2013. 1:58PM
To: Rich and Terri
From: Meghan
Hi Rich and Terri,

Please forgive me for the long absence. I think, in a way, I did not handle your son's death well at all–especially after the trial. A 20-year sentence seemed like such a slap in the face after such a heartless action. Drinking or not, the eyes of the law would view everyone equally, and when it comes to murder, that should mean life for a life taken.

I treasured every update you gave me about you and your family. My mom and I think of you so, so often. In fact, when I told her you wrote me over the weekend, she encouraged me to try to move forward by writing back -not that I thought you think any less of me for the sentence that was handed down by the panel, but because I feel so sad about Ryan. His picture is beside me every day in my office. I carry the "Fleet Feet" sports card in my running shoes when I go out on long runs. I got it in Appleton on West College Ave when Sofia and I visited you. I keep it with me on those runs and when I deploy because it reminds me that, no matter how tough things get, that night in July 2009 at Fort Hood, Texas, Ryan had it tougher. It is so strange–I never met him, yet he is with me every day. Literally. Every day. I have not stopped prosecuting cases since I became a prosecutor in 2009. I arrived at Fort Hood only three weeks before Ryan was murdered. So, your son has really impacted me every step of the way in my career as a prosecutor. His life and senseless death are the reasons I keep doing what I am doing.

Since I left Fort Hood in August 2011, I came to Germany to be the Special Victim Prosecutor (sexual assaults, homicide, child abuse cases) for the US Army Europe and Afghanistan/Kuwait. The cases are tough and tragic, but helping these families and victims keeps me going.

Thank you so much for asking about my mom.

Regarding the increase in sentence, I will look into it. I have never heard of it in a military court, though. Likewise, I will look into whether the state of Texas could prosecute him as well. Usually, states can prosecute even if the military has already prosecuted, but I would need to find out if that holds true with a conviction in military court. I will GLADLY look into both issues. I can also tell you that MAJ Michaels will be here with me in Germany in less than two months. What a small world! I haven't seen him since we flew together to Iraq in September 2010.

Thank you so much for writing. This was very therapeutic for me and so kind of you. I will send you some pictures in a follow-up email. I will look for you on Facebook too, so we can stay in touch personally more frequently. Please keep me posted on your trip to Italy. It is a hop-skip-and-a-jump from here ;)

Please give Adam my warmest regards– "Meet Me in St. Louis" is one of my favorite movies. I always love the song the father sings at the piano on Christmas Eve. It is called "You and I" and it makes me pine for the days when things seemed simpler and the world was not so full of rage, hate and crime.

Enough of that for now. I will do some research and get back to you. Much love to you both,

Meghan

My left knee has a scar, but I haven't been feeling any pain for quite a few weeks. I am amazed. The physical therapist warned me that no two knee surgeries are the same. Again, I get prepped, have the surgery, and wake up with my right knee all bandaged up. But something is different.

Joyce calls me to find out how I am doing. "I am disheartened, Joyce," I begin. "The physicians, again, keep me in the hospital an extra day. The results for oxygen level and CAT scan on my chest are good. It is the blood pressure that would jump around for an hour or so then settle in. I conclude it is anxiety because there is nothing physical once the blood pressure settles."

Joyce asks, "Could it be the anxiety is elevated due to the pain?"

"That would be my guess," I reply. "This ain't fun. I am homebound and can't do much of anything. I recently went to my first visit to the physical therapist. I am gritting my teeth, leaning on my walker, but couldn't stop the tears because of the pain. I do have a good therapist, I think. Oh, Darlene is so gentle with me. She told me she will handle me with kid gloves. She said it will heal but will just take longer. I so very much want to believe her."

The right knee surgery recovery is a lot more painful than the left knee. Tomorrow when I go for a checkup, I will ask to up my pain medication. The only relief is when I am laying down. If I lay for hours, then get up to walk with my walker, it is unbearable. I will need to experiment, I guess. I can't take this much longer. On top of this, my eczema is slowly getting worse.

On Fox News one May evening, someone was interviewing Chris Stevens's mother. Ambassador Stevens was one of four killed by terrorists in Benghazi. His mother was saying how she will no longer speak to or hear her son. That the government and Mrs. Clinton have taken that away from her. She continues to ask what if it was Mrs. Clinton's daughter in that situation? She kept talking, and I just break down. She won't look at Mother's Day the same way. The anger, the feeling of unfairness and why, why did this happen? My heart went out to her because I know what she'll have to go through.

I do have my embarrassing moments. We're at a gathering of motorcycle friends on a camping weekend in May. Rich and I take the car there for the day.

At one point, I find Jill and after small talk, I ask, "Could you do me a favor and ask your husband to please not call me at 6:00AM since I am not awake at that time?"

Jill replies, "Oh, yes, I tell him not to call people so early, but he's up at 5:00 in the morning and thinks everyone is up by 7:00."

"I don't sleep well some nights and tend to sleep late in the morning when I've had a sleepless night. Maybe it is because of my medications," I explain.

"What time do you think Dave could call or text you?"

"After 10:00AM might be okay."

She is surprised by my answer. Then my tears start to fall. I stay silent because she doesn't know how sometimes I can't get Ryan out of my mind and have a difficult time falling asleep.

Mark, who is standing near us, starts making funny remarks about his sleeping habits because he works nights. I know he knew I was crying. He's trying to help me pull it together.

Jill walks away, but I feel I need to explain my reaction. I don't like leaving things hanging, so I approach Jill and whisper in her ear, "It's sometimes Ryan."

She hugs me and whispers back, "I knew it the minute I saw you react. I guess men just don't think of that kind of thing. Don't feel bad. I'll talk to Dave."

"I don't want to hurt Dave's feelings, but I really do not have good sleeping habits. I try to regulate my sleep, but I just can't seem to get it in a good pattern."

This gets me to wonder if I am not normal. Should I, by now, be able to cope with Ryan's death? At least to stop crying so much? After all this time, should I talk to someone? I feel talking to my friends helps but come to think of it, I haven't talked to anyone about it for a long time. I tend to write. Should I see a professional? What would I say? A person cannot erase a loved one out of the mind. I can never forget Ryan. Through the tough times and easy times, Ryan was a part of our lives. As long as we fight for justice for Ryan, it will be painful. But this pain will not stop me. Ryan deserves to be treated like a human being whose life was cut short by a premeditated murder. Abadia was not aiming at Ryan, so premeditated was not on the table. I know Ryan was not the intended target. Ryan showed his courage. Twenty years minus those for one lame reason or another is not justice. It is not justice. I cannot change the sentence but will keep Abadia in prison as long as we can.

It's July 12. Ryan would be 34 years old. How old that sounds, but then I remember my mom saying the same thing when she'd ask me my age.

We all seem to be participating in life a little more. I don't think about Abadia as much if at all but do worry about Ryan's friends who keep me posted on Facebook. Greg Owens seems to be taking it hardest, but that doesn't surprise me. Owens has a lot on his plate. I see moments of healing from him, but not completely. It was a traumatic event.

CHAPTER 76

To our surprise, Adam checks out the army and the navy in June. Because he is 30 years old, not every military branch would take him. The idea of running around in a desert did not appeal to him. Adam thinks a ship would suit him better.

Sitting outside on a warm August day, I share with Joyce of Adam's decision to go into the Navy. "I have stupid thoughts running around in my head, Joyce. I want to have an open mind about it all." I have to pause to compose myself.

"Terri, this change in Adam's life may be what he needs. Joining the military is quite a step, and you know it won't be easy. Adam will have different experiences. Don't assume Adam will get into a similar situation as Ryan. He went into the Navy which, to me, is on board ships or in submarines, not a face-to-face combat. Just see what he chooses to do. Don't work yourself in a tizzy until you learn more about it."

"Adam already told me he will try not to get in a job that means shooting or being shot at. I am sure it is a different feeling when you are on a ship shooting miles away at a target not distinct or you have no close interaction. I don't want to discourage him by telling him my concerns. I want to be supportive. After all, he is getting out of his dead-end job and actually making a plausible career."

Adam scored very well on the Navy's exams, of course, so has a large selection of jobs (or ratings) he can choose from. I have read descriptions online of the two he says sound interesting to him. One rating he is considering is gathering intel to share with others, so correct decisions can be made on warships. Adam thinks he'll be in a cozy room not near any engagements. The other advanced electronic computer field seems like making sure the computer programs onboard a ship or submarine are updated. He will take out the unneeded programs and put in what is needed for the mission. That doesn't sound too scary.

I am throwing myself into volunteering at the Military Veterans Museum and Education Center (MVMEC). It does help me feel I am productive even though it is taking years to finish a small portion of the museum so we can finally open.

The Italian trip all began with a conversation last winter with friends from the Gold Wing group. On August 25, John, Kathy, Rich and I let the excursion begin. We fly from Green Bay to Chicago to Newark to Rome. The itinerary takes us site seeing in Rome, Lucca, an Excursion to Cinque Terre & Pisa, then Siena, San Gimignano, Verrazzano Castle, Florence, Verona, Venice Island, Assisi Orvieto and back to Rome. Busy, busy, busy! I have blisters on my feet and put on band aids every chance I get.

Six days into our ten-day trip, I find a note slipped under the door. I am thinking it is a bill slipped under the door by mistake. I see it's a telegram so I open it and stopped breathing. It is saying that Adam will ship out next week for boot camp and to call him. I want nothing but to be there for him and hated the thought of sending him off without us there. The parallels between Ryan going to boot camp and Adam now heading to boot camp pops into my head.

I immediately call our son once I figured how to get a connection overseas. "Adam? This is Mom. We got a telegram this morning about you going to boot camp earlier than originally scheduled. Is that true? What's going on?" I stammer.

"Yeah, it took me by surprise, too. I leave on Wednesday. Mom, I got the job I was hoping for! This makes me happy," he announces excitedly.

"What can we do to help? I mean, as much as I want to be there, we can't jump on a plane and fly home in time," I sigh.

"Right now, I am trying to sell my large household items. I'll probably leave what I can't get rid of. I've got to clean the apartment and clear it with the landlord, turn off cable and maybe utilities."

"Adam, listen. Leave the apartment cleanup and check out to us. I am assuming your landlord already knows." He confirms this.

"I am kind of excited, Mom. It will be different," Adam confides.

I can barely speak. "We will call in a couple of days when you have a better handle on what is going on. We are proud of you, Adam, and love you very much."

Later in the morning while on the tour bus, our tour guide asks me if I am alright, and this struck me as strange. Was she asking about my blisters, or did she find out about Adam from her agency? I am vague in my response trying to figure the next step.

While running around Florence, I have a moment with our tour guide.

After telling her about the telegram, I ask, "I need to talk to my son, but how do I make phone calls? I know I spent a lot of money on the few minutes I talked with him this morning."

Her eyes brighten and she responds, "Yes, there is a much better way. I can buy for you a phone card for twenty euros and the calls will be cheaper."

I give her the money and after about an hour she brings me a card and explains how to use it.

At breakfast the next day she asks, "Is it because of Iraq? Is Adam forced into the military?"

"No, no, not at all. He joined voluntarily," I reply. "He looked into other branches of service and the Navy appealed to him. He thought he would have a better future than what he is doing now which is driving large trucks for a trucking company. There's more advancement and better pay as time goes on."

We are now home, and Adam is gone. A couple of days later, Adam calls to request Ryan's proof of citizenship because Ryan was born in Germany. He said he can't talk now, so the conversation is very short.

We mail a copy off along with a death certificate. His being gone didn't sink in until we went to his apartment to clean it up.

Apparently, not high on his list was to clean his apartment at all. I gather his belongings in boxes. I haul his clothes and bedding home and tackle all of Adam's washable stuff. As soon as I bring the basket of dried clothes into the dining area, a strange, awful sensation hits me.

The day we were told of Ryan's death, I had been doing laundry and began folding things on the table. I never had folded clothes on the dining room table. This creepy feeling of doom was with me all day today as I fold Adam's belongings on the table. I keep telling myself how stupid the idea is. I can't believe it bothers me so much.

In the pile of mail the Post Office collected for us, we get a packet from The United States Amy Court of Criminal Appeals. A cover letter reads:

Dear Mr. and Mrs. Schlack:
The US Army Court of Appeals (ACCA) completed its appellate review and affirmed both the findings of guilty and the sentence approved by the convening authority (commanding general). A copy of ACCA's decision is enclosed. SPC Barto Abadia has 60 days from the date of receipt of ACCA's decision to appeal to the next higher court, the US Court of Appeals for the Armed Forces (CAAF). Unlike ACCA, CAAF does not grant an automatic review.

I will contact you only if CAAF grants a review. If CAAF denies his petition for review, the appellate process will be complete. Once the appellate process is complete, a final order will be issued, executing Bardo Abadia's bad conduct discharge from the Army.

There was also an enclosed packet from the US Army Court of Criminal Appeals dated August 22, 2013. It explains that the ACCA completed its appellate review and agrees with the sentencing. In the summary, the tragic events are relayed. He was charged with inter alia, premeditated murder of SPC Schlack under Article 118, UCMJ. I look up "inter alia" and it means "among other things".

The merits case is summarized, in other words, the defense's strategy to determine Abadia's state of mind. There are all the psychologists' and psychiatrists' statements included from the trial transcripts.

The Court of Appeals continued:

The malingering diagnosis was one of the primary bases of Dr. Barker's opinion that Abadia did not suffer from a severe disease or mental defect. At the outset of the testimony, the doctor explained, "malingering…is considered a core competency in forensic psychiatry", and that he has received training in the assessment and detection of malingering.

Defense counsel objected several times to Dr. Barker's testimony. The first objection occurred when Dr. Barker testified that he was "startled" when Abadia told him he regretted throwing out his gun.

Q: What was your reaction to Specialist Abadia saying this?
A: I was startled. I was honestly startled. Again, in my experience, when it comes to trying to detect whether someone is telling me the whole truth, no one's ever gonna come out and tell me, "Oh, I'm lying to you." No one ever says that. What you have to rely on when you're trying to detect whether someone is telling you the whole truth—
CDC: Objection—
A: …is one—
CDC: Objection, Your Honor.
MJ: What's the basis?
CDC: He's trying to act as a human lie detector.
MJ: Sustained.
Q: Doctor Barker, why don't you cast it in terms of malingering, the forensic term?

The next defense objection occurred when Dr. Barker described the testing of malingering memory he performed on Abadia and the resulting scores.

A summary follows. The prosecutor was asking what the scores indicated. Dr. Barker replied it is suggestive of malingering. This is where the defense objected again about the doctor being a human lie detector. The prosecutor rephrased and asked if the doctor meant that he was malingering on these tests in which Barker replied in the affirmative. The judge overruled.

"The third objection occurred as Barker discussed Abadia's performance on the Structured Inventory Malingered Symptology (SIMS) test, which is a validated test for malingering. Previously, Dr. Barker stressed that Abadia's SIMS score suggested of malingering but was not by any means definitive. However, the defense objected when Dr. Barker gave his conclusions based on the test results."

Q: So what did you conclude from this result?

A: Just that, again, it's just one more data point—when I'm trying to decide whether a particular defendant or accused is malingering their presentation. I'm looking for a convergence of data that are going to either come down on saying yes, the person is attempting to tell the truth, or no—

CDC: Objection, Your Honor—

A: —a person is not exactly saying the whole truth.

CDC: Objection. He has just stated exactly the basis for the earlier objection.

The judge sustained then turned to the panel members instructing them that only they can determine the credibility of any witness or any evidence. The judge continued that it is improper for another witness to give an opinion on what they believe is a lie or what they believe is truth. Disregard that testimony if they took it that way. The panel indicated that they will adhere to the judge's curative instruction.

The judge sustained the defense's objection when Dr. Barker testified "drinking voluntarily, you knowingly take upon yourself consequences."

The judge sustained the defense when Dr. Barker compared California's mental illness definition to the military's definition.

The defense counsel asked for a mistrial citing Dr. Barker's repeated "human lie detector" testimony and Military Rule of Evidence 403. Defense argued that a curative instruction could not cure the prejudice because of the doctor's three comments. The judge denied the mistrial.

Dr. Barker summed up the basis of his opinion that Abadia did appreciate the wrongfulness of his conduct at the time of the shooting. The prosecution asked on what he based his opinion and Dr. Barker replied by citing actions of Abadia such as picking up the weapon himself, leaves the scene, doesn't stay or call 911, doesn't attempt to assist his friend, and throwing the murder weapon out of the car at some point at some distance from the scene. In his opinion, these are the actions of a man attempting to evade justice. And again the defense objects and the judge sustained, but did instruct the panel to disregard Barker's last statement.

At the end of the trial, the panel found Abadia not guilty of premeditated murder, but guilty of a lesser-included offense of unpremeditated murder. There was a four-page written discussion which referenced various cases, but the Court of Appeals agreed with the findings.

CHAPTER 77

The Victim/Witness Notification of Inmate Status arrives in the mail. Abadia will go in front of the Board on November 19. That means we plan another trip to DC in March.

My oldest brother and sister are getting up in age and Shirley mentioned a few months ago she wants to go see Jerry, but her husband has no desire to go. I offhandedly say, "If you want to go, let's go. I'll take you."

"Really? Really, are you serious?" Shirley asks excitedly.

"Sure, why not?" I reply. So, we tentatively plan for October.

October arrives and on the first of October we head for Texas with a few stops planned as we go. Oh, there is a hitch. About two months ago, Jerry lets the family know he is collecting books to send to a new library built in Uganda where he knows the initiator of the idea. Trying to be helpful, I pick up boxes and boxes of books for elementary, high school and some college how-to books. The day before we leave, I am snuggly packing boxes of books and carefully packing books on the floor in the back, on the seats and the backend of my SUV. I need to save room for our luggage, so warn Shirley to pack carefully.

As we head to Texas, we research what monuments or sites we might want to see on the way. Shirley is excited to get there, so we make only a few stops, one being in Oklahoma City and two stops to visit friends of hers as well as her daughter Michelle and family.

We get a very warm welcome from Jerry and Rita and relax awhile to catch up on the latest news. At one point, Jerry suggests we get the luggage and whatever books I brought out of the SUV.

"Oh, my gosh," Jerry exclaims then whistles. "How many boxes have you got here?"

"Let's get them out of the car and count," I jokingly say.

It takes us several trips hauling book boxes from the car to the house. There are quite a few on the floor of the car and they are all fished out. We have a lovely and fun visit with Jerry and Rita. Our activities include going out to eat while watching the beautiful sunset, going to a comedy play, visiting Luckenbach and other historical cities and museums and browsing in a town with interesting shops.

Shirley and I have a safe trip back arriving home the third week in October.

For me, it's jumping in the car soon afterward for another road trip. Rich and I head to Great Lakes Naval Base near Chicago, Illinois, to see Adam graduate from Basic Training on November 1. Adam told us he will be in the group at the end coming into the gymnasium then to look for him at an end corner. Not difficult to spot him at all. Besides being the tallest, he looks so much like Ryan, it amazes me.

I wonder what Ryan would think about all this. He isn't here to witness this change of life for Adam. He won't be here to tease Adam or feel proud of his younger brother. It is hard again to think it is just the three of us. There is such a big hole in our lives.

If we don't get out of this seemingly endless war, I don't know if I could handle Adam in harm's way. I tell myself he'd be on a ship and not on the ground. I don't know much about his upcoming job to know where he'll be. It is the unknown that worries me. It may not be as I fear.

In no time at all, it's Thanksgiving. Adam calls to tell us he will be coming home on December 23 for Christmas. He plans to get a one-way ticket from Pensacola to Milwaukee. He plans to take his car back with him.

I decide we need to change Ryan's bedroom completely–take off the wallpaper, paint the walls, get Ryan's big chest the Army gave us out of there, and the window treatments. To begin this plan, I went in with a couple boxes and start emptying the dresser. That is harder than I thought. The high school yearbooks, the German leather shorts, and hat I had him wear for his two-year-old photo, the directions for cameras and game systems, papers, papers and more papers I guess I shoved out of my mind. I get emotional and have a "calm yourself" time. The anger returns, the hopelessness of it all. It just isn't fair is what I do know. I end up walking out of the room.

We are so naïve with the workings of parole hearings. There are two meetings of the Board after a certain number of years. We figure out after a year or two that the November one is where Abadia has his say. Then we have our chance usually in March. To whom do we send the Witness/Victim statements and my journal? I have only been sending it to the March Board. Does the November Board see the same material? Should I send the November Board a copy so it is more up to date?

Rich and I went to Ryan's grave and placed a Christmas wreath next to his stone. I feel such a weight. I miss his smile and how I was in awe of the man he had become. So very proud of him.

We are thrilled to have Adam home for Christmas. We do all the things he wants to do as a family like visit relatives, go to a movie or two, and shop, then in the evening, he goes off with friends.

On Christmas Day, as every year, we visit Ryan. I recall the first time we did this, and I couldn't get past why I was seeing my son's name on a gravestone. Of course, we haul out "A Christmas Story" and "National Lampoon's Christmas" and settle in for the evening.

CHAPTER 78

2014

For the third year in a row, we leave the snow in Wisconsin. I have to get a handle on the bronchitis and pink eye I am suffering with. We seem to both deal with one ailment or another lately.

Our first goal is Pensacola, Florida, to visit with Adam. Of course, time is spent at the Naval Aviation Museum which is quite an impressive place. Rich and I then travel straight to Washington, DC, to the Parole and Clemency Board scheduled this time for March 6.

This time, the Board hearing is in a different building than the past two years, but it is not difficult to find. Essentially, the three of us write something. I read Adam's and my contribution, and Rich reads his own.

PAROLE AND CLEMENCY BOARD
March 6, 2014
By Richard Schlack

I spent 1968 to 1972 in the Marine Corps. From 1970 to 1972, I was assigned as permanent personnel to the Marine Corps brig on Camp Lejeune, North Carolina. During that time, I saw men march off to their court marshals almost every day. When they returned, I found out what their sentences were. In many cases, they were given Bad Conduct Discharges for going AWOL over

30 days or possession of drugs. No one ever got a Bad Conduct Discharge for a guilty conviction of murder.

Abadia committed murder. The worst crime a person can commit. It was brought out at the trial that it would have been multiple murders if the gun had not jammed that night. Abadia's sentence was twenty years and a Bad Conduct Discharge. It should have been Life and a Dishonorable Discharge. The punishment should fit the crime.

In the past few years, Abadia has requested to have his sentence reduced by half and an upgrade of his discharge. These requests were denied. And, again, Abadia's request for clemency or parole should be denied.

PAROLE AND CLEMENCY BOARD
March 6, 2014
By Adam Schlack

Every once in a while, I'll hear a song or a joke and for just a split second I think, "I can't wait to share that with Ryan." References or reminders of things so specific to our shared experiences that I know only Ryan would be able to fully appreciate them. But the split second always passes, and I'm left with the thought, "No, I can't do that. Ryan is gone."

The thought is followed by me thinking about all he has missed in the almost five years since he was taken from us. Among his friends and family there have been marriages, divorces, career changes, and children born, one who was named in Ryan's honor.

Of all the things that have happened with the people he hung out with, we are forced to only speculate about what he would have done himself. Would he have a post-military career by now? Would he have a girlfriend or wife or a family of his own? I think sometimes about how all those possibilities are absent from the world all because of the impulsive decision of one man.

Barto Abadia's actions that night tore a hole in my life and the lives of Ryan's family and friends. Barto, the bully and killer, will someday be returned to his family, but Ryan, who did nothing wrong, will not. The sentence given, in my opinion, was too light for his crime. On top of that, his annual requests to lessen his time in prison shows me his total lack of remorse.

I know that the day is coming when I will be told that Abadia is being let out of prison. He will return home and hug his family. I can only hope that this day does not arrive for many, many years. All the celebrating and the "Welcome Homes" one day going on at the Abadia household, the hole Abadia made will still be there, and Ryan, my brother, will still be gone.

PAROLE AND CLEMENCY BOARD
March 6, 2014
By Terri Schlack

Children grow up so fast. You watch your child grow into little individuals with his or her own walk, talk, facial expressions and his or her ever-inquisitive mind. As your child grows older and matures, he or she makes decisions. Yes, you advise and suggest, but in the long run, you know it is time for your son or daughter to learn cause and effect. All the time, you are there to watch that life as years go by. You will always be a part of that life. At least, that is what I thought and was looking forward to.

But something happens that you cannot ever imagine and you cannot control, change or repair. This incident changes every aspect of your life and, consequently, the lives of family and friends. In the beginning, you feel emptiness that you can barely deal with. I am here to tell you a loss will never go away or get lost in memories. The feeling does, for lack of a better word, "lighten" but that is not consistent. It is helpful that friends and family can digest it better because in some ways, they help put my life back together.

It has now been 4 years and 8 months since Abadia murdered Ryan. We have worries we never dreamed we'd have or something happens that would never have occurred if Ryan didn't die. A few examples:

- How is Adam, now our only son, really handling his brother's death? Very, very rarely, he brings up things concerning Ryan, but not about how he is coping.
- Are Ryan's friends who were witnesses getting the help they need? Sometimes the Facebook comments concern me. One comment from

Greg Owens was, "Abadia ruined my life…" How can you not be concerned?

- Is it wrong of me to keep track of Ryan's friends on Facebook? Two have taken themselves off my Facebook this past year, but that doesn't stop me from wondering.
- There has been a divorce, and Owens is still stumbling through life and doesn't seem to know what to do with himself. However, two days ago, Owens's Facebook page's comment was encouraging.
- I'll have memories of Ryan and me singing together loudly in the car when I hear "Horse With No Name". Or the song "Gotta Be Somebody" by Nickleback. Ryan had this song playing on his social page, "MySpace". In fact, I recently was in a restroom freshening up when I realized that the Nickleback's song was playing throughout the restaurant. I went into a stall and cried.
- I can't look at a red Mustang convertible without thinking of Ryan's car that he treasured and had driven to the party that July night.
- For some reason, I feel awkward going to a family gathering; like there's a bit of a strain in the air. Nobody really wants that, but my family can't help that this is my life now.

Then unexplained things come about. You see, an hour or so before we received the news of Ryan's murder, I was folding clothes on the table. Now, I don't think I have ever done that since I tend to listen to news on the TV in the living room while doing my folding. It has taken me a long time- many months-and I still would hesitate at the table but couldn't bring myself to fold clothes on the table. I thought it might jinx Adam. How stupid! I know this is ridiculous and superstitious. I am an educated person. No matter. I don't fold clothes on the table.

With Adam joining the Navy in September, I admit that in the deep little recesses of my mind, I worry I will lose him. I know I shouldn't think that way. It's just as likely Adam will lose us. Then I cry over that because he will be alone to deal with it.

One day, Fox News was interviewing Ambassador Chris Steven's mother. She was saying how she no longer will speak to or hear her son. As she continued, I began to cry for her because I know she won't feel the same on Mother's Day or Christmas or all the other family gatherings.

When reading a book or watching a movie and there is a death, I find myself comparing the feeling the characters are describing to how I feel. I admit I read "The Army Times" to see if I can find similar incidences to Ryan's and their outcomes. It really weighs on my mind that Abadia received only 20 years and a Bad Conduct Discharge for three charges-bringing a weapon on post, threatening a soldier, and murdering my son. I look at 20 years and think, really? For 3 crimes? How did that panel add that up? No one explained it to us. No one ever will.

Yes, I think of Ryan a minimum of once a day. Yes, it cuts deeper at some times than others. I know my life has been forever changed and how I perceive things may not be the way others could understand. I know my husband's and my son's lives are changed forever, and I feel so helpless because I can't fix it or make it better. I accept my loss is not something that will go away. It will be with my husband, my son and myself forever.

We will continue to attend the Parole and Clemency Hearings as long as we can. I hope with all my heart that we meet yearly at least until the year 2029.

I am reading "The Death of Punishment: Searching for Justice Among the Worst of the Worst" by Robert Blecker. I thought of Abadia as I read this through the eyes of a convict.

> "… How [the criminal] thinks, what he feels as he kills, why he kills - a criminal's attitude and values determine his behavior. Beyond the intent to cause death or an extreme recklessness that makes him guilty of murder, the killer's thoughts and feelings, his motives for the killing dictate the punishment he deserves. Motive-what moves him to act- offers from intent. He may kill intentionally from a variety of motives - fear, anger, jealously, greed, pity, or even love. A killer's motive stems from his character, that cluster of attitudes that mostly persists through time and defines each of us as a unique individual. Is he selfish, cruel, cold, or cowardly?" (pgs. 33-34) "…attitude and values determine his behavior."

Children are taught values at home. Before going out into the work world, children have what values they would be taught embedded in their character. My point of view is that Abadia wanted to come out on top. The fight Owens and he had prior to Ryan getting to the house was not settled in his eyes. Someone separated Abadia and Owens, and I think Abadia was thinking how could he get back at Owens rather than trying to calm himself down. That was what the fight was about; not being a good battle buddy. As he walked to the car, Abadia had to be thinking how he was going to best Owens. The gun was in the car. The gun could certainly show Owens who won this argument.

Meanwhile, the building is running tests on the fire alarms and loud, irritating sounds interrupt. I have to stop reading my part three times. Things like that can do something to concentration.

At the end of our statements, the sole female on the board remarks, "I read your journal completely. It touched me deeply." She then began to shed some tears and wipe them away.

A second person stated, "I also read the whole thing. I learned some things you told about."

The chairman of the board who is the same one I was impressed with at the first Board hearing was still onboard. He remarks, "As much as we would like, we do not have the power to lengthen the sentencing."

Rich responds, "We know that. We just look to keep Abadia in prison and do all of his 20 years, if at all possible. We know there is the 'get out early for good behavior' and recommendations from the warden." But silently we are thinking, Abadia won't screw up. He knows how to play the game.

CHAPTER 79

Shortly after coming home, we go to Ryan's gravesite and take the Christmas wreath off. I'll wait until the spring weather is mostly over or by Memorial Day to put something out again.

I give Ron Holland until April, when I feel I need to call him to find out what the end decision was concerning Abadia.

"Oh, Mrs. Schlack, I apologize for not getting back to you. The thing is there have been cuts in staff and down-sizing. I cannot tell you what Abadia wanted, but if you would call in a few weeks, I should have the information."

I said I'd call in about a month. Rich recalls we could call the board in DC, but I really don't want to bother them. I also know Mr. Holland can tell me specifics as to what Abadia asked for. I don't know if the Board can or will. I am in favor of sticking with a sure thing.

On Easter morning, I am scratching my stomach and can't stand the pain. "Oh, Rich, I am plagued by the worst eczema I have ever had. Can you see it? It is now spots of itchiness on my sides and a few spots on my back. When I scratch it, it gets ten times worse. I think I have an inkling of how people with shingles must feel. It seems when I first get these red, itchy spots, they would fade away sometimes, but now, they don't. I swear a couple of spots got larger."

Rich examines my back. "I'll put some of that cream on the back ones. When did this round start?"

"I noticed it right after the Clemency and Parole Meeting. The tube of that Triamcinolone Acetonide Cream is on the bathroom counter."

"Do I rub on a lot of it or what?" Rich asks.

"I think it takes a bit more applications than usual. You can help put it on later today if it acts up," I express with a sigh as he smears it on me. Rich does not like having any cream or lotion on his hands, so having him rub some meds on me is very appreciated.

The museum opening has been giving me problems. I am seemingly spending my life there trying to get the gift shop up and running. I tell people I should bring a cot in and sleep overnight. Maybe too much pressure for me to handle. I know my anxiety is up. Do I need to rethink my involvement? Not take on so much. In the next instance, I know I do it in memory of Ryan. This is what I knew I wanted to do after Ryan died. I need to keep busy. I can't do the sitting in front of a TV or playing solitaire all day long like my husband tends to do.

This isn't healthy for Rich, I know, but he really needs to find something to do. For the first few years that we participated in the museum, he would help me. I really needed him with hauling the heavy stuff. Now that we no longer travel to places, he is not on board. I am hoping he will take an interest in photography again. Good thing he walks on the treadmill. A colleague long ago told me, don't let your husband have nothing to do or he'll die. That is what happened to her husband a few years after he retired from the service.

Rich is crabby and moody lately since we returned from DC. He has been getting very critical of the museum and sometimes on little picky things. I just want him to stop it. I try to remember he is doing so well on his diet, losing 35 pounds, and I'd be a bit cranky, too. But he's acting different. He was mad at me not too long ago and didn't talk to me for 3 or 4 days. I still don't know why. Good thing I didn't react or life would be hell. Is attending the Clemency & Parole Hearing more stressful or becoming more than he can handle? Something to think and worry about.

Mother's Day. What do I think about? One of the first things I usually think about is how the trial ran over Mother's Day. The panel heard closing arguments then they said we can finish on Monday. That's it. They could have deliberated Friday night or Saturday morning, but, no, they didn't want to do that. The panel made us wait over 2 days to finish the trial to find out what they would decide. Imagine spending Mother's Day in a hotel room. The anguish, the tension, the helplessness were all the three of us felt all weekend.

Rich's sister Ellen, her husband Jim, their daughter Jodi, and her two kids come to visit today. As we are talking in our living room, Jim gets up to look at Ryan's challenge coins that are encased in a glass container on display.

"Rich, what's all these medals here?" Jim asks curiously.

"They are called challenge coins, Jim," explains Rich. "When someone dies, each commander of a unit presents a coin that commemorates that commander's unit. In this case these coins were laid at the base of the Soldier's Cross the chapel had made in honor of Ryan as part of the services they held. You can get them for other reasons, too, like for a job well done or you buy them yourself as a momento. The ones you see can only be gotten by the commanders of the units."

"What's a Soldier's Cross?" Ellen asks.

Rich turns to her and says, "You've seen a rifle on its end with boots at the base and a helmet resting on the butt of the rifle, right? That's a Soldier's Cross, but there are other names for it." Ellen nods.

"I know the story of the challenge coins," I begin. "In World War I, a lieutenant who was from a wealthy family wanted his men to remember their time in the war and the comradery, so he had coins made up to hand out to each man in his unit. The pilots were sent out to do a mission and one pilot got shot down. He was surrounded by foreign soldiers and men with no uniforms who were aiming rifles at him and speaking to him in a strange language. Maybe they didn't know what country he was from. This might be the end for him.

"He began shouting, 'American! I am an American!'

"'Prove it! Prove it!' shouted the soldiers. Everything he brought along was destroyed in the plane crash. But suddenly he remembered his coin in a pocket. Slowly he pulls out the challenge coin and the French examine it then start to put down their rifles, slap him on the back and welcome him. The Frenchmen took him to their village, and they had wine to celebrate.

"After that, a custom was started. A soldier can challenge any other soldiers in a bar to get out a challenge coin. If a serviceman could not produce a coin, that serviceman had to buy all the others a drink. At least that's the story I read."

After more talking, we find out Jim and Ellen have never seen the taped Memorial Service done at Ft. Hood. I ask if they'd like to see it, and all said yes. I get it out, and yes, it brings tears.

Getting into the car to go to lunch with them, Rich says quietly, "It's hard to watch the tape."

It is June and I can wait no longer. I call the Clemency and Parole Board in Washington, DC, and talk to Ms. Curtis. When asked what Abadia asked for, she said all she can tell me is he was denied everything he requested. She did not tell me specifics.

Rich and I pack up and head straight to Pensacola for Adam's graduation from his school. The affair is short, even acknowledging parents who had served in the military by having them stand. There is a final resignation which is to refuse to even consider Adam will be harmed. It wouldn't be fair to him to know I am worried beyond the "normal" anxiety a mother feels. As time goes on and I get a better handle on what he does and where he is stationed, I will feel less stress.

Adam can leave Pensacola, Florida, now that he's finished CTM A School where he learned the basics of doing his job. He was there for seven months. Then he spends two weeks hanging out at home and having fun with friends.

All good things come to an end. Adam's car is packed up with his belongings, but we take his large TV in our car. In our caravan of two cars, we are driving into Burlington, Illinois and the rain is so heavy, we lose sight of Adam. Apparently, he turned off a wrong exit but calls us, and we eventually get together again. Yep, we get separated again, so we had to turn around and go east on Hwy 20. The drive went better from that point.

We stay for a short time. Once he is settled into his new home at Groton, Connecticut, we leave and are home by Friday the 13th of June.

The antidepressant meds are increased because I am feeling so down and having anxiety attacks too often. Now, I think it is helping. My goal is to get off these pills, but I hate feeling depressed and I hate the panic attacks.

Finally, out of patience, I call Mr. Holland again. This time he could give me the information that we desire. Yes, he had to find it and call me back, but he did call about five minutes later.

Mr. Holland relays to us, "Abadia asked for a three-year reduction in his sentence, and an administrative discharge in lieu of the bad conduct discharge–which means asking for a less than honorable discharge, and custody elevated to minimum security rather than a medium." Mr. Holland confirmed all were denied.

I try not to get all upset about what Abadia asks for. I really should not care what he asks for. The "denied" word is what I want to hear. At the same time, I know he is getting closer to his release, so I feel a heightened panic knowing that one of these years, he'll get what he wants. I don't want to dwell on that.

CHAPTER 80

July means Ryan's birthday. He would be 35 years old. We jump on our motorcycles, and with a group of friends, head to Minnesota. Operating a bike doesn't require a lot of physical movement. In other words, there is a lot of sitting which means half your brain is thinking while the other half watches the road and other drivers. Consequentially, though I try hard not to let it happen, tears build. It isn't as if anyone can notice with my helmet on and riding in a staggered formation. So, it lasts awhile, then I pull myself together.

At the end of the day, we are around a campfire and we celebrate two friends' birthdays with cake and ice cream. As I eat the cake, I think of Ryan.

Adam puts a Roman numeral "5" on Facebook. Nothing else. People know what that means. A few friends made comments:

"I'd like to think he's somewhere winning War Hammer games."

"My heart goes out to you and your parents today. Praying you'll find peace."

"It's hard to believe. Thinking of you and your awesome parents."

"Ahhh…Adam. I know it doesn't get any easier. I'm so sorry. Hugs to u, cousin."

One time Ryan, Rich, and I were having a conversation about people breaking laws and guilty verdicts and endless appeals. I clearly remember Ryan saying, "If there was absolutely no doubt a person committed a murder, that killer should be shot, too."

It surprised me because Ryan was such a gentle soul. I don't think if he was ever in a physical fight or provoked, he would be aggressive or verbal. That is why joining the Army was such a surprise–yet, what he chose was a non-combative job. Although because of not always having computers or high-tech equipment to repair, soldiers would be put on gate guard duty or some other behind-the-scenes position in Iraq.

About a month later, I visit Ryan's grave again. There are no leaves left on the few remaining real flowers which still have some blossoms. A little strange, I think. The plastic red flowers are fading and should be replaced.

An eerie sensation strikes me, my whole being. It could be an out-of-body experience; I am not sure. As I am looking at the gravestone with Ryan's name on it, this weird feeling strikes when I realize that my son's name is on this stone. It's almost like it is the first time I am seeing it. That I should be surprised or something. It lasts just a moment but throws me for a loop. It is beyond strange.

It occurs to me. Is this Ryan's soul? I have been thinking of this in the wrong way. Don't think about a buried son. The heart and soul of Ryan is not dead, but in a manner of speaking, still working, but in a different way. His love and his soul are touching others who remember him and what he did for them, or with him, or his effect on them. All these beautiful letters and stories from people whose lives had been affected by Ryan. He has left a mark on other's lives. I need to think this through more.

It looks like a beautiful fall day is upon us so Rich leaves early on his motorcycle for a place in southern Wisconsin to take pictures. He leaves in a very upbeat mood doing the two things he loves–photography and motorcycling. I haven't seen him like this in a long while. I am tickled. I do wish there will be more days for him like this. Not that he is moping around, but I don't always see him even a little excited. His sense of humor is making a slow comeback. It kind of crept up while I wasn't paying attention. We used to make each other laugh a lot.

I have been getting anxiety attacks for the past couple of weeks–more often than I would like. I don't like them at all but am considering taking a half pill more of my anti-depressant. Some time ago I increased it by half a pill and it seemed to be doing its job.

Adam invited us to visit in the fall. We decide to visit Adam in Groton, Connecticut, in early October. We take our Chevy Equinox since it is pretty good on mileage and stop in Sandusky, Ohio, overnight. We hope to make it to Groton the next day but stopped in Albany, New York, instead. While waiting for Adam to get out of work, we check in at the Navy Lodge. Adam introduces us to the Groton Family Restaurant, and it becomes a must-go place every time we are in Groton.

As a family, we do the usual, go out to eat, take in movies, shop at the NEX (Navy Exchange), find local sights to see including a casino and the USS Nautilus, Library and Museum, and watch TV in the evening.

We leave Groton and I am driving. I am tired of the music being played so ask Rich to put in a CD. He puts some CDs in the player and after a while, I find I am listening to the Dixie Chicks. I know there is a song I skip since Ryan died, but I'm thinking it has been five years. Surely, I'll be fine. The song talks about a "travelin' soldier". Sure enough, the song is in the second verse when the waterworks start.

Getting back into my life, I go to work at the Military Veterans Museum checking over the gift shop and setting out new merchandise recently ordered. Five members of the Blue Star Mothers group are here as well. They are fixing a lunch for the vocational tech students who are planting greenery near the front door area. I overhear a man and two women talking about the Blue Star Mothers.

At one point the man asks, "Well, what about the Gold Star?" He must have thought that was better than blue just by the way he said it.

Both women replied, "No, no, we don't want that." and other comments I couldn't hear.

After the students were fed and the Blue Star Moms were cleaning up, one turns to me and says, "Hey, Terri, maybe you should join the Blue Star Moms. "

I smile and reply, "I am proud of Adam going into the Navy." But I am thinking I am also a Gold Star Mom and that all would be too difficult. I walk away before I embarrass myself.

I take a moment to watch the flags flying at half-staff at the museum. It is for a Wisconsin soldier killed. I thought of my sons.

CHAPTER 81

Does Abadia ever think anymore of what he did on that July 17th? Does he have a clue what lives he's changed forever? He won't ever hurt inside like Rich, Adam, and I do. I doubt he feels much of anything except figuring ways to get what he wants one of these years.

Still, even now, the realization of Ryan's death comes on so strong still at times, I feel like screaming. I never do, but it takes a while to calm down.

October 21, 2014
To: Ron Holland
From: Terri Schlack
Subject: A Question
Mr. Holland,
The enclosure relates to the case of US vs. Barto Abadia. The court date was in early May 2010 and took place at Fort Hood, TX. My husband and I received a notification that Abadia is scheduled to meet a Service Clemency and Parole Board on November 18, 2014.

I have been keeping a journal of sorts since Ryan's murder. Since I was not knowledgeable about how things "work", I always sent my journal to the offices in Washington, DC, around February. Last March, Ms. Curtis informed me I should be sending copies to you, so these get into the hands of the Service Clemency and Parole Board in Leavenworth.

From this point on, unless I hear differently, I will be sending you a partial copy of my journal in hopes it will be included in any paperwork the Board looks over. I will, of course, send it once I receive the "Victim/Witness Notification of Inmate Status" form.

Thank you, Mr. Holland, for always keeping us informed and being kind whenever we call with questions or clarifications.

Respectfully,
Terri Schlack
Enclosure: Terri Schlack's Journal March 9, 2014–October 20, 2014

November equals Adam's birthday. Today our son calls to tell us he would be hard to reach since he is working in Virginia for the next couple of weeks. Wishes of Happy Birthday are bestowed on him.

Just yesterday, Rich matted and framed the group pictures taken at boot camp graduation of Adam at his Navy graduation, Ryan at his Army graduation, and himself at his Marine graduation. They are hanging at the top of the stairs very prominently. I am not too crazy about that, but it obviously is important to my husband. Call it Rich's way of making a connection.

Last week, Owens wrote a message on Facebook to ask how I felt if he could come and visit Ryan's grave in January. If he feels he needs to do that, then I'm all for it. I really hope Owens can make a good life for himself. All of Ryan's friends who were there that night spent a year in Iraq just prior. To survive that war-torn country and come home to experience a friend get killed by a fellow soldier just a month later. That is hard to comprehend.

Rich and I go to Ryan's gravestone and place the Christmas wreath next to it. I am overcome by a strange feeling. I can't put my finger on it, but for just a split second, it's like I didn't know Ryan has died. It is such fear for a split second, I think I froze from fear. Then the creepy feeling passes and things are back to reality.

This is the second time. Will this feeling occur again? But then I think of Ryan's heart and soul theory I thought about the first time this happened. Maybe this time it is a nudge to think more about it.

On the TV news one night in early December, a newscaster reports a mandatory release date is given for a convict. The convict raped and killed a 6-year-old girl. He was sentenced to 40 years and now will get out at 28 years.

"I never heard of a mandatory release date. Why make a big deal out of the initial sentence when there is this release date shorter than the actual sentence, Rich?" I wonder aloud.

"Remember I have told you that prisoners get out early. You can figure Abadia will serve half of the 20 years," he calmly reminds me.

"Okay, then what is this about getting out early for good behavior or being an exemplary prisoner? Do these instances make the sentence shorter than the mandatory release date?" I ask.

"I'm not sure how that all works," Rich responds.

I must see if there is any information on the most recent "Victim/Witness Notification of Inmate Status". It does say in one of the boxes that there is a "Minimum Release Date" of 2025/09/21.

Adam is home on leave during the Christmas holidays. This made the holidays a happier time. We go to movies and visit family. We eat out but I also make his favorite meals. He goes to visit his friends when he can.

Adam tells us he will be stationed in Groton his whole enlistment time which is until September 2017. I know he wants to get on an aircraft carrier or submarine badly, but I am secretly glad he is stateside. The world is just too crazy right now. If he gets stationed in another country, I hope it is a safe place.

Prior to taking Adam to the airport for his flight back to Groton, we stop at Ryan's gravesite. It hasn't snowed in a while so the grass is brown. The Christmas wreath looks out of place somehow. We will have to take it down before we head south. Adam put his arm around me as we stand before the gravesite and tears fall. I think about Adam and maybe he will find a woman to marry someday and have a happy life.

CHAPTER 82

2015

Rich and I plan another Winter Get-Away. We use his Nissan Pathfinder this time and take off in minus 6-degree weather on January 6. When we go southeast, we visit friends and relatives, but the tourist spots are a visit to Parris Island in Port Royal, South Carolina, a Union Cemetery located along our route, Patrick Air Force Base located near Cocoa Beach, Florida and on to Homestead Air Force Reserve near Homestead, Florida.

In Key West, my hip is giving me trouble. Rich says his back is not the best and another day his heart is acting up. What a pair we make!

The second night we are in the Keys, my nose starts bleeding. I wake up with my pillow soaked with blood so badly I have to throw it out. No more dawdling. I have to go see a doctor. The first clinic says to stop the aspirin and Aleve. This doesn't help at all. The next clinic tells me to coat the inside of my nose with Vaseline. By now I sleep sitting up on the couch with pillows to prop me.

My nose is creating such problems! One day at Wal-Mart, I bend over to look at something on a low shelf outside the store and the bleeding starts a drip at a time. Christmas cards for 10 cents a box! I am really making a mess so put the five boxes down before blood gets on them and go back to the car to grab tissues. I can't get it to stop and it's getting worse. I pinch my nose with one hand and hold a tissue in the other. What a sight! I can't swap tissues fast enough. Luckily, the parking spot next to our car is not being used, so I sit with the car door open, turned so I drip onto the asphalt parking lot. Of course, some fool hedges into the parking slot slowly, but I be damned if I close my door. He pulls the truck in and slithers out his door. I am dripping so badly and have a huge puddle of blood growing by the second. Bloody tissues are piling up on the ground.

Not two minutes later, a guy comes up asking me for money. Here I am, blood pouring out my nose, a bit pre-occupied, and he has the balls to ask me for money.

The middle-aged man begins to explain his problem. "I sure could use it because I locked my keys in the car. The $3 is to take the bus home so I can get my spare keys."

I try to tell him, "I don't have any money. I have bigger problems right now."

"Aw, just $3. I'm a Marine vet. Won't you help a Marine veteran?" he asks.

"Listen, go away or go in Wal-Mart and ask them to make an announcement for Rich to go to his car," I struggle to say. By this time globs of blood come out. I find pinching my nose does no good. But the man appears to leave.

Suddenly, I hear Rich say something as he is walking toward the car. I hear the man talking to Rich probably begging for money. Rich always wears a cap with the Army or Marine logo on it which prompts the guy to say he is a veteran.

The guy says, "Hey, I served, too. I am a Marine veteran." I couldn't hear clearly what he is saying but would bet he was telling Rich he did this in the Marines and that in the Marines.

For some reason, he is bugging me. Just for spite, I ask, "What unit were you in?" He ignores me. I ask him two or three times. I know I am flustering him because he gives me a disgusted look.

Finally, he turns to me and asks, "Why do you keep asking me that? What difference does it make?"

"I am just curious," I explain. "I think it is important if you are asking me to believe you."

"Well, I don't remember right now," he says. "I was in the Paratroopers and I..." I didn't hear the rest because in my mind I am thinking, "Wrong answer, you dickhead!"

And just for an added irritant, I say, "Semper Fi!"

He says nothing. Now, I know I shouldn't say that all-important phrase because I have no right to do so. He should have set me straight because I am not a Marine or returned the greeting just in case he thought I was a Marine. Rich gives him a couple of bucks, and I am furious, but my nose is my bigger problem now.

As he gets into the car, Rich grins at me and says, "The jackass doesn't know military. He was mixing Marine units with Army units. He was a Paratrooper. Right. What an idiot!"

I cough up crud, so Rich finds a bag I can spit into. As I lean my head against the headrest, I realize the bleeding is stopping. "Well, let's go back to the camping area where we are staying in a mobile home so I can clean up."

It is while we are in Key West, Adam calls and tells us about a girl he met. He is infatuated with her and is giddy with the thought he may have found the right one.

We leave Key West on the 2nd of February and drive to Fort Benning, Plaines, Georgia, and another air force base.

I am getting headaches with these nosebleeds, but my nose doesn't bleed as often. The nosebleeds didn't completely stop, so on Tuesday I go to NE Georgia Urgent Care and spent four and a half hours there. The next morning, I have to be in Gainsville to get the inner part of my nose cauterized. I was not an ambitious person for the rest of the day. We take off for Tococa, Georgia, where Currahee Mountain as seen in the "Band of Brothers" is located; a must-see miniseries. Then we head back to Wisconsin.

Adam calls as we are on the road to say it is not meant to be, so he thinks it is the end of the girl. He sounds disappointed, but I tell him he is a good catch and just don't be in a hurry. It'll happen.

It is time to write a Victim Impact Statement for the next Parole Hearing. The bottom line is I am having trouble writing anything new to say at the Parole Board Hearings. I am sure by reading my speeches to the Board, the current members will certainly know what it is I am hoping for, pleading for, and what is uppermost in my mind when it comes to Abadia's sentence. Mr. Andraschko has been the chair since the beginning. Only the Board members seem to change. I feel confident Mr. Andraschko has a good read on us, so the point is the other members need to understand this frustration and the weight on our shoulders as each year passes.

Rich and I jump in the car on Monday, March 2, and head for DC with our overnight stay in Sandusky, Ohio. The weather is a concern and forecasts are not making it any better. The next morning, with the weather getting worse the more east we go, we decide to see how far we get.

About two hours into the drive, a Mr. Williams calls my cell. "Hello Mrs. Schlack. I am a secretary from the Clemency and Parole Board office. I am calling because DC is expecting a snowstorm or ice storm on Thursday, so it isn't possible to have the meeting on Thursday. You see, DC shuts down when there's bad weather."

I ask, "Is it possible to postpone until Friday? We are about 300 miles out of DC."

He pauses a second then states, "I'll see if I can put a plan together. Thank you. Goodbye."

About one hundred miles out from DC, Mr. Williams calls and asks, "Hello, Mrs. Schlack. Will you be available at 11:00AM tomorrow?"

"Yes, we sure can, Mr. Williams."

My next problem is to find people to work my shifts at the museum on Saturday and Sunday because with the nasty weather, I wasn't sure I'd be home. I am having a terrible time but finally two volunteers help me out.

The next morning, I ask the hotel desk to call a cab. I am so surprised that one cab slowed down then kept driving. The nerve of the guy! I ask the clerk to call a cab once more. This time we get one and it takes about 10 minutes to get to Crystal City. Since we came early, we roam around and find a place to eat lunch after the Parole Board Hearing.

After making the phone call from the lobby, William comes to escort us to the conference room. I misunderstood thinking Williams is his last name, but he laughs and says I can call him William. He is younger than I thought, dressed well and is as polite as can be. Not soon after, another woman is escorted into the room with us. Her name is Taylor and for a moment, I think she is here to defend Abadia. Listening to her talk to someone she calls William, I find she is here for another case.

The two Williams, last names Blake and Wheeler, leave us to get things prepared. Rich and I have a friendly conversation when the conversation turns into why she is here.

Mrs. Taylor sighs and quietly says, "My daughter got raped when she was twelve years old. She is twenty-four now, but the guilty guy is up for parole. He also recently switched into the federal prison system."

Rich and I are called a little after 11:00AM into the Board room. This time there were three colonels, one civilian and the chairman on the board.

CHAPTER 83

Adam nor Rich want to write or say anything. Adam says he'd only repeat himself from prior times he has contributed. He says nothing has changed. Rich says he feels the way I do and, besides, I say it better.

We find out that next year is the first time Abadia can ask for parole. Prior to this, his request was always about leniency. I probably will worry myself sick if we don't show up at this important crossroad.

CLEMENCY AND PAROLE BOARD
By Terri Schlack
March 5, 2015

In May 2010, when the weeklong trial came to an end, I went into a small room off the courtroom that was assigned to us, sat down and decompressed. I was trying so hard to keep myself together during the trial; it wore me out mentally and physically. Sitting there, I hadn't realized how wound up I was, so I told myself to let it go. It's over. Take a minute to settle. As I said, I felt I was decompressing. A huge weight has been lifted.

A few minutes later, the head of the panel, a colonel, came into the room. She was speaking to me and said something like - Sometimes unfortunate accidents such as this happen. It's just a sad, sad accident. She said more, but I couldn't focus. I was trying to understand what she was saying. Finally, I heard, "Don't you agree?" I was in a state of shock and didn't think I comprehended what she was saying. Then I felt my head actually nodding, yes, very slightly, although I didn't command it to. She said something quietly then left before I could get myself composed and respond to her. My mind started screaming, "Wait! No! Why did Abadia go back to the car for his gun? Don't you see? How is that an accident?" I felt paralyzed.

This incident pops in my head at times and, like a few other things I wish I'd done differently, I wished I had kept myself from decompressing long enough to respond to that colonel. It gets me wondering if others think that it was an accident. The others on the panel must have thought so. I just don't see it. How I wish I could have gotten up to confront that colonel.

For the past five years, we have been in communication with this Parole and Clemency Board either in person or via teleconferencing. Each time we present our reasons why Abadia should not receive his request for leniency or early discharge from Leavenworth.

The reasons include:

- Abadia took a young, productive man's life
- The murderer threatened another soldier, a comrade at arms

- This unrepentant person willingly broke the rule of no weapons are to be brought on post
- Three crimes in which he was found guilty
- Does Abadia think about what he did that July night every day?
- Does Abadia have a clue the lives he has changed forever?
- What else? What else is affected by his crimes?
- Abadia can see an end to his sentence; Ryan does not have that luxury. No matter how tough life gets for Abadia, he still has a future; my son does not have that luxury.
- Abadia's family will have him back home someday; Ryan's family does not have that luxury.
- Even now, Abadia's family and friends can see him face-to-face, talk with him and spend times with him; Ryan's family and friends do not have that luxury.
- Abadia's family may not have him present at holidays and family events, but he is just a phone call away; Ryan's family does not have that luxury.
- Abadia's friends will have him back home someday to hang out, laughing and joking; Ryan's friends do not have that luxury.
- I am guessing Abadia's friends more than likely have not experienced trauma; Ryan's friends did not have that luxury.
- Ryan's Army friends still try to cope with what they had experienced and struggle at times while Ryan's Wisconsin friends try to come to terms with what happened.

- Abadia's family and friends will get past this point in time; Ryan's family and friends do not have that luxury.
- Abadia's family and friends will never hurt like Ryan's family and friends.

As you may have realized, there is the rock-thrown-in-a-pool-of-water ripple effect to what had happened on July 17, 2009. Although the ripple isn't as strong and noticeable as a couple years ago, this horror has ripples that are still defined close to its center.

Because we feel the Board needs a hint at what we have gone through and are still dealing with, this Board receives copies of my journal. The entries in the journal also make you aware of how Ryan's murder affects not only the immediate family, but people around us.

My sister-in-law once said to me, "We want our Terri back." This caught me by surprise because I thought I was doing well, masking how I truly feel. I questioned her about why she said that, and her reply was that she doesn't think I am as I used to be. No high energy; no funny comments. She said it was hard to describe.

Then there are Ryan's friends, Adam's friends, and our friends. Ryan and Adam hung out with the same people. I noticed the last time Adam was home, he didn't spend as much time with those friends they had in common. Adam is making new friends in his "new" life, and I think that has helped.

In November or December of last year, Greg Owens, the man Ryan pushed out of the way of the bullet, asked if he could come to visit Ryan's grave in late December or early January. I emailed him back and said, sure, it was perfectly all right. He never came, at least not that I am aware of. I figure it is still too difficult for him.

And then there are the people we all worked with. I was still teaching and, thankfully, I had a few people at work I could confide in and depend on if I needed help to get through the long days. Now, when former co-workers see me, I still get hugs and a sincere concern about how I am doing. I also have a close friend who lost a daughter who was fatally shot as well. We keep in touch with each other a lot more than we used to.

The Patriot Guard's leader for our area, Wayne Midlands, still stops by Ryan's grave when he is in town. We never even knew Wayne prior to his calling us to see if we would like an escort to the burial site and veterans standing with flags along the funeral home's drive.

Flowers are left each year by Ryan's gravestone. We don't know who does that, but surely, he or she is affected by Ryan's death. We suspect it is Wayne.

One thing that is not going away or cannot be ignored is the eczema I suffer with. Old spots are getting larger and the spots are increasing in number. I know it goes into what I call 'hibernation at times' when I am not as stressed. I have talked with my doctor and her suggestion is to not be put under undue stress. She knows my husband and I go every year in front of the Clemency and Parole Board here in DC and has suggested I not go. It would be an experiment to see if this yearly event has any bearing on this health issue. Personally, I am not sure if I would be feeling more stressed, but I can still send my journal so feel like I am doing something. I guess I need to consider this because the eczema can itch for weeks and weeks before I feel relief.

Rich and I feel we have presented everything we can, so you, the Clemency and Parole Board, can see our side of things. We know Abadia is getting closer to his minimum time in prison, so I feel a heightened panic knowing that is coming up one of these years.

CHAPTER 84

With the serious snowstorm coming in, Rich and I decide to stay Thursday night. On Friday, our car is packed by 8:00AM and off we go.

It is slow going in town; ice is on the roads, but the wheel tracks are better than expected. There is an on-ramp that looked pretty steep. In fact, a little truck in front of us is sliding and spinning the wheels and going nowhere.

Rich jumps out of the car at the same time a man from a construction crew walks down the ramp and both give the truck a good push. Now it is our turn. We are halfway up the ramp and ice stops us from proceeding. The driver behind us and the construction guy push our car and we are on our way. It renews the spirit to find there are some good people yet.

Highway speeds are 25 mph until the more west we head the better the roads get. Our usual stop in Sandusky is a welcome sight, but better yet, we decide to stay there on Friday. Saturday is uneventful, and we're happy to pull into our driveway on Saturday afternoon.

Once again, my plan is to tackle Ryan's things within a few days. "Rich, I feel like I should organize the photos, letters, emails, and whatever belonging to Ryan or about Ryan," I say in a slightly demanding voice. "The box has been sitting on top of Ryan's footlocker all this time. This has been on my mind for a while."

Rich doesn't say a thing, so I guess he is okay with it. I put some things in the footlocker. There is a lot of shredding, but lots to keep and file with similar items. Ryan's wooden footlocker is now organized.

For two years, Rich would include the Soldier's Cross in a community weekend display in a park where others put up some remembrance of their military son or daughter. But now the Cross is in a room in the basement. Rich would like to display it, but where?

"Here's a thought. What about the military museum?" I throw out to Rich.

"Wouldn't you have to talk to someone?" Rich questions.

"Well, sure. I will talk to the president and VP. That's all it will take I would think," I reply.

When I approach him with the idea, the president exclaims, "That is wonderful. We have been looking for a Soldier's Cross for some time now. We didn't have a clue where to begin to look." It is now displayed in the Military Veterans Museum & Education's entranceway with an explanation of purpose. It is a much more suited use than sitting in the basement.

Three weeks after our annual DC trip, Rich gets ahold of Mr. Holland's office, but he finds out another person took Mr. Holland's place; a Mrs. Brenda Salazar. He leaves a message and hangs around the rest of the day to wait for the return call. Rich is doing a slow burn because she doesn't call.

This morning Salazar calls. I just have a feeling this would happen, but I also thought, "Don't feel so negative." With a new person taking over, you just know that person is going to follow the rules. I guess she never heard of "If you don't ask, do it anyway. You can always say, "Oh, well, I didn't know." If those who make the rules could walk in our shoes, would the rule of not sharing what the murderer asked for even exist? I suspect not. What do those people think we are going to do if they told us? We already know that the sentence can't be extended. It is really much more aggravating this way.

Our lives are torn up as it is, and we put up with the pressure of hearing that Abadia has asked for yet another parole hearing which is usually in November, then we set up a meeting with the Army Clemency and Parole Board in DC which is more time spent waiting, and the only thing that feels like something has been done is when we hear Abadia's request has been denied and we find out specifics. This year it's like you get half of something you want, but you can't get the other half no matter what. Being told what he's asked for puts a finality on it for at least another year. When I 'talk' to Ryan, I picture him feeling satisfied for another year.

I know for a fact everyone I share this experience with is going to say, "Why not? Don't you have rights? Why wouldn't they tell you what he wanted? This is not right." Of course, we agree with them. But our hands feel tied because we can't reach out and get an answer.

On a Saturday morning in April, my siblings and spouses gather for a breakfast, the first since last year. The weather is nice again and the winter snow is finished. The purpose is to get together once a month to get caught up in all our lives. I have a bit of news for them to "chew on".

"Oh, by the way, everyone, Adam is engaged!" I announce to the table.

The first question from everyone's mouth is, "Oh, and when is the wedding?"

"April 25," I smile with pride.

My sister says, "Oh, 2016?"

I calmly say, "No, this year."

Then there is a pause as they are doing the math. The expression on their faces are priceless. "Well," Gib says with surprise, "That's a week away!"

"Ah-huh," I nonchalantly say. It has been many years since there was a wedding in the family.

Rich and I get everything in order prior to leaving, so the mail has been stopped and the house will be looked after. It takes us two days to get to Connecticut in the pouring rain. We check into the Navy Lodge on base.

"Hey there, Adam," I greet him on the phone after we check in.

"Hi, Mom. Are you here in Groton yet?" asks Adam anxiously.

"Yes, we are settled in at the Navy Lodge," I inform him. "Is there a plan for this evening?"

Adam responds, "Yes, actually. I just got home from work, so give us a half hour and we will pick you up and go to dinner. How does that sound?"

"Great, sounds good. See you soon. We are in Room 201," I reply.

We go to Groton Family Restaurant which serves very good food. At first, the conversation is centered on catching up with what is going on lately then turns to finding out about the bride's family and her work. The evening went well.

Waiting in the doctor's waiting room the next day, Rich and I meet Adam's mother-in-law for the first time. She seems quiet and nervous. It was difficult getting her to talk. I am hoping she'll become more comfortable once she meets us more often.

We all get to go to the first sonogram which is exciting. I have never been on this end of it all before. Adam seems very attentive to his partner which I am happy to see. Seeing the little person got a lot of "ooohs" and "aaahs" and pointing at the screen.

Prior to going, Rich and I had hauled most of what Adam asked us to bring as well as some surprises. We carefully packed it into our car for the trip east.

Once we got to Adam's apartment, Rich and I carried the packages into the living room. "Adam, we have brought all the items you asked us to bring, but there are some surprises. These are things I have saved all these years to give to you and your wife when you get married. Today is the day."

Adam was so very surprised that I had kept all those youthful items and artwork from elementary school. "Thank you, Mom and Dad," Adam bursts out. His wife-to-be had a surprised look on her face but says nothing. Later, I find out she hates surprises.

"You don't have to do this, but it might make it interesting. Choose two packages a day to open, and Adam will tell the story about it to you or explanations of it. But here is one to open now." I hand them a big box. Inside is Adam's baby blanket, a gift my sixth-grade class made while I was on maternity leave. It is a lot of little squares filled with pillow stuffing and sewn together in a blanket. The squares are lots of different youthful material. The other side is solid. Both of them were in awe that I kept it and were pleased with the unusual baby gift.

Adam and wife-to-be kept us busy before the wedding. Adam takes us to the Foxwood Casino where the wedding will take place. The Casino is huge with lots of shopping places and many restaurants, all quite impressive. We tour a few submarines and battleships which Rich is very interested in and couldn't stop talking about. We eat out most every meal when we are with them, and did some shopping for baby and mommy.

We have nice conversations but some information about herself doesn't add up. Rich says the same thing. Already I am thinking Adam doesn't deserve to be lied to.

April 25, 2015, is the wedding day at the casino and it turns out better as the day goes on. For such a small affair, I can't believe the problems. The bride's hairdresser did not show up. Her mother, grandmother and the few uninvited relatives are late in arriving and the Justice of the Peace can't stay much longer to wait for them. But once the ceremony starts, everything smooths out. The dinner for ten of us is spectacular in that it is served like a course meal which is very fancy to me. We meet an aunt and uncle of Adam's wife which is unexpected; to Wifey as well. Her side is not conversationalists, so the meal is very quiet. We get group pictures as we exchange cameras with each other. I end the evening as sick with stomach pains as I can remember. We say our goodbyes and leave on Monday, still sick and now Rich has issues, too.

Ryan would cross my mind during those days, and I am sad he didn't get to see his brother get married or meet her. Ryan is in my heart during the wedding day and, as at all family gatherings, I feel we aren't complete.

On the national news in mid-May, there is talk of sending more ships to the waters touching the Middle East. I know Adam told me he is not firmly experienced at his job to have to go on a ship. I should not worry.

I am having panic attacks so I increase my anti-depressants. I can't figure out why the attacks. A doctor's appointment is just days away. The PA prescribes an additional anxiety suppressant pill to take.

On Memorial Day, a flowerpot of huge white geraniums is next to Ryan's gravestone. A couple of weeks later, Joyce and I visit Ryan's grave after a lunch date and another potted flower arrangement, this time in red, is there. It warms my heart to think others think of him, too.

June is creeping up fast. We are getting ready to go to Branson, Missouri, and what pops into my head? The last time we planned a motorcycle trip to Branson, the day before we were to leave, three soldiers came knocking on our door. Kind of gets me in a different frame of mind. Like this is an omen for something not good. I should get that out of my head. Our trip goes well and nothing terrible happens.

On TV, someone said, "It leaves a hole in my heart that will always be there." The speaker is saying this about the shooting death of a loved one. I think this is eloquent and so true.

Ryan would have turned 36 years old on the 12th of July. It doesn't help to think what his life would be like. It is more of a fact that is just out there. I try not to ponder it as July passes.

Today is the 18th. Six years ago. I just miss him and the relationship that we would have had. He was funny when he was in a good mood. He brooded a lot during his high school. After the Army, I could see such a change; more easy-going, more relaxed, more willing to talk with me, not at me. No one has any idea how I wanted him to finish his stop-loss year and come home in September. This was robbed from me. I just knew things changed for the better between us.

Adam converses with us every week. With his new life of marriage and upcoming child, we are hanging on every word. This family is evolving, and this brings a good feeling, something to be happy about.

The land around the Military Museum has been cleaned up and I think it is about time to use the nursery gift certificate from my siblings to buy a tree or two.

I walk into the house and find Rich in the living room. "Hey, guess what? The two red maple trees are finally planted."

"Oh, yeah?" Rich replies.

As time goes on, it takes me by surprise when I go to the museum that I actually feel a comfort. I don't know if that's the right word; a kind of serenity, maybe, or a peaceful feeling when I see the trees. One tree is close to the entryway, so I pass it as I go to and from my car. It even makes me smile sometimes. Just like at the funeral, I wanted all the green plants and sent most of the flowers to a nun's nursing home nearby.

When the Soldier's Cross Rich made was first placed in the museum entrance, I didn't really look at it. Or, if I did, I looked away quickly. Today, I actually touch it for the first time and read the two dog tags put on the rifle with a chain. When I come in to volunteer now, I even look at it and think, "Hello, Ryan."

I think the times, they are a'changing.

CHAPTER 85

Things in general do not feel like it is happening in quick secession anymore. It seemed we just deal with one thing and another comes right behind. After all, it has been six years since Ryan died and, at this juncture, events happen, but they can be dealt with. Significant events are talked about from here on which shows our lives are calming down and manageable.

I surprise myself today. I put together a poem. I haven't written anything since Ryan died. This one is simple but conveys a humorous message. It is a thank you for the September birthday wishes sent to me, and I posted it on Facebook.

You all made my day
With the wishes you sent.
And I gotta say
I know what you meant.
You're thinking, "Go play!
Go have your day's fun!
No time to delay
Your day's almost done."
As I ponder my wishes
I know now what I want.
Forget the damn dishes
And crawl back to bed.

I should mail my journal out to Leavenworth. Right around this time, I get uptight and nervous wondering what Abadia's outcome will be. When I get the "Notification of Prisoner Status", I immediately look for the "Minimum Release Date" wondering if that is truly the minimal. The maximum is four years later. Then, I think of those two soldiers who had committed a very similar crime in about the same way and how they got life. Where is the fairness? If I were those two criminals, I'd throw a fit and make it a point every time I met with the board.

I haven't had itching problems until just lately. I can't say it has gotten worse, thank goodness, but holding its own. We'll see as we go through November to March, if that is still the case.

Now I am in a bit of a panic. I get another letter from Brenda Salazar, the new Victim/Witness Assistance Coordinator, that says I can submit a "Victim/Witness Impact Statement" but I already got one from her in September. That letter states Abadia will have a Clemency and Parole Board on Nov. 19. Now this November letter says Abadia will have a Clemency and Parole Board on Jan. 21, 2016. I need to call her and find out what is going on. I shiver a bit thinking the stress this causes; we aren't privileged enough to be privy to the outcomes. Well, she is new. She doesn't get it.

A week later, out of nowhere, a friend Becca calls to see if we can meet. It has been a long time since we've talked. We meet and relatively early in the conversation, Becca starts telling me about her father dying in January 2014.

"Terri, I want to share this with you. Just recently, I went to a psychic gathering with friends," Becca begins. "I really don't believe in that stuff but went with a few friends as a skeptic. But Terri, the psychic told me things about my dad that no one would have known. The psychic got one thing wrong, but the couple of things she did know took my friends aback. So, a person wonders, you know?"

Sometimes I think a presence of some sort is flitting around my brain. It penetrates my consciousness. Could this presence be of Ryan? I'd say this has been going on for a month or a bit more. My mom had died in 2007 and I don't get that sense about her.

Later in November, Adam calls and invites us to the birth of their daughter. As soon as we can, we pack up the car and drive out to Groton, Connecticut.

On Thanksgiving Day, Rich is in the waiting room, and I am with Adam to watch the birth of Violet. It is special because for one reason or another I couldn't see my own sons being born. We did the pictures thing and the holding and feeding thing and everything grandparents do to become a part of the baby's life. Violet Ryan Schlack is as cute a baby as you'll ever see.

We are invited to Violet's First Christmas, so we fly out there for a few days to enjoy being grandparents. The cameras never stop flashing. The time is so magical, and we act like the typical first-time grandparents the whole time. I even am inspired to write a poem.

'Twas the night before Christmas
And all through Schlack's home
The smells of spaghetti
And pecan pie did roam.
The white tree was trimmed up
With ornaments and lights
And there's Grandma and Grandpa
Fresh off their long flight.
WOW! The weather was so warm
No rain was coming down.
Not a heavy coat nor mittens
Worn by anyone in town.
'Twas the night before Christmas
Mommy made us a great meal
Daddy served a local tasty wine
Pecan pie sealed the deal.
Sweet Violet, our first grandchild
Was a bit cranky this night.
She soon will be one month
And to Grandma, is a delight.

We watched a Christmas movie
The Lampoon one with Chevy Chase.
Lots of talking and reminiscing
The evening's end we had to face.
'Twas four days after Christmas
As Grandpa drove us from sight.
Merry Christmas to all
And to all a good night!

A couple of days after Christmas, Adam and his wife present Rich with a birthday cake. He thought that was a funny thing being all the excitement going on around us.

There is a blizzard all day today and is supposed to go into tomorrow. Days like these give me time to think. My mind rambling all over the place. Changes are occurring in our lives–wonderful, life-changing occurrences. I haven't seen Rich so happy in a very long while. Adam and his wife now have Violet Ryan in all our lives. Adam is happily married and will make a fantastic dad. He can't get enough of holding Violet and asking how he can help. Even Rich, who thinks babies break like a thin piece of ice, holds Violet. It is truly difficult to leave Groton.

Since she was born, every other day, if not every 3rd day, we get pictures of Violet, but to see and hold her is an overload of emotional experience. To see Adam still enthralled with the baby is good for the soul.

One evening, Rich caught me teary-eyed and asked what was wrong. I just had to say "Ryan" and he understood. He then said, "Now we have Violet Ryan." I get what he meant even though I was thinking in terms of Ryan missing this time in his brother's life. Rich is thinking Violet may fill the hole in our lives even if by a little bit. This could be true. Who knew a person could feel so over the top with love and joy?

CHAPTER 86

2016

It starts to snow when we leave for points south in January, but slowly the clouds are less ominous, and the sun finally pulls itself out from behind the clouds.

We are in Sedona, Arizona, for a week. I am to sign some form as part of checking in. Who reads forms? According to the small print on the form, we have to listen to a promoter regarding time shares in these apartments or we would not get back our $100 deposit. I am a tightwad enough to do this.

After sitting with this promoter, he begins to get a bit nasty. This is probably because we are polite but constantly say we are not interested. Rich and I did our usual bantering back and forth in a teasing way like the whole thing is a joke.

At one point, the pompous salesman says in a cocky voice, "We have to talk about Wyndham Resorts for 90 minutes before I will release you. No, we cannot talk about the weather or Sedona in general. We talk time shares."

The promoter suddenly looks closely at Rich's jacket. "What is that on your jacket?"

Looking more closely at Rich, I see he is wearing his jacket with Ryan's name, date of birth and death and the Soldier's Cross embroidered on it. A feeling of sadness washes over me like someone just dumped a pail of water over me. I can't sit at the table for one second longer, so I get up out of my seat and head to anyplace out of this room.

I walk through corridors and finally find a counter where women are doing secretarial work on the other side. Plunking myself down on a chair in front of this counter, I ask if anyone has tissues as the tears begin. Both women look at me, concerned, and hand me a box. It took quite a while to stop and control my breath. Where did that come from? I feel I didn't want to share our lives with this jerk. Could that have been it?

After about 15 minutes, it surely is time to go back to the promoter and Rich. My intent is to get Rich out of there. The promoter sees my red splotchy face and me dabbing my face with tissue. As I am very near his table, he says he'll let us go and hope we enjoy our stay.

On the same trip, one evening while at a hotel, Rich happens to be flipping channels and stops on a story about James Foley, the photojournalist, who was beheaded by ISIS for the world to see. This happened in August 2014.

His mother is being interviewed and says, "I learned about him as an adult through his friends." Her son was gone for years, and she could see changes when he'd visit but not near the changes she heard from friends. I feel a kinship with her.

Over the course of the trip, Rich and I have been talking about what to say at the Parole and Clemency Hearing. We both agree we have said everything we can. We decide to send a letter with my journal.

January 7, 2016
To the Clemency and Parole Board,
Accompanying this letter is a journal I have kept for the 2015 year regarding the effect Ryan's murder has had on family members, friends, and mostly myself. This is an ongoing journal. The previous years should be in your file already so I will not send the entire piece.

My husband and I decided that we will not be appearing before the Board this year primarily because we have said everything we can about it. Aside from meeting with the Board every year, only something such as a journal can give you insight since it is written during intervals throughout the year.

If you are new to this Board, please see if you can read my journal from beginning to end so you have the whole picture. If you are acquainted with this case, I assume a skimming of previous years will refresh your memory.

Respectfully,
Terri and Richard Schlack

We are home by mid-February from the trip to the southwest. I open an email from Ms. Salazar. My reaction is one of shock.

January 2016
To: Richard Schlack
From: Ms. Salazar
Subject: Abadia's Request
Mr. Schlack,

I have a request from Inmate Abadia. He has completed a letter to you and your wife with his counselor. I was asked if you would accept it. I have tried calling. Will you email me or call me to let me know if this is something you would like to have or even talk about? I know this is very hard for you and your wife. Let me know your thoughts.

Mrs. Brenda Salazar
Victim Witness/Sex Offender Registration Coordinator

"What do you make of this email, Rich?" I question.

"I saw it on my phone," he calmly replies.

"How do you want to reply? I have a couple of ideas, but it is addressed to you, so you should respond, I think."

Rich states, "I refuse to acknowledge the inmate so won't bother responding." Well then, that's how it will be handled.

What is Salazar thinking? In her defense, I suppose she has to be sure the inmate does not have his rights violated. What to hell do I care!

"Here's what I think of it," Rich quips. "Abadia is trying to contact us because it has something to do with him getting paroled."

We want justice done. We want Ryan's life to have meant something. His death should not be shrugged off as someone making an insane choice. If it isn't clear by now, know that I am thinking of the other two soldiers who did a very, very similar crime and received life. On top of that, those two committed ONE crime, not the THREE that Abadia did.

About a week later, I am in shock over an article. I can't believe what I am reading! I am catching up on the January/February 2016 Army Times because we were gone. Right there it talks about "Military judges would be empowered in several new ways, to include having control over the sentencing phase of trials." I know it won't change Abadia's sentence but, finally someone sees through an insincere panel, or a panel who seemingly was compelled to go along with the highest-ranking officer, or a panel who just wanted to finish up their last case since they have been serving as a panel pool for the past six months. Finally, the sentences would or could be more in line with each other. Then came the deflating part. I show Rich the article thinking he would be as excited as I am.

Rich says, "Yeah, but I had looked up how long Leavenworth prisoners serve their time compared to their actual sentence and the average is half the sentence." That means in 2020, Abadia will potentially get out. That's only in four years. It is just not right."

I still have a sliver of hope that if the judges are given more influence in the sentencing portion of the trial, judges can pad on more years if the prisoner serves half. It won't happen to Abadia, but maybe in the future. Passing this law doesn't come soon enough for me.

A couple weeks prior to the March Parole & Clemency Board Hearing, Ms. Curtis calls and says, "Hello, Mrs. Schlack. This is Ms. Curtis. How are you doing?"

"I am as well as can be expected, Ms. Curtis. I hope all is well with you," I reply.

"I am doing fine but I am calling because I am checking to be sure you will not be attending the Clemency and Parole Board this year," she states in a quizzical manner, like she's almost sad about it.

I sigh and say, "No, Ms. Curtis, we will not be attending the Board this year. Between my husband's health and the fact that I think my journal says it all, our speeches may turn into repeating ourselves."

"Oh, okay," she comments.

"But I will tell you that I only hope that the Board did not grant his request because then I will feel that we did not do enough. I can't bear that thought."

"Mrs. Schlack, please listen. I have never heard of someone getting paroled on the first board hearing. You shouldn't worry or give it a thought," Ms. Curtis says in a soothing manner.

"Well, thank you so much for all you have done, Ms. Curtis. Should I have any questions, I will call. Take care. Good bye," I say softly.

"You, too, Mrs. Schlack," she replies.

I hope Abadia will be in until 2023. Is his max in 2029? That would be 20 years. I shouldn't be thinking like this so much. I need to remember to take this one year at a time and do what I can to be sure he puts in his full time. If this sounds like I want revenge, then try losing a child by the hands of a killer.

We both need a Violet-fix, and it is February, but we will risk it. We head to Groton only to run into a snowstorm somewhere in Indiana so we stopped for two nights. It was a good thing to do because we didn't know what to expect beyond Indiana.

CHAPTER 87

By mid-March 2016, the Parole Hearing had to have taken place. Things are different. We are focusing on Adam, his wife and our first grandchild. We want to visit them in Connecticut whenever we can.

Things also will not change. I think about the journal and feel it does still give insight into how Abadia's crimes affect us. How else will the Boards know?

As was stated in a poem, "there is no pushing through" to get to the other side. There is no other side. "Grief is not something you complete. But, rather, you endure,… (It is) an element of yourself–An alteration of your being. A new way of seeing. A new definition of self."

Here's a thought. Let's try weaning myself off the anti-depressants. My brain says I can do this. My hope is this is the time to do it.

It's late March when we attend my uncle's funeral. He was in the Battle of the Bulge. The last song during the Catholic service is a patriotic song; can't recall the title, but I sing the words in my head and, of course, sniffle during the song. This also means there is a 21-gun salute. I am trying hard to think this honored my uncle, but all I think of is Ryan. I am glad to be standing at the back of the crowd. Two sisters-in-law hear my sniffles and stand close. I calm down before we leave to go to the luncheon.

Two weeks later, I attend the funeral of one of the dearest men I have ever known. Larry is one of those guys that you take an instant liking to. There is a special place in my heart for this man I met at the Military Veterans Museum where he was a docent and I as cashier. I knew we would get along famously because he started to tease me the first day we worked together, and we would make jokes the whole time we volunteered. He was a 20-year Marine and was proud of every minute.

All I know about his family is that his wife is sick with cancer again. He told me a few months ago that I was the only person outside the family he told that his own cancer came back. But in the same breath, he said, "And we will beat it this time, too!"

The service is held at the same funeral home where we had Ryan's service. As soon as I walk into the viewing room, my eyes water, and I scold myself in my head for letting it happen. There is a receiving line, and I make a guess as to who is family. Sure enough, tears start as I talk to Larry's daughter. Apologizing for my tears which I can't find how to explain, his children say they are glad I came to pay respects. Embarrassed and mortified, it is difficult to confront Larry's wife. She doesn't have to see a stranger crying at her husband's funeral. I leave right afterward because I know I can't stay.

Three weeks later is the funeral of a 21-year-old, Rich's sister's grandchild. I did go through the receiving line. Rich's nephew John sees me and as I am next in line, he starts to cry so hard. I knew I'd have that effect on him, so I try to be strong. I hold him as tight as I can for a long time. A thought flies through my mind that I am taking too long in line, but it flies right out just as fast. His wife comes next to us.

"How did you get through it?" the parents ask me. I didn't want my thoughts to go too far back into that dark time. I try to respond with advice.

I reply, "It's hard as hell, but you can do it. You have a strong support group of family and friends who love you. Take it one day at a time. Don't even think about next week or next month. Just one day at a time. You'll think stupid things, crazy things. You might blame each other and then you look for who to blame. This will test a marriage, but you have been together for a long time. You have family near you. I know you have a supportive family, but if you need to talk in a week, or even in a month, I will be here for you."

"Yes, yes, thank you. We just may take you up on your offer." I hope they are not thinking I have the golden answer. I have none.

We are happy to find out that benches are finally being ordered for the Memorial Plaza at the Military Veterans Museum & Education Center to be placed around the Flag Plaza.

"I have been waiting about five years for this day, Rich. Let's see if there are any benches in," I plead.

We pull up to the Flag Plaza and see a board member supervising and other guys working on setting up the first of the benches. The Board member calls us over then suggests, "I know you are planning to get a bench. You should plan something for Ryan's bench then take it to the stone engraver. It only takes about a week."

So, Rich puts the idea on paper and takes it to the stone engraver. Next week, we are to go back to see the layout for the bench. Ryan received two challenge coins exactly the same. One will be encased in the bench. It is a large coin, so it really adds to the design. It is a couple weeks before the bench is placed.

It's Memorial Day, so Rich goes to the cemetery early. He puts out a picture of Ryan on an easel, Ryan's medals with flag case and the Soldier's Cross.

Rich calls me on the phone. "Hey, it's me."

"Yes, I figured that out. Where are you?" I chuckle.

"Come to the cemetery. The presentation will start in a few minutes. You'll see my car parked in the next lane where the veterans' gravestones are."

I race out to the cemetery and the Annual Oshkosh Procession is underway. We sit where we can watch the items Rich set up in front of the gravestone. Many people would stop to look and point. I mention to Rich that it would be cool if we started something for the next year's Memorial Day event.

June is a great month for traveling so Adam and family are visiting now. Sitting in the living room, I happen to open my Facebook. Greg Owens was on Facebook yesterday evening and sounded so suicidal. It scares me.

"Adam, contact Greg to see if you might help him. I see friends of Greg are trying to encourage him to call them or to hang in there."

Adam texts him, but he is resistant at first about responding to questions. Greg's mom texts to say he has been drinking and having a bad day. Greg texts Adam, "I miss Ryan's friendship. We were going to do so many things together since Minnesota is just a day's drive away. I think I will sleep now."

After Adam reads that to me, I have Adam text Greg's mom to say he should be watched closely.

My annoying eczema is on the rise again. Not as bad as previous years, but it raises its ugly head; nudging the rough patches. I am wondering why it is in a hibernation until now. Then it occurs to me that July is coming up fast.

I get a notice that the insurance says I have to find another cream for the eczema. I won't. I know this works on the god-awful itching. I will pay out of my pocket if I can get the doctor to write a prescription for me. Sometimes I scratch so hard, I draw blood.

CHAPTER 88

It is July 11 and I'm riding in the car with Rich. I don't know why, but as I am sitting in the passenger seat, I am confused that I can't figure out how old Ryan will be tomorrow.

Getting frustrated, I bluster, "Why can't I figure out how old Ryan will be?" My eyes leak.

Rich turns to me and says, "He will be 37 years old tomorrow." Then, like always, he tries to get me thinking of other things. How do I stop this crying all the damn time?

I accept Ryan isn't going to walk through the door and call out to me. I accept Ryan won't be in his bedroom stretched out on the bed reading a book or hovering over his notebooks writing strategies on those games his friends played with him. I accept Ryan is no longer in the army gone to a foreign land or stationed stateside somewhere. I have visited Ryan's gravesite to know he is truly gone. But Ryan will never, ever leave my heart and mind.

I begin to wean myself off the anti-depression pills. I want to see if it makes any difference. Here's to hoping I won't need them.

What crossed my mind recently is what Abadia's mom is thinking about this all - being quite a few years into his sentence. His mother was not in the courtroom during the trial because she was one who was called to testify during the trial, so she wasn't allowed. Does she think he'll do his time and then it'll be okay? Maybe she thinks he can put it behind him when he gets out. Does she really see what he has done?

Will she really trust him now that he killed another man? Does she know he is not the person she thinks he is? Does she ever think of Ryan?

I have been getting more emotional more easily over things that make me even a bit sad. My eczema irritates more often. It must be close to the time we get the November letter saying Abadia is asking for something and wants to go in front of the Parole Board.

The nurse practitioner told me long ago that the eczema may very well come from stress. My new doctor doesn't agree, so I ask her why do I get eczema the first time in my life after Ryan's murder? It comes back with a vengeance in July and after Christmas. She didn't have an answer.

John, Rich's nephew, texts, "I'm sitting in my car at work and like a ton of bricks, it hits me. Is it always like this?"

My returning text says, "John, the feeling sort of changes, but thoughts of your son will never leave your heart. Time will help, but it is so easy to say and so very hard to do."

Attending a Veteran's Day Program in November at Perry Tipler Middle School, I listen to a speaker that I suggested to the school organizer but have never heard in person. The first time I had contact with John Reemer, I had called him on the phone regarding this speaking engagement. Right off, I liked him and knew he would be a good candidate as a speaker.

One part of the program was the playing of taps. I never expected to hear Taps today. This is the day we remember veterans who survived. On Memorial Day, taps are played. I am sitting in some chairs that were set up for veterans, but because I had a boot on due to a recent foot surgery and had to use the knee stroller, I take a chair. The alternative was bleachers with all the students. The audience is asked to stand for taps and the tears roll. Becca comes with me, touches my hand trying to comfort me, but I feel embarrassed. We are in the middle of a gym full of middle school students and people could see me since we sit where no one else does, in front of crowded bleachers. I think of Ryan, which is so easy to do. I try to concentrate on other things around me.

Thankfully, Taps isn't a long piece. I focus on what is happening next—more music from the school orchestra.

It came; the notice from DC about Abadia. I send the journal that tells of what our lives were like this past year.

Lots of celebrations packed into these days when Adam and his family visit. Adam, his wife, and Violet fly home so we celebrate Adam's birthday, Thanksgiving, Violet's birthday, Christmas, and Rich's birthday. We have birthday cakes, birthday gifts, turkey with all the trimming, Christmas gifts and Christmas dinner. I even put together a little fun for Adam and his wife like I had done with Ryan and Adam some Christmases. They are given a hint written as a poem which told them to go into the house where they'd find a present. With the present is another clue, so they had to figure where that place was in the house and find another gift and clue. The clues had them running in circles which made it fun for Rich and me as well.

Adam's family, Rich, and I put a Christmas wreath by Ryan's grave. With Adam and his family here to visit, a person might think it would be hard to do. Surprisingly, it lightens the weight for a bit of time.

CHAPTER 89

2017

It is Rich's idea to get a recreational vehicle for our trips south. He found one last summer that seemed to meet our needs. The 2007 Georgie Boy had less than 10,000 miles, garaged when not in use, seemingly well maintained and fit into our price range. We would be its third owners. Rich found something he can tinker with and learn about and spend time with, so for this I am happy.

My plan this first RVing year is going somewhere in the south to experience as many campgrounds as we can especially military ones to see which ones we like. This first winter trip we are moving sometimes as often as after a week to find out what we want in a campground and scheduled our winter trip from mid-December to mid-March. One unexpected experience was there were a couple times we had to unhitch the Equinox from the RV because we couldn't backup or turn tightly.

Rich loves RV camping, and I put up with it although I am questioning my sanity. On practically the whole trip, there would be nights in a row that I muffled my sobbing in bed and sometimes crying out loud. This is not good for Rich or me.

Some mornings, I just do not want to get up and start the day. Getting ready many mornings, I force myself to get up. Why? Maybe there is a correlation between not really liking RVing and my awful mood. A time or two I told Rich I am not 100% on this idea. But then, I think, he needs something positive going on in his life and who am I to take that away? There are no words to describe the change in me now that we are on our way home. I cannot wait to jump out and run into the house. If I could hug it, I know I would.

Some thoughts of mine scare me. I feel unstable; I don't care if I die sometimes. But thinking of whom I would leave behind brings me back to somewhat saner thinking.

I see the Physician's Assistant at the end of April which won't come soon enough. Maybe I need to get back on some anti-depressants. This is a hell I dread every morning. These days, I monitor and check how I am feeling. What can I do or what should I get involved in to help me feel better? I seem to fight every morning to have a half-way decent day.

To get into living, I set up some lunch and dinner dates with friends or relatives for April. I take a trip to the library to get some books. I try to work on the museum projects I spearheaded.

Rich and I have been back about two weeks. I reflect on our RV trip. I think I went too long for the first time in an RV. The confinement got to me, or maybe the lack of doing things. Is this god-awful feeling going to happen when we go again in December? If I can't get out of this funk, what do I tell Rich? I hope my pity party is over. I can't stand being in the room with myself.

The Physician's Assistant puts me back on the anti-depressant/anxiety pills. I think they are starting to kick in. I don't feel absolutely miserable, although I am up most of the night and sleep the morning away.

Maybe it is time to get professional help. Is it too late to do something like this? Admitting this is not easy, but this anxiety and depression has got to stop. I hate the depressed feeling more than the "pressure" of meeting a stranger and talking about my issues. I figure if this is going to work, I better just jump in and do it. In May, when I set up an appointment, I am told there are three visits scheduled, each about a week apart.

The first session is all assessing and coming up with how to approach this depression. There is very little of what I imagine it would be like. Of course, there is the informal evaluation, but I think we could get into it a bit, but, no, we save that for next time. It isn't the expectation of what a person sees on TV nor has anyone ever talked with me about this experience.

During the second session, the psychiatrist begins with conversing and I describe to him the issues in my life. Good thing the tissue box is handy because I do a lot of crying. But what's new? I didn't know what to expect from therapy, but halfway through, I know this isn't for me. One thing is I have been educated and well-read enough to know the strategies he is using. Somehow, that bothers me. It annoys me so much I couldn't wait to end the second session. I knew he and I were not a good fit.

Prior to going to the third session with the psychiatrist, I began to look at what is going on with me. I feel a bit of confidence that I can deal with this myself and make a plan to fix myself. When I walk into the psychiatrist's office, I already know this is my last time with him.

After talking with the psychiatrist for about fifteen minutes, I finally share my thoughts. "I think I am getting a handle on this. Maybe I have a clear head now to face this. My plan is to see what I can manage on my own."

"Well, I am glad you feel that way. I do not want to be a hindrance. If you ever need to talk, I have all the data I need and we can pick up again. What do you think?"

"I feel I have alternatives now. It didn't seem that way a month ago," I respond.

The session ended early, and I feel good about myself. Is it the antidepressants kicking in? It could be, and I don't care that it is. The hole I was in has a light at the end of it. However, I am leaving the door open though, as a safety net.

About a week later, the phone rings. "Hello, is this Mrs. Schlack?"

"Yes," I respond hesitantly because the voice is not familiar.

"Mrs. Schlack, I am SGT Black from the Criminal Investigation Division of Ft. Hood. I am calling to find out if you want the remains of the evidence from Ryan's murder sent to you or we can dispose of it."

I hear Rich pick up the other phone so I let him do the talking. I am ready to say no. To my surprise, he says, "Yes, please send it to us."

"Alright, Mr. Schlack. I will mail it and the package should get to you in a week. Have a nice day. Goodbye."

After we all hung up, I walk in the living room to Rich. "Why would you want something like that back?" I ask, astounded. "Do you think there is more than just clothing being sent? It's been eight years. Why, after all this time?"

Calmly, Rich answers, "I think there are a couple of things we never got back. One thing is the car keys. When the commander couldn't find the keys, they had to be with Ryan's belongings somewhere. This is the last of his things. Wouldn't it make sense to find the keys still at the house?"

"To be honest, I never thought of that," I admit.

Getting a start on my upcoming May garage sale, I'm in the basement reaching to the very back of a high shelf and pull out a huge African mask Ryan made in high school. Why save it? I wrestle with this but, today I make the decision to discard it. Ryan enjoyed it while it was up on the wall in his room and that was great. Now the room is a half office and half baby room when Violet comes to visit. There is now baby room décor on half of it and a table with a phone and computer opposite it.

CHAPTER 90

Joyce and I are on the phone talking about nothing in particular. Then she asks, "Did I tell you about a Veterans Memorial Honor Wall that is being designed within the hallways of the Oshkosh West High School by a teacher?"

"No, Joyce, you haven't. What do you know about it?" I inquire.

"One of the high school teachers is looking for anybody who graduated from Oshkosh West or the old Oshkosh High School and is or was a veteran from any US war. My husband is on the wall."

This piqued my interest. "How did you find out about it? Who do I contact?" I ask her.

"Well, I think my husband found out from some golfing buddies, but you can get online and submit Ryan's and Adam's names. I would do that if I were you," she suggests.

I answer, "Well, I'm going to get right on that. Do you know the website or who to contact?"

"I'll look it up for you and get right back to you, okay?"

Joyce tells me to google Oshkosh West High School Veterans Memorial. I contact the teacher on the website but still need to get more information from the teacher. I also discover the teacher is a veteran of the Iraq War which I appreciate.

"Hello, Mrs. Schlack. I am calling regarding the nameplates you wish to put on the Veterans Memorial Wall. You said in the online form that you want to talk about how much room is on the nameplate because your description for Ryan's may not fit. Can I ask what your concern is?"

"Yes, thank you for calling. You see, my son had returned from his second tour in Iraq.

"He did come home on leave and the day he returned to post, he was invited to a party, a block party. There was an argument that broke out. It got carried to outside where one soldier went to his car to get a gun and it is believed he had every intention of shooting the guy he was arguing with. My son saw what was going to happen in the corner of his eye and pushed the soldier out of harm's way. Instead, Ryan took the bullet and died. I am not sure how many letters would go on the nameplate. There is already the name, rank, and the years in service."

In a quiet tone, the teacher said, "I am so sorry for your loss. I can't imagine what you have gone through. Let's see, what do you think of 'Killed in training' or 'Killed on duty?'"

"I guess I want to think about this," I reply. "Ryan's death is not the norm. I feel 'Killed in Training' sounds like he was still in boot camp; not that he finished two tours in Iraq. My thought is something like 'Died saving another.' Something like that. How about if I get back to you about this? Do I have time or is there a deadline?"

"Oh, no, there is no deadline. This is an ongoing project. Yes, Mrs. Schlack, do get back to me," he said.

Rich and I talk about how Ryan died and word it to put on the name plate. We decide on "2009–Died saving another soldier". I call the high school teacher and he said that sounds very good. He will see that it gets done.

Greg Owens posts a note with a picture of Ryan on Memorial Day. I see that those who were with Ryan on that day also acknowledge this posting.

> "This Memorial Day weekend, I'll greatly be thinking of my friend Sergeant Ryan Schlack, who gave his life saving mine. It was an honor to serve with him and calling him friend. Pushing me out of harm's way sacrificing his own life makes him the most courageous man and the greatest hero in my eyes. I miss him greatly."

We, well, I, make a big change in our lives. I wonder what Ryan would think of our life-changing decision; we get a seven-week-old yellow lab. The whole purpose of the dog is first, Rich always wanted a dog but was realistic to know we moved too much, and we both worked even after he retired from the Army. Second and most importantly, this is a great way to get Rich out of the damn Lazy Boy and away from the television.

I see a text from Ted Thurston, a friend who trains dogs. "I will soon be having some puppies available." Immediately, I call him.

"Hey, Ted, I see you have some puppies available. Can I put my name on the list of potential buyers, please?"

"Gee, Terri, mine are not quite ready. Still needs momma for a couple weeks. I do know of someone who has puppies that are ready to go. How about if I bring one over in a couple of days?"

Not too long after Memorial Day, there is a knock on our front door and in Ted's arms is a beautiful yellow lab. Without a moment's hesitation, Rich says, "We'll take her." Casey becomes part of the family. Casey, born on April 8, 2017, is named after an army base in Korea where Rich got stationed in 1974, before we got married.

A day after we get Casey, Rich tears a muscle so is out of commission for a few weeks. The puppy is totally mine to care for since Rich has to stay off his leg and is basically bedridden. Since this is our first puppy, who knew what to expect? We sure didn't. Then there's the lawn cutting and trimming and whatever needs to be done with the cars. I must be sure all my ducks are in a row because I turn 65 which means looking into setting up a new military ID, Tricare for Life, finding a new dentist due to signing up for the Tricare dental program and the list goes on.

I find myself looking at the website of the Oshkosh High/West Veterans Honor Wall. There is a sub-page on Ryan, so I click on it. That leads me to something from the Patriot Guard that is placed there. On the top of that page, there is a picture with Ryan's name under a photo. The problem is that the photo is not of Ryan; looks similar, but it isn't Ryan.

I send an email to the teacher who is spearheading this project and tell him of the error and see if he can fix it. I also send two pictures of Ryan for him to use if he can fix it.

July 12 and it's Ryan's birthday. There is crying and thinking and missing Ryan so much, it hurts. Even after all this time. It is futile, but I do it anyway. There is Ryan's photo book about his first years in the army which lies near the burial flag in a wooden case on a shelf in the living room. I haven't looked at it for a very long time but feel the urge to do so. I pick it up and go slowly through each page in the photo album.

A person calls on the phone. Rich and I answer at the same time on different phones. The caller asks if Ryan is home. I let Rich talk. He says the coldest "no" I have ever heard from him. We both then hang up. It's been eight years.

Adam and his family are now stationed in Hawaii near Pearl Harbor, so we jump on a plane and spend two weeks enjoying Violet and what Hawaii offers in terms of tourist traps. It is something different for us since we are not sun-loving. Hawaii is a place to experience, and Adam makes it a fun and adventurous trip. Violet is growing and I so wish we lived in closer proximity. She truly is the light of my life.

On more than one occasion, Casey, our 6-month-old yellow lab, will go upstairs to Ryan's door and bark once or twice like there is something/someone in there. I wonder what is going on in her head. I open the door and she sniffs around until she is satisfied.

The "Opening" for the Veterans Memorial Honor Wall in Oshkosh West High School is on November 11. There are tables set up in the Oshkosh West High School hallway outside the auditorium where the Military Veterans Museum & Educational Center display various artifacts from World War I, World War II, the Korean War, Vietnam War and the Iraq/Afghanistan Wars. I worked very hard to have booklets briefly describing the items on display so we didn't need lots of volunteers standing near each war's display. There were three of us that could wander from table to table to answer questions.

When it is quiet due to most everyone in the auditorium, I sneak in to listen to what is going on. There is a request from the speaker to stand if you were in World War II. Then he asks about the Korean War, and of course, the first groups are small.

In a video, there were veterans from all branches being shown on a huge screen. I leave but come back to hear the speaker ask for all Gold Star Mothers to stand so I do. In a few moments, I see a video of men and women who have been killed in action and Ryan's picture appears; the one of him in his uniform all formal and not smiling. It makes me sad to think he is in that category of men. It seems a very appreciated project from the audience based on the clapping at the end of the program and overhearing what people are saying while walking out.

We finally did get the notice that Abadia's request for parole will be on January 4, 2018. I send in my journal to the Board.

Thoughts of putting the Christmas wreath next to Ryan's gravestone is on my mind. Rich says he does not want to put the responsibility of taking it down on anyone, so he says no.

I ask how he is feeling about Ryan at this point in time. "I think of Ryan every day. It hurts. I can't talk about it," is his answer.

At the end of 2017, the RV trip to the southwest means traveling about 250–300 miles a day. Casey does fine traveling except when she throws up or has diarrhea in the evenings. Our adventure takes us to Fort Scott Air Force Base, Tinker Air Force Base, Kirtland Air Force Base and our first stop to live for a while is Nellis Air Force Base in Las Vegas. Then we stay for a time on the RV Fam-Camps at Davis-Monthan Air Force Base near Tucson, Arizona, and at Fort Huachuca, Arizona.

Our Christmas décor in the Georgie Boy RV is Ryan's eight-inch-tall Christmas tree with tiny bulbs and a few little lights. Next to it stands Ryan's tiny old-style Santa. We sent these to Ryan on his first Iraq tour.

CHAPTER 91

2018 -2019

We arrive home in March and there is a message on our answering machine when we get home. The message is from a Special Agent Johnson from Ft. Hood, Texas.

Rich calls the Special Agent. "I would like to speak to a Special Agent Johnson."

"Yes, this is he. Is this Mr. Schlack?" asks Johnson.

"Yes," Rich replies.

"Mr. Schlack, we still have some evidence from Ryan's murder that we can now release. I am calling to find out if you would like what we have or we can dispose of it if you wish."

"Again?" Rich sounds surprised. "What's going on? We had a call in April or May of last year about this same thing. We received nothing."

"Well, sir, sometimes it's hard to find. I'll send this off today," Johnson quickly said then signs off.

Rich looks at the phone and says, "What a putz."

About a week later, there is a call for the second time in three days asking for Ryan, and I ask who she is. This time the caller speaks so fast, but I catch the word "research." I ask her to take Ryan's name off the list because he has died almost nine years ago. She mumbles something, but I was already hanging up.

We did receive the box from Ft. Hood's CID. There are Ryan's blue jeans, socks, tennis shoes and his underwear which are full of dried blood in the box. Imagine receiving a box of a murdered person's clothing. Shocking, sad, eerie, a little sickening, a bit disgusting, all swirling in a pool of emotions. Trying hard not to feel anything, I dispose of the clothes. No car keys or any other such items are found in that box.

At the museum in April, the board holds a presentation that introduces the new Iraq/Afghanistan War display focusing on two soldiers in the same company who had died in Iraq within months of each other. Both parents donate some artifacts so the President of the Museum decided to have a public event inviting the families of the two young men and the public.

Of course, my interest is up, so I go to this event. Basically, the MVMEC President talks about the two men and how the museum acquired the start of honoring those who serve in Iraq. Before this, the museum did not have enough artifacts to design a display for the Gulf, Iraq or Afghanistan Wars.

After the presentation, a woman seated next to me asks, "Are you a family member of either of these two men?"

I reply, "No, I am not. I did want to be here to kind of honor my son who died after doing two tours in Iraq."

She looked a little puzzled because she hears the "after doing two tours". She asks, "Can you tell me how it happened?"

I surprisingly do a good job of telling Ryan's story with not a lot of detail, though. As I am talking, it seems I attract a few other people. She wants to ask me more, but I excuse myself and go hide among the gift shop shelving to compose myself. It is so uncomfortable and embarrassing tearing up in front of strangers. Eventually, I slip out the door.

On May 31, Adam and our granddaughter Violet, now age 2 ½, visit from Hawaii. They flew in on a red-eye flight and both were very tired. Punkin' is the sweetest, most loquacious, beautiful little girl ever. She gets many compliments about her blue eyes and curly blond hair everywhere we go. Her vocabulary far exceeds a typical child her age, at least to my thinking. She sees a photo of Ryan in the bedroom, points to it and says, "That's Daddy!" Wow, that blows me away since I don't think of Adam as looking like his older brother now. But Violet insisted.

While in the bedroom one day, Adam is showing Violet the family pictures on the wall. There's a small collection of photos as the boys were growing up within each frame - one for Ryan, one for Adam and one for our family. Adam is telling Violet that one frame was of Uncle Ryan. Now there's a thought. Ryan in the role of uncle. That made me smile. He would have doted on her big time.

We did all kinds of visiting and playing in children's museums and seeing a movie. It is the best time we have had in a long while.

Sometime in late June, I receive a telemarketing call asking if she can speak to Ryan. I swear it is the same voice I heard a few months ago. At that time, I was firm in telling her to take Ryan off her list because he's deceased. This time I get a little rattled and just hang up.

When it's July, I know I should be ready for a card or two remembering Ryan from other Gold Star mothers. How many people do I know that get one of these kinds of cards? The thought crosses my mind that too many mothers and fathers get a card like this.

It reminds me of times when the question asked is, "How many children do you have?" My answer is I had two boys. Ryan would be ___ years old and Adam is now ___ years old" and then I talk about Adam. I don't want to dwell too long for fear the waterworks will start.

After Rich first hears me answer that question, he pulls me aside and says to me, "Say we have one child because that way we don't have to explain." But I don't agree. Ryan lives in my heart.

CHAPTER 92

On one August day, Adam leaves Hawaii to fly to Japan to board his submarine. This is his first deployment and will be gone for who knows how many months. We are not told anything definite. It brings memories of Ryan's first deployment and how we were able to go to Texas and see him off.

Now the worrying begins. I do get an iMessage from Adam. He is in Tokyo waiting for a bus so we talk. This will be a little more stressful because we can't talk to him or get any communication until the submarine comes up. I will think positively. What else can I do?

My care package for Adam containing silly notes, cards, jokes, and pictures arrives in Hawaii a day too late. His wife says she can send it with another sailor who will leave tomorrow to board the sub.

I could send Ryan boxes of stupid stuff at any time. For Adam, I had to think in terms of five or six months of writing and sending funny things for him to open as time goes by. Also, the package had to be flat so no candy bars or silly gifts.

Frequently my brother Gib's daughter-in-law posts things about missing her son that are heartbreaking. She posted a picture on Facebook of a man walking up heaven's steps in the clouds and who reminds me so much of Ryan. I cry when I see this.

Another parole hearing letter arrives. It will take place in February. I have a bad feeling about this hearing.

On Facebook, Greg Owens says his little dachshund died. I can tell by the Facebook entries he is having a very, very tough time with it. He brings up Ryan's name and how he just can't seem to take it. I figure the little dachshund was his service dog. Owens can't seem to get himself moving in a better direction. I truly hope he seeks professional support. I send a reply saying how sorry I am that his dog died.

Rich and I get a notice that Abadia has been approved for custody level, which means he is under minimal supervision and can be granted other privileges. "I can't say I have no feeling about this," I say to Rich. "Minimal supervision" and "privileges" are vague terms. I'm thinking he doesn't have freedom from the Disciplinary Barracks, whatever that looks like, and has to answer to someone yet. He isn't free to do as he pleases. Is he?"

"He can get an apartment, get a job, and pretty much be out on his own. He will probably have to just check in with someone, but there are never enough parole officers to do a good job of keeping tabs on the parolees and do we even know if ankle monitors are done," Rich informs me.

"It is still an insult to think Abadia is not confined anymore," I mumble.

Rich speaks up, "The worthless piece of s — should be in jail or shot."

"I want Abadia to stay in a prison cell longer," is my comment. The unsettling thing that has crossed my mind is if Abadia might track us down and harm us because he spent those years in prison. Blame us for his mess.

Am I holding a grudge? I have been preparing mentally for Abadia's release because it is inevitable and that I will have to accept it.

A weird incidence occurs when Rich and I are at a dealership filling out the paperwork for a new vehicle. Rich is signing his name, and it needs a date.

"What's the date today?" Rich asks.

The car dealer automatically says, "July 12."

I am a bit startled by the realization that it is Ryan's birthday, and I didn't think about it today. That's a first. I am "lost" for a moment but recover. The dealer gives me a strange look because I think he saw me bolt a little when he said the date.

Ryan would be 40 years old. The new vehicle is not at all important to me for the rest of the day.

Adam puts simply "X" on a posting. Yes, my son, it has been ten years. I know Adam is still hurting.

CHAPTER 93

2020

It is spring of 2020 and we find out Adam's family will be moving back to Groton, Connecticut, from Hawaii. He gave up the house in March and planned to stay with friends a couple weeks before they come here to stay awhile. Then the Navy changed his orders due to COVID so Adam had to stay until July. His family needed a place to live and the best plan was to have Mommy and Violet come stay with us starting in March until July. We welcome the two with open arms.

After two more changes of orders, Adam can finally get out of Hawaii in September. Spending six months with Mommy and Violet, I find I don't feel comfortable with Adam's wife. Will this feeling pass? Though, I loved fussing over Violet.

Although we get it in the summer, our Christmas gift to ourselves is the 2019 Winnebago Adventurer RV. We leave for our snow birding in mid-November and decide to stay in Las Vegas to see how we like staying in one place. We walk The Strip one or two times. COVID hit everywhere so we leave in late March for home. Downtown Vegas is a ghost town.

I think it's time to cut this connection to the person who murdered my son, Ryan. Now that I think about it, the journal I write is something a bit therapeutic. No need to write a journal anymore because Abadia is out for all intents and purposes.

A slow process I am going through is getting off of the antidepressants. The sleepless nights are still with me. The eczema has been gone for the last year. The aches are not as severe. Exercise and maybe eating better could remedy some of this.

Adam and I are talking and it strikes me to ask, "How are you feeling about Ryan now and hearing Abadia is basically no longer in prison?"

Immediately he says, "I feel disappointed. I expected him to stay in at least 14 years. Mom, I wonder what Ryan would think about me becoming a 'dad'. I am a little concerned about when Dad and you grow old or when you both die. I don't have Ryan to talk to about decisions that have to be made. I will most likely have a wife who can help me through this time when it comes. Maybe even Violet will be old enough to help her dad."

Rich can't really put into words how he feels. He says it upsets him and he gets angry every time he dwells on it. He doesn't want to talk about it.

Ryan is in our hearts as we know he would always be. Adam is an attentive son. He has brought a new life to our family and we couldn't be happier about that. Rich is still his quiet self and still tough to read.

Sure, those tears will fall, but it's just me. That's the way I'm built. Is there a different outlook? It is hard to describe but can tell you it's better. I feel like doing things like write, volunteer on a couple of committees at the museum, and doing a better job of keeping in touch with my family and friends. Volunteering at the museum is a lifeline because I needed to do something to make my thoughts go in another direction. My sense of humor may even be back. No more antidepressants for me. This is great!

Is the feeling I have now due to the passage of time? Is it because I "let go" of Abadia? That maybe a part of it.

EPILOGUE

2021

One hope I have is that the judicial system puts the sentencing phase of the trial into the hands of the military judge. I truly believe Abadia would have received a stronger sentence. The commanders on a panel have no background in the law and surely do not consider its implications. On top of that, they are not doing the accused or the victim's family any favors. Yes, commanders do impose sentences of a sort onto guilty soldiers. That does not make them experts. Or is it because there are no guidelines for the length of incarceration and the panel pulls a number out of the air?

Our counsel becomes an assistant to a US attorney and was involved in 2021 serving 90 days on President Biden's Independent Review Commission on Sexual Assault in the Military. It was recommended taking prosecutorial decisions away from commanding officers and putting them into the hands of trained military prosecutors. This recommendation focuses on those who are guilty of spousal abuse, child abuse and the like. But this is one small step in the right direction.

Another of my hopes is dealing with the accused committing a crime while drunk. That person should not have the right to drive, carry a weapon, or be in a situation that harms someone. Yes, there are laws, but are they tough enough? Yes, the military has been known to kick out those who are caught driving drunk but to give bad conduct and not a dishonorable discharge to those who kill? What about heavy inebriation in general?

The "Notification to Victim/Witness of Prisoner Status" was received in April 2021 and stated that Barto Abadia will be paroled on May 3, 2021, and released in Santa Fe, New Mexico.

The final hope is that the best military in the world follows its own words.

In the Soldier's Code it says:

"I will treat others with dignity and respect and expect others to do the same."

In the Army Values the definition of loyalty is:

"Bear true faith and allegiance to the US Constitution, the Army, your unit and other soldiers."

"Respect: Treat people as they should be treated."

"Honor: Live up to all the Army Values."

APPENDIX A

ARMY RANKS

<u>LOWER ENLISTED</u>
- E1 - PVT - Private
- E2 - PV2 - Private 2
- E3 - PFC - Private First Class

<u>NON-COMMISSIONED OFFICERS</u>
- E4 - SPC/CPL - Specialist/Corporal
- E5 - SGT - Sergeant
- E6 - SSGT - Staff Sergeant

<u>SENIOR NON-COMMISSIONED OFFICERS</u>
- E7 - SFC - Sergeant First Class
- E8 - MSG/1SGT - Master Sergeant/First Sergeant
- E9 - SGM/ CSM - Sergeant Major/Command Sergeant Major

<u>WARRANT OFFICERS</u>
- WO1–Warrant Officer 1
- WO2–Chief Warrant Officer 2
- WO3–Chief Warrant Officer 3
- WO4–Chief Warrant Officer 4
- WO5–Chief Warrant Officer 5

<u>OFFICERS</u>
- 2LT–Second Lieutenant
- 1LT–First Lieutenant
- CPT–Captain
- MAJ–Major
- LCT–Lieutenant Colonel
- COL–Colonel
- BG–Brigadier General (wears 1 star)
- MG–Major General
- LTG–Lieutenant General
- GEN–General (wears 4 stars)
- GA–General of the Army (wears 5 stars)

ABOUT THE AUTHOR

Terri Schlack grew up in Wisconsin and, after college, got married. Due to Rich's army career, they lived in Kansas, Texas, and Germany. Along the way two sons were born. Terri earned her Bachelor's degree in Wisconsin and later, her Master of Education degree in Texas. Her 35 years of teaching included grade three through college. When Rich retired in 1990, they moved back to Wisconsin. Terri has written poems, plays, parodies, speeches and short stories to use with teaching, for school events and for a motorcycle association's newsletters. Terri loved to teach but after Ryan's death, found her heart wasn't in it so she retired in 2010. Terri then volunteered at the Military Veterans Museum & Education Center in Oshkosh, WI where she is still very active. To keep writing, she is editor of the museum newsletter. Terri has written a book about the museum, which was published in 2024.

NOTE FROM TERRI SCHLACK

Word-of-mouth is crucial for any author to succeed. If you enjoyed *Afterward*, please leave a review online—anywhere you are able. Even if it's just a sentence or two. It would make all the difference and would be very much appreciated.

Thanks!
Terri Schlack

We hope you enjoyed reading this title from:

www.blackrosewriting.com

Subscribe to our mailing list – *The Rosevine* – and receive **FREE** books, daily deals, and stay current with news about upcoming releases and our hottest authors.
Scan the QR code below to sign up.

Already a subscriber? Please accept a sincere thank you for being a fan of Black Rose Writing authors.

View other Black Rose Writing titles at www.blackrosewriting.com/books and use promo code **PRINT** to receive a **20% discount** when purchasing.

www.ingramcontent.com/pod-product-compliance
Lightning Source LLC
Chambersburg PA
CBHW030539080526
44585CB00012B/196